# PAUL BROWN

THE RISE AND FALL
AND RISE AGAIN
OF FOOTBALL'S MOST
INNOVATIVE COACH

*Andrew O'Toole*

CLERISY PRESS

Published by Clerisy Press
Printed in the United States of America
Distributed by Publishers Group West
First edition, first printing

For further information, contact the publisher at:
Clerisy Press
1700 Madison Road
Cincinnati, OH 45206
www.clerisypress.com

Library of Congress Cataloging-in-Publication Data
    O'Toole, Andrew.
        Paul Brown: the rise and fall and rise again of football's most innovative coach/
    by Andrew O'Toole.—1st ed. p. cm.
        ISBN 978-1-57860-319-0 (cloth)
        ISBN 978-1-57860-357-2 (paper)
        1. Brown, Paul, 1908– 2. Football coaches–United States–Biography. I. Title.
        GV939.B77076 2008
        796.332092–dc22
        [B]
                        2008021985

Edited by Jack Heffron, Steve Watkins, and Donna Poehner
Cover designed by Stephen Sullivan
Interior design by Annie Long
Photo Credits: The photos on pages 331, 410, and 412 appear courtesy of Mary Brown.
    All other photos appear courtesy of the Paul E. Brown Museum.

For my girl, Mickie

You are the Everything

# TABLE OF CONTENTS

# ACKNOWLEDGMENTS

When I first approached this project I had a predetermined image of Paul Brown. I understood him to be the preeminent architect of professional football, but also etched in my mind was the vision of a cold, calculating autocrat. My impressions, while not totally off base, were incomplete. I learned through numerous interviews with men and women who knew Paul personally and professionally that Brown was a multifaceted person. In addition to being a football genius who demanded complete control, he also was charming, engaging, and loyal. He could also be a dictator within the realms of his football world, and his genial disposition would turn frosty when confronted with a question to his rule. Brilliant and petty. Innovative and stubborn. Professionally, Paul Brown was a dichotomy, and this book primarily deals with the professional side of the man.

Writing a book of this nature and breadth is impossible without the assistance of others. I would like to thank Mike Brown for taking the time to sit and talk with me on several occasions, sharing memories and thoughts of his father. Mike also generously allowed me to explore the Paul Brown Collection at the Bengals offices. I appreciate that Mike did not try to steer me in any direction during the course of my research, nor did he try to influence my opinions or the conclusions I've drawn.

This book is primarily a contemporary account of Brown's life. I did, however, conduct a number of interviews to augment Paul's story. A complete listing of interview subjects is located in the bibliography, and I am grateful to everyone who gave of their time and patiently answered my questions. I would especially like to thank Paul's widow, Mary, who was kind enough to regale me with remembrances of her life with PB.

I would like to thank the following people who helped me in the course of my research.

Heather Cole—Miami University

Jim Anderson—St. Louis Cardinals

Therese Gonzalez—Great Lakes Naval Museum and Archives

Judith Adkins—National Archives

Kristen Wilhelm—National Archives

Ray Stein—*Columbus Dispatch*

Chick Ludwig—*Dayton Daily News*

Eric Ball—Cincinnati Bengals

Jack Brennan—Cincinnati Bengals

Bill Conlin—*Philadelphia Daily News*

Janet H. Stuckey—Head of Special Collections & Archives,
          Miami University

Steve Stout—*Urbana Daily Citizen*

Gene Boerner—Paul E. Brown Museum

Junie Studer, the keeper of Massillon Tiger history, supplied me with tales of Massillon football and also opened his vast archives for my use.

Dino Lucarelli of the Cleveland Browns. Dino is a great ambassador of Browns football and has been enormously helpful and encouraging to me. Thanks for everything, Dino.

PJ Combs of the Cincinnati Bengals. PJ has been there for me, just an e-mail or a phone call away, ready to help me with any question or request I might have. I appreciate all your help, PJ.

Thanks and love to Courtney.

And lastly, my girl Mickie, You and me, it's a beautiful thing, this life we have.

Upon arriving in heaven, a football fan was pleased to discover a football game being played. He looked around and surveyed the gridiron of rapture. There, roaming one sideline, was a mythical figure dressed in a camel-hair coat and snap-brim felt hat coaching one of the teams.

"That looks like Paul Brown," the fan excitedly said to an angel seated next to him.

"No," the angel replied, "that's not Paul Brown. That's God. He thinks he's Paul Brown."

*Popular joke of the Paul Brown era,*
*usually credited to Chuck Heaton of the* Cleveland Plain Dealer.

# PROLOGUE: Living Again

*Everything is black and white.*
*In life, there are no shades of gray.*

It's a cold world. It's an even colder business. You give your life to something; you devote yourself to this football, but where are you at the end of the day? You wind up with your possessions stuffed in a couple of cardboard boxes callously dumped outside your office, your old office. Your old office, your old job. . . . Nothing that was, is.

Seventeen years and this is all that's left: a carton of memories, reminiscence of faded glory.

From 1946 until January of 1963, Paul Brown was an imperious presence in Cleveland. His rule as head coach of the Cleveland Browns was an autocracy, a dictatorship that bred seven championships during his reign. His Browns were the only champion the now defunct All American Football Conference had ever known. And when Cleveland moved to the National Football League in 1950, the Browns shocked the more established NFL teams by winning their championship. This achievement, however, didn't surprise Brown. No, he expected success.

"Paul is a lot more than a coach in Cleveland," one of his players once remarked. "He signs you to a contract; he coaches you on the field; he tells you what to eat; and he tells you when to get up and when to go to bed."

For seventeen years things were done his way. The right way. . . the only way. Brown had been persuaded to the pro game by Mickey McBride, a Cleveland businessman with diverse interests and questionable legitimacy. McBride gave Brown carte blanche and then sat back as the club won and won, the championships kept coming practically to the point of tedium. The initial infatuation McBride had for the sport faded, and eventually he sold his interest to a group of investors headed by Dave

1

Jones. Little changed in the years that followed. Jones receded into the background, while Brown remained the face of the team.

Like all things good, the championship run dried up. And the Jones group, too, ultimately tired of the game. Change came again, and, like before, Brown saw no reason to think his role would be any different no matter who purchased the team. In fact, this new owner, this Art Modell, admitted that Paul Brown was a big reason for his interest in purchasing the Cleveland Browns. They were the New York Yankees of football, he said, and Brown was the architect behind their unparalleled success. But, by 1961 when Modell bought the club, Brown's team had fallen on hard times. The franchise hadn't reached the postseason since 1957. Before long, Brown's timeworn methods were being questioned. In the press box, in the bleachers, even in his own locker room, Brown's techniques were coming under scrutiny like never before. This criticism increased until it reached a crescendo at the close of the 1962 season.

And then a door to his life closed, and it would stay closed. Some names would never be uttered by Paul Brown again. Or if they were, they were part of a biting invective.

—⁂—

Paul Brown stood on the dais overlooking a packed ballroom in Cincinnati's Sheraton Gibson Hotel. The date was September 26, 1967. Following a four-and-a-half year forced exile from his chosen profession, Brown was bringing pro football to the Queen City. Football's greatest innovator had returned to the game, and the state, that had brought him glory. Looking out over the room, Paul was awash with emotion.

"This is like coming home," Brown told the gathering of Cincinnati business leaders.

Nearly two years of fervent politicking culminated with Paul's declaration from the podium that early-fall afternoon. With the endorsement of Pete Rozelle, the commissioner of the National Football League, Brown and his financial backers had been awarded the American Football League's tenth franchise. Though others had invested, and invested heavily, in the endeavor, Brown wanted to set the record straight. "I appoint the board of directors," he told reporters following the announcement. "I wouldn't have come back unless I was in complete charge. The players know they cannot bypass me or go to the general manager or the owners. It gives me great advantage over other coaches."

"This is the way it must be," Paul continued. "Any other way and in time you'll see the whole structure begin to crumble, and all at once a good team will begin to slide. It's inevitable. Look at the history of great football teams, and you'll see all the authority concentrated in the coach."[1]

Brown's words were born of experience. He had, at one time, autonomy in Cleveland. And then, practically overnight, a fresh-talking, fast-living salesman ingratiated himself with Brown's players and usurped his powers. Art Modell bought the Cleveland Browns fair and square. Hell, Brown even signed off on the deal and made himself more than a few bucks in the process. But what came along with this Modell blindsided Brown.

The discord between the two men went deeper than a simple clash of personalities. In addition to distinct philosophies and styles, two impressive egos had collided. Each man was a success in his chosen field, but Modell and Brown reached the summit from different points on the map. "One was from knowledge and experience," Paul would later say, "The other from a complete lack of either."

The lessons learned in those last, bitter days in Cleveland had left an enduring mark on Brown. At endgame, of course, that carpetbagger was still there in Cleveland running the team named for Paul Brown, while he was left here, standing in a hotel ballroom, ready to start anew. History, Paul vowed, would not be repeated. This new beginning, this second chance was all he'd ever hoped for. A rebirth—it was all anyone could ever wish for.

Indeed, "This is like coming home," Brown told those gathered in the ballroom. "I'm living again."

Paul E. Brown, age six months,
fourteen days.

# one  PAULIE BOY

**Through the stillness of night** came a lonesome whistle, a shrill cry calling out through the tranquility. Cutting through the dark was a familiar roar, a rhythmic clatter, the cadence of steel wheels rolling on iron rails resonated in the calm of night . . . rumbling, rumbling . . . carrying possibility, hope, destiny, stirring the romantic minded, rousing exotic dreams inside a young man.

Paul Eugene Brown was born on September 7, 1908, in Norwalk, Ohio. The Brown family home sat on 7 Elm Street, just a couple of blocks to the south of the Wheeling and Lake Erie line, where Paul's father, Lester, worked as a dispatcher. Lester Browne was a first-generation American of English ancestry. At some point, Lester dropped the "e" from his surname for reasons unknown. He was a precise, meticulous man, qualities necessary in his line of employ. He was also a modest, unassuming man. A man of values emblematic of Middle America, and Lester Brown impressed upon his son these principles which had served him so well.

Located in north-central Ohio, fifty-five miles to the east of Toledo, and fifty-five miles to the west of Cleveland, Norwalk was an ideal playground for a young boy. Paul discovered the joys of small-town life.

Fishing on the Vermilion River, hiking in nearby woods, and playing sports all occupied Paul's time. When he was six, his father gave him his first football, which Paul played with until the bladder gave out. Resourcefully, Paul gave the ball new life by stuffing the deflated pigskin with rags and old socks. When that ball finally gave out for good, he took a stocking cap and filled it with leaves. It wasn't exactly regulation, but the makeshift "ball" served its purpose. Sport had captured Paul's attention and focus, but his parents emphasized the necessity of proper education.

Born in nearby Milan, Ida Sherwood Brown, like her husband Lester, came from English descent. Theirs was a marriage of equality, though Lester

Paulie Boy at three.

was indisputably the head of the Brown household. Each parent fostered on Paul and their daughter Marian unconditional love as well as discipline and order.

In 1915, while Paul was in the fourth grade, Lester was transferred to Brewster, Ohio, an important division point on the Wheeling and Lake Erie line. He found a new home for his family in nearby Massillon, on Grant Street. Massillon was a bigger version of Norwalk, another idyllic American town for a boy to be raised in. Wide, tree-lined avenues checkered the town, and the Lincoln Highway cut through the heart of it. It was a steel town, home to Republic Steel. It was a town dotted with churches as varied as those who worshiped within their walls. It was also a football town, home of the Massillon Tigers of the American Professional Football

Brown with his first football.

Association. And Paul found that, just like Norwalk, Massillon offered a precocious boy ample opportunity to find new adventures.

In his new hometown, Paul fell in with a group of young boys: Del Halpin, Harry Stroble, Warren Ott, and Jim Hollinger. The boys did what boys do. There was sport; every conceivable game was played in the parks of Massillon. Sometimes their endeavors were a bit more dangerous, including leaping from the Lorain Avenue fire escape while using an umbrella as a parachute. Such daredevil escapades were rare, though the boys did occasionally take in a Tiger football game without the benefit of a ticket. There was a flat-bottomed boat the boys kept to shuttle across the Tuscarawas River. Once safely on the other side, they "scrambled" up the bank to the stadium. As luck would have it, the security guard was easily distracted, allowing the boys to worm their way under the fencing, and "presto,"[1] they found their way inside the ballpark. Brown often loafed at the west-side fire house, where the walls of the station were decorated with photographs of Massillon Tigers. He would sit for hours, watching the firemen during their work day and gazing at the photos of his football heroes, studying the pictures and daydreaming about maybe one day joining them on that wall.

The love of sport began early and was documented when someone snapped a shot of Paulie at age five trying to hike a football.

Paul's first opportunity to play ball in an organized fashion occurred when Lorin Andrews Junior High was closed for a period of time to erect a new building. Transferred to Edmond Jones, Paulie Boy, "full of vim and vigor," went out for the school football team. Being much smaller than his school mates, Paul played, but sparingly. He did find one sport in which his slight frame was an advantage: pole vaulting. Brown developed a reputation in junior high, so much so that Washington High's track coach, Dave Stewart, was coaxed into seeing this kid at Edmond Jones pole vault. Stewart, who also coached football and basketball at the high school, was impressed by what he saw. He told Paul that he looked forward to coaching him when Paul reached Washington High.

Track was the only varsity sport Paul was eligible to play in his freshman year. And, at the year-end sports award banquet, Brown received his first varsity letter. Paul had hoped that Lester and Ida might buy him his first pair of long pants for the special event, but no such luck. He stepped up to the makeshift stage assembled in the school auditorium wearing his "freshly washed knickers" and accepted the valued prize from Coach Stewart. Ida took the orange varsity M and sewed it on a white sweater, which Paul proceeded to wear practically every waking moment.

The last months before Paul's sophomore year in high school were rife with thoughts of Dave Stewart's football camp. Every summer, two weeks before the start of the school year, Stewart would hold a camp for prospective members of the varsity football team. It cost each boy $5 a week for food for the fourteen-day camp. Though a wispy 120 pounds, Paul naturally assumed he would be invited to Turkey Foot Lake along

"A banty rooster" Washington High Quarterback.

with the rest of the boys, giving no thought to his diminutive size or the possibility of being overlooked. The night before the boys of Massillon made off for Turkey Foot Lake, Paul packed his bags in anticipation. He awoke the following morning earlier than usual, having barely slept a wink. Following a light breakfast, Brown went to the front stoop and waited for his ride, the ride he assumed would be coming for him. All morning, Paul sat with his bag, patiently waiting.

"I guess they didn't even know I was alive," Brown later remembered.

All that Paul wanted had been pulled out from under him. Not yet fourteen years old, all Brown aspired to was wrapped up in the game of

From left to right Paulie Smith, Elwood Kammer,
Vince Define, Paul Brown. 1924.

football. For a couple of days, Paul neither ate nor slept. Sympathizing with his devastated son, Lester placed Paul in the family car and drove to Turkey Foot. Arriving at the Stewart's camp, Lester approached the coach.

"Please take him, if for nothing more than a water boy," Brown asked. "He's driving us crazy."

Stewart looked the boy over and warned Lester that his son could get hurt. Football players do not discriminate, the coach explained. They'll hit a small kid every bit as hard as they will a big kid. Despite his and Ida's misgivings, Lester knew this had been all Paul thought about for months. If he got hurt, it would be a life lesson. The elder Brown gave Stewart ten dollars for the two-week encampment and returned home to Massillon.

For the moment, Paul's place on the team did not matter; he was part of a team. Stewart put Brown on the fifth string of the Tigers squad

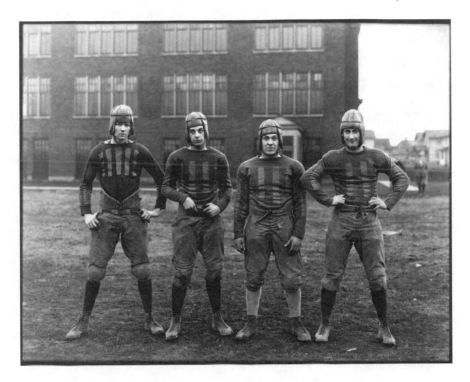

The Tiger backfield before the 1925 McKinley game.
From left to right, Artie McConnell, Paul Brown,
Whitey Laughlin, Elwood Kammer.

as a quarterback. From the bench, Paul took in everything: the play on the field and, more importantly, the decisions made by his coach. In the season's sixth game, with the Tigers holding a substantial lead against Wellstone High, Stewart gave Brown his chance in game conditions. Improbably, with Lester and Ida sitting in the stands of Agathon Field, Paul threw a touchdown pass. That brief moment of glory was nearly the extent of playing time Brown saw as a sophomore. Still, Stewart saw something in the slight but eager Brown.

"He was like a banty rooster," Stewart later recalled, "full of authority and self-confidence." The coach was taken by Paul's innate ability to take charge on the field. His voice, full of authority, provided inspiration to his teammates and, by the start of his junior year, Brown was Washington High's starting quarterback.

1925 Massillon football team.

"The kids believed in him and he ran them like a Napoleon,"[2] Stewart said.

As he gained experience, Paul's confidence grew. At one point, Brown sent a lineman from the huddle to the bench with instructions for Stewart to send in a substitute.

"He's taken over the world," the coach thought to himself.

But Brown's judgment proved correct and Stewart began trusting Brown's instinct more and more. The jug-eared Stewart played some collegiate ball at Grove City College. And, at a time when eligibility and background checks were uncommon, Stewart also played occasionally for Bethany College. As the coach of all sports at Washington High, Stewart offered guidance and leadership to his players. He was a bachelor with time on his hands and a love of sport to share. Occasionally, he would round up three or four of his boys and take them all to a nearby college contest. An uncommon bond was forming between the coach and his quarterback, however. Stewart would often pick Brown up and take him for a drive around Stark County. As they rode through the countryside, the two would talk football and game strategy.

As an adult, Brown acknowledged the impact his coach had upon his life. "Dave Stewart was wonderful," he said. "He gave me a love of football and winning."

Winning . . . Stewart may have taught Paul about football, but Brown's thirst for competition originated with his mother. Ida loved games of all sorts. Checkers and bridge were two of her favorites, games she taught her Paulie boy to play . . . and win. As soon as he came through the door, home from school, Ida called out, "Let's go, Paulie." Even when she sat with her son, Ida played to win. This trait, this thirst for competition, was embedded in Paul. Never sit down without the expectation of success. When you take the field, anticipate victory.

Brown lettered in track, basketball, where he served as the Tigers' designated free-throw shooter, and football. But it was the last sport that enthralled Paul. He continued to hone his quarterbacking skills into his senior year. "I could throw the ball," he would later boast. But few colleges would take a chance on a 120-pound banty rooster.

1925 Massillon basketball squad. Top row fourth from left, coach Dave Stewart; bottom row, fourth from left, Paul Brown.

It was Lester's wish that his son attend Ohio State University. He had hopes that his Paul would develop a love of the law and perhaps seek a career in the profession after gaining his degree. Scholastically speaking, Paul was indifferent to OSU. And the law, well, that was Lester's dream. But the chance of suiting up and playing for the Buckeyes certainly drew Paul's interest. He accepted his father's aspiration, and, several days shy of his seventeenth birthday, Paul boarded a train bound for Columbus. Four hours later, he was on campus, and it didn't take much longer than that for Paul to become homesick. Previously, he had never been away from Lester and Ida for any extended length of time. For a while, every Sunday Brown would take a four-mile hike to the Pennsylvania Station hoping to see the train from Massillon come rolling in. Any little sign from home. Not only was he missing Ida's home cooking, but Brown wasn't permitted to try out for the Buckeyes football squad. Too small, he was told. And by the end of the school year, Brown knew he had had enough of Ohio State. To his father's consternation, Brown wanted to transfer. Previously he had been to Oxford, Ohio, visiting a friend from Norwalk who was attending Miami University. Brown was taken by the campus. "I became enamored with the place," Brown explained. "I really thought it looked the way a school should look."

This is where he wanted to go to college. Though not pleased with his son's decision, Lester was assuaged when he learned all of the credits Brown accumulated at Ohio State would transfer to Miami.

—⚏—

In the fall of '26, Brown again took a train from Massillon. This time his destination was Hamilton, Ohio. From there, Brown shared a bus filled with Miami students. On this final leg of the journey, Brown was introduced to the infectious school spirit found at Miami. As the bus made its way up a hill near the campus, a student rose from his seat and shouted, "Crimson Towers, everybody up!" Upon that command every occupant on the bus stood and sang the Miami fight song. Though he didn't know the tune or the words, Brown was entranced. In stark contrast to Ohio State's large, formidable campus, Oxford was a quaint, picturesque college town nestled on the southwestern border where Ohio meets Indiana.

At Miami, Brown majored in English and history, and he joined a fraternity, Delta Kappa Epsilon, where he served as house manager for his room and board. Of all the things he would take away from his days at Oxford, nothing stuck in Brown's memory more than the words of wisdom uttered by Elizabeth Hamilong, a Miami dean.

"The eternal verities will always prevail. Such things as truth, honesty, and good character will never change. No matter how people and times change."

Because he was a transfer student, Brown was not eligible to play varsity football for Miami's Big Red in his sophomore year. He did, however, play for the freshman team in 1926, which permitted him the chance to stay in shape and prepare for his junior year. Miami's frosh coach, Merlin Detmer, gave Brown the smallest available jersey, number 38. He continued to grow . . . slowly. Over the course of his sophomore year, Brown enjoyed a growth spurt that saw him go from 136 pounds to a robust 144. By the time fall rolled around once again, Brown was ready to compete for the varsity squad. And luck was on his side when, the week before Big Red's first game of the 1928 season, the young man battling Brown for the quarterback position suffered a torn Achilles tendon, abruptly ending his football career. Thrust into the starting position behind center, Brown excelled in his first collegiate game.

"Brown at quarter was another of the outstanding players in the Defiance contest," reported the school paper as Brown led the Big Red to a 42-0 victory. "If Saturday is an indication, the other teams of the Buckeye Conference are going to have considerable to worry about in this respect this year."

The effusive praise continued. "Brown's broken field running is some of the best seen on Miami Field in recent years. His ability to elude tacklers is almost uncanny and his passing and punting are likewise strong features in his play."

The biggest game of the '28 season was an 18-0 win over Wittenberg in which Brown threw two touchdowns to Jimmy Gordon. Both scores were completed without the approval of Coach Chet Pittser, when Paulie tossed aside the coach's play and called his own. Luckily for Brown, Pittser

1928 Miami University.

was a calm, conservative man. As a football coach, Pittser was a disciple of innovative Illinois coach Bob Zuppke. The Zuppke style had the quarterback lining up behind center, but before the ball was snapped, he shifted to either tailback or fullback. From that position the quarterback could run, pass, or block for another back.

Brown tested Pittser's patience on numerous occasions, and the two touchdown passes in the Wittenberg game are just a couple of examples. While playing under Dave Stewart, Brown was encouraged to use his instinct, and often Brown would improvise. In one contest, Miami's opponents had vowed to hit Brown hard enough to force the diminutive quarterback from the game. Big Red players staunchly protected their teammate throughout the game, and Pittser, too, tried to shield Brown from harm.

"Let the ball go," Pittser instructed the punt-returning Brown. "I don't want them ganging up on you."

Brown followed his coach's orders until late in the contest. Then, Miami's opponent surrounded a punted ball believing that Brown again would allow the kick to roll to a stop. Instead, Brown skirted between the defenders, scooped up the football, and scooted a fair distance downfield before being brought down. Though he defied his coach frequently, Brown liked to remember that his calls were successful more often than not. His untamed style of play earned Brown a spot on the Associated Press's All-Buckeye team.

Brown also went out for the Big Red baseball team in the spring. As Miami's starting center fielder, Brown employed a style of play reminiscent of John McGraw's New York Giants. "Get 'em on and move 'em over." He could lay down a bunt effectively and had a knack for getting on base while not possessing much power at the plate.

But Brown had something more important than "moving them over" on his mind when the school year ended. During a periodic fire drill in the midst of his junior year at Washington High, Paul found himself standing next to a striking, effervescent young girl. Kathryn Kester was a petite, blue-eyed beauty with light brown hair. A year younger than Paul, Katy was equally smitten. She returned home that afternoon and told her parents that she had met the boy she would marry. A courtship began: ice cream socials, ice skating, and an occasional movie at the Lincoln Theater.

They continued to date through high school, and when Paul went to Ohio State during Katy's senior year, they spent the summer together at the Kester's Turkey Foot Lake cottage. Simultaneous with Paul's transfer to Miami, Katy enrolled at Western Reserve Nursing School in Cleveland. Despite the geographic distance between them, their love deepened and the question of marriage arose. Both Paul and Katy acknowledged the wish to exchange wedding vows. Standing in their way, though, were the rules of both of their schools. Like a number of institutions of the day, Western Reserve and Miami each forbade marriage until their students graduated. Following Paul's junior year at Oxford, however, the couple decided to take the leap nonetheless. And on June 10, 1929, with their parents' blessing, Paul and Katy were married at St. Matthew's Episcopal Church in Wheeling, West Virginia. For the time being, however, the marriage would have to be their secret.

Come September, Katy returned to Western Reserve for her final year of schooling, while Paul headed to Oxford and his senior year. Yes, Brown would still play football, but he would forgo baseball in order to concentrate on his studies. He was hitting the books, and the extra effort paid off with straight B's in courses during his senior year. He was through with baseball, but on the gridiron, Brown continued to excel.

"Brown was well-liked by the boys," teammate Willie Wertz remembered. "As a quarterback, he was the team leader. . . . Of course Brown made a mistake occasionally, but on the whole he used good judgment. He wasn't a great player, but a mighty good one."

The Big Red went 13-4 with Brown behind center in his two varsity seasons. Brown's senior season was capped with a brilliant 6-0 Thanksgiving Day win over the University of Cincinnati.

Brown graduated from Miami in the spring of 1930, just months after the Great Crash. He had the grades to qualify for a Rhodes scholarship, but when an unexpected offer arose, Brown had to reconsider his career path. Dave Stewart left Massillon in 1925 and returned to his hometown of Sharon, Pennsylvania, where he coached the local high school team. In each of the previous few summers, Brown came to Sharon and helped his old coach prepare for the upcoming season. The experience exhilarated Brown. He had never thought of coaching as a career option, but watching Stewart at work gave him cause to pause.

A coaching vacancy came open at Severn Military Academy in Maryland, which served as a prep school for the nearby Naval Academy in Annapolis. After Stewart wrote a glowing letter of recommendation to the school's headmaster, Roland Teal, the position of backfield coach was offered to Brown. Any job in those times of desperation was worth having. Though the pay was modest, $1,200 annually, an apartment was provided for the Browns. The deal was sealed when Katy was offered a position working in the school's infirmary. The team's head coach was suffering from cancer, and shortly after the start of the school year, passed away. The position fell to Brown, who turned twenty-one the first day on the job. "I was nervous," he would later admit, "but I was so young and full of it I just forged ahead."

In addition to coaching the football squad, Brown taught grammar, English literature, and history. Though in his two years at Severn Brown's team won sixteen and lost only one while also tying one, Brown was frustrated by the lack of enthusiasm expressed for the football program by the school administration and alumni. He wasn't necessarily looking to move on, but when an opportunity arose, he couldn't turn away.

In Massillon, interest in the Washington High football program steadily increased under Dave Stewart. An estimated 1,000 fans traveled to Erie in 1925 to watch the Tigers take on Erie Academy High. And then, after Stewart left for Lock Haven, Pennsylvania, where he stayed for two years before moving on to Sharon, Pennsylvania, Massillon football stagnated over the ensuing six years. As the Tiger's fortunes steadily plummeted, the Massillon Field bleachers played host to plenty of empty seats. The program was soon operating in the red, and team uniforms were worn and ragged.

Finally, following the 1931 season, when Elmer McGrew's team went 2-6-2, the school board gathered and discussed the situation. Do we want to field a quality program or abandon football altogether? What was unanimous among board members was the belief that status quo would not suffice.

Massillon school superintendent Dr. Richard Bell placed a call to Dave Stewart. "Who would you recommend for the post," Bell asked.

Without a moment's hesitation, Stewart responded, "Hire Brown."

Paul and Katy Brown.

# two    TIGER TOWN

Coming home was like a dream.

A dream indeed, but still, the job Brown was coming home to was formidable. The football program Brown inherited at Washington High was in complete disrepair. The 1931 Tigers won but two contests while playing before crowds that usually averaged little more than 1,000. Tiger Stadium was in shambles; the stands were dilapidated and the field was speckled with dust and cluttered with rocks. Football finances were in the red. In an attempt to increase attendance, school officials tried night football, but that experiment was met with relative indifference. Due to the widening effects of the Depression, the school hadn't purchased new football uniforms since 1929.

It was a challenge, certainly, and Brown eagerly stepped up to this challenge. With the backing of Dr. Bell and the other members of the Massillon school board, Brown began organizing and implementing his own program at Washington High. The school system had three junior high schools—Edmund Jones, Longfellow, and Lorin Andrews—and the coach at each school used his own scheme. Kids came through the Massillon system and reached Washington High having learned varying techniques and methods along the way. Brown instituted structure to the slapdash program. Each school would have a head coach and an assistant, men who met with Brown's approval. These coaches were also required to attend regular summits with Brown. Most importantly, the same system used by Brown at the varsity level would be employed at all three junior highs.

The program was open to every male student from the sixth grade through the ninth. And every boy who came out for the squad made the team. Brown, perhaps thinking back to his own youth when he was prejudged purely because of his size, vowed never to underestimate a young man solely at a glance. He wanted the football program to be fun for the kids, but he was also grooming players for the next level of play. By the time a boy reached his freshman year, Brown and his assistants had identified the finest players in Massillon.

Luther Emery of the *Massillon Independent* ran into Brown at Lincoln Park shortly after Brown was named the Tigers' head coach. Emery started in the newspaper business at the age of seven when he started peddling copies of the *Cleveland Plain Dealer.* He joined the *Evening Independent* in June 1926 as a reporter and, in a short time, became the paper's first photographer. On this day, though, Emery wasn't out chasing a story, but he stumbled upon one nonetheless.

A gang of grade-schoolers were playing a game of football as Brown stood back watching the undisciplined contest before him. Emery came up and introduced himself. The two men were acquainted with one another from years before, when they were part of the gangs filling Massillon's playgrounds. Brown and Emery met initially when Luther was among a group of boys playing their own pickup game of football. When one of the kids was called home for supper, Brown asked if he could join in. Looking over the smallish Brown, the boys hesitated briefly before allowing Brown into the mix. This was the beginning of a friendship that would continue to develop as each boy progressed through Washington High. And now that they were joined together again, Emery, using his bully pulpit at the *Independent,* would be Brown's biggest booster in town.

Emery and Brown left Lincoln Park and took a stroll along Massillon's tree-lined streets. As they conversed, Emery picked Brown's mind. He was going to emulate Chick Meehan's dominating program at New York University, Brown explained. His boys would stand during timeouts, and there would be no water! While most teams would have a manager dart out with a water bucket during a timeout in play, Brown wouldn't even have water available on the sideline. He picked up this concept from Meehan, but Meehan took stringency a step further. He would have his players jump rope when they reached the sideline. Even Brown thought this practice was a bit extreme. But there would be discipline, this much Brown promised Emery.

Before the first practice, Brown tossed all the ragged uniforms into a large pile. The first-string players had first dibs on the better jerseys; the rest of the squad grabbed the leftovers. This act was the only time Brown showed favoritism to any member of his team. There were rules to be obeyed, and they were to be followed by everyone.

"Of course we have no smoking or drinking at any time," Brown told his players. "Any boy found guilty of either is out, definitely and completely. That's the law."

And the law, as Massillon players quickly learned, was Paul Brown.

"During the football season we have some additional rules. We don't ride in an automobile, don't go to dances, don't have dates. ...The boys are off the streets at 9:30 and in bed by 10."

"What happens if a boy breaks training?" Brown asked rhetorically.

"If he does, he is a forgotten man. He just disappears from the squad. There is no trouble about it."

Though they were dressed like ragamuffins, and they played on a ramshackle field, Brown's Tigers burst out of the gates by winning their first five games and tying their sixth. Brown's young charges came crashing back to reality in the season's second half, however. Massillon lost its last four games while scoring only six points over the final five contests. Before the season finale against McKinley, Brown approached Dr. Bell with an unusual proposal. "What if we charged $1 for admission?" Brown asked. Though demand for the Canton game was always high, this was a daring proposition in the midst of the Depression. Still, Bell believed it was worth a try. The gamble paid off for the program; nearly $4,000 was made off of the evening's attendance, from which new Tiger uniforms were purchased.

Midway through the schedule, Brown found it necessary to assert his authority. He inherited two assistant coaches, John Tannehill and Wallace Clay. For Clay, coaching was purely a secondary responsibility. His farming and family obligations took precedence over Massillon football. In the early weeks of the season, Clay arrived late for practice, increasingly testing Brown's patience. Finally, halfway through the season, Brown's patience gave way when Clay, late once again, strolled onto the practice field still wearing his work boots.

Brown walked over to his coach. "Wallace, we can't have this," Brown said. "You have to be here on time like everyone else."

The very next day Clay was tardy again.

That was the final straw. "Wallace, that'll be all," Brown said.

Clay didn't believe Brown had any power over him. "You can't fire me," he protested.

Brown responded with a severe glare, "Don't think I can't," he snapped.

Clay took his complaint to Dr. Bell, who shortly afterward called Brown into his office. "Wallace said you fired him," Bell said.

"This is true," Brown admitted. "Everyone on my staff must be dedicated to his job. Clay isn't. It is important to establish discipline. He was arriving late."

"Well," Bell said with some contemplation, "What would you say if I said to you, 'You're fired'?"

"That's your privilege sir," Brown responded, "but I wouldn't do it if I were you."

Though he didn't care for the manner in which Brown handled the affair, Bell had no intention of calling Brown's bluff. The Tiger's 5-4-1 record was mediocre, but it was a step up for a program that had hit rock bottom. And Bell instinctively could tell that Brown was a leader of men. Such faith began to bear fruit in year two of Brown's rule as the Tigers continued their progress with an 8-2 record. It was the second loss that riled the Washington High faithful, however. Massillon concluded Brown's first season with a 19-0 loss to Canton McKinley's Bulldogs, and the Tigers fared no better in 1933 when they closed out the schedule with a 21-0 defeat at the hands of Canton. Losing to McKinley was unpardonable. Even Elmer McGrew beat the Bulldogs in his last three tries. Eight wins were fine, but until this Brown beats McKinley…

Despite the marked improvement, there were even some calls for Brown's head, but Brown had a new ally at Washington High. Before the 1933 school year, L.J. Smith was hired as the superintendent of Massillon city schools. Immediately, Smith and Brown hit it off. The men had identical goals: a prosperous Washington High School, both on the football field and in the classroom. And it was Smith who called off the hounds when some wanted Brown removed as the Tigers coach. He saw something in Brown, much like Dave Stewart before and Dr. Bell more recently. There was a distinct plan in place, and Smith wasn't going to make a knee-jerk decision based solely on a loss or two to McKinley.

Dr. Bell, as well, remained in Brown's corner. "P," Bell told Brown, "the hammers are never very far beneath the surface."

Bell and Stewart may have placed their faith in Brown, but quite a few Tiger fans remained skeptical. Some were so disturbed by recent Massillon efforts against McKinley that a movement was begun to have the Canton series canceled. The possibility troubled admirers of scholastic athletics. One such aficionado, Roy D. Moore, the publisher of the *Canton Repository,* stepped forward in an effort to stifle the campaign. Moore brought the school boards of both McKinley and Massillon together at Canton's Onesta Hotel. By evening's end, it was agreed the rivalry would continue.

Brown would continue on as well. In fact, he was given even more accountability at Washington High. The football program, of course, was his domain. But beginning with the 1934 school year, Brown became the school's director of athletics, which charged him with the responsibility of every major sport at Massillon. He had already begun coaching the Tiger basketball team a year earlier, guiding the cagers to the state tournament. Success on the hardwood, however, wouldn't quell the call for Brown's head. An idea was conceived by Karl Young, a member of the board of education. Young thought of the formation of a "booster" club, which would bring supporters of the football program together with Brown.

The group was created in the summer of '34 with the objective of promoting "school and everything good in the community." It would cost twenty-five cents to become a booster, and the fee entitled each member to a seat in a preferred section at Tiger Stadium for the opening game. More importantly, with membership came the privilege of hearing firsthand from Brown explanations and the rationale behind his decisions.

Brown's most ardent critics, some of whom were self-anointed football experts, would have their second-guesses answered directly by Brown.

On September 12, the Washington High Booster Club met for the first time at the school's gymnasium. Many of the school's oldest and most loyal fans were among the one hundred in the audience listening to Brown as he described what they could expect at these booster meetings. It was to be a roundtable discussion of the team's play, with straightforward man-to-man answers, Brown explained. Why this fellow didn't play. Why this fellow was taken out of the game. Why Massillon punted when they did, and why this play failed to work. All these subjects and more would be tackled on a weekly basis at these meetings.

Having dispatched Tannehill and Clay, Brown introduced his cur-rent assistants: C.C. Widdoes, the former Longfellow junior high coach, and Hugh McGranahan, who was new to Massillon. Brown then brought up most of his first-string players, who, after taking a bow, demonstrated several shifts and formations that would be used in the upcoming season. After that display, Brown used a blackboard to explain some offensive and defensive formations before closing his presentation by discussing various players, their personalities, and why he chose to use them as he did.

Beyond the X's and O's, the Booster Club served a vital role to the team and community. It was learned that a few players lacked proper clothing, and in those terrible days of want, a good meal was hard to come by for too many of Brown's kids. The Boosters's first project was to give needy players a lunch at the YMCA, while some families received a milk delivery to their homes.

Watching the development of the Tiger football program from a dis-tance was an old friend and counselor. Brown had continued to stay in con-tact with Dave Stewart, as the two wrote numerous letters to one another updating each other on their respective teams. In a correspondence dated October 23 and addressed to "Brownie," Stewart dissected the upcoming season and analyzed Massillon's future opponents. "I am [glad] to see that your team is functioning in high gear," Stewart penned. "You will have no trouble till the Canton game and you even have a chance there."[1]

Much as Stewart predicted, Brown's 1934 Tigers played nine consecutive games without being scored upon as they prepared to face McKinley. The state title was on the line, as McKinley was also unbeaten—the first time in the series history that both Canton and Massillon entered the contest undefeated. The game generated unprecedented anticipation and publicity. Tiger Stadium's seating capacity had been enlarged from 10,000 to 22,000, and every one of the newly added seats was occupied for the contest.

A reporter from Toledo sat in the press box, sending a play-by-play account of the action back to his newsroom via telegraph. Before the largest crowd to witness a sporting event in Stark County history, McKinley took the opening kickoff and drove down the field across the Tigers' goal line. Massillon responded to these, the first points surrendered all season, with a touchdown of their own, but the Tigers failed on the extra point. The 7-6 Canton lead held until halftime. In the second-half, however, it was all Bulldogs. McKinley shut down Massillon's offense following the Tigers initial drive and added two touchdowns following the intermission as well. The Bulldogs took the game, 21-6, and with the victory came the state title for Canton.

The frustrating loss to McKinley notwithstanding, the Massillon program turned a corner in 1934. Brown had found himself as a teacher and motivator. He brought both players and parents together and spoke to them as a group. "We're going to pick the best players regardless of who they are," he emphasized. Brown made it perfectly clear: He ran the program. A player's background would not be taken into consideration when Brown selected his team. Nor would a boy's race be a deciding factor. What mattered was a player's ability and dedication. There would be no interference from the school board, the boosters, or parents. The final word in all things Massillon football would be Paul Brown's word.

Prior to the beginning of the '35 season, Brown sat down and wrote a long hand letter to August Morningstar. The note informed Augie that Brown had named him team captain, and with that designation came vast responsibility.

This honor, Brown informed Morningstar, was "an all-year job."

"You are my 'contact' man," Brown wrote. "You are naturally closer to all the boys than I am. I can get close, but I can't be one of them very well anymore."

Brown then offered Augie a litany of suggestions: "Avoid any act that would permit suspicion of 'growing ego.' Do not get the big head in other words. Be Democratic.

"On the field you have no real authority—you function only by example—you are another player.

"Be cheerful and Spartan like in your attitude no matter how hard the work-out has been or no matter how tired you are. Constantly remind the boys of the axiom: 'Drive yourself in practice and you won't have to in games.'

"Sing and have fun in the showers. Keep your talk clean."

And there was a code to follow:

- The team comes first.
- Set an example not only as a football player.
- Be alert for opportunities to better the team.
- Be in all instances a sportsman and a gentleman.

Augie's letter was unique, but the message was similar to the one Brown penned each summer to prospective participants of Washington High's football program. In his missive, Brown advised the young men what was expected of them and what they could expect from their coach.

"The team is not made by any man yet," Brown explained. "Your success and the success of your team depend upon what shape you report in—and the go-get-'em attitude that it takes to win. Do your exercise daily—work at your football—think about your football. . . . Your coaching staff will give everything they have to help you win. We'll not overlook one single little point that might make you better or save you a beating. The rest is up to you. Train, think football, sacrifice for your team and stick together. We have just one objective—the undefeated State championship."[2]

"Undefeated" and "State champion!" Brown certainly set his sights high, but he had reason to believe in his team. Following the 1933 season, Brown and his staff attended a coaching clinic at Ohio University. Brown came away from the clinic convinced that legendary coach Jock Sutherland's single-wing offense should be adopted by his squad. Previously, Brown employed the double-wing system at Massillon with a degree of success. The switch to Sutherland's innovative scheme, however, altered the Tigers' fortunes exponentially. Speed was a prerequisite in this style of offense. Running out of the single wing, the Tigers implemented a unique shift and kept opponents befuddled with deceptive ball-handling. Brown's team became known for their precise timing, effective blocking, and sure tackling.

Brown's adoption of Sutherland's system played a part in Massillon's resurgence, but most importantly, by 1935, Brown had four years to implement his own teachings. He introduced to the game the "playbook": a small ring notebook in which each member of the Tigers diagramed plays taught to them by Brown in a classroom. Brown was teaching the game by rote; he wanted his players to see the play illustrated, hear it described, illustrate the play in their playbooks, and physically perform it on the field. Through repetition, Brown believed his players would see the play before it happened. Four years of Massillon boys had been schooled in the Paul Brown way of football, and the tutoring began to show on the field.

A couple of days before Massillon faced Niles High School in the season's ninth week, Brown became very ill. Dr. Bell was summoned, took one look at Brown and ordered the coach, "You can't go to Niles."

Ridiculous, Brown responded, "I have to."

"I'm the doctor and you're not going to Niles," Bell told him. "Remember this, Paul, we are all useful, but no one is necessary."

Reluctantly, Brown heeded Bell's orders, but he insisted on being called at halftime. Perhaps his coaches would need some instruction or his boys some words of wisdom. The evening of the game, Brown sat by the phone impatiently.

"What's the score?" Brown snapped when the ring finally came.

"47-0, coach" Hugh McGanahan replied. The Tigers were on the way to a 72-0 romp. Brown settled back into his bed. He smiled and remembered Dr. Bell's words, "no one is necessary."

The Tigers went through their '35 schedule unscathed. Their bril-

liant year was capped with a 6-0 victory over McKinley. It was Massillon's
first undefeated season in thirteen years. Determining a champion was far
from a scientific undertaking. Writers throughout Ohio allied with the
Associated Press submitted their choice for state champ. There had been
occasions when the AP scribes couldn't arrive at a consensus. But this year
there was no doubt. The Massillon Tigers were the finest team in all of
Ohio. Brown's first win over McKinley clinched his first state title. It also
marked the first occasion that Brown's assistants had seen him smile.

The Booster Club continued to grow with the Tigers' rising fortune. The Monday evening meetings had become a premier social event
in Massillon. During the season, the boosters gathered as Brown showed
game films and discussed events from the preceding weekend's game.
Members of the boosters became a network of informants who helped
Brown enforce his ban on dating, attending dances, or riding in cars.
Brown often said that one of his players couldn't hope to break a training
rule and get away with the transgression. "Every waitress in town knows
every boy, and if a boy broke training, I would know about it soon."

Indeed, it seemed as if the whole town played a part in the Tigers'
success. Washington High followed up its first state title by rolling through
its schedule unbeaten in 1936 while allowing only fourteen points all season en route to their second Ohio high school championship. Massillon
entered 1937 having won twenty straight contests, and twenty-nine of
its previous thirty games. All this could come to a sudden halt, Brown
warned, before the 1937 schedule was set to begin.

The boosters gathered in the school's study hall, jammed tightly into
the undersized classroom. Chairs were scarce, so boosters made do by sitting on tables, window sills, and stood lining the walls of the room. What
they heard from Brown was foreboding. He told the crowd that they
wouldn't be seeing the recently graduated Charley Anderson or Michael
Byelene on the field leading the Tigers to glory.

"Those days are gone," Brown stated. "We will not be what we were
last year. We will not run up the scores we did last year, but we will be a
hard, driving club."

Brown couldn't exactly set up the Tigers as underdogs for the com-

The mayor of Tiger Town.

ing season, but he did hope to curtail expectations as best he could. In the two previous seasons, Massillon outscored its opponents 483-13 and 443-14, respectively. This dominance certainly couldn't last. Maybe the scores wouldn't be so lopsided, but Brown had brought a divergent look to the Tigers' schedule in 1937.

Massillon was slated to play three out-of-state opponents: Horace Mann from Gary, Indiana; the Cedar Rapids, Iowa, Thunderbolts; and, for the second consecutive year, New Castle High School from Pennsylvania. The practice of playing non-Ohio schools started in 1934 when Brown's mentor, Dave Stewart, brought his Sharon High School club to Massillon for a sort of homecoming. But Brown wasn't looking solely beyond the state's borders for more exotic and challenging opponents. Brown was also scheduling the best in-state schools he could arrange. In 1937, one of those opponents was a highly touted Mansfield team.

Heading into the Mansfield game, Brown was concerned that his team was taking the Hornets too lightly. Brown's fears were realized when Mansfield ended the Tigers' twenty-one-game winning streak by battling Massillon to a 6-6 stalemate. Brown bristled afterward. "Now you see what happens when everybody is telling them they will win by twenty-nine points," he said.

The Tigers righted themselves and reeled off four consecutive wins before falling to an out-of-state opponent, New Castle High School of Pennsylvania. The loss didn't hurt Massillon in their drive for another championship, and the Tigers swept through their final three games to post an 8-1-1 record. A tie and a loss certainly were not what Massillon fans had come to expect, but the record was good enough to once again earn the Tigers the state title.

Football, Brown believed, should be entertaining. Winning football, obviously, was the most important aspect of the entertainment package, but Brown wanted it all. At his urging, Washington High put together a band. This would be no ordinary high school marching band. In 1938, George "Red" Bird was hired as bandmaster and, almost overnight, the Tiger Swing Band became as big a draw as Brown's football team.

Led by four majorettes in their oh-so-short skirts, Red Bird's Swing Band entranced audiences with their eye-catching uniforms, fancy formations, perfectly executed maneuvers, and up-tempo tunes. Brown suggested to Bird that the band try a New Orleans jazz standard, "Tiger Rag," as a fight song, and before long the tune became a Massillon standard.

While attending a University of Pittsburgh game with L. J. Smith, a thought crossed Brown's mind and the seeds of another Massillon institution were sown. Looking down on the field, Brown and Smith were amused by the poorly outfitted Panther mascot. Both men chuckled over the unrealistic and dilapidated costume, and an idea came to Brown, "Why can't we have a tiger skin, L.J.? An authentic tiger skin?"

Smith thought the suggestion was intriguing and took the thought with him to the athletic board when they returned home. Within two weeks Washington High had a real tiger-skin suit, which was first inhabited by Paul "Pep" Paulson. *Obie,* as the mascot came to be known (orange and black; OB) began to lead the Tigers on the field before each game.

Pomp and circumstance was nice, but without proper execution on the field it was all just window dressing. To properly prepare his Tigers, Brown rode the team hard. "Block your man," Brown would exhort his players, "even if he runs up into the stands—go up there and block him."

On one occasion, lightning was flashing in the skies above Jones Field while the Tigers were in the midst of a practice session. Rather than pull the Tigers from the mud-saturated surface, Brown told his players, "We'll continue to practice." He reasoned, "We might have game conditions like this." And so, the Tigers continued on.

"The Tigers are the best uniformed football team I know of," Brown stated with more than a hint of pride. It cost approximately $120 to outfit a Tiger, and every uniform was tailor-made for each individual. As far as Brown was concerned, this was money well spent. He wanted his players to not only perform like champions, but to look the part also. Away from the field, too, Brown wanted his boys to look sharp. He had pants and sweaters tailored for each player. It was also made clear, Brown didn't want any girls flirting around any of his boys. "I don't want any moonstruck players," he would say. However, at the close of each season, Brown rewarded his Tigers with a "football prom." The dance was the social event of the school year as a nationally known orchestra was brought in, refreshments served and, for the first time in many months, Tiger players could relax, have a good time, and finally acknowledge the existence of girls again.

"We have the toughest schedule to ever face a high school team," Brown wrote to prospective Washington High School players in the summer of '38. He then proceeded to list the formidable teams dotting the Tigers' fall calendar, "and lastly, and most important, Canton McKinley, the toughest, strongest and biggest team we will have to play. We would rather win the last one than all the others put together.

"We are the defending state champions," Brown reminded his Tigers, "at the top of the heap."

But this past success meant nothing in the coming year. "You must win it on your own merit." And to win, he then prompted his readers, took hard work, rigid training, and a strict discipline. "You represent the finest football town in the country," Brown wrote in conclusion. "Don't disappoint your people."[3]

The new Massillon Tiger was introduced before the opening game as the band belted out "Hold That Tiger," but there was no holding these Bengals. Not this year.

"They play like a college team," McKeesport coach Jim Stinson remarked after his team fell to Massillon, 19-7. Stinson's team was the first of three Pennsylvanian schools on Washington High's 1938 schedule. From McKeesport to the traditional season-ending clash with McKinley, the Tigers won with machine-like regularity, as they dominated opponents and entertained spectators with their sharp execution and adroit ball handling. Against the Bulldogs, the Tigers protected a 12-0 second-half lead with three successful goal-line stands. It was a championship performance on a grand stage.

—w—

Massillon had outgrown old Tiger Stadium. The capacity of the field had been enlarged so often, one observer noted, "that the stands looked like a jigsaw puzzle." One portion of the wooden bleachers was badly rotted and condemned. It had become quite obvious that a new facility was sorely needed. However, there was no room for expansion on the site of Edwin Ave. and Third Street, that much was certain. Along with Dr. Bell, Brown began scouting the surrounding area. Eight acres was the estimated amount of land needed for the new stadium. When Brown was shown a large parcel of land in southeast Massillon, he surveyed the scene with a long look.

"How much is available?" he asked.

"One hundred and twenty acres," Brown was told

Cost be damned. "Get it all," Paul implored. He was visualizing the future of Washington High's sports: the stadium and a baseball field. But admittedly, Brown did not think in terms of school expansion. The financial quandary, which hadn't concerned Brown in the first place, was solved when the citizens of Massillon approved a bond issue. Construction began almost immediately upon consummation of the real estate deal. A five-month Public Works Administration and Works Progress Administration project saw a vacant field sprinkled with a handful of trees transformed into the finest high school stadium in Ohio. The finished product was state of the art, unlike any high school facility in the land, boasting a training room, a large locker room, and a classroom for Massillon players. Above each light pole flew a pennant in the color of each school on the Tiger schedule. The press box was almost as large as Pitt Stadium's media area, and Massillon could boast of having the only tarpaulin in Ohio, with the exception of Ohio State. There was also an electronic scoreboard, which cost $2,000 alone. Besides giving the score, the fancy scoreboard told yardage needed for a first down, the period, and time remaining in the quarter. And on May 19, 1939, grass was sown at the new field in preparation for the stadium's first contest.

Four months later the new ballpark was christened in splendid style. The playing field was illuminated with 120,000 watts of light shimmering down on the spectacular show. The ceremonies began as the drum corps of Massillon American Legion No. 221 marched on the field, followed by the Tiger Swing Band, and the Sons of V.F.W. drum corp. The musicians gathered together on the northern end of the field as Obie stormed through a banner, which was said to be a copy of the original architecture design. Pinky Hunter, a radio announcer from Cleveland's WHK, emceed the festivities, the first half hour of which was broadcast on his home station.

Following Obie's appearance, Brown's players burst onto the field. The Tigers came out in three groups, at intervals of ninety seconds. They marched the length of the gridiron and waited for the starting eleven to make their entrance. The bands from both schools put on fabulous shows, priming the crowd of 15,000 for the main event of the evening: the game. Cleveland Cathedral Latin had won their previous seventeen contests, and twenty-seven of their last twenty-eight. Still, the Lions were no match for the Tigers, who out gained their guests on the ground, 310 yards to 45, on their way to a 40-13 victory. Massillon then breezed through the next eight games, allowing only six points in the process. Only Canton McKinley stood between the Tigers and their fifth consecutive championship. There was talk at the time of a "Buckeye Bowl," a post-season scrap that would bring together the state's two best scholastic teams at Ohio Stadium. Such speculation died out quickly when Brown immediately vetoed the idea insofar as Washington High was concerned. No, Brown stated emphatically, the Tiger's season ended with Canton. Only McKinley stood between Massillon and their fifth consecutive championship.

The red and black togged Bulldogs once again had a fine team, and if anything, the rivalry had gotten more heated. The evening before the game, Brown rode out to Fawcett Stadium; he wanted to test the turf in order to know what type of shoes his players needed the next day. Upon returning to his car, Brown found that each of his car's four tires had been relieved of their air by mischievous Bulldog enthusiasts. Brown had the last laugh the following afternoon when his Tigers came out on top 20-6. The win, however, had been anything but easy.

"That ought to be a good lesson to Massillon fans," Brown commented following the final gun. "There's never anything but a tough Canton McKinley game."

—⁂—

For some time, the question had been bandied about . . . could Massillon beat a college outfit? Such a thought seemed absurd. On the scholastic level, the Tigers were as fine a team as ever assembled on Ohio soil, but a college club? That prospect seemed far fetched. Experience and size alone would put Massillon at a severe disadvantage.  In the spring of 1940, however, Brown scheduled a practice game against the Kent University Golden Flashes and had a verbal agreement with the University of Akron for another. Before the game, Kent released publicity material that proclaimed the Golden Flashes to be, "the best Kent team in history."

The contest, played under regulation rules, was never close. At the close of the six-period exhibition, the Tigers were leading 47-0. Not everyone, though, was taken by the dominating Massillon performance. One day after the contest Jim Schlemmer of the *Akron Beacon Journal* took Brown to task for putting his team up against a college club.

"Our respect for Paul Brown is great, but we don't give him any credit for scheduling a game such as this. We don't believe he put his team's reputation on the spot, but he did risk its physical well-being."

Schlemmer's position had merit. But the novelty of a high school team defeating a college team, even in an exhibition, was hard to ignore. In the aftermath of the Kent-Massillon game, Akron pulled out of their commitment and canceled their meeting with Washington High. After witnessing the Kent debacle, Akron officials acknowledged the reality that nothing could be gained from playing a high school team.

"The fundamental idea of matching a big college team with a little high school team is bad," Schlemmer wrote. "We hope the thing goes no further. The next college squad will try even harder than the Flashes did yesterday to mess up the schoolboys and whether or not they succeeded, both teams are likely to be the loser."

One thing was decided by the peculiar exhibition: "Massillon can beat an ordinary college team and do it handily."

—☩—

In the fall of '40, *Life* magazine featured a profile on the Massillon Tigers. The whole town celebrated the flattering exposure in the popular newsweekly. Inside every restaurant, drug store, and newsstand, copies of the magazine were placed on display—opened to the two page-spread celebrating Massillon's eleven.

Life was far from the only periodical keyed into the Massillon story. *The Saturday Evening Post* told its readers about the phenomenal high school team in middle Ohio. The *Philadelphia Inquirer* devoted a full page to the Tigers, while Chester Smith of the *Pittsburgh Press* made the leisurely drive to Massillon. Smith had heard of the happenings in Stark County and the sports editor of the *Press* wanted to see first-hand what the fuss was all about.

"It is whispered here and there," Smith wrote, "Coach Brown teethes the town's boys on shin guards and old shoulder pads, so that by the time they reach high school age, they walk the streets in huddles and signal for a fair catch every time the local trolley comes along."

Smith's writing, while tongue in cheek, displayed just how some questioned how Brown put together his teams. Surely it couldn't all be above board.

In a letter dated August 22, 1940, Brown wrote, "Dear George, we will go on a one week's fishing trip." The fishing expedition Brown referred to was to take place a week from the coming Monday, and George wasn't to tell anyone but his parents of the trip, "because some people will misconstrue things and call it a football camp."

Brown informed young George on what to pack for the seven-day excursion. "One or two blankets and a pillow, swimming trunks, fishing equipment, your football shoes, towel, an old set of knife fork and spoon, glasses and soup bowl." The need for football shoes wasn't explained by Brown in his letter, but the note's recipient understood the implication. There would be fishing on the fishing trip, but there would also be football, which was in violation of the Ohio high school regulations.

Massillon's extraordinary string of state titles placed the program under intense scrutiny. Critics heard whispers of the team's fishing trips, but extra training couldn't be the sole reason for Paul's success. Surely state association rules were being violated, or at a minimum, bent. One often-heard accusation was that Brown scouted players outside the school district. If Paul found a player of particular talent, he offered to find the boy's father a job in Massillon.

"It seems Massillon goes about gathering material for its elevens much as do many colleges," Bill McKinnon wrote in the *Columbus Dispatch*. McKinnon then played out in print a hypothetical of Paul bringing a football standout from Portsmouth to Massillon by finding his father some work. Or maybe, McKinnon speculated, a widowed mother needed some financial assistance to keep her and her football-playing son in Massillon. Whatever it took to keep the best players in town, so the story went, Brown would see to it. McKinnon explained that he'd gotten his information from "travelers" who had been to Massillon; hardly a concrete source. The rumors were just that—rumors. Nothing of ill-repute was ever substantiated and Paul dismissed all accusations. Everyone who played for Brown at Washington High did so "legitimately," he insisted.

The *Columbus Dispatch* piece by McKinnon created a maelstrom of letters from Massillon supporters. The deluge of protest prompted McKinnon to recant his charges several days later. No one supported Brown and the school's football program more than Luther Emery. The newsman made no attempt to hide his passion. Emery was a Tiger booster, and if that fact bled through in his work, so be it. Using his forum in the *Independent*, Emery extolled the virtues of Brown, but he was far from alone. In the eyes of his fellow townspeople, Brown could do no wrong. It was damn near impossible to find someone, anyone, in Massillon saying a disparaging word about Brown. How could they? Revenue generated by the program entirely supported the astronomy club (they even had a telescope!), basketball, junior school athletics, and equipped the Tiger Band. In addition, football funded the camera club, the model airplane club, the traveling debate team, speech study, and nature study expedition. Guest speakers for chapel were also paid for by the football program. Indeed, Tiger football bettered the school and altered the environment of the town.

The success came through hard work and diligence as well as Brown's unconventional method of analyzing his players' mental capabilities. Each Tiger had his IQ tested prior to the season. Intelligence on the playing field was as important as ability, Brown believed. He wanted bright boys who could think on their feet. But he also wanted them resilient.

"We never substitute because a man is tired," Brown bragged. "There is no water for the players during the entire game. We don't even possess a water bucket. We have one rule which we are careful to follow. When the ball is dead, our men are all up on their feet. Any man who is down when the ball is dead is hurt."

This hard-nosed approach, too, came under fire by Brown's detractors. Washington High wasn't the military; these were just boys who wanted to play a little football. Paul ignored such carping. It was his team and he would run it as he saw fit. His response to critics was found on the field. Brown was confident in his boys' abilities and did not blush at pitting them against quality opponents. The 1940 schedule again was chock-full of excellent teams. First up were the powerful Cathedral Latin Lions of Cleveland, whom the Tigers dismantled, 64-0. In the aftermath, a local writer speculated, "Coach Brown is going to have a rather difficult time trying to convince a lot of fans that his 1940 team isn't possibly just a teeny-weeny bit better than any of his preceding state champions."

They made it look so easy, even opposing coaches watched in awe and appreciation.

"The boys and I want to congratulate your boys and you on your fine football team," Weirton's coach, Carl Harrill, wrote to Brown after his team fell 48-0 to the Tigers. "It is the best high school team I have ever seen or ever hope to see. My boys suggested you play West Virginia University. We have never seen such deception, speed, and blocking. It is the finest job of coaching I have seen in college or high school."[4]

Later in the season, Toledo Waite's team bus rolled into town bearing a large banner, which was draped over the side of the vehicle. "State Champions!" the sign declared, and the vehicle's occupants were in agreement with the statement. Waite, with its nineteen-game winning streak, had pushed for a match with Massillon. The Indians, not the Tigers, earned the designation as the champions of Ohio, Toledo fans believed. In the days leading up to the November 1 contest, Toledo newspapers belittled the Washington High program. Waite needed to travel far and wide to find an opponent worthy of its abilities. Texas, New York, California … certainly some small-time outfit from a two-bit town like Massillon had no chance against the mighty Toledo Waite Indians.

More than fifty newspaper credentials were issued for the showdown at Tiger Stadium, which was played in a steady rain. And Brown, who had little to say before the game, was uncharacteristically sarcastic following the Tigers' 28-0 victory.

"Let them go to Honolulu or the South Seas for their opponents from here on out, and let them claim the international championship if they want," Brown said, sticking the needle into his defeated foe. "We didn't win as decisively as the boys wanted but, in view of the playing conditions, which were so definitely against us, we should be satisfied."[5]

Waite's coach, Jack Mellenkopf, returned home and graciously took the time to pen Paul a note following the stinging defeat.

"If there is a team in the United States that can touch you, I'd like to see it," Mellenkopf wrote. The Indians' coach then extolled the many virtues of Brown's players before closing the letter with an intriguing suggestion.

"Dismiss it from your mind, if you care to, but I sincerely believe it would be profitable to you, to Massillon, and a great many high school coaches in the Middle West." Mellenkopf proposed that in the coming spring Brown "hold a football coaching school. Invite coaches to come in at a fee and observe."

Such a thought was hardly revolutionary. Other highly touted coaches had put on teaching clinics, much like Jock Sutherland's, which Brown had attended. But Brown hadn't given a thought to hosting such an event. The idea was appealing, certainly, but he took the suggestion and put it aside, for the moment.

—⁂—

The stage was set for the most anticipated McKinley-Massillon game to date. Like the Tigers, the Bulldogs were also undefeated in nine games and every ticket that could be had for the contest was scooped up weeks in advance. For much of the week, as a blanket of snow covered the rest of town, a tarpaulin protected the playing field. Still, as a precaution extra security was also in place outside Tiger Stadium. There would be no mischief as guards were stationed outside the field to prevent anyone from entering the grounds.

A couple of days before the game, Brown's five-year-old boy, Mike, climbed a ladder up to the roof of the family's garage. In a burst of inspiration, Mike stripped the linen from his bed and fashioned a cape from a bed sheet in the hopes of channeling Superman. Rather than soar like his comic book hero, however, Mike crashed down into the unforgiving ground. Later at the Massillon Community Hospital, while being treated for a broken leg, Mike looked to his father. "I'll bet you're glad it was me instead of Horace Gillom." Brown's response went unrecorded, but he, indeed, needed the third member of the football-playing Gilloms. Jake and Odell had both preceded Horace at Massillon, but the youngest of the Gillom brothers was also the most talented of the group.

Come game time, dignity and appearance were forgotten by spectators as they bundled up in anything that would keep the frigid breezes at bay. As they struggled to keep warm, fans watched a closely contested battle. Following a scoreless first quarter, Bulldog halfback Athie Garrison made a scintillating 31-yard dash into the end zone. The Garrison touchdown put McKinley up 6-0, marking the first time Massillon had trailed all season. Hell, they were the first points yielded by the Tigers all season. The Bulldog lead held briefly. Shortly before intermission, Tommy James connected with Horace Gillom for a 25-yard touchdown pass. Gillom crossed the goal line with forty-five seconds remaining in the first half. Following the successful extra point, the Tigers never looked back. Even the great Jim Thorpe sitting on the Bulldog bench couldn't provide the necessary inspiration for the McKinley eleven. The Tigers were ahead 34-6 as the game clock hit zero.

"It's the best football team I've ever coached," Brown told reporters inside a jubilant Tiger locker room. "When a team can be hit on the chin and come back like this one did, it really has something."

They drew the curtain on a magnificent season with a banquet sponsored by the Tiger Booster Club. A crowd of more than 1,000 gathered in the school auditorium as Governor Bricker declared the Tigers as "one of the best, if not the best football team in Ohio."

Hanging behind the dais as the governor spoke was a large banner that counted off the Tigers' championships, 1935, 1936, 1937 ... "It is encouraging in the midst of troubled days to find a spirit and enthusiasm such as is being manifested here tonight," Bricker said.

Ohio State coach Francis Schmidt was also in attendance and spoke directly to the team. But it was Massillon's own coach who tempered the enthusiasm. "This record can't go on forever," Brown told the packed hall. "I hope we can keep amusing you next year and that you will enjoy it as much as you did this year."

—∿—

"We're just a normal family," Katy informed a visiting reporter from the *Independent*. With two precocious young boys and a terrier they named Suzy Q, the Browns resembled the All-American family. In a house filled with athletically inclined boys, Katy fit in well. She displayed prowess in the swimming pool, and passed her love of ice skating on to Robin.

How did she feel about her sons becoming involved in football, the journalist asked. "If they are athletically inclined, I believe there is no cleaner or more character-building sport they could participate in," Katy replied. "The game will give them the 'give and take' so important in life. I should be proud if they do play football provided they play it well."

Her boys were too young for organized football just yet. Mike was only five, and Robin nine, but the older sibling had already taken a liking to skiing as well as ice skating and had joined the boys choir at the Episcopal Church. He had recently tried out for the sixth-grade basketball team, but because he was only in the third grade, Robin was dismissed from the squad.

On a personal note, the article stated that the petite Mrs. Brown was partial to brown and blue tailored suits and liked costume jewelry. She seldom wore her hair in the same style more than once and liked nothing better than to arrange it in a new coiffure. Her partiality to blue was shown in her home, where the blue carpets contrasted nicely with the yellow print drapes. Katy liked to cook and loved to whip up Paul's favorite chocolate cake, but "I haven't time for gardening, nor very much for reading, though I like both."[6]

As they slipped into their second decade of marriage, Paul and Katy were living an idyllic life. Several months earlier, in the midst of the previous summer Paul spent several days in Columbus with Katy, working on his master's degree at OSU. The topic of Brown's thesis, "A Survey of the State High School Libraries," though dour, kept the couple busy researching, typing, and retyping. One afternoon, to escape the stifling

Big shoes to fill.

heat of their rented apartment, Paul and Katy took a leisurely walk along the Olentangy River. Eventually they came upon Ohio Stadium and Paul could not resist the urge to take a peek.

"Let's take a look inside," he said to Katy.

Through the unguarded gates they went, and as they walked deeper into the massive stadium, the Browns realized they were all alone. Not a soul was to be found.

They walked across the turf to the Buckeyes' side of the field and sat on a bench in silence for awhile, taking in the view from every angle. From the bench, Paul took Katy by the hand and led her up a mountain of stairs, all the way to the top of the bowl. Again they sat, quietly soaking in the ambiance. With some reluctance, Paul prepared to leave the building, but before walking through the gates, he turned and took one final glance at the never-ending expanse of bleachers surrounding the beautiful emerald turf.

"You know Katy, I've got a feeling that some day I'm going to be running this show,"[7] he said.

# three    LEAN AND HUNGRY

One of the most sought-after and gratifying jobs in collegiate football was the head coaching position at Ohio State University. It was also one of the most pressurized and unforgiving in the business. In Columbus, success was a relative measure.

On December 16, 1940, Francis Schmidt resigned his position as the Buckeyes' head football coach. The decision to resign, Schmidt explained, came "to beat the athletic board to the punch."[1] It's not as if his term as the Buckeye coach had been a failure. To the contrary, Schmidt's seven-year record of 30-9-1 in Big Ten competition was more than respectable. He was also the only Ohio State coach to ever beat Michigan four years in a row as well as the only coach to end his tenure with more victories over the Wolverines than losses. Unfortunately, the Buckeyes lost their most recent meeting with Michigan on November 23, 40-0. With Brown watching from the Ohio Stadium stands, the Wolverines' domination was complete and total. For all the good Schmidt had done while at Ohio State, the High Street quarterbacks—the rabid Ohio State fans—were calling for his head even before the debacle against Michigan. With his violent temper and vile vocabulary, Schmidt had many detractors. Even Brown occasionally steered his Massillon players away from OSU and Schmidt. And Buckeye players were on the verge of a mutiny as the 1940 season concluded.

"He worked his boys until they were sick of football," the *OSU Monthly* reported. "He never talked or thought about anything else than plays and football, 365 days a year."[2]

Whether he was fired or resigned mattered little. Schmidt was now gone and Buckeye boosters had high hopes and expectations for his replacement. The wish list was long, and for the most part, impractical.

They wanted a big name. Maybe a Jock Sutherland or Clark Shaughnessy; either man would be a nice fit. Unfortunately, those men were under contract elsewhere and weren't available for hiring. Whoever was selected would need to meet certain requirements. For years, OSU administrators wanted a coach who also served as a physical education tutor, rather than functioning solely as a full-time football coach. The administration wasn't altering this prerequisite while searching for the next coach. "He must be an educator," one board member said, "a teacher, a physical education professor preferably."

The university's athletic director, Lynn St. John, had already begun the search using this, as well as his own personal criteria, in the quest. The leading candidate was Don Farout of Missouri, but also under consideration were George Hauser, a line coach at Minnesota, and Alan Holman, head coach at Marshall. Off St. John's radar but on the minds of several in the Columbus press was the high school coach from Massillon: "the Massillon Miracle Man," as so many liked to write. St. John entered the process searching for a coach with college experience, but outside pressure forced him to take Brown into consideration. What began in the local media, with writers caught up in the Horatio Alger aspect to Brown's story, quickly spread to the Ohio High School Football Coaches Association, which announced its endorsement of Brown for the position. The association applied pressure upon Ohio State with the implied threat of withholding the state's best prospects if Brown were not hired. On the other hand, if Brown were named, the coaches association would steer Ohio's best prep stars to the university.

The bullying tactics of the association annoyed St. John, but there was little he could do but play along. St. John was granted permission to speak with a number of candidates: Holman, Farout, Hauser, and also Brown. In fact, on December 21, Brown became the first "official" interview. Over the course of the next ten days, all the other leading candidates were also screened. Each day brought a new name to the headlines. To the dismay of St. John, the Columbus papers were beginning to dictate the direction of the process. The *Citizen* and the *Dispatch* were both now declaring Brown to be the leading candidate just two weeks into the search. On the 30th, Brown, along with L.J. Smith, met with J. Lewis Morrill. Morrill served as the university's vice president as well as the athletic board chairman. Brown and Morrill had met previously, but only in casual circumstances. Their second encounter, however, found the two men and Smith holed up together for more than two hours. Asked afterward if he was impressed by Brown, Morrill smiled and replied, "very much." The grin indicated he was being questioned by a pro-Brown reporter. Still Morrill refused to discuss the situation further.

This is not at all what St. John had envisioned. Circumstances were quickly spinning out of his control. Brown had made a very good impression on members of the board, and now his office was being overwhelmed by letters and telegrams from influential alumni endorsing Brown for the job.

*"I am writing this note with respect to Paul Brown of Massillon, Ohio. I have known Paul since his high school days and have followed his great success as a coach of the Massillon High School football team. He is a grand young fellow, with outstanding ability, as his record proves, and I hope he will fit into your picture at Ohio State."* [3]

—Paul Fairless, president of U.S. Steel

The same day that Paul met with Morrill, Wes Fesler withdrew his name from consideration. He recently signed a three-year contract with Connecticut Wesleyan and would not break his commitment. With his list of candidates narrowed, St. John called Faurot in for a second interview. But by this time the final choice was a forgone conclusion. This thought was only reinforced when St. John and Jim Remnick traveled to Massillon and paid a surprise visit to Brown on January 6. St. John wanted to talk with Brown and his three top assistants: Carrol Widdoes, Hugh McGranahan, and Fritz Heisler. From noon until early evening, St. John spoke with the coaches individually and as a group. For the better part of the afternoon he was educated first hand to the coaching values of Brown and his assistants, and was also treated to a taste of this football philosophy in action when Brown showed film of several Tiger games. Before departing, St. John told Brown that Brown would be asked to come to Columbus "within the next few days."

Throughout the whole process, Brown had remained mum. His was a respectful silence as well as strategic. He certainly didn't want to act presumptuous. And Brown also didn't want to appear to be campaigning for the position. Silence, then, was the best course of action. But following St. John's visit to Massillon, Brown felt the need to address the fears of an "anti-Brown" faction out there, a group that feared he would bring his entire staff to Columbus.

"The men who have worked with me at Massillon are very valuable because of their intimate knowledge of my playing style and my organization methods," he said. With that said, Brown admitted that he would "certainly want more than a staff of high school coaches to go with me."

No other candidate was laying out his place for the press. In fact, no one else seemed to be talking at all. Though George Hauser did have strong faculty support, once he removed himself from consideration all eyes then turned to Brown. In his contact with board members, Brown not only demonstrated that he was a gentleman capable of representing the university in any capacity, but he had also impressed them with deep football knowledge and a keen organizational ability. Indeed, he was the favorite, this Brown understood, and it would be foolish for anyone to think that he wasn't thinking ahead.

"I would have to get the feel of the situation in Columbus before I would make any move toward selecting aides," he said. "I don't want anybody to presume I would be so rash as to move in a high school staff to assume complete charge of a Western Conference football squad."[4]

St. John continued to look at other candidates, but the athletic director seemingly was the only person in Columbus still searching.

Within days, Brown returned to Columbus for his sixth and seventh interviews. On January 1, there was a luncheon with St. John and members of the athletic board. Following the meeting at the Faculty Club, Brown

Paul meeting with Lynn St. John at the Hotel New Yorker,
December 29, 1940.

headed to Akron where his Tigers lost to Canton McKinley 24-23 on the
hardwood. He returned to campus the next morning and met with several
board members who were unable to attend the previous day's luncheon.
The busy day closed when Paul and Katy, accompanied by St. John, attended the Ohio State-Northwestern basketball game. The evening was
something of a celebratory night. Though a contract hadn't been officially
offered, the job was all but given to Brown that afternoon. The particulars
would be worked out over the weekend. His responsibilities as Massillon's
basketball coach wouldn't be a problem, according to Brown.

"I can be released from those duties without delay and without placing any handicap upon the team," he said. Though Brown had shepherd-
ed the Tiger cagers to the state tournament the previous four seasons,
he hadn't actually been coaching the team during the current campaign,
anyhow. That obligation fell to Carroll Widdoes and Bill Rohr. "I have

retained my title so that there would be one central point of authority for our entire athletic set-up,"[5] Brown explained.

Brown also admitted that he had made preliminary inquiries into the availabilities of several men, but wouldn't elaborate any further. "It would be injudicious to approach them at this time," he said.

The month-long search, the weeks of speculation and debate ended shortly after noon on January 14. Following a luncheon meeting at the Faculty Club, St. John announced that the board had come to an agreement.

"The athletic board voted unanimously to recommend Paul Eugene Brown to the board of trustees. We hope he will be a long-time coach at Ohio State,"[6] St. John said.

That same afternoon, Brown was a guest speaker at a meeting of the Agonis and Lions clubs at the Chittenden Hotel. He had just concluded a twenty-five-minute address when word of his appointment was passed to Brown. As word spread throughout the hotel ballroom, well-wishers surrounded him and mobbed him with their congratulations. He, of course, was asked to say a few words to those gathered in the hall.

"I'm grateful for the splendid way in which I've been received," Brown told the group. "I'll try hard and my teams will try hard to deserve your full cooperation and support.[7]

"I'm prepared to take over my work here immediately. . . . (I) will devote every bit of my ability and energy toward showing that Ohio State's confidence in me has not been misplaced. There's much to be done and I'm ready to roll up my sleeves and tackle it."[8]

Brown, flush with emotion, shook countless hands. "You know," he told the press who had gathered at the luncheon, "Fritz Crisler remarked long ago the hardest part of accepting a job such as this is living through the turmoil that comes immediately after the appointment."

—⁂—

Luther Emery called Katy at home. He caught her as she was ready to walk out the door for an appointment at the beauty parlor.

"A choice has been made," Emery told Katy.

Ida Bell Brown and Lester Brown learning their
son had been named to the OSU post.

"Which way?" she asked.

"Paul has been named," he informed her.

Thrilled by the news, Katy decided she was too excited to sit at home and rushed out the door to keep her engagement.

The job was his, finally. He had dreamed of this moment for years. At just thirty-two years old, Brown was the youngest coach in the history of the Western Conference. Indeed, Brown's entire adult life was spent preparing for this moment. The groundwork was laid in Massillon, and Brown would bring the theories that worked so well at Washington High to Columbus. But first, he needed to make certain that those remaining skeptics were won over. Brown well understood that a few vocal High Street quarterbacks could make his job hell if they weren't on board. Over the next several months, Brown would speak before countless alumni groups in every corner of the state, wooing the few unconverted. The campaign began just hours after he was named the Buckeyes coach, in the evening of January 14. He had previously agreed to speak at a father-son gathering at Temple Israel, and even after a busy day, Brown kept his appointment. This was the perfect venue to begin spreading the word.

The size of the audience swelled, as could be expected, following the announcement made earlier that afternoon. Present in the crowd were a number of Brown's players. Some, like Earl Martin, had played for Brown at Massillon. But for the other boys, this was a new, energizing experience. By the close of Brown's brief talk, the whole auditorium was ready to take the field.

"I'm here," Brown began, "to speak not in terms of would be and if, but in terms of we will."

Then he laid it out, point by point, of what he expected from his players. "If our boys don't want to keep in condition and refuse to do what is right, I don't care who he is or what he is, he'll be a forgotten man," Brown said. "He'll leave the squad never to come back . . . There will be no water out there for you fellows. You'll get it when you really need it. And if a boy is hurt, I'll decide whether he is to be removed. I'll go on the field and determine his condition."

It would be no picnic, Brown assured his players, but if you come prepared, listen to instruction, and execute, the results would show.

"I'll never lie to you, and I'll know soon enough if you're lying to me," he said.

Brown had heard the stories; coaching the Buckeyes wasn't a job for the faint of heart. He not only was ready for the scrutiny and criticism, he welcomed it. "They tell me Columbus is tough on a football coach," he said. "If that's true, so much the better. That's swell. It shows the folks here are interested in their team."[9]

His confidence was undeniable. The enthusiasm, infectious. The passion, impossible to deny. Everywhere he went, Brown captivated audiences. He seemed to say all the right things, and nothing was more important to the Buckeye faithful than the team from up north. Seven years earlier, Francis Schmidt was disdainful when speaking of the Michigan rivalry. "They put on their pants one leg at a time just as we do," Schmidt said dismissively.

Brown wouldn't crack wise about such a serious subject. "We'll prepare all season with the thought in mind that we'd rather beat Michigan than any other team on the schedule."[10]

As far as Brown was concerned, from border to border, the entire state was Buckeye recruiting domain. Why should any of Ohio's top prospects leave the state to go to college? Brown applied pressure on his old colleagues to send their boys to Columbus. And to help him locate and land the finest recruits, Brown divided the state up into sections and gave each of his assistants their own area to recruit. He had finally settled on his assistants in early February. The men Brown asked to serve with him on his staff were of varied experience. "I rise or fall," he explained, "with these selections." Two, Fritz Mackey and Eddie Blickle, were holdovers from the Schmidt staff. Three men had served under Brown in Massillon: Fritz Heisler, Hugh McGranahan, and C.C. Widdoes. Trevor Rees coached at East Cleveland High, and Paul Bixler was the assistant football coach at Colgate. One thing they all had in common was their youth. "Not one of them was forced upon me," Brown made certain to tell.

—⚉—

Brown was formally introduced to the student body on February 5 before a large rally at Men's Gymnasium sponsored by The Lantern. The stands at the Commerce Auditorium were stacked to the rafters, as Brown won over the audience with his calm confidence and friendly demeanor.

"Have fun with us. The team and coaches are going to have fun, because next fall we are going to do just two things: study, that's why we're here, and play football for pleasure. No black cigars, no beer, no running around. Anybody who cheats his body cheats the school and cheats the team.

"We'll fight for you, and we'd like to have you pull for us. Laugh with us when we win, and cry with us when we lose. Don't be too sophisticated to cheer for your team. Cheering for your team, pulling for your school, getting into the spirit of things are some of the things you come to college to do. Don't go cynical, or ten years from now you'll realize how much you cheated yourself out of the joy and fun of college years.

"We may not win every game, but if ever a better team takes us to the one yard line we'll show them how far one yard is, 'cause we'll bump 'em nose to nose for every inch of the distance.

"Let me introduce Kate, my wife. I'm Paul, and she is Kate. When you pass us on campus, why, say hello to us, 'cause we're gonna say hello to you. You'll be amazed how many of you we're going to get to know personally."[11]

At the close of Brown's impromptu speech, the entire auditorium sprung to its collective feet, ready to go to battle (or rather, cheer the battlers on) for the man.

During the first week of February, Paul and Katy finished moving their belongings into the Upper Arlington home they had decided upon. Brown had little time to relax with his family in their new home. Alumni in Akron, Youngstown, Cincinnati, Canton, Toledo, and Cleveland had all requested Brown's attendance at meetings held in his honor. Paul grudgingly agreed to a limited number of such gatherings, preferring to establish himself on campus first. But first he needed to say goodbye to Massillon.

—∞—

On Valentine's Day, the Stark County Ohio State Alumni Club held a dinner in Brown's honor. More than 250 people assembled at the Belden Hotel in Massillon, where they feted Brown and sent him on his way to Columbus. L.J. Smith offered a toast to the departing coach. "Paul has been a grand man to work with," the superintendent of schools said, "and he has done much for the entire school system at Massillon. I am confident he will do the same for Ohio State. He not only is a great football coach, but also a splendid teacher, and his career at Ohio State can be nothing but brilliant."

Brown was visibly moved by the evening. The silver coffee service given to him and Katy was nice, but the outpouring of sincere regard all evening touched him. "This seems to be the parting of the ways, and I don't know whether it is a sad or happy occasion," Brown told the gathering of friends before him. He was moving on, moving on to the job he coveted more than any other, but Massillon was more than a stepping stone to Paul. It was more than a by-station on the way to the big time. To Brown Massillon was home. "This completes nine happy, long years. . . . This is a wonderful community. I want for my own part and for my assistants to thank you for everything. It's been wonderful. It has always been the finest town I know of. It has the finest enthusiasm, loyalty, and spirit. You are always welcome at Columbus and I still know Massillon as my home."[12]

During the final week of March, Brown and members of his staff traveled to twenty Ohio communities, in addition to Detroit, to address meetings arranged by the university's alumni office. Brown divided the state into districts and designated each of his seven assistants to their own area. He himself covered the northeast quadrant of the state, at Celina on March 24, Akron on the 25th, Zanesville the 26th, Findlay the 27th, and Cleveland on the 28th.

In the ensuing weeks Brown continued his "get-acquainted" tour when he traveled to Newark, Toledo, Norwalk, Hamilton, Dayton, and Detroit, before taking a vacation from such diplomatic tasks. Throughout the state, Brown made a favorable impression that included Dayton, where journalist Jack Frong, who normally found much to criticize about OSU football, sang Brown's praises.

"We like Paul Brown's methods and we don't mind telling you that he made a tremendous impression," Franz wrote, "not upon us, but upon everyone who listened to him last night. Even our most rabid downtown coaches came up to us after Brown's little address to tell us he was OK in their book. Unless we're dead wrong, Paul Brown will prove to be the most popular football coach Ohio State ever had. He's certainly got what it takes in our book."[13]

All this traveling and visiting throughout the state was something of an evil necessity that came with the job. That's not to say Brown didn't enjoy getting out and meeting the alumni, but it was coaching that he lived for. There were a few weeks of indoor drills in late February, but the real stuff, spring outdoor practice, began April 3.

More than 200 Buckeye enthusiasts endured a damp cold breeze while sitting under an overcast sky in order to be on hand for the team's first spring practice. Brown's scheduled four o'clock practice began at precisely four o'clock. A lecture from the new coach began the proceedings, followed by a succinct lesson on the chalkboard. He then proceeded to have his players run from the lecture room to the practice field.

The practice consisted of wind sprints, kicking and passing drills, calisthenics and "talking" practice. The regimen proved too taxing for several lineman who opted to catch a breather while seated on the ground. Brown took note of the malingerers. "On your feet," he commanded. "You can't play football lying on the ground. You'll have to get in shape to be on your feet all the time."[14]

At the conclusion of practice, Brown offered little praise of the eighty-three prospective Buckeye players, whom he deemed "too porky."[15]

—⁂—

Eighty-two players reported to spring practice. "That squad," Brown explained, "was at maximum only for the first week." It seems that a number of the boys didn't actually want to toil and sweat on the practice field, "but rather wished to talk about being on the football squad." A number of the upper-classmen present were dubious of a high school coach making a successful jump to Ohio State. Brown showed his new team a film of the Massillon Tigers at work. The speed and execution of the high school boys impressed even the most cynical Buckeye, earning Brown their immediate respect and deference.

The number of boys at Paul's disposal as the new school year approached was much smaller. On August 2, Brown sent out letters to thirty-seven members of the football team. In the note, he demanded that his players report to their first practice on September 10. The Brown family then went on vacation to the Eastern seaboard before Brown and his

Stepping onto the OSU practice field for the first time.
Brown, followed by Paul Bixler, Fred Mackey, and Carrol Widdoes.

coaches began final preparations for the coming season. The squad he had at his disposal was just forty players, easily the smallest squad in the Big Ten. In comparison, Minnesota had sixty-seven, Northwestern sixty-five, Illinois sixty-three, Michigan and Purdue each had sixty, while Iowa, Wisconsin, and Indiana had fifty-seven, fifty-five, and forty-three, respectively. The dearth of manpower worried Brown not one bit.

"We're satisfied to work with a group of forty," he said. "We can give every one of these boys personal attention and they all know that their chances of breaking into games are good. That keeps their interest and is something that a kid on some of those bigger squads can't feel."[16]

The Bucks opened the 1941 season on September 27 against the Missouri Tigers. Brown's counterpart was, ironically, Don Faurot, his chief competition for the Buckeye position. Ohio State entered the game unranked against a formidable opponent in Missouri.

His initial foray onto the lush, emerald, Ohio Stadium field, would have been memorable regardless, but events conspired to make Brown's debut as the Buckeyes head coach truly memorable. Even before the opening kickoff, actually before Brown had entered the stadium, strange happenings made the day unforgettable.

As the team bus approached the Horseshoe, Paul spotted several old acquaintances from Massillon standing outside the park waiting to enter. Brown asked the driver to pull over so he could get out and greet his friends. When Paul was done chatting he realized that the bus and its police escort had already entered the stadium. The attendant, not recognizing the Buckeyes' new head coach, asked Brown for his ticket.

"I don't have a ticket, I'm the new coach."

"Is that right?" the guard replied, quite unconvinced. "Well, I'm President Roosevelt, but you must have a ticket if you want to see today's game."

Nothing he could say would convince the dogged sentinel. Thankfully, Brown was able to rouse someone in the locker room above the entry, who promptly made certain he was let through the gate.

Once inside, Brown struggled to contain his glee and exhilaration.

Led by their youthful coach, the Buckeyes took the field in their crisp home scarlet jerseys. Brown looked just as fresh as his boys. In a starched white shirt, covert cloth suit, and green hat, Brown may have been the sharpest dressed man in the stadium. In his exuberance, Paul embarrassingly found himself in the middle of the field with his players just prior to kickoff. With great zeal, Brown made his way to his proper station, the sideline, "hopping and skipping all the way."

It wasn't until he sat on the bench awaiting the kickoff that his nervousness began to show. "He jerked up his socks, crossed and re-crossed his legs, clasped and re-clasped his hands," one observer noted. Brown sat on the edge of the bench, nothing occupying his hands, no program, no charts . . . he leaned forward, staring intently ahead, lost in thought.

During a break in the contest, Brown walked over to the bench and picked up the phone connected to the coaches' box above. Carroll Widdoes, upstairs spotting plays, stopped the discourse for a moment. "Hey Paul," Brown's assistant said, "Have you stopped to think where you're sitting?"

"No," Brown replied after a reflective pause, "I hadn't stopped to think about it, Wid."

After the final gun, however, Brown allowed the emotion of the day to wash over him. A photographer approached and asked the beaming Brown to smile for the camera. "If I could make it any bigger, I would," Brown answered, referring to the grin which already stretched from ear to ear.

Brown's first victory didn't come without a bit of suspense; it was a nail-biter through and through. "Man, I'm not used to this sort of stuff," Brown said in the locker room following the 12-7 Ohio State win. "If it's always going to be like that, I'll lose ten years off my life."

It was back to work the next day, though. "Sure, I was glad to get off to a winning start," Brown admitted. "But the team that beat Missouri isn't the kind of an outfit that I hope eventually to give to Ohio State fans. The team Saturday didn't represent what I want and what I'll strive doubly hard to develop in the weeks to come. Against the Tigers, we lacked balance, and naturally, that's a sign of weakness."[17]

Next up was the Southern California Trojans and a trip to Los Angeles. To compete with a strong USC team, Brown well understood that the Buckeyes must step up their game, but the task wouldn't be easy. After working out Monday and Tuesday, Brown and his team embarked for the coast Wednesday morning. The Buckeyes were venturing west in style, in an all-steel, diesel-powered streamliner. The team occupied three sleeping cars, a diner, and an observation car that the boys used for studying and to listen to an occasional lecture from their coach. The club car included a sandwich bar, a barber shop, and a shower, in addition to "lounging" facilities for more than two dozen.

It was a working trip for the team. The players still had to keep up their studies, and the team also held practice sessions, in Chicago on Thursday and Albuquerque Friday. Following the stopover in Albuquer-

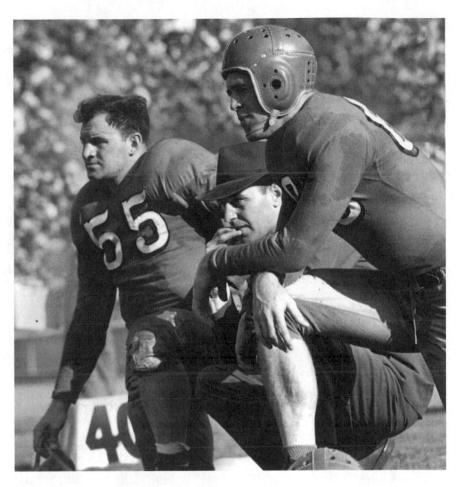

October 4, 1941, Brown (center) watching his Buckeyes shock the
USC Trojans with John Hallabrin (number 55) and Thomas Kinkade.

que, where the Bucks drilled at the University of New Mexico, the players
boarded the train sporting ten-gallon Stetsons and "talking like characters
out of a Zane Grey novel."

Paul certainly had his team loose and relaxed, but few believed his team
stood a chance against the Trojans. An Ohio State team had never before
won on the West Coast and expectations were that the Buckeyes wouldn't
on this occasion, either. That USC was riddled with injuries didn't lessen the
shock of the outcome at Los Angeles Memorial Coliseum. A 33-0 Buckeye
whitewashing of the Trojans was more than Brown could have hoped for.

"It was one of those things when everything went right for us," Brown offered. "The Trojans were crippled and—perhaps—they thought because they had been favorites, they could win without too much effort."[18]

Afterward, the dressing room was alive with the hum of victory. With unrepentant joy, giddy Buckeyes sang a disjointed tune about "... the whole state of Michigan." On the field, a group of alumni made their way down from the stands and joyously danced around Brown, smothering the coach with appreciative kisses. Though thoroughly embarrassed by the outpouring of affection, Brown savored every moment of the triumph. It had been only two games, but Brown couldn't help but feel validation. Those skeptics who questioned whether a "high school" coach could cut it in the big time were silenced for the moment.

—⁂—

The victory was sweet, indeed. But the time for celebrating had passed, Brown told his players as they made their way back home. "We've got to learn there is no 'get-rich-quick' in football. Games are won the hard way, so for the rest of the week after we get back home, we're going right back to the fundamentals."

Convincing these young men that there was still work to do following two stirring victories would prove a difficult task. These were the moments when Brown's motivational and teaching skills would be tested. "We're still a long ways from a football team," Brown continued. "I hope we will be one in a few more weeks. We're better than we were, but we're still a long ways from being what we'd like to be."

His words of warning were heard, but still the festive atmosphere on the Bucks' train continued. The *Dispatch* sent a photographer to Logansport to meet the team and take some shots of the celebratory ride home. Captured by the staff photographer was a beaming Brown, gaily sporting a Stetson. It was a far cry from his usual ball cap, or sideline fedora, but for the occasion the look was just fine. The festive trip home reached its climax as the train rolled into Columbus's Union Depot at 6:38 Wednesday evening. Twenty thousand fans were at the station to greet the Buckeyes.

The welcome home was overwhelming for the players as well as their normally taciturn coach. Briefly, Brown spoke to the boisterous crowd.

"I never have seen so much ado about a football game," Brown said about the festive din, "but I like it."

Still, he assured all, resting on their laurels was not an option for the Buckeyes. "Tomorrow we're going back to work in the mud up at the stadium."

The Buckeyes then had two weeks off between the USC game and the Buckeyes' Western Conference opener against Purdue, which gave Ohio State fans plenty of time to celebrate and speculate. These heightened expectations concerned Brown. One of his main priorities became trying to dampen this unbridled optimism. The scores of the first two contests were deceptive, he said unconvincingly. Their defense, in particular, was lacking. Lacking "the edge," according to Brown, "you have to have."

The Buckeyes made it three straight to start the year when they eeked out a 16-14 win against Purdue's Boilermakers. However, seven days later, Brown's personal thirty-six game winning streak was stopped by Northwestern, 14-7. The jauntiness that filled the Buckeye locker room following each of their first three games was conspicuously absent in the stadium tower. With immense gall, a photographer approached Brown in the locker room. Could we have a smile, Paul? He asked hopefully.

"I'm afraid I can't," Brown replied with great courtesy. "I don't feel like smiling right now."

He then turned his attention to the beat reporters hovering nearby. "We—the boys and I—are going out of this tower with our noses in the air and try to lick someone else. . . . We died by inches," he explained, "but dammit, we died."[19]

Two days later, Brown was still put off by the loss. He complained at a press luncheon that he was frustrated with some of the players held over from the Schmidt regime. It was the little things that were bothering him, he confessed, something as simple as breaking a huddle. "It isn't the way I want it. It isn't the kind of football we like. But habits are hard to break."

Brown spent much of the summer and fall trying to clean up the residue of Schmidt's hard-nosed approach to coaching. There was much about his predecessor's tactics that left Brown wanting. The gutter talk used by Schmidt himself was not tolerated by Brown. Foul language—in a game, on the practice field, or in the locker room—was forbidden. In fact, uncouth behavior of any type was unacceptable. Brown expected his players to carry themselves in an urbane manner. Skipping class and snubbing studies were things of the past. Under Brown's watch, school work took precedence; football practice was scheduled around class.

The very afternoon that Brown carped about the lack of discipline, Charlie Anderson, one of Brown's kids from Massillon, arrived late to the team's Monday meeting. In fact, Anderson had been something of a problem for Brown the whole year. He blatantly cut classes and was on the verge of being kicked out of the university. There were other transgressions also. Anderson had been seen frequenting a night spot in season, and once Charlie nearly came to blows with a teammate while the team practiced at the University of Chicago on the way to California. This latest infraction was the last straw, however. Anderson was unrepentant, and the complete lack of remorse forced Brown's hand. That it was one of his Massillon boys especially pained Brown, but he had to prove that he pulled no favorites.

Anderson was dismissed, the official statement explained, "for the welfare of the Ohio State football squad and for the future of Ohio State football." Brown's decision to remove Anderson from the Buckeye squad caused a ripple of concern in the press. Locally, given Anderson's behavior all season, Columbus scribes had anticipated such an action. Still, such a drastic verdict right in the middle of the schedule shook the squad. But the decision established that Brown was in complete control, and that no individual player was bigger than the team. It was exactly the effect Brown wanted to fashion.

—⚬—

The loss of Anderson and the ensuing controversy didn't affect the team on the playing field. Apparently, the defeat to Northwestern was just a hiccup. The Buckeyes proceeded to win their first ever game at Pitt Stadium, which was followed by a barnburner against Wisconsin (a 46-34 win over the Badgers) and a 12-7 triumph over Illinois. One thing was consistent each week. For attribution, Brown's comments following a game were to the point and often unimaginative. Even in victory, his remarks veered to the negative. What he saw as a coach was where his team needed to improve. That's what needed to be emphasized. Brown's standards were extraordinarily high; he expected more than just a win. After the Illinois contest, he quipped, "we continued our policy of making every one of our opponents look good." It had been a victory, but a complacent one. Certainly, Brown was pleased when he looked up and realized his Buckeyes were 6-1 heading into the Michigan game, but stressing the positive was superfluous in the glow of victory.

"It's just one problem we haven't been able to lick yet," Brown told a Varsity O gathering following the Illinois contest. "We just can't stand to be favored, and anyway that whole set up is wrong. The sooner everyone gets used to the idea of taking the game as it's played and not as it looked on paper on Friday and Saturday morning, the happier we will be."[20]

Brown certainly didn't need to worry about his team being over-confident before heading to Ann Arbor November 22. Michigan had won the three previous meetings, and the Wolverines were thirteen point favorites this season over the Buckeyes. The expectation was Michigan's vaunted defense would be too much for Ohio State to negotiate. To the great surprise of almost every one of the nearly 86,000 in attendance, the Buckeyes stood up to the stronger, faster, and more talented Wolverines. With "deception and courage," Ohio State fought Michigan to a 20-20 deadlock.

At times throughout the season, Brown had struggled to elicit a smile following a win. On this day, however, Brown burst onto the field at the sound of the final gun and merrily ran to his players. He made no attempt to conceal his joy, as he hugged and backslapped his boys who were equally animated. It wasn't a victory on the scoreboard, but the draw was a testament to the Buckeyes' hard work and diligence.

Validation. He felt it on the train ride home from California, and Brown certainly felt it now. He sold his system: to his players, his assistants, the alumni, hell, even most of the press . . . everyone bought into Brown's system. A team that hadn't been expected to finish in the top half of the Western Conference closed the year in a second-place tie with Michigan, trailing only the Minnesota Gophers in the standings.

Two nights later, at the season ending Appreciation Dinner, standing before 1,100 banqueters in the men's gymnasium, Brown bared his sentiments. The entire room burst into enthusiastic cheers when Brown was introduced by toastmaster Jack Fullen.

"I'm rather embarrassed at all this," a seemingly self-conscious Brown said as he stepped to the podium. "This being a nameplate and accepting all the plaudits because I'm no more a part of the show than any one of my staff and any of the members of my team. It concerns me when they make too much ado over one man. We all work together and one man is just as much responsible for the success of the group as another."

Brown then introduced each member of his staff, and called up his twelve seniors. It was then that his voice began to crack with emotion, displaying as much feeling as he'd ever publicly demonstrated. "They've been wonderful, just wonderful, and I'll never forget them," Brown said while looking over at his players. "As you can see, they're the apple of my eye, and I'll always remember them most because they represent a sort of a landmark. They were my first at Ohio State and they were so cooperative and so willing."

He then turned and spoke to the seniors directly. "I can't tell you how much I sincerely feel toward you. You were so perfectly swell."[21]

Off the record, Brown loosened up some and allowed the writers covering the football program a peek at his personality. Brown cultivated good relationships with most of the men who covered the Buckeyes on a daily basis. With Paul Hornung of the *Dispatch*, Brown developed a warm friendship, a relationship that would serve both men well professionally and personally. Hornung was an affable sort, a bit mousy. Never had a bad thing to say, or write, about anyone. Brown certainly liked Hornung's non-

Brown talking with newsmen.

controversial coverage of the Buckeyes. The reporter was always there, waiting for the coach. Following a game, after practice, it never mattered how long it took for Brown to come out of his office, Hornung was there waiting. Off the record, or on, Hornung protected Brown

The *Dispatch's* beat reporter wasn't the only predisposed voice in the Columbus press corps. Lew Byrer, the sports editor of the *Citizen,* was the veteran of the local sports scene. He favored short sentences in his short columns. Fond of a good cigar, Byrer was fonder still of a good drink. These were the days when sportswriters carried a fifth of whiskey in their briefcase and once safely seated in the press box, they broke out the bottle and got to work. Byrer certainly wasn't alone in his love of drink. His contemporaries in town, Bob Hooey, sports editor of the *Journal,* and Russ Needham, of the *Dispatch,* were both hard-drinking old hands around the Horseshoe.

The rotund Needham was a blustery sort. Full of himself, cocky, boastful, Needham's was usually the loudest voice in the press box. And in print he, more than any of his colleagues, found reason to criticize the Buckeyes' head coach. Still, none of the press box barons could find much fault with Brown's first year in Columbus. It was inarguably a successful campaign, one that harbored promise for bigger things to come.

# four   WE WON, WE WON

As he did at Washington High each summer, Brown sent a letter to every member of his football team. Dated August 14, Brown's 1942 edition expressed the most rudimentary expectations he had for his team.

"We are faced with a long and difficult schedule," he wrote. "A great experience awaits you—you must be at your best both physically and mentally. It is absolutely imperative that you work out daily. If you report out of condition, you simply do not represent our type of men—and we can not use you. You have so much at stake—plan for it—enjoy it—look it right in the eye knowing that you have gone 'all out.'"[1]

Prior to taking the field for the first time, Brown gathered his players together. Shortly after the Buckeyes tied Michigan the previous November, America was attacked by the Japanese. The events of December 7 would have unforeseen impact on all their lives. But for the moment, the war was put out of mind.

He approached this meeting as he always did; there would be no pep talk. That is not Brown's style. He welcomed his players, who sat before him in classroom desks. In effect, that is what the Buckeye meeting room was— a classroom. Each OSU player was handed his own loose-leaf notebook filled with blank paper. While listening to their coach, the Buckeyes were expected to take notes and diagram plays. With the opening game against the soldiers of Fort Knox fast approaching, the Buckeyes were running short of time to prepare. Brown gave the players "about a play and a half a day."

Two days before the Buckeyes' initial practice, Ohio State players were introduced to the Columbus media. Watching his players as they posed for photographs and answered reporters' questions, Brown shook his head. They were, "too small an outfit for a Big Ten team," he said. The sessions helped put a face on the names that the public would be hearing throughout the autumn and also gave writers a brief look into the personalities of the young men playing each Saturday. An introduction was necessary as many of the stars who comprised the '41 team were gone, including Jack Graf, Tom Kinkade, Dick Fischer, and Jim Daniell. Brown's 1942 outfit included just eight lettermen and a slew of sophomores. Twenty-three to be exact; a group that boasted such promising players as Dante Lavelli, Bill Willis, and Massillon's own Tommy James. This session was essentially the last opportunity the press would have to directly contact the players. This edict was strictly enforced by Brown. He was the face of the team; he was the voice of the team.

*Esquire* magazine had conducted a preseason poll of football experts that placed Ohio State sixth in the country behind Minnesota, Notre Dame, Great Lakes Naval Academy, Penn, and Army. Where his team would be at the end of the year, Brown wasn't certain, but he did like what he'd seen on the practice field. This group of boys had something special, something that he couldn't quite put his finger on. Before sending his players out onto the Ohio Stadium turf against Ft. Knox, Paul came as close to an inspirational talk as he would all season.

"I don't know how good a team you are, but I don't know of one better."

Brown certainly knew Fort Knox wouldn't be a proper challenge; the 59-0 victory in a relentless downpour was little more than a scrimmage for the Buckeyes against an overmatched opponent. "It gave us a taste of opposition," he explained. "That's all we needed. Just something to break the monotony of practice."[2]

But next up was a decidedly tougher opponent, Indiana University, a much better measuring stick. On paper, at least, the Hoosiers were the superior squad. They were bigger, more experienced, and boasted star back Billy Hillenbrand. Indeed, it was one of the finest Indiana teams in years. On a hot, sultry October afternoon, more than 8,000 high school students from throughout the state were in the stands as guests of Ohio State, watching a stirring Buckeyes 32-21 victory.

"Our boys have more innards than a pirate," Brown gushed following the final gun. "When a team comes from behind twice to win, it has what it takes. That was one of the best contests I've ever seen."[3]

Following the exhilarating victory over Indiana, Ohio State took Southern California, 28-12. The game wasn't as close as the score would indicate. The Buckeyes' thorough domination over the Trojans propelled them to number one in the Associated Press collegiate poll. Ohio State followed that victory with a 26-0 win at Purdue, the same Boilermaker team that upset Northwestern one week earlier.

"That one next week, that's the one I want!" Paul was heard to proclaim at the sound of the final gun. Brown had October 24 at Northwestern circled since the Buckeyes' schedule was released. "Northwestern was the only team that licked us. I hate to get licked and I've waited the whole year to play this game. My boys know how I'm thinking on it and our purpose is clear.[4]

"We'd been waiting a year for this, and you know how it is when you want something badly. You're afraid you won't get it."[5]

Against a formidable Northwestern team led by its star quarterback, "Automatic" Otto Graham, the Buckeyes and Brown had their revenge, 20-6. And, as sweet as the victory over the Purple Wildcats was, Brown had to quell the celebration, his own and his players. Northwestern was far from the conclusion of the season and next up was a trip to Madison, Wisconsin, always a difficult proposition for Ohio State.

— ᴍ —

The war hadn't yet made a conspicuous difference on the field, but restrictions on travel placed visiting teams at a distinct disadvantage. In the past, when in Madison, Ohio State teams were housed outside of town from the time of the arrival until game time. But such accommodations required two buses to transport the team. In this time of war, however, superfluous transportation was not allowed. Consequently, the Buckeyes stayed at a Madison hotel where the corridors inside, and the street outside, rang with the din of merrymakers celebrating Halloween far into the night. Worse than losing sleep, however, on their trip to Madison, the Buckeyes' water supply had been placed in an old rusty tank which hadn't been properly flushed and cleaned before being filled with the fresh water.

Nearly the entire Ohio State squad suffered from a bout of dysentery after drinking the water.

A sleepless night and a roster of boys weakened by illness had a definite effect on the game. The "Wausau Wiggler," Elroy Hirsch, had runs of 53, 21, 20, and 34 yards for the Badgers. Hirsch was a wonder; he was the finest, most spectacular running back the Buckeyes had faced since Red Grange toted the ball for Illinois in the '20s. And though he didn't do it alone, Hirsch was a key factor in the Badgers' clear-cut, 17-7 victory.

"They seemed to anticipate what we were trying to do and met it," Brown admitted. He was gracious in defeat, but he couldn't help but wonder what would have happened had his squad been healthy.

"Half my kids were downright sick at halftime, and for some of them it was the second week in a row that this thing had happened," Brown explained. "Don't misunderstand me, we met a good team—easily the best we've played so far—but we might have shown a little more life if we hadn't been physically weak."[6]

Ohio State recovered from the disappointing loss by beating Pitt, 59-19, and Illinois, 44-20. The Illinois contest was held at Cleveland's "Lake Front Stadium," Paul's first victory in the city of Cleveland, to place OSU at the top of the Big Ten with only Michigan standing between the Buckeyes and a Western Conference title.

"The squad is in fine shape," Paul said in midweek. "They know what they're up against Saturday; they have their eyes open and their feet on the ground. THE WORST THING, THE VERY WORST THING WE CAN GET IS A LICKIN'."

Northwestern was retribution, but Michigan was a blood feud.

"This is THE game on our schedule. Set your hearts on winning it and on having your best day that day. We want to win this game more than all others put together."[7]

Only rain marred one of the greatest days and sweetest victories in Ohio State history. "We won, we won!" the exuberant Bucks hollered as they hoisted Brown to their shoulders and carried him across the field to the locker room.

Dave Stewart (center) flanked by two of his protégés: Brown (left)
and Wisconsin coach Harry Stuhldreher.

Brown was downright giddy when he spoke with the press. "Were
you ever so muddy and didn't give a darn? Boy, it's wonderful!" he said
about the 21-7 victory.

"We waited so long time for this one. We pointed for it, we planned
for it. We thought about this a great deal. This meant everything to us."[8]
A Big Ten championship! A victory over Michigan!

Traditionally, the Michigan game concluded Ohio State's regular
season. However, St. John added a contest in '42 against a service school,
the Iowa Pre-Flight Seahawks. There was certainly the risk of a Buckeye
letdown following an emotionally charged win over their arch rival. Besides, the Seahawks weren't a pushover. The Iowa roster, "the Green Bay
Packers in Navy Blue," was filled with quality players.

"We might get beat 100-0 and I'm not kidding about that," Brown
said from the Buckeye dressing room. With his familiar felt hat perched
on his head, Paul sat on the trainer's table with his legs crossed, unwrap-
ping a stick of gum. "They're pointing for us and we haven't even thought

about them. Michigan is the game we wanted and we're just playing out the string now. We shot the works today and there's just not much excuse for getting up again."

Was this a shocking admission by Brown, or was Paul simply downplaying his team's chances, as he was wont to do? It was becoming an old song. According to Brown, the Buckeyes were the underdog nearly every weekend. And, when they won, they were an overachieving bunch, his boys. Though not the band of underdogs Paul made them out to be this group was a special bunch.

The annual "Senior Tackle" was held on November 27, two days before the Seahawk game. The yearly tradition took a poignant turn when Paul spoke to his players for the last time. The seniors, Les Harvath, Bill Vickroy, and Dan McCafferty, were the primary audience of the speech, but Brown understood the talk pertained to many other boys before him. Many of the young men would answer the call of their country and would not return in the fall. The specter of war had been successfully cast into the recesses of most players' consciousness during the season. The reality was before them now, and Paul wouldn't skirt the issue any longer. The moment took on an air of solemnity as Brown began to speak.

"This is the last practice you'll have with us, the last time this particular group will be together for practice as a football squad. . . . I want you always to think of us and to come back to visit us as often as you can. You'll always be our boys, a part of Ohio State football. Don't forget that.

"This is a solemn occasion, because it ends a phase in your lives. You're going to be away from all this. In normal times, you'd be taking up your life's work, but this is war time and this is different.

"You're going into another game—a bigger, more serious game. The game you're going into, they play for keeps with killing and dying and risk to your very lives. But I want you to play it the same way you played football here—with courage, unafraid. When the going gets the toughest, look it right in the eye and keep plugging away all the harder—give it everything you've got.

"There'll always be troubles—wives dying, kids getting hurt and killed—a lot of things. The going will be rough sometimes, but I want you to meet that, too, with your chins up and driving for all that's in you. I never want to hear of any of you committing suicide because the going got too rough. I'd be ashamed of that. Never, never quit."[9]

For the moment football seemed insignificant, if just for the moment.

—⁂—

The apprehension Brown expressed earlier in the week, the fear that his team would let down following the Michigan win was unfounded. The Buckeyes had a great week of practice that culminated with a resounding victory over the service school. At the conclusion, Ohio State's three seniors were carried off the field by their teammates. Brown himself was practically giddy as he greeted the Columbus press corps. He bounced into the locker room and found a cozy spot on a bench. On this day, Brown was particularly expansive.

"Funny ball game," he said with a smile. "Not funny, Ha! Ha! But funny, good."

What a great game, indeed. "Say," Brown said as if struck by a thought, "what was our score anyway? I got too excited to look at the final."

"42 to 12," the reporters chimed in unison.

With a nod and a twinkle in his eye, Brown had one more thing to add. "I couldn't say it before, but now that it's all over I can be frank—we've got a great football team, a great one!"[10] It was a fact Paul wouldn't admit all year, but now, even the most cynical couldn't deny the Buckeyes' eminence.

Two days later, 700 OSU fans gathered in the Men's Gymnasium for three hours to celebrate the Buckeyes' wonderful season.

Speaking of his coaching staff, Brown began, "When we go out on the field, our plans represent the crystallized thoughts of these seven men, my partners in every sense of the word. We're together not only on the football field but all the way. I wouldn't trade any of 'em for any man on any staff in the country."

Brown then turned and called on his seniors to come forward. "You fellows carry a whole lot of responsibility. In the fraternity houses you're tops, back home you're heroes. But just one thing, don't get too big to live."

It was a bit anticlimactic when the news came the next day announcing that Ohio State was selected as the top team in the nation by members of the Associated Press. Two teams were ranked ahead of the Buckeyes leading into the season's final week, Boston College and Georgia Tech. Ohio State's victory over Iowa Pre-Flight, coupled with losses by both Georgia Tech and Boston College, made a national championship a foregone conclusion. For Brown, there was little time to celebrate. He was in Cleveland when the announcement came, the first of many stops for him in the month of December. Lorain, Wooster, Toledo, Philadelphia, New York, and Baltimore were just a few of the towns and cities Brown visited as he spent much of December visiting Buckeye Booster Clubs

In the midst of the many Booster Club appearances, Brown traveled to Chicago for the Western Conference meetings. While stationed at the Palmer House, he was approached by several universities with job offers, including California and Southern California. Learning of this, OSU president Howard Bevis vowed not to let Brown go without a fight. "To keep a coach like Paul Brown, Ohio State would pay what is necessary,"[11] Bevis told newsmen. No, as far as Bevis was concerned, Brown was a Buckeye for life.

—m—

Lester Brown wanted his son to become a lawyer. Though he turned into one of the Massillon Tigers' biggest boosters, Lester held out hope that coaching was just a passing fancy for Paul, even as the younger Brown became the most successful high school coach in the country. Lester's tune changed when Ohio State tapped Paul to coach the Buckeyes. He rabidly followed the Bucks, and no one was happier or prouder than Lester when OSU marched to a national championship. Sadly, on January 30, 1943, just two months after Ohio State captured the title, and shortly after Katy delivered his third grandson, Pete, Lester Brown passed away. (*The Lantern* had held a poll and it was decided that should Katy give birth to a girl, and the Browns should name the baby Scarlet Gray.)

—m—

"Athletic director St. John feels that we should go along with our plans," Paul Brown said, "and so we're expecting to have just the best football team we can have under the circumstances."[12]

Under normal conditions, Ohio State would have returned thirty-nine members of their national championship team. But with the mobilization for war in full realization, these were far from normal times. The Western Conference faculty representatives and athletic directors gathered in late February for a special conference. The meeting was convened to discuss the Big Ten's ban on freshman participation in varsity sports. The decision was made with great reluctance, but wholly out of necessity. The move made available a large number of players who were under the draft age. According to conference statistics, the average age of incoming freshmen was 17 ½ years—assuring them at least six months of varsity competition. This judgment kept alive the possibility of a Big Ten season in the autumn.

Brown, who had invited eighty-five players to spring practice, was pragmatically optimistic. "I believe we'll have football next fall all right, but it will be football after a fashion," he said. "The clean-cut precision play will be missing. The teams won't be as good.[13]

"We have responsibilities we cannot neglect. We are not concerned with the caliber of players or the size of crowds. These are immaterial in these times.

"The football men now are in the van of the thousands who are defending our nation. Thousands of youngsters will follow in their steps. They must not be deprived of the advantages others have had."

The difficulties of fielding a competitive team concerned Brown, but for the time being he put a rosy spin on the trying circumstances. "We believe Ohio State will put on the field a squad comparable to the teams representing Michigan, Northwestern, Minnesota and other opponents."

But this Brown did not believe.

Nearly all Ohio universities gave up football for the duration. Many student athletes enrolled in officer's training programs which allowed them a year of football if they attended a university that had advanced Navy and ROTC programs. In the Big Ten, Purdue, Northwestern, and Michigan had Navy V-12 programs that helped keep their football programs afloat. These Navy training programs in some instances had men with pro ball experience, which put these universities at a considerable competitive advantage. This, Brown believed, was inherently unfair. It was unfair to the kids. It was unfair to the spirit of competition. And though Brown left the thought unspoken, it was unfair to him. While many of Brown's players were enrolled in an ROTC program, Ohio State did not offer an advanced program, leaving the pool of available players severely limited. Still, suspending the football program wasn't an option given serious consideration by Ohio State officials. The administration argued that the continuation of the football program was imperative. A sense of normalcy was vital to the community's well-being. This argument fell flat with Brown. It was a money grab by the university. Simple as that. He was being forced to field an inferior product. The perfectionist in him was offended by this prospect and the reality of the situation.

Several weeks before the opener against the Iowa Pre-Flight Seahawks, Brown attended the first press luncheon of the season at the Faculty Club. After he revealed the Buckeyes' official roster, Paul came clean about his team's chances, and it wasn't pretty. It was the fewest number of players he'd ever started a season with, Brown complained, and there was no telling how many more would be called up to serve before the schedule was played out. That afternoon was just the start of his campaign to prepare the Scarlet faithful not to set their expectations too high.

"Why," Brown moaned following the first real scrimmage, "on nearly every play there was someone who didn't know his assignment. Boy, we have a long way to go."

These Bucks were young, inexperienced, too small . . . the list of deficiencies was lengthy and Brown did not tire of rehashing them. Still, the public wasn't buying all that Brown was peddling. After all, weren't his words eerily similar before the 1941 season? And how did that turn out? Those Buckeyes performed beyond all expectations. The song was similar prior to Brown's second year in Columbus; again he played down the Bucks prospects.

When the team came around to playing for real, the veracity of Brown's forecast was substantiated. They lacked ability, experience, and poise, but the Baby Bucks were full of enthusiasm. Still, vim wasn't near enough to still the Seahawk onslaught. Iowa Pre-Flight pushed Ohio State up and down the field. The 28-13 score would have been worse had the Seahawks coach, Lt. Don Faurot, not pulled back the reins and showed some mercy for Brown's boys. Iowa's average age was more than a half-dozen years older than the Buckeyes. The Seahawks even had a handful of former pro players take the field.

"You can't fight a war with a BB gun against an 18-inch howitzer," Brown said afterward.

Jack Clowser of the *Cleveland Press* searched throughout the Buckeye locker room for Brown. After some diligence, Clowser finally located him in the equipment room, one floor above the players' dressing quarters. Brown's head was in his hands. That the result was anticipated didn't lighten his disappointment. A loss was a loss. Each one stung regardless of expectation.

"You know," Brown said, looking up at the writer, "losing is like dying a little."

Oh, but what a difference a week made. A 27-6 drubbing of Missouri momentarily cured Brown's doldrums. "I feel better," he said, cracking a smile for the first time in seven days. "I was encouraged this afternoon."[14]

The Bucks were more ebullient than their subdued coach. Plenty of hearty back-slapping took place throughout the Ohio State locker room, and a rousing chorus of "Hail, Hail, the Gang's All Here" heard in the showers capped the post-game celebration.

Two days after the stirring victory, the first top-twenty poll of the season was released. Though it was only October 5, the Buckeyes were the highest ranked "civilian" team. The other nineteen schools were either Navy or Army teams or schools that had been augmented by the addition of Navy recruits. This modest high was quickly tempered. The next four weeks brought four losses. Great Lakes, Purdue, Northwestern, and Indiana all proved too much for the Bucks. The effort against the Great Lakes sailors pleased Brown well enough ("It's the first time I've ever taken a licking and been glad to say afterwards I was satisfied."[15]). The following week against Purdue, "we got licked." This was a fact, a fact that Brown repeated over and over in the dressing room. "Every Saturday afternoon until the season ends will find our kids outmanned."[16] Against Northwestern, Wildcats quarterback Otto Graham loomed large. With his legs and arms, number 48 kept the Buckeyes off balance all afternoon.

"The thing happened which we feared," Brown said. "We're butchered up to such an extent that we'll have to fight for our lives against the teams that are in our own class: Indiana, Pitt, and Illinois."

Brown sat on a dressing room table covered with folded scarlet jerseys. His eyes sparked with fight yet were shaded with the inevitable truth he couldn't deny. "But I can't give them one bit of hell. I'll never kick on their effort. Those boys will fight every week. They'll never quit on me."

The toughest part of their schedule was behind them. The Bucks looked next to "the 4F's of Indiana." Though Indiana was more in Ohio State's league, the Hoosiers got the best of Brown's boys, 20-14. Another loss, a heartbreaking loss, to a team with a roster also depleted by the war effort. OSU experts were looking in the annals to see if the university had ever equaled this poor a start, five losses in six games. "We've become one for the books," Brown acknowledged. "But there's nothing we can do about it."[17] Even a resounding 46-6 beating of the Pitt Panthers couldn't shake Brown's malaise. Instead of reveling in the victory, he empathized with his counterpart at Pitt, Clark Shaughnessy. He had been on the other side of the ledger too many times in the past weeks. Victory was sweet, but some of the thrill was stripped from winning when the opponent was completely overmatched. Pitt was the worst team Ohio State had played in many years.

The lopsided score over the Panthers inspired a reporter to ask Brown, "Do you think your team can defeat Michigan, Coach?"

Staring at his inquisitor, Paul paused momentarily before replying, "We shouldn't even be playing Michigan."[18]

The backlash was bound to come. Brown's continual griping and "beefing" about the Buckeyes' tough schedule and the higher powers that forced his team to face better schools nearly every week wore on some of the men who covered Ohio State football. Though the criticism was far from rampant, Brown had begun to receive some of his first negative press.

Boys were dying in North Africa and in the South Pacific, yet Brown kept harping about how iniquitous it was that his Buckeyes had to play better programs. This 1943 season would be the last chance for many players to compete in intercollegiate sports. The call to serve would come for many of these Baby Bucks, and this experience of representing Ohio State on the football field would be cherished for a lifetime. The defeats to superior teams, which Brown found humiliating, were seen by his players as an experience of a lifetime. The victories, rare as they were, became moments of exhilaration for Brown's youthful squad.

One week following the victory at Pittsburgh, the Buckeyes came home and played a thrilling contest against Illinois, one that ended in chaos and a white lie.

With the game knotted at 26, the Buckeyes attempted a last-second pass that fell incomplete in the Illini end zone. The clock had run out and both schools left the playing field and entered their locker rooms. Remaining on the field was an official's penalty flag, which was thrown during the course of the final play and went unnoticed by all with the exception of the field judge who threw the marker. The referee notified his fellow officials that Illinois was offside on the last play and the game could not end on a defensive penalty.

Both teams were alerted to the situation and slowly returned to the field. The ball was placed on the Illini 21 and, unlike the previous play, Brown opted to go for a field goal. In an attempt to calm his placekicker, freshman John Stungis, who had never been asked to try a field goal, Brown toyed with the truth a little.

"Nothing to it, John. I've never missed one of these."

Emboldened, Stungis' kick soared through the uprights, giving the Buckeyes an improbable victory. While his teammates celebrated around him, a jovial Stungis embraced Brown.

"I'm even with you coach. I never missed one either."

"No," Brown told Stungis, "you're ahead of me, John. I never even tried one."[19]

So much had changed. Sometimes it seemed as if nothing remained the same. There would be no senior tackle this year, and for good rea-

Brown watching his Buckeyes (date unknown).

son. "We don't have but five juniors on the squad, let alone any seniors," Brown explained.

The annual football banquet also was scaled back. Rather than 1,500 attendees gathering in the gymnasium for a dinner and festivities, the event was held at University Hall Chapel after dinner was enjoyed at home. Even the trip to Michigan was a drastic change compared to past excursions. An Ohio State team before the war traveled by Pullman, stayed at the best hotels, and ate the finest of food. This fall the Buckeyes traveled by day coach, ate box lunches on the train, doubled and tripled up in hotels, and took what they could get in the way of meals in hotel dining rooms. Even the rivalry with Michigan seemed diminished this time around. The Wolverines won, and won big, 45-7, handing the Buckeyes their worst defeat of a long season. The victory for Michigan had lost some of its luster. Wolverine fans didn't need Paul Brown to remind them that they'd won with the use of "lend-lease" players.

As he walked off the playing field at Michigan Stadium, Brown did not view the season as a success. How could he? After all, his Bucks only won three games, and that is why you play the game, to win, isn't it? Not all were seeing the year as a failure, however. One of Brown's critics, Franklin Lewis of the *Cleveland Press,* was also one of his strongest boosters. Lewis viewed the just-concluded campaign as a learning experience for the young Buckeyes, and for Brown, a coaching job he could be proud of.

"As a football coach, Brown did a good job, a job that should bring the applause of Ohio State alumni," Lewis claimed. In his column, the Cleveland writer stated that of the nine games played by the Buckeyes, only once did Brown field a team unfit for play and that was the final contest in Ann Arbor.

"The team he sent against Michigan was not a good team even at the price of this year's Buckeye material," Lewis continued. And while he hoped the Buckeye players learned from the trying season, Lewis believed that their coach, no matter his previous successes, had some room for personal improvement. "I admire Brown because he wants to win," Lewis admitted, "and I think he did a commendable job this year. But he is not too old to take some instruction in public relations."[20]

On December 1, Brown and Lynn St. John began a ten-day trip that took them through Pittsburgh, Philadelphia, Baltimore, Washington, and upstate New York to meet with alumni in each of those cities. At each stop Brown spoke with radio and print media. He was asked a wide array of questions, ranging from last season's struggles, to rule changes for 1944, to the future of college ball. The crisis for intercollegiate football had passed, Brown said. Next season would see a leveling off of talent. They wouldn't have to worry about a repeat of this year's Baby Bucks, he assured alumni. But to Brown's surprise, at every stop he was greeted warmly. No alumni on the entire trip gave him a hard time for Ohio State's 3-9 season.

"You're slipping," Brown kidded one crowd. "What? No nomination for a new coach? You're slipping."[21]

—⚹—

Brown had registered for the military draft back in 1939, but as the sole provider to a wife and three children, there was seemingly little chance that he would be called on to serve. To the surprise of many, however, on

February 12 the Massillon draft board reclassified Brown from 3-A to 1-A. Before the day was through, Ohio State president Howard Bevis requested that the draft board defer Brown. The appeal, Bevis explained, wasn't because Brown coached football, but "because he is part of the physical instruction forces of the university."[22] This occupational deferment was a customary course of action that Ohio State used for its entire faculty. Without delay, Brown asked that the university officials drop the appeal.

"I requested no one to request a deferment for me," Brown said in a released statement. "I wanted to and still want to be treated like the rest of the fellows."[23]

The Western Conference held its annual meeting at Chicago's Windemere Hotel on the weekend of March 9 and 10. Though he knew his time as Buckeye coach was short, Brown attended the conference along with Lynn St. John. Camaraderie was never apparent between Brown and Ohio State's athletic director; theirs was a working relationship solely, and civility was the extent each would reach. Though they had never seen eye to eye, at the Chicago gathering Brown couldn't help but discern an appreciable coldness coming from St. John. For the moment, however, Brown had other concerns. He was due in Columbus on Monday for his pre-induction physical. The Navy it would be, but when was the question. Brown had at least the required twenty-one days before being called for induction, though, depending on the Massillon Draft Board's needs, it could stretch to six weeks before he was called.

Slightly more than a month had passed when Brown received his commission on Thursday, April 14. Along with his orders to report to Great Lakes Training Base in Illinois, Brown was instructed to leave Columbus by midnight that coming Sunday. His final three days at Ohio State were hectic and full. The telephone at both his office and home rang continuously with calls from members of the press. Some were just wishing Brown well, others were hoping for an interview. For the most part, he turned down all such requests. His schedule the last week in Columbus was occupied with the mundane and essential. Foremost was making the preparations to smooth the way for an easy transition for the next Buckeye coach. The job of selecting his successor was handed to Brown by the Athletic Board, and the choice was a simple one. His long-time associate Carroll Widdoes would serve as the interim head coach while Brown was away. Widdoes was "a man who has had experience in all phases of football coaching, a man well qualified to carry on for Ohio State,"[24] according to Brown.

He didn't rebuff all requests by the press. Before leaving town, Brown agreed to pose for a few photos dressed in his Navy blues, which he had just purchased. "I only got this suit an hour ago," he explained, "and I had a little difficulty getting into it. It's stiff and new like. I hope there aren't any price tags showing. This business has really moved in a rush."

In a rush, indeed. On his last day on campus, Brown consented to an interview with a student reporter from the *OSU Monthly*. These were the happiest times of his life and though it was hardly newsworthy, Paul wanted to reminisce for awhile. He knew these days would never, could never, come again.

"It was so darned hot it was tough to work on a thesis," Brown said, recalling his time spent in Columbus several years earlier when he was trying to earn his master's degree. "And of all subjects I had chosen to do, 'A Survey of the State High School Libraries.' Now don't laugh. It's true."

Brown then thought about the long walk he and Katy took one afternoon. The stroll that took the couple along the Olentangy and then to Ohio Stadium; he remembered that day like it was yesterday. That day when he and his Katy sat high in the bleachers and looked down on the majestic field. . . .

"You know Katy; I've got a feeling that someday I am going to be running this show."

That was all he'd ever wanted, and he got it; the job of a lifetime, and he rode it to the top of the college game. But on this day, as he gathered his belongings for his journey to Great Lakes, Brown couldn't help but wonder if these were his last moments at Ohio State, if, no matter what the administration said, if he would be welcomed back once his service to the Navy was fulfilled.

Before he boarded the train, all of Brown's players stopped by. Some came alone, others in pairs. They each filed into Brown's Athletic Building office to bid their coach farewell.

"The only job I ever wanted."

To Bill Willis, Brown's all-conference tackle, Brown joked, "Gee, I hope they don't assign me to scout Ohio State or send Great Lakes against Ohio State on game day."

"Hmm, yes sir," Willis agreed. "That would really be something."

"But if they do give me that game," Paul said, "you know, Bill, what I'm going to have our linemen do? They're going to try to trap you on every play."

Willis took his coach's playful bait. "Boy, that would be something. I'd like to see 'em try and do it."

"Yes," Brown agreed, "'try and do it' is the right expression. In the last two seasons of ball, I guess you can count on one hand the number of times you've been trapped."

And with that, Brown stuck out his hand. "So long, Bill."

"So long, coach."[25]

At 11:30 that evening, Brown's train pulled out of Columbus.

Great Lakes already had a football coach, a good one at that. Lt. Tony Hinkle had served as the Bluejackets head coach for the past two years and before he entered the service was an assistant under George Halas with the Chicago Bears. Despite conjecture by some in the press that Brown would take over the lead position, station commander R.R.M. Emmett announce that Brown would serve as an assistant to Hinkle. And this was the chain of command on the football field until mid-October, when Lt. Hinkle was transferred to sea duty in the South Pacific.

The family quarters, 65-C, sat overlooking Lake Michigan. The nice view was augmented by friendly neighbors, helpful with any needs the Browns might have in their new environs. One neighbor, fellow Miami University alum Weeb Ewbank, helped the Brown family get acclimated to military base surroundings. Paul and Weeb went back a number of years, when both men played on Miami's baseball team. Ewbank's duties at Great Lakes were serving as the head of the Shore Patrol, and he eventually served on Brown's football staff.

Brown's boys adjusted to life on the base with ease. Robin and Mike had free rein to roam, play, watch, and learn. Major league ballplayers by the score were assigned to the base, including Bob Feller, Schoolboy Rowe, and Mickey Cochrane. Young Mike had the great thrill of serving as batboy on Feller's baseball team. And at night, anti-aircraft guns practiced out on Lake Michigan, filling the sky with a spectacular fireworks display.

Things were different here at Great Lakes, though. Brown's duties went beyond simply coaching. He also served as battalion commander. Prior to games he would leave the locker room before his team took the field to oversee the sailors as they were seated in the grandstand. Following the final gun, after his players returned to their clubhouse, Brown remained behind to dismiss the sailors. Strictly following protocol, Admiral Emmett would exit, followed by senior officers, and so on down the line. Brown remained on the field until the last company filed out of the stadium.

He may have been thousands of miles from the front, but Brown knew that many of the young men who passed through the base would indeed serve in combat. And he understood that many of those fresh-

Lieutenant Paul E. Brown.

scrubbed faces wouldn't return from battle. The dichotomy was vexing. Admiral Emmett wanted Brown to field a winning team and allowed Brown wide rein to find the best players available. Do whatever it took to get the finest players, Emmett told Brown, whatever it took within the rules. It was good for morale, the admiral explained.

Never one to need great encouragement to field a good football team, Brown was brightened knowing that he and his commanding officer were on the same page. He put himself on the lookout for any athlete coming through the base. Brown would pull their jackets, and the sailors were held over until Brown and his staff analyzed their ability. The men who qualified were assigned temporary duty to the football team.

It wasn't Ohio State, but it was football, and it was competition.

# five    FIRST GET A BALL

**Prior to the war,** professional football struggled to hold the attention of sports fans. Baseball, of course, reigned supreme. Prizefighting, too, enraptured a significant portion of the public. And when it came to football, people preferred the collegiate fashion over the style played by professionals. Three years of absolute war did little to expand interest in the National Football League. Investing in a professional football team was a dubious endeavor. Indeed, reportedly the Chicago Bears, Green Bay Packers, New York Giants, and Washington Redskins were the only money-making outfits in the established ten-team NFL.

Still, the war would conclude eventually, and the most optimistic saw the end coming within the year. Astute businessmen understood that the men returning from overseas would want to be entertained when they came home. Escapism and a return to normalcy would be in great demand. Speculators looked for an avenue to exploit, and to the great surprise of many, professional football was the path to possible riches.

In the fall of '44 three different groups announced plans to challenge the NFL's monopoly on pro football. Though the revelation seemed ridiculous to some observers, a boom for the sport was anticipated by investors. Others believed they could capitalize on the game to a greater extent than the NFL owners had ever attempted. It largely came down to promotion, and since the established NFL hadn't exactly built an extensive or loyal fan base, the opportunity lay there for the adventurous sort to stake a foothold and compete with the NFL on equal or near-equal footing.

The United States Football League was to be headed by Red Grange, professional football's first bona fide star. With headquarters in Chicago, the league granted franchises in Akron, Baltimore, Boston, Philadelphia, Washington, Chicago, New York, and Honolulu. The association, according to Grange, had been in the planning stages for two years. In addition to placing a team on the exotic island of Hawaii, the United States League hoped to garner attention by playing as many night games as possible. This idea would not only be novel, but it would help avoid direct competition with the NFL.

Another circuit, the Trans-America League, would begin play "when war conditions permit." Its hook: the Trans-America teams would travel from town to town almost exclusively by air. Teams were to be placed in New York, Boston, Baltimore, Philadelphia, Miami, Dallas, Houston, and Los Angeles. A Trans-America by-law decreed that its teams would not be controlled by one individual. Rather, every club would have a group of five or more investors holding an interest in each club.

The Trans-America and United States proposals each made headlines and garnered some attention, but neither had firm financial backing. Seemingly, they were held together solely with frayed string, hot air, and a fervent wish.

The third group was the most intriguing, and it offered the most promise to actually one day take the field. The assemblage was organized by Arch Ward. Ward's talents extended beyond his role as the *Chicago Tribune's* sports editor; he also operated as an innovator and promoter. The forty-seven-year-old Ward's resume went well past the usual wordsmith's work. His promotional mind was behind the creation of the baseball All-Star Game in 1933 and the Collegiate All-Star contest the following year. Later, in 1941, Ward rejected a ten-year, $250,000 offer to become commissioner of the NFL. His latest idea began to take shape on June 4, 1944, in St. Louis, when Ward met with men representing interests in New York, San Francisco, Los Angeles, and Chicago. Not present but in the fold was Arthur "Mickey" McBride, the prospective owner of a Cleveland franchise who gave power of attorney to Ward. Little was decided upon at this initial meeting other than the name of the new league they all hoped to form: the All-America Football Conference.

For three months Ward worked quietly behind the scenes finding firm backing for the individual franchises before making the venture public.

Following a September 3 meeting held in Chicago, Ward used the pages of the *Chicago Tribune* to announce the formation of his newest endeavor. The second summit shed a little more light on the makeup and aspirations of the league. Ward promised a "coast to coast" football league, with seven cities already on board with substantial backing, and the hope that eventually they would reach eight to ten franchises.

Two noteworthy resolutions were adopted at the Chicago conference:

- No club will be allowed to employ a coach or player under contract to any team in the National Football League.
- No player will be admitted into the organization who has college eligibility remaining.

───※───

The hope existed among league executives that an affiliation of sorts could be built with the NFL, and a determining World Series-like championship game would result. Still, members of the NFL didn't take the threat very serious. Chile Walsh, the general manager of the Cleveland Rams, didn't believe a market existed for another league. "Football needs good businessmen behind the franchisees, and good businessmen inspecting the books of the National League don't find the game very tempting," Walsh said. "We're lucky, we've got some club owners with imagination and business sense in addition to a love for football, but there aren't many of that kind around. I doubt that a new league would find enough of them to constitute a very serious threat to us."[1]

The league's ownership was a varied group, but a common trait bound the men together. They hoped that their deep pockets made up for their lack of experience in professional football. Oilman James Brueil bought the Buffalo club. Lumber magnate Anthony Morabito purchased San Francisco. A movie conglomerate, which included Louis B. Mayer and Don Ameche, purchased the Los Angeles franchise. John Keeshin, a racetrack owner and trucking industrialist, controlled the Chicago Rockets. Dan Topping of baseball's New York Yankees headed the AAFC team of the same name.* And, in Cleveland, a shrewd, vibrant businessman threw his hat into the ring.

—∞—

Mickey McBride offered a simple explanation for investing in Ward's fledgling league, "I wanted to get into it because people said it was impossible."

Five years earlier, McBride made an attempt to buy the Cleveland Rams of the NFL, only to be rebuffed. The rejection was a blessing of sorts for McBride. The Rams were a losing proposition on the field and at the gate. For awhile they played their home contests at a high school stadium where the majority of the bleachers remained unoccupied. McBride pushed the prospect of football ownership out of his mind until he learned of Ward's latest brainchild. He went to Ed McAuley of the *Cleveland News* and asked the writer his thoughts on bringing a new professional football outfit to town.

"Mickey," McAuley answered, "I wouldn't advise anyone to go into business which depends for its success on anything so unpredictable as Cleveland's weather in the fall."

"Well," McBride asked, "how much did the Rams lose last year?"

"I heard they lost about $20,000."

"Oh hell," Mickey roared. "I thought they lost some money. I wouldn't mind dropping a hundred thousand a year for a couple of seasons if I could get this thing rolling."[2]

With this newfound information in hand, McBride headed to Chicago to meet with Arch Ward in person. The two men had never met before McBride entered Ward's office and requested a franchise for Cleveland. Ward had several concerns, all of which centered on McBride's financial wherewithal. McBride guaranteed Ward that with him, cash wouldn't be a problem. Within a week, McBride had the reply he anticipated. He would be the man behind the Cleveland outfit in the AAFC.

—∞—

Short, stocky, and bursting with ambition, McBride well knew how to hustle a buck and did so successfully with his wide-ranging business interests. He owned taxicab companies in Cleveland, Akron, and Canton, real estate in Chicago, Cleveland, and Florida. There was a radio station, a printing company, and a race wire syndicate. These varied ventures occasionally brought McBride in cahoots with an element of society that sometimes skirted legality to make a dollar. He crossed paths with some characters of ill repute early on. Indeed he came up through the take-no-prisoners world of newspaper circulation, where strong arm tactics were the rule, where it took muscle and nerve to hold street corners.

In the years prior to the emergence of radio, newspapers held a monopoly on the media. Within major cities, competition was fierce between dailies, and politicians understood the enormous influence newsprint held over voters. Newspaper circulation wars erupted as gangs were hired to stake a claim on the choicest street corners where vendors could hawk their wares.

The son of an Irish immigrant, McBride was born in the stockyard district of Chicago in 1888. He quit school following the fourth grade to pursue a career peddling newspapers. He started at age seven and would exchange a paper for a streetcar transfer, which he obtained from commuters who had no need for the extra ride. The paper cost Mickey a half-cent. To regular customers he sold the transfers for two-and-a-half cents. He proved so adept at pushing newspapers that before his twenty-second birthday, McBride had become the circulation manager of the *Chicago American.* Two years later, in 1913, McBride moved to Cleveland where he became the circulation director of the *Cleveland News* for the princely pay of $10,000 annually.

In 1930 Dan Sherby and his father, Harry, entered the Cleveland cab business. Several companies were then competing for the town's hack business, and the Sherbys had nothing but trouble. There was labor violence against the Sherby cabs. In the midst of a strike by Sherby's cab drivers in 1931, McBride stepped in and helped the father and son out. McBride then acquired control of the Tone Cab Corporation by obtaining fifty-one percent of the stock. Sherby retained minority interest. After McBride bought in, the cab drivers' strike ended immediately. By 1934 McBride consolidated with Yellow and Zone Cab companies. He and Sherby then had a monopoly on the business in Cleveland. Since that deal, Sherby and McBride became partners in virtually every one of McBride's Ohio ventures.

He also entered into real estate speculation throughout Cleveland. "I bought real estate here from the time I arrived," McBride acknowledged. "I used to spend my Sundays getting around town and looking at properties. I watched where things were growing and where they weren't.

"I've made a lot of money, yes," McBride admitted. "I've worked hard—and I've been lucky.

"But," he added for emphasis, "I'm not in anything kinky, I don't need to be. Everything is here in the books. I pay my taxes and stay square with the government. When I hit the pillow at night, I sleep sound." He paused for a moment before insisting, "Nothing is bothering me."

—⁓—

He had his hand in a lot of things, that's for sure. He certainly knew how to make a buck, but this football racket was all new to him. To make a go at this game, McBride decided on a formula to make it work. First, get the best coach available. Then, once that coach is under contract, give him the authority and money needed to bring in the finest players available. Make the game an entertaining venture for the fans. Complement the football team with quality on-field entertainment. And finally, publicize and promote this spectacular product.

He wanted a marquee name to govern his team. A national figure with a winning track record was a prerequisite, and the man he wanted, the only man he sought for the job, was Frank Leahy of Notre Dame. In fact, at the time, Leahy was the only football coach McBride had ever heard of. McBride's football knowledge didn't extend far beyond South Bend and the Fighting Irish. His boys attended Notre Dame and it was Arthur Jr. who convinced his dad to take in an Irish game one fall afternoon. McBride was hooked. The pageantry. The glory. Yes, Leahy was the man for the job, but convincing the coach to risk his reputation and take the chance on the pro game, that would take some doing.

Leahy was serving in the Navy and was on a leave of absence from Notre Dame when McBride approached him with an offer to run his club. The two men came to a handshake agreement. Word of the contract quickly reached Notre Dame's president, Reverend John Cavanaugh, who was distraught at the thought of losing Leahy.

Cavanaugh approached McBride and explained to him how vital Leahy was to the university and pleaded with McBride not to take the Irish coach. McBride was swayed, with his boys enrolled at South Bend. He hated to think his hold on Leahy would cause them any unease on campus. After some deliberation, McBride decided to release Leahy from their agreement. Now where to turn? His reserve of coaching candidates now barren, McBride again sought advice from a Cleveland sportswriter. On this occasion, he turned to John Dietrich of the *Plain Dealer.*

"Who's the best coach in the country? McBride asked the scribe.

Dietrich, a veteran football reporter, didn't hesitate before responding. "Paul Brown," he said, and then began to recount to the football novice, McBride, Brown's impressive resume. By the time Dietrich had finished extolling Brown's numerous achievements, McBride's interest was stoked.

McBride left the *Plain Dealer* offices and quickly made arrangements to travel to Chicago. With his newly acquired information, he dropped in on Arch Ward. He wanted Ward's advice on how to secure Brown as his head coach. McBride had gone to the proper source. Ward was pleased with McBride's choice. Ward had gotten to know Brown while Paul was stationed at Great Lakes. What a coup this would be, the promoter thought. If Brown would agree to coach the Cleveland franchise, his name would bring instant recognition and prestige to Ward's league.

The two men sat for awhile and discussed exactly what McBride was willing to offer to entice Brown to make the leap from college to the pros. McBride was willing to pay whatever it took. The numbers McBride bandied about staggered Ward. The more he thought about it, the more Ward thought this just might be doable.

If you would like, Ward offered, I'll serve as the middleman for you.

—⚹—

That Ohio State had booked a game against Paul Brown and Great Lakes was purely coincidental. Originally, the Buckeyes were slated to play

Northwestern on October 21. However, due to a conflict, Northwestern asked to be released from the obligation. Since OSU did not have a service team on its schedule, as was required by the Big Ten for the duration of the war, it consented to Northwestern's request. St. John did not wish to play Iowa Pre-Flight again, so the Ohio State athletic director looked to Great Lakes. At the time of the scheduling change, Lt. Hinkle was serving as the Blue Jackets head coach. Now, however, with Paul Brown leading Great Lakes, the buildup to the game was altered considerably.

In the week before the match-up, Brown dismissed his team's chances against such a formidable opponent. It was the same old song from the coach, and many critics were tired of the refrain. His smaller, less experienced boys didn't stand a chance Saturday.

"We haven't the speed to cope with Ohio State," Brown moaned. "We haven't a back as fast as Havarth. We may be able to stop him but if we do, one of those other fast backs will get away and make trouble for us."[3]

Upon hearing such talk from Brown all week, Russ Needham took him to task in the *Columbus Dispatch*.

"He's just a youngster as big college coaches go, but the man from Massillon takes a back seat to no one where the shedding of verbal tears is concerned," Needham said. "And he's doing a first rate job of wailing over this one."[4]

Still, Columbus was happy to have Brown return home, if only for a day and on the wrong sideline. More than 73,000 fans filled Ohio Stadium to welcome Brown home and root for their Bucks, who were undefeated in three tries so far. Certainly, Brown was torn. Those were his Buckeyes he would be facing Saturday, but he wasn't the only one whose allegiance was frayed. "You might as well know, Daddy," Mike told his father, "I'm rooting for Ohio State."

Surprisingly, Great Lakes made the contest interesting while battling Ohio State to a 6-6 tie as the game entered the fourth quarter. The Buckeyes' dominant offensive line pushed the Blue Jackets around in the final stanza, though. Ohio State managed to cross the goal line three times in the final fifteen minutes, making the final score 26-6. At the conclusion of

On the sideline as Great Lakes falls to Ohio State.

the game, Buckeye players swarmed around Brown. With a warm smile, he accepted the well-wishes in good spirits, but Brown's mood darkened when he approached Carroll Widdoes.

"You cut me to pieces. I'll fix you," he said, while jabbing a finger at his old friend.[5] The grin returned by the time Brown reached the Great Lakes dressing room. "Do you believe me now?" Brown asked of the reporters circled around him. "I told you what would happen and you laughed at me. You just can't take a bunch of kids and work with them for five or six weeks and get them ready to cope with the sort of football that is played in the Big Ten."

The loss rankled. The desire to win just didn't burn in his players as it did in Brown. Admittedly, he struggled with the lack of enthusiasm many of his players exhibited. Certainly, he acknowledged, the import of football games paled in comparison to what many of the sailors would face once they shipped out. Still, Brown could never square himself with this lack of passion.

"It's just a different situation," Brown remarked of his position at Great Lakes. "You just get along the best you can."[6]

How much longer the war would last, no one knew for certain. But as 1944 drew to a close, and Brown's Great Lakes team concluded its season, he began to contemplate what the post-war world would hold for him. His uncertainty of returning to Ohio State only intensified when Carroll Widdoes was named coach of the year following a perfect 9-0 season and a Big Nine championship. Given what he knew, and presuming what he believed, Brown wondered if anyone would remember his name once this war was over.

—⁓—

Shortly after the start of the New Year, Ward paid a visit to Great Lakes. While Brown was pleased to see his friend, within moments Brown's head was spinning with the news Ward carried.

A new league? Professional football? How much money did you say?

Ward laid everything out for Brown, but the information was all too much to absorb during their short meeting. Brown promised to mull over the proposal but declined to make any promises.

The pros had never held any interest for Brown. Artistically, the game wasn't as pleasing to the eye, he believed. Besides that, professional leagues had long struggled financially and few towns were as dubious in the support of the pros as Cleveland had been. Still, the numbers Ward laid out for him were intriguing. He would be a fool not to at least consider the offer. First, though, Brown wanted to give Ohio State the chance to invite him back when the Navy granted his discharge.

—⁓—

On Saturday, February 3, Brown traveled by train to Chicago, where the Western Conference athletic directors were meeting. The unease between Paul Brown and Lynn St. John had not lessened in the previous twelve months. Indeed, as the two men sat down to talk at the Hotel Sherman, the tension was palpable. If anything, it intensified as Brown told St. John of Arch Ward's proposal.

The offer: $15,000 a year, plus a monthly stipend of $1,000 for the duration of the war, in addition to part ownership in the new team.

Shaking his head in disbelief, St. John assured Brown that the university would be unable to match such terms. Perhaps they could meet the annual salary of $15,000, but the other perks, of course, were beyond reach. He would take the information back to Columbus, St. John told Brown, and see what the board proposed. They left things at that. St. John returned to Ohio State at the close of the meetings, while Brown headed back to the naval base.

Three days and Brown heard nothing from St. John or any other university representative. In the meantime, Brown was contacted yet again by Ward. The promoter had been persistent. He had been in close contact with Brown over the previous few weeks, having made several trips to Great Lakes. In addition to bragging about the strong financial backing of the league owners, Ward stroked Brown's expanding ego. With his soft sell, Ward tried to convince Brown that his coaching talents deserved a bigger stage than was offered in Columbus. But Ward was beginning to get antsy. No other team had yet signed a coach. For all intents and purposes, Ward's new league had vanished from the news. He and McBride needed Brown more than Brown needed them. If not Ohio State, then surely some other school would pursue Brown's services when they became available. McBride had upped the ante. The offer was sweetened to $25,000 a year, but they needed an answer.

What will it be? Ward pressed: we need to know if you're with us. Brown hesitated. One more day, Brown said. I would like to know if the board will tender me an offer.

—m—

Brown's apparent good fortune was also kismet for St. John. The board would never approve $25,000, or anything near that figure. The athletic director could allow Brown to move on without fear of backlash from the press or OSU alumni. St. John had Brown forced down his throat four years earlier by the press, high school coaches, and alumni. He sat by as Brown's personality and popularity eclipsed his own in Columbus and throughout the entire state. Their work relationship was strained; their personal relationship, nonexistent. And now St. John could allow Brown to move on without ever having to make a decision between Widdoes and Brown. The choice had been made for him when Mickey McBride upped the ante. While Brown sat waiting for a call at Great Lakes, St. John sat silently in Columbus, biding his time, forcing Brown to come to a resolution.

—⚮—

Five days passed, and Brown heard nothing from St. John, nor had any other university official reached out to him. All Paul wanted was an offer, a respectable salary. Coaching the Buckeyes was the only job Brown had ever wanted. He consulted with Katy by phone, but she offered little more than support for whatever he chose. "You do whatever you want to do,"[7] Katy said. The money and the perks promised by McBride were too great to overlook. But his heart belonged to High Street, and Brown struggled to reconcile the diverging feelings. But, Brown came to realize, St. John had left him with no option. He called Ward, and a meeting was set up in Chicago for the next day, February 8.

If he was anything but sure of his decision, Brown effectively buried all vacillation. Dressed in his Navy blues, Brown sat in Arch Ward's Tribune Tower office and placed his signature beneath the terms that made him the wealthiest football coach in the land. Photographers captured Mickey McBride peering over Brown's right shoulder as if to make certain the deed was realized. For the reporters present, Brown aired none of the frustration he felt toward the lack of negotiation with OSU or enmity he personally felt toward his antagonist, Lynn St. John.

"I leave Ohio State reluctantly," Brown said. "The time has arrived for me to decide whether I was to continue as a professor or a businessman. I simply couldn't turn down the deal in fairness to my family."[8]

Indeed, it was a bittersweet moment for Brown as he sat in Ward's Tribune Tower office and signed on to coach the Cleveland outfit in this new, risky endeavor. He had never had much use for the pro game and now he was a part of it, a vital part of it.

"I have every confidence in professional football and especially in the future of the All-America Conference," he said. "I am convinced that professional football and college football will continue to prosper side by side.[9]

"I will have complete freedom to pick my own coaching staff," Brown explained, "as well as the business staff, and, of course, our players."[10]

McBride spoke to the handful of reporters in the room. "I have one ambition; to give Cleveland a championship team in professional football. . . .We are going to do our part to see that it will be a valuable contribution to the post-war sporting scene." Proudly, and with a degree of braggado-cio, McBride revealed the startling terms of agreement. In addition to the $25,000 yearly salary, Brown would receive five percent ownership in the franchise and a monthly retainer of $1,500 for the duration of his stay in the Navy. McBride freely admitted his ignorance concerning the adminis-tration of a football club and readily ceded to Brown complete autonomy, including the right to hire and fire all personnel on and off the field.

For the most part, Brown's decision was met with understanding. On its editorial page, the *Columbus Dispatch* sympathized with Brown's posi-tion. "Idealism butters no bread, and the difference between a five-year con-tract at a much higher salary and a succession of year-by-year agreements was too much to be overlooked by any conscientious family man."[11]

But not everyone thought chasing a buck was admirable. Nor was everyone privy to St. John's behind-the-scenes antics. There was an air of belittlement in the prose of some. "Pay for play." Columbus was a college town, a town which devoted twelve months a year to Buckeye football, a town with an inferiority complex. Jim Schlemmer of the *Akron Beacon Journal,* once one of his biggest fans, was now one of Paul's biggest critics.

Every man has a price, Schlemmer admitted, but it was reprehen-sible that a college coach who sold his program to the alumni, the student body, and his players would leave, "purely for personal gain. . . . There are ethics involved here; ethics, or lack of them, which show only too clearly what some persons will do with and for money."[12]

The news made a bigger splash than Ward could have hoped. All the nation's leading newspapers led their sports sections with banner headlines announcing the AAFC's coup. A couple of writers traveled to Great Lakes and still more telephoned. For the moment, Brown was the sport story in the country. "It will be a tough go," he told John Dietrich of Cleveland's *Plain Dealer,* "but that's the way I like it. I realize it will take more than a year or two to build, but we're not going to waste any time."[13]

In between answering the telephone, accepting congratulations from well-wishers, and speaking with Ed Prell of the *Chicago Tribune,* Brown sat down to pen a letter to Lynn St. John. It was Brown's official notification of resignation. In the note he reminisced about the good days at Ohio State, the big victories, and again Brown emphasized that he was reluctant to leave Columbus. "I hope Saint understands," Brown murmured to Prell as he sealed the envelope.

"I plan to carry through on the same idealism I had at Ohio State," Brown said.

Pro gridders carried the unsettling image of hard-drinking, cigar-chomping ruffians. Brown hoped to bring the enthusiasm, energy, and yes, naïveté of the collegiate athlete to his Cleveland operation. "I want our boys to be high-class and will pick them on the basis of personality as much as ability. With them I will have the same relationship as I had with the boys at Ohio State. After all, they will be former collegians and only slightly older."[14]

―ɯ―

Immediately, Brown threw himself headlong into the daunting task of building an organization from the ground up. He began by starting the formation of his staff. Over the next few weeks, Brown hired several assistants, including John Brickles, Creighton Miller, and Bob Voights.

On the last day of March, Brown, in Cleveland thanks to a forty-eight-hour leave from Great Lakes, was a guest of Mickey McBride's at a press-radio luncheon held at the Hotel Cleveland. It was Brown's coming out, of sorts, in the city. Before more than seventy local sports and civic leaders, Brown gave a short talk that touched on several topics. Though it was only in the infant stages, the team was beginning to come together, Brown explained. Though it looked as if the league wouldn't kickoff in the fall, he said, "I have great hope that we will start operating in '46."

Whenever the games began, Brown promised, he would bring a winner to town, "If I have to lose football games to make money, we won't make it. And Arthur," Brown said, looking down the dais to McBride, "we'll build a winner here if it takes every cent you've got."[15]

McBride could only hope Brown was joking, but his new coach was already proving to be very good at spending someone else's money. Brown revealed to the luncheon crowd that he'd signed the one player he coveted more than any other, old Buckeye nemesis Otto Graham. The former Northwestern quarterback had recently been assigned to Glenview air station just outside of Chicago. One weekend Brown made a foray to the air base and paid a visit to the former Northwestern star. He told Graham about the Cleveland club in the new league, and that he would be running the Cleveland edition on the circuit. He was very interested in Graham's services, Brown told him. Not only that, they were willing to pay for it, now. Though Graham had been drafted by the Detroit Lions of the NFL, he was never offered a contract. When Brown reached out and made Graham an unusual offer consisting of a $1,000 bonus, a $250-a-month retainer while he remained in the service, and a $7,500 salary, Graham couldn't resist. The particulars of the deal weren't revealed that evening at the Hotel Cleveland. "The greatest thing to come from Waukegan since Jack Benny" was coming to Cleveland. Brown's audience had no idea the import of what they'd just been told. That would have to come in time.

—⁂—

It was all very interesting, Brown's plans for this new Cleveland team, but the Ohio State question still burned. "I didn't leave on the spur of the moment," he said. "It was a situation in which I had been very happy. . . . I left voluntarily and with no regrets. I did not leave altogether for financial reasons. I thought I had an opportunity to do something in professional football. It's a new and unexplained world and I decided I'd like to see what makes it tick."

And, Brown believed, his old world could live peacefully with his new.

"There is no conflict between professional and intercollegiate football. Intercollegiate and pro football are two phases of the same thing."[16]

A letter from Columbus businessman Bob Hill acknowledged a raging debate in the state capital over Brown's departure from the university. "I talked to Paul Hornung several times, but his hands are tied," Hill wrote to Brown. "He is still working for Russ (Needham), you know. The only sportswriter in town showing any signs of 'guts' up to now is Lew (Byrer). The people in Columbus and in Ohio are not getting a true picture of this. . . . I think it is time that the athletic department is blasted wide open."[17]

—⚬—

Brown spent every free moment away from his duties planning and developing the team, pinpointing the players he would like to have, as well as forecasting who would be available at the end of the war. Since Brown had no experience in the pro game, he knew little about what comprised a successful professional player. To remedy this deficiency, he relied on instinct. He wanted players who not only had ability, but those whose passion for the game exceeded their want of a paycheck. For players he didn't personally coach, or coach against, Brown considered recommendations from men whose opinions he respected.

When exactly Brown decided his next course of action is uncertain. Perhaps the thought process began in late March when Lynn St. John released a lengthy, detailed chronicle of the events which led to Brown's jump to the professional ranks. At the time, St. John released an obligatory statement expressing his regret over Brown's decision. A few short weeks later, however, St. John told the OSU Alumni magazine his side of the affair. His telling, which was picked up by most Ohio newspapers, was vitriolic. The blame was placed entirely on Brown's shoulders. He was money-hungry, and the university could do nothing to please him. In fact, Brown didn't even allow Ohio State the opportunity to make a counter offer, according to St. John.

"Ohio State University is counting itself exceedingly fortunate in having Paul Brown eliminate himself from the university picture," St. John wrote.

The athletic director didn't confine his diatribe to the present. No, St. John reached back several years to an issue that still grated. . . . Having Paul Brown forced upon him by the Ohio high school coaches. In fact, St. John asserted that Brown orchestrated the campaign personally.

"One further thing that came to light following Paul Brown's move to the pros was the announced support of the Ohio High School Coaches Association boosting Paul Brown for the Ohio State job was conceived by Paul Brown and engineered by him as a means of ensuring his appointment to the Ohio State post. This action was definitely resented by a considerable group of the Ohio high school coaches who evidently knew Paul Brown better than those of us at the Ohio State University knew him."[18]

Brown offered no response; at least not publicly. What Brown did do was set on a course that would further enflame the passions between Columbus and he. Virtually every evening Brown would communicate with John Brickles on the telephone and transmit his desires to the assistant. Brickles was an old friend of Brown's, a rival high school coach from New Philadelphia. In the winter of '45 Brickles was coaching basketball at West Virginia University when Brown offered him a position with the Cleveland organization. If he would be allowed to finish out the season with his basketball team, Brickles asked, he would gladly accept the proposal. Immediately following the conclusion of West Virginia's schedule, Brickles relocated to Cleveland and set up team offices in the Leader Building. From there he became Brown's point man in contacting prospective players.

For years Brown had kept a detailed record of the many players he'd seen through the years. From Massillon, to the Western Conference to his experience at Great Lakes, Brown had notes on every intriguing or great talent he'd seen through the years. Brown gave Brickles a lengthy list of names, and asked his assistant to contact the men. The same enticement used to lure Graham, a signing bonus and monthly retainer for the duration of military service, was open for other prospective players. Letters were sent to a number of men serving in the armed forces, including John Winkler, a fullback from Ohio State's 1942 squad, and Lou Groza, also a freshman on the '42 team. Both men had college eligibility remaining. The seemingly innocuous epistles stirred up a firestorm of malevolence. Not surprisingly, the most boisterous protest emanated from Columbus.  Brown targeted these and several other former Buckeyes with college eligibility remaining, including Dante Lavelli, Lin Houston, and Gene Fekete.

St. John exploded. The gloves came off and the animosity spilled out into the open. Whatever goodwill had existed between Brown and Ohio State had evaporated

Buckeye assistant Ernie Godfrey raged, "When Brown starts going after boys like that he's in for it. We're ready for the biggest knockdown and drag-out fight you ever saw."

Though less acrimonious than Godfrey, Carrol Widdoes was equally distressed by the turn of events. "When Paul was here, he frequently told his boys to get their college education first and then turn to professional sports if they felt they really wanted to. Now he's coaxing the boys who were here a year or two ago to play pro football at the end of the war."[19]

Reached for comment at Great Lakes, Brown defended himself. His ideals remained, he claimed. The AAFC wouldn't begin play until 1946, and by then the college classes of all the men in question will have graduated.

"My attitude toward boys getting their education first hasn't changed one bit," he said. "The fact that a boy plays professional football does not mean he cannot continue his education. I don't know anything about men being approached with contracts. I haven't talked with any of them. Our league will not operate until the 1946 season and the availability of those

1942 freshmen now in the service is contingent upon how long it takes to whip the Japanese."

Brown's plea of ignorance was disingenuous. Nothing was being done in Cleveland without his approval. Mailed with the return address of 405 N. Leader Building, Cleveland, the letters, all the letters, were sent under the direction of Brown who implicitly told Brickles which players to approach. But so, too, the howls of protest from the collegiate field were self-serving. Groza had planned on returning to OSU following the war and pursuing his degree. For a kid who grew up across the street from a steel mill, the bonus and the monthly stipend proved too much to ignore. Groza's story was much like other players reached by Brickles. Groza had spent time on Okinawa. Dante Lavelli lived through hell in Belgium during the Battle of the Bulge. These were no longer school boys, but rather men who lived through the ravages of war. Sure, some may have re-enrolled in school when peace finally came, but they all deserved the opportunity to earn a living. Any reasonable man would recognize that.

—⁂—

On April 21, Brown traveled to Chicago for a long weekend of league meetings at the Palmer House. The Cleveland delegation, consisting of Brown, McBride, and Brickles, as well as stockholders Ray T. Miler and Dan Sherby, made up the largest group at the conference. With league President James Crowley serving in the Pacific, presiding over the confab was vice president and co-owner of the Los Angeles franchise, Christy Walsh. Over the course of four days, representatives for seven teams discussed a wide variety of issues and came away from the meeting with a league constitution and a firm belief in the AAFC's equal ranking with the NFL, "for the good of the public and the two leagues."

While the two other prospective leagues that announced their intentions to challenge the NFL the previous autumn had gone by the wayside, the All America Conference steadfastly considered its league to be on a par with the established National circuit.** The constitution adopted in Chicago took into consideration the excessive travel that would encompass a coast-to-coast league. Surprisingly, a $15,000 guarantee for visiting teams was agreed upon, a decision that would assist the weaker franchises. Pointedly missing from the by-laws was the prohibition of signing players with college eligibility remaining, not exactly what Arch Ward promised some months earlier when announcing the formation of his league. But circumstances change, and the reality of competing with the NFL proved that luring players back from the service was the most practical avenue available. If not that, then perhaps raiding the ranks of the NFL would be necessary. This was a circumstance the AAFC was trying to avoid, which is why Walsh, Brown, and Chicago president John L. Keeshin privately and publicly requested a meeting with NFL Commissioner Elmer Layden.

There was much to discuss: a common player draft, coordinating schedules, outlawing player raiding, and considering inter-league contests. But there would no tête-à-tête. Layden's office initially stalled when contacted. The commissioner was "out to lunch," his secretary feebly claimed. Persistence finally elicited a statement from Layden.

"All I know of new leagues is what I read in the newspapers," he claimed. "There is nothing for the National Football League to talk about as far as new leagues are concerned, until someone gets a football and plays a game."[20]

Over the next few weeks Layden repeated variations of the assertion. The catchiest was his advice that the new league "first get a ball, then make a schedule, and then play a game." This declaration would be repeated often.

Tell them to get a ball!

## six   **HEY ELMER**

"The man who said that wars are 'hell' was certainly right," Brown wrote in a June 6 letter to Robin Priday, a member of his '42 championship club. "In my particular case, it broke up the vast dreams I had for a dynasty at OSU. It is a long story that only time will bring to light."

The war in Europe came to a close in May while victory in the Pacific arrived in August. Still, Brown would remain in the service for the foreseeable future. Another Bluejacket season was on the horizon, and though Brown's mind may have been preoccupied with building an organization in Cleveland, his duty demanded he field the finest team possible at Great Lakes.

Unlike the previous year, when Tony Hinkle put together the Bluejacket squad before he was shipped out to the Pacific, the task fell entirely on Brown's shoulders in 1945. As the new season approached, Brown was enthused about his team's prospects. A number of elite college stars had come through Great Lakes and had their jackets pulled. Brown felt confident that he would field one of the country's finest teams. His hopes for a dominant season faded, however, when a Great Lakes officer was transferred to Fleet City in San Francisco. One by one, Brown helplessly watched as his players were mysteriously relocated to Fleet City. As the first game inched closer, Brown realized he had been stripped of nearly every quality player.

Nearly 300 sailors came out for the initial practice. Eventually Brown whittled the number down to fifty men. One player stood head and shoulders above all others, however. Left untouched in the great exodus to Fleet City was fullback Marion Motley. Though Motley had played college ball at the University of Nevada, he had not been at the school long enough to build a reputation, which would have gotten him transferred to the San Francisco base.

Motley was inducted into the Navy on Christmas Day, 1944, and had been immediately assigned to Great Lakes. Ever on the alert for quality players coming through the base, Brown saw Marion's file and made a mental note. He remembered Motley when the fullback played against Massillon for Canton McKinley. Brown sent a memo to Motley asking him to stop by his office. Brown was pleased by what he saw. Motley, at a lean 225 pounds, was in playing shape. Without a second thought, Brown designated Motley for the "ship's company."

In addition to losing players, Great Lakes was losing games from its schedule. Originally, the Bluejackets were slated to play twelve contests. Shortly before the start of the season, the number of games was reduced to ten, eight against university squads and two versus army outfits. Still, though his roster had been ravaged and the schedule cut, Brown prepared his players for battle as he always had. Each afternoon the Bluejackets were put through the rigors of a Paul Brown practice. Day after day Brown ran his players through the training camp grind under the blazing August sun. Brown wasn't the only one absorbed with the team's performance on the practice field. Outside the fence every day stood a man studying Brown's players and Brown himself. He was there each day, like clockwork, enraptured by the monotonous display before him.

Who was this fella watching his team every day? Brown asked a commanding officer to check out this guy. Maybe he was a spy; you could never be too careful.

Brown was given the information he requested. His name was Blanton Collier, and he was at Great Lakes on an outpatient basis. And, the officer told Brown, "he knows as much football as you."

Intrigued, Brown extended an invitation for Collier to meet with him in Brown's office.

What's your background? Brown asked. Collier was modest. There wasn't much to tell. He had taught mathematics and coached both basketball and football at Paris High School in Paris, Kentucky. He played some "midget" football at Georgetown University in his home state of Kentucky. Blanton, like Brown, was diminutive: 5' 10" and 160 pounds sopping wet.

Collier's passion for the game was apparent to Brown, as was his intellect for the technical side of football. He could use the assistance with the Bluejackets, Brown surmised. Perhaps Collier would like to join his staff?

Blanton couldn't believe his good fortune. The proposition was more than he had ever hoped for. Collier was just biding time watching Brown run his team through practice, hoping to learn a thing or two from Brown, but an offer to coach alongside him. . . . Collier jumped at the opportunity.

Their first game was coming up quickly, Brown explained, and there was much to do in little time. Great Lakes had one final tune-up against the College All-Stars before heading to Ann Arbor for the season opening clash with Michigan on September 15. The 25-2 drubbing by the Wolverines over the outmanned Bluejackets didn't sting quite like a loss to the maize and blue did in Columbus.

Michigan and Notre Dame served as bookends to the Great Lakes schedule. As the December 1 game with Notre Dame neared, the ever-cautious Brown slipped into the realm of paranoia. While he ran his players through their drills, Brown had the field encircled by shore patrol personnel. Before the start of each practice session, Brown bellowed, "About face!" and the patrol would turn away from the field in unison. "No one," Brown explained, "friend or foe saw our practices."[1]

The atmosphere at Ross Field for the season's biggest and final contest was festive. About 22,000 sailors were in the stands boisterously cheering on their brethren as the Bluejackets overwhelmed the Irish with four fourth-quarter touchdowns in the course of a 39-7 win.

The victory satisfied Brown as much as any in his career. His team had played as one, with commitment and desire. Equally thrilled with the win was Admiral Emmett, who presented Brown and each of the Bluejacket players with a wristwatch commemorating the event and their service at Great Lakes. Brown appreciated the gesture, as well as the support given him by the admiral throughout his nearly two years on the base. Most importantly to Brown, Emmett had always kept his word. Brown was given one directive, to win football games, and he had won the biggest one, against Notre Dame's Fighting Irish.

It was his last contest in the amateur ranks. It was also the last game played at Ross Field; the edifice was torn down a week after the Notre Dame contest. So much was changing. The war was over, and with it wartime football. A return to normalcy was everyone's hope.

—⁂—

A few days later, Chile Walsh spoke with the *Cleveland News*. The Rams' general manager had no intention of playing nice with this new Cleveland team.

"Look at it this way," Walsh explained. "Suppose you spent twenty-five years, tough losing years, building up a business. Suppose you finally get it on a basis where you could see some hope of profitability, suppose you had the respect and goodwill of the community. Now suppose some fellow came in and said he was going into the same business, but he wanted to cooperate with you. He wanted to use your program, your methods—all the things you had built up in a quarter of a century."[2]

The message was delivered, Walsh was very clear, yet McBride still reached out to his intercity rivals. "I want to be congenial and I hope they feel the same way," McBride said, and then offered an olive branch: a proposal that the two Cleveland teams have home schedules that would not conflict. "If not," McBride warned ominously, "it will be a dogfight."[3]

And then the Rams abandoned the battle. A month after Walsh's declaration of autonomy, Dan Reeves picked up and moved his team across the country to Los Angeles. Brown, McBride, and their still unnamed club now had the town to themselves.

But a name was necessary. A call was sent out to the area's fans soliciting suggestions. Over 8,500 entries were received and on June 8, 1945, three judges—former Cleveland Indian Tris Speaker, Judge James C. Connell, and athletic great Stan Cofall—selected the entry of Ensign John J. Harnett. Harnett's winning submission of "Panthers" earned him a $1,100 bond. Thus the franchise would be known as the Cleveland Panthers—for all of nine weeks, that is.

Sometime over the course of the summer, Brown was educated to the history of professional football in Cleveland. With this edification came the knowledge that there was a previous incarnation of the Cleveland Panthers. The first Panthers struggled on the playing field, and over the period of seven years they accumulated an inglorious record of 13-45-3 before disbanding.

"I won't start out with anything associated with our enterprise that smacks of failure," Brown told McBride. "The old Panther team failed. I want no part of that name."

Wanting in no way to rankle his coach, McBride recalled the judging committee and asked them to decide upon another name. On this occasion the triumvirate decided upon the designation "Browns." Modestly, Brown's initial instinct was to object to the proposal. After some prodding, however, he did relent. The team would be the Cleveland Browns.* It was an unusual designation, certainly. In the norm, teams weren't named for coaches. But the new league had no bigger marketing tool than Brown, and such was the respect Brown garnered, and the reverence he was given in Ohio, that an exception was made in Cleveland.

—⁓—

A strange turn of events in Columbus brought Brown firmly in the midst of Ohio State politics once again. Through an intermediary, Brown passed on his opinion on the surprising resignation of Carrol Widdoes as the Buckeyes' head coach. Following the '45 Ohio State season Widdoes asked permission to step down and take back his position as backfield coach. A 16-2 record in two seasons notwithstanding, Widdoes found the spotlight as Buckeye head coach too much. Brown couldn't resist commenting on the strange circumstances. Why Brown felt the need to interject his thoughts on the matter is a good question. The animus between him and Lynn St. John ran deep, certainly. Perhaps Brown couldn't keep from sticking a needle in his old nemesis.

The commentary, relayed in a column by Joe Aston of the *Cincinnati Post* was pointed. In the January 14 piece, Brown was quoted as believing that "there will be no permanent peace for Ohio State football until St. John 'and his crowd' are out of the picture." Brown also blamed St. John for "what happened to him and Widdoes." Beyond criticizing St. John, Brown also questioned some of Widdoes's decision-making after taking over for Brown as Buckeye head coach. The obvious pro-Brown lilt to Aston's piece, plus the writer's recitation of the events that pushed Brown into the pros, put St. John on the attack.

St. John's response came in the form of a lengthy note to the alumni who made the *Cincinnati Post* article available to him. The letter, which St. John had reprinted in the *OSU Monthly,* was embarrassing in its vitriol. "It is certainly a shame for anyone, even for Joe Aston, who is writing sports, to be so misled by a gross misrepresentation of facts and to put himself in a position to write such a malicious column in an effort to build up a chap of the character of Paul Brown who has, by his false statements, definitely unfitted himself for all time to come for holding any position in a respectable institution.

"[Brown] is definitely unable to accept any criticism for any of his actions," St. John continued, "but on the other hand, must always find somebody to be the goat in an attempt to justify whatever he does.

"Brown was money mad and nothing could keep him away from cashing in on McBride's offer of $1,000 a month when he was in the service and $25,000 for five years after he got out of the service."

St. John also accused Brown of "tearing down Widdoes once he left Columbus, doing everything he could to create dissension on the Buckeyes."

"The Ohio State University," St. John continued, "will be here doing business at the old stand and turning out winning teams long after Paul Brown is forgotten."

The give and take, the tit for tat, between Brown and St. John was shameful in its immaturity. Two colossal egos colliding, each man not satisfied until his version of the truth had been disseminated. Some in the Columbus press speculated that Brown was positioning himself for a return to Columbus once St. John retired from his position as athletic director. Such a possibility vexed St. John. Ohio State mustn't be stained by a man with the porous character of Brown. The record must be set straight, and St. John went to excruciating lengths to poison the waters in the hopes that he could prevent a Columbus homecoming for Brown.

When word of St. John's dispatch reached Brown at Great Lakes, he shook his head in wonder. "I don't know what Saint's objective is, but it seems a shame that a high-class school like Ohio State should have to try to discredit a person who has been out of his employ for over a year. They must be having real trouble covering up their own situation. . . . Maybe the series of events that followed my leaving might give some insight as to why I really left. St. John is a bitter foe of professional football and I seem to be in the middle of the two."

As this storm of controversy played out, Brown's days in the service were coming to an end. He spent his final month at Great Lakes chasing down players for the team. On February 13, Lou Groza officially signed on to play for the Cleveland Browns, foregoing his planned return to

Ohio State. A few days before Groza, Brown signed two members of the Rams backfield, Tom Colella and Don Greenwood. He would soon entice two other Rams, offensive linemen Mike Scarry, and Chet Adams. Earlier, Brown had declared that he wouldn't raid the Rams' roster. The Cleveland Rams, that is. The legality of Brown's raid was another matter, but that was a problem for the coming months.

World War II came to a close for Brown on March 2 when he received his discharge from the Navy. Relieved of his duties to the country, Brown was now officially the head coach of the football team that bore his name. Even with all the preparations made in the previous months, the to-do list awaiting Brown was staggering. High among Brown's priorities was finding a home for his family. He and Katy scouted the Cleveland area for a few weeks before deciding on a house in suburban Shaker Heights.

On the professional level, Brown added one more name to his coaching staff: Blanton Collier. A friendship was born at Great Lakes; Collier and Brown were kindred spirits. Football was the common bond, but the relationship went well beyond the X's and O's of the game. Brown also took the time out to write a letter to each man on the Browns roster. The note was an introduction of sorts. He wanted his men to know what was expected of them, and, by God, they had better be prepared when they arrived for training camp.

"Regardless of how good a friend of mine you might be or how much of a football name you might have," Brown wrote forebodingly, "it means nothing when it comes to making this football team. To make the squad you must earn the right."

—⚋—

On the eve of training camp, a photograph of Brown appeared in the *Cleveland Press*. In the picture, a beaming Brown was caught holding an overflowing armful of footballs. "Hey Elmer!" the caption below read, "Now they've got a ball."

They had a ball. In fact they had twelve dozen, as well as 288 pairs of shoes, 102 helmets, 2,500 cleats. . . .They also had a place to prepare for the upcoming season, Bowling Green State University. The decision to train at Bowling Green was made several months earlier, in April. The university had served as the summer home for the Rams a year earlier and was well-equipped to accommodate a football team in training. The gorgeous campus with its beautiful lush lawns offered a tranquil backdrop for the birth of the Cleveland Browns. The team was housed in the Alpha Xi sorority house, a spacious three-story building. They would take their meals at the Falcon's Nest, in the Student Union building. The players housed in the sorority house were, for the most part, just home from the war. Many of them arrive with their belongings stuffed in their duffle bags salvaged from the service.

As he had done with all of his teams in the past, Brown stood in front of the classroom and addressed his players to start the new season. For almost two hours, Brown covered a wide array of subjects

"We'll start just as we started when I coached at Massillon," he began. "It'll be just like it was there, at Ohio State and at Great Lakes and those of you who were with me at those places know exactly what I mean. We'll coach the pro team the same way we coached the others. That means we'll start right on the ground floor with fundamentals."[4]

Brown distributed notebooks to each player and informed them that they were to write down everything they heard from either him or any of his assistants. The books were to be brought to every team meeting, where they were expected to diagram each play drawn up on the blackboard in their playbooks. Brown wanted his players to understand the complete concept of every individual play. The playbooks would eventually be examined by Brown and his staff, and the player was graded on neatness and accuracy. In fact, the players were graded on numerous matters, including IQ tests.

—◦—

## Rules

T-shirts in camp, jackets and ties in public.

No smoking in the locker room or dining hall.

Dress shirt or sport shirt to the evening meal.

All players must be in their rooms by 10:30, lights out by 11.

Of course there were players who drank and some that smoked, but none dared take a puff or imbibe within Brown's sight. There were other policies, too. Brown was one who held onto the belief that sexual activity sapped an athlete's strength. He instituted the "Tuesday Rule." Wedded players were instructed to abstain from marital relations after Tuesday every week. Brown never felt the need to order the bachelors on his team to also refrain. Their virtue, apparently, was beyond reproach.

"We've got money invested in you, and on paper it looks as if we would have a good team. But we won't be able to use you if you've lost the fire you had when you were in college. We're starting from scratch, and I want you to think in terms of being the best. We'll settle for nothing less than a winner. We want to be the best. When you think of baseball, you immediately think of the New York Yankees. When you think of boxing, it's Joe Louis. One of these days when people think of football, I want them to think of the Cleveland Browns."

The New York Yankees of professional football; that was the standard. And Brown was determined that his team would look, act, and play the part.

He wanted his to be the most amateur in pro ball: players with a love for the game; a desire to succeed. He wanted money to be secondary; winning must be the first priority. Idyllic, indeed, and everything Brown did was with the intent to make the Browns more "collegiate." The old standard exhibited by the pros was inadequate, obsolete. In Cleveland, there was a blank slate, a new benchmark.

Even the practices were run with precision. The Browns practiced their practice. How they ran on the field, where each unit went on the field for their warm-ups, every minute detail was covered by Brown. Repetition was the key, down to the time of practice, one o'clock, the same as Sunday's kickoff. Brown wanted his players mentally and physically conditioned.

The night before a game the team was sequestered together in a hotel, even for home games. Dinner and a movie every week was the routine. Camaraderie was built, which was the goal, but Brown also knew where all his players were the night before a game. His opponents were possibly prowling taverns, or finding some other avenue of trouble, while Brown's men were sitting together through a lighthearted film. Everything was done with a purpose; even the most seemingly mundane tasks had a function.

The stars were aligned. The post-war boom promised a startling growth in the popularity of pro football. Cleveland was a city starving for sporting success, and with McBride's deep pockets, the Browns had all the resources necessary to build a winning franchise. And Brown insisted that this team go first class—the finest hotels, hot meals on airplanes, jackets for players on the road. McBride wholeheartedly agreed and opened his pocketbook. Little things, like a good meal on airplanes, made an impression on players. And simple things, like jackets worn by his players, gave the Browns an appearance of dignity in the careworn world of professional football.

The assistants Brown selected to fill out his staff were chosen with care and great thought. The Browns' assistants weren't just former college players with some coaching experience, but they were also teachers, either in high school or college. Brown delegated authority; assistants were given responsibility and expected to fulfill the job at hand. It was a team effort. Offensively, Otto Graham and Blanton Collier called the majority of the plays. Seated in the press box with binoculars, play sheets, and a phone connected to the bench, Collier would send specific offensive sequences to Graham, who spoke with Collier by phone while the Cleveland defense was on the field. All other professional teams engaged their assistants on a part-time basis, but this wouldn't do for Brown. Brown went to McBride and convinced him to make his staff full-time employees. The only explanation McBride asked for was, why the need for all these "second coaches." Brown continued the football education of McBride while emptying poor Mickey's wallet.

McBride had complete faith in Brown's vision and gamely agreed to all of Brown's initiatives. To promote his team, however, McBride had a few ideas of his own. He hired twenty girls with telephone sales experience. They called every house and business in Cleveland. The callers stirred civic pride. While his girls hustled ticket sales, McBride blanketed the state with billboard advertising. On game days, he planned on advertising on every Cleveland radio station. He placarded streetcars and his

Mickey McBride with one of his fleets of taxi cabs.

own line of cabs. He set up ticket stations in Akron, Canton, Columbus, Youngstown, Massillon, Sandusky, Elyria, and Lorain.

"You have to spend money to make money," McBride explained, repeating the well-worn mantra.

The question was posed to James Crowley, the new league's commissioner: Would the All-America Conference allow Negro players in the league? The topic was particularly pertinent in the summer of 1946 because Jackie Robinson had become the first Negro to play professional baseball in the modern era. Robinson was performing for the Montreal Royals, the top minor-league club of the Brooklyn Dodgers. Though a sprinkling of blacks participated in the formative years of the NFL during the twenties and early thirties, no players of color had played in the pros since 1933, when Joe Lillard played for the Chicago Cardinals and Ray

Kemp was a member of the Pittsburgh Pirates.** How about this new circuit?

There was "no rule that bars a Negro athlete from playing," Crowley stated. "The AAFC is just what the name implies; it is All-American in every aspect."

The commissioner's words rang hollow. None of the eight teams in his league made any move to integrate their clubs, despite the AAFC's declaration that theirs, unlike the rival NFL, would be an equal-opportunity operation. When questioned on the subject by the Cleveland media, Brown was straightforward with reporters.

"I'm only interested in selecting the best football player," Brown said before the start of camp. "I don't care about their color, nationality, or religion."

Knowing Brown's history and his willingness to field integrated teams, the *Call and Post* enthusiastically reported, "Brown was emphatic in his declaration that his team would 'go the limit' to add Negro stars to his team." Yet when the Cleveland Browns opened camp, the roster was as lily white as the rest of the AAFC. That's not to say Brown wasn't approached. Shortly before embarking for Bowling Green, Brown received a letter from Marion Motley, who wrote requesting an opportunity to try out for Brown's new team.

The inquiry was answered by Brown with a note explaining that the Cleveland club already had its fill of backs.

Brown also heard from his former standout tackle at Ohio State, Bill Willis. Willis phoned Brown and asked if there was a possibility of catching on with the new Cleveland team. "I'll give you a call," was all the commitment Brown could muster. Willis interpreted Brown's perfunctory reply as a brushoff. Knowing that the NFL wasn't an option, Willis contacted the Montreal Alouettes of the Canadian Football League, who offered the lineman a tryout. His bags were packed when Willis received a call, not from Brown, but rather Paul Hornung of the *Columbus Dispatch*. Hornung deeply admired Willis's play at Ohio State and had remained a friend and confidant of Brown's. The writer strongly suggested that Willis drop his plans to go to Montreal.

"Come up to Bowling Green," Hornung said.

"I can't do that," Willis replied. "I wouldn't feel right walking into camp without being invited."

"Now wait a minute," the scribe advised. "You just get here. You take my word for it that you can make this ball club. And, as a matter of fact, I'll stake my reputation on it."

Still reluctant, Willis told Hornung, "Look, I have a plane ticket to go to Canada. If I go to the Browns' camp it's going to cost me expenses."

Undeterred, Hornung continued to press. "Never mind about that. You just be here."

Willis heeded Hornung's advice and canceled his trip to Montreal. On August 1 Willis arrived at Bowling Green just as practice was coming to a close. From across the field Brown noticed Willis. Curiously, Brown showed no sign of surprise when he approached and shook Bill's hand. "Do you think you can still play football?" Brown asked, knowing that Willis had been coaching the game at Kentucky State.

"I don't know, I think so," he replied.

"Well, go get a uniform and be out here tomorrow."

Willis's impact was immediately felt. He lined up opposite Mo Scarry and proceeded to go up, over, and around the center. On one snap Willis reached over Scarry and grabbed Otto Graham by the belt before the quarterback could release the ball.

Bill's initial jump off the ball was so quick that Brown was forced to closely study the line of scrimmage and see if Willis was gaining an advantage from leaping offside. Brown's scrutiny did not uncover any infractions on Willis's part, but he did learn that his own quarterback's stance was contributing to the problem. The quarterback's feet normally were in a parallel position, but Brown asked Graham to place his right foot slightly behind the left in order to push off and move away from the line of scrimmage quicker. This stance, in time, would become the norm around the league.

Brown could not discount Willis's extraordinary performance. There was no doubt that he possessed the talent to make the team. Brown offered the tackle a $4,000 contract with the stipulation that he not inform anyone of the agreement. "An announcement would be made at the proper time," Brown told his newest player.

The next thought for Brown was how to handle this delicate situation. Just weeks earlier, Marion Motley had expressed interest in playing for his team and, Brown reasoned, he wasn't overly impressed with the fullbacks on the roster. Besides, and this was no small point, he needed a roommate for Willis. At Brown's instruction, John Brickles phoned Motley at his home in Canton. He was working in a steel mill in his hometown and playing semi-pro baseball on the side, but Motley said he'd toss that aside. I'll be in Bowling Green by afternoon, he told Brickles. Motley packed a bag and hopped a ride with his cousin.

"He could play a game tomorrow," Brown declared after watching Motley go through drills with the rest of the squad during their August 12 practice. "We have the same plays, the same formation, the same signals we used at Great Lakes."[5]

The final rosters were far from being set, but every man in the Browns' locker room recognized the talent of Motley and Willis. Though Brown had comprised the team with a great number of men who played in the Big Ten, where most teams were integrated, a couple members of the Browns weren't pleased with the new addition to the squad. Brown caught wind of the dissatisfaction and called his team together. His statement was simple and to the point:

"If you can't get along with your teammates, you won't be here."

No word of race was mentioned, but every man in the room understood Brown's intent. The disgruntled were few, and not one soul uttered even a murmur of protest. It was Brown's locker room. It was his team, and his word was final. What was out of Brown's control was the reaction of players around the league. He called Motley and Willis into his office before the first exhibition game. The difficulties that lie ahead were vast. Brown addressed this burden with his players.

"You know that you're going to be in scrapes," Brown advised the young men. "People are going to be calling you names. They're going to be nasty, but you're going to have to stick it out."[6]

Quite possibly Brown's hesitation in bringing Motley and Willis to Bowling Green was deliberate. Perhaps having a Negro on the roster at the start of camp would have brought too much scrutiny from the press. As it was, the news that Brown was integrating the Browns was, for the most part, overlooked. Overlooked, that is, with the exception of the *Call and Post,* which widely heralded Brown's noble decision. Negro fans from all over Northeast Ohio had already developed "a strong attachment" for the Browns, Cleveland Jackson wrote in the pages of the *Call and Post.* Building a devoted fan base among Negroes across the country was a welcomed by-product of Brown's desire to field the best team possible.

—⁓—

The Browns' first victory came before they even played a game. On the eve of the season, federal judge Emerich H. Freed denied an injunction sought by the Los Angeles Rams. They initiated the action earlier in the summer, hoping to restrict Chet Adams from taking the field with the Browns. The Rams' petition alleged that "by offers of more money and argument and persuasion, the Browns induced Adams to breach his contract." Two weeks into camp, the Rams were granted subpoenas for depositions by Adams, Brown, and McBride, as well as the scout who signed Adams, Red Conkright. The Browns' argument was simple and swayed the judge; the Cleveland Rams and the Los Angeles Rams were not the same entity. Freed, in his ruling, proclaimed that the Cleveland Rams ceased to exist when Dan Reeves picked up stakes and moved his team to Los Angeles.

McBride's intense promotional efforts paid off immediately.

For their home games, the Browns played in Cleveland's Municipal Stadium, which was built in 1931 in the hope of attracting the 1932 Summer Olympics. The Games went to Los Angeles, and the enormous ballpark hosted modest crowds for occasional Indians games. Municipal Stadium had never seen such a crowd when 60,135 turned out for the Browns' first contest against the Miami Seahawks. Team public relations men relished reporting that the opening day crowd was just 12,000 fewer than had attended all four of the departed Rams' home contests the previous season.

All suspense vanished from the game just three-and-a-half minutes into the contest when Cliff Lewis hit Mac Speedie with a 16-yard touchdown pass. The Seahawks were everything the Browns were not. While Cleveland played with pristine precision, Miami resembled a second-rate semi-pro outfit. The Browns dominated on the field, 44-0, and also in entertainment value. The play of Brown's men was ballyhooed in postgame commentary, as was Red Bird's Musical Majorettes. The Majorettes, a group of women thirty strong, put on a halftime show that practically overshadowed the contest itself.

Bird answered when McBride called upon him to organize a marching band. And what a band Bird scratched together. He auditioned more than two hundred girls before whittling the applicants down to thirty of the most talented. "It takes a certain type of girl for the band," Bird acknowledged. "They have to be strong in order to stand the tough workouts."[7]

Prior to the Majorettes' official debut at Cleveland Stadium, Bird ran them through grueling nine-to-five practice sessions, five days a week. The arduous preparation paid off in spades as Bird's band received glowing reviews in the next day's papers.

"To say that George 'Red' Bird's Musical Majorettes made a distinct hit with the fans is putting it mildly," Dan Taylor wrote in the Cleveland Press. "After the gaily clad, high-stepping, precision-marching young ladies treated the assemblage to a snappy thirty-minute show between the halves, they drew an ovation that was louder and longer than any offense during the night to the athletes."[8]

Red Bird and his girls were of no concern to Brown. In fact, none of the promotional gimmicks had any bearing on Brown. He left that stuff to Mickey. Though he appreciated the professional showmanship, to Brown it was the game that mattered; it was all that mattered. "We aren't kidding ourselves about the game tonight," Brown said from his office following the contest. "Miami wasn't as tough as we expected, but it won't be that easy every week."[9]

The Seahawks were definitely the dreck of the circuit, but the Miami franchise wasn't the only deficient member of the AAFC. Just one month into the season, the viability of the novice league was in question. A distinct chasm of talent existed between the teams at the top of the standings and those bringing up the rear. The Chicago Rockets failed to live up to the high expectations held by league hierarchy, and the team failed miserably in conjuring up interest in a city vital for the well-being of the AAFC. Across the country, the Los Angeles Dons, a preseason favorite by many who forecast such things, were another disappointment.

And in Cleveland, the Browns were rolling through their opponents. With the exception of the October 12 7-0 victory over the Yankees, all were by lopsided scores. It took just a few weeks for Gordon Cobbledick to declare, however facetiously, "Break up the Browns." The *Plain Dealer* columnist worried that the Browns were so far ahead of their competition that interest in the conference would be "destroyed."

"Perhaps this state of affairs is not surprising," Cobbledick wrote in reference to the struggling franchises in the AAFC. "It could hardly have been expected that a league which, until this fall, existed only on paper, would spring into life on the gridiron as a well-balanced organization."

Well-balanced the All America Conference was not. While the Browns dominated the Western Division, the New York Yankees were running away with the East.

—⁂—

The integration of the Cleveland Browns, Brown insisted, was not a social statement. There were no pious histrionics on the part of Brown, nor did he issue any self-serving pronouncements. Willis and Motley were football players, football players who made the Cleveland Browns a better team. Each man performed exceptionally well under trying circumstances while earning the respect of his teammates. Opponents spewed invective at Willis and Motley. "Nigger" and "coon" were just a sampling of the revolting epithets spewed at them. The abuse went beyond words, though. Flagrant elbows to the face, dirty blows after the whistle blew, and fingers crushed maliciously under stomping feet were also common. Brown asked his players not to retaliate, and both Willis and Motley complied. Each man understood that retaliation could set back the chance of another Negro man reaching the pro game for another decade.

Much of their groundbreaking experience went unnoticed by the crowd and was unreported by the press. An issue that did get debated in the papers was the late-season game scheduled in Miami. As early as mid-August the *Call and Post* had expressed concern about the contest. "No reports have been received to date about the attitude of Miami officials on the possibilities of two Negroes playing in the scheduled December 2nd game between the two teams," the newspaper reported.

As the season wore on and the game approached, the *Call and Post* began to speculate on whether Willis and Motley would even accompany the team to Florida. The writers of the paper wanted Brown to force the hand of Miami officials. Leave it to Florida politicians to enforce their segregation laws. "Let the Southern folks expel the players from the field," the editorial read. "Let them be shown up as a group of contemptible so-and-so's when they send the local gendarmes to take Willis and Motley off the football field, every newspaper in the country will take up the hue and cry which will be heard around the world."

Though the *Call and Post* was optimistic in its belief that Brown would do the right thing, the *Plain Dealer*'s Gordon Cobbledick argued that the subject wasn't even up for debate. "The fact is that Brown could not, even if he wished, expose his star fullback and his great tackle to the kind of treatment they'd receive in Miami," the columnist opined. "A Florida state law forbids mixing of the races in sports events. Brown was aware of the statute when he signed Willis and Motley to contracts and got them to understand that they could not play in Miami."[10]

When word of his decision was publicized, numerous letters poured into Brown's office chiding him for not planning on taking his Negro stars to Miami. There was some call for Brown to make a statement and forfeit the game. Kept from the press, though, was a letter received by Marion Motley several days before the game. "You black son of a bitch," it read, "you come down here and run across the goal line, you'll be a dead son-of-a-bitch."

With Willis at his side, Marion took the letter to Brown. Brown asked the two men what they wanted to do, and both Willis and Motley agreed that they would prefer not to travel to Florida. The decision was made. The news of Motley's letter was kept from the public. Instead, Brown released a statement which, rather than condemn the bigotry that made his decision necessary, placated the existing Jim Crow laws.

"Florida has a state law regarding that situation and we just can't do anything about it," Brown explained. "We had no argument about not using them. We know we can't and that's all there is to it. We can't change the laws or argue about it."

It was the low point of what had been a special season. With Willis and Motley left behind in Cleveland, the Browns ran through the Seahawks with ease, 34-0. Florida's segregation laws notwithstanding, the year had been an overwhelming success for the Browns and Brown. In early December, Brown sat down with Herman Goldstein of the *Cleveland News*. Perhaps it was premature, but Brown offered thoughts and evaluations on his inaugural season in the pro game. "It's been more than I dared hope for," Brown said. With one contest at Brooklyn remaining, the Browns had already clinched the Western Division and were assured a place in the December 22 championship game.

"We worked this year with pros the same way fundamentally we had worked in high school and college football," he said. "We worked the players individually by positions, something few pro clubs do, and it turned out as we thought it should.[11]

"When we beat San Francisco out in California," Brown said, "that was a crucial game for us. We had lost two straight games, and we had injuries. When the boys came through I was satisfied we had it." It was the victory over the 49ers that clinched the division for Cleveland, but that win came in the wake of two consecutive defeats, the second of which was at the hands of a much inferior team, the Los Angeles Dons. After the loss to Los Angeles, Brown's players were expecting a dressing down. Even the

Cleveland writers who traveled to the coast knew what they'd hear from Brown. "We stunk out the joint," Brown would say. They already had their stories ready to go before speaking with the coach.

But what they saw and heard was another side of their stern coach. Psychology was an important aspect to Brown's coaching style, and he wasn't going to beat his team while they were down. Instead, as the Browns' bus arrived at the L.A. airport, Brown stood and spoke to his players. "I thought we played a good football game today and were beaten by the breaks of the game. But I don't want anybody to talk about it. Let's not talk about anybody. We coaches probably made some mistakes, too. It's all part of the business. Now let's all keep our heads up."[12]

The talk had the effect Brown hoped. Cleveland went on a five-game winning streak to close out the regular season. However, on the eve of December 14, three members of the Browns had a night on the town. Jim Daniell was behind the wheel with two passengers, Lou Rymkus and Mac Speedie. The three Browns were cruising through downtown Cleveland when they came upon a police cruiser in the street blocking the lane. Daniell laid on the horn, whether by complete lack of judgment or arrogance fueled by intemperance. Whatever the reason, Daniell successfully garnered the attention of the police officer ahead.

Annoyed at Daniell's impatience, the officer exited his vehicle and took all three men to the local station house. Daniell was charged with public intoxication while his companions were both charged with disorderly conduct.*** Unfortunately for Daniell, news of his indiscretion reached the Cleveland newspapers. The next morning the town woke to the *Plain Dealer's* headline: "Cleveland Brown Captain Arrested for Drunken Driving."

The team was scheduled to meet for a nine o'clock practice at League Park. As usual everyone was in their seat on time, but a murmur ran through the room as Brown entered. Brown stepped to his podium and looked to Daniell.

"Jim, is what I read in the paper true?"

"Yes, sir," answered Daniell.

1946 Cleveland Browns coaching staff. From left to right:
Red Conkright, Blanton Collier, Creighton Miller, Fritz Heisler,
Bob Voights, Paul Brown, and John Brickles.

"Okay, then you're through."

Startled by Brown's terse manner and abrupt pronouncement, Daniell asked, "Do you want to hear my side of the story?"

Brown fixed a steely gaze upon Daniell. There was no need for further explanation. "No," Brown said. "You're through. Get out of here."

Though kicking Daniell off the team left Brown shorthanded heading into the most important game of the year, the act was deliberate. Curiously, Speedie and Rymkus escaped Brown's wrath. Brown knew he had the player to step in and take over for Daniell without missing a beat. More importantly, the decision became legendary among Cleveland players. For years to come, Brown's teams would talk about the time captain Jim Daniell was released from the squad on the eve of a championship game. Brown's reputation as a stern disciplinarian was etched in stone and the decision fell into coaching lore.

It was a cold business, and Brown offered no contrition for his decision. "We run the team on a certain basis," Brown explained, "and it's up to the players to observe the rules or take the consequences. Daniell is not being made an example. He's simply getting what's coming to him."

If the Browns had developed a rivalry in their brief existence, the New York Yankees surely fit the bill. On the field, Cleveland defeated New York three times, including an exhibition game at Akron's Rubber Bowl. Still, Yankee coach Ray Flaherty showed no respect for Brown's team. Flaherty was a veteran of the NFL and disdained the competition he faced in the new league. Following their September 29 24-7 defeat to the Browns, Flaherty upbraided his team for losing "to a bunch of podunks coached by a high school coach." Word of Flaherty's comments reached Brown, who then began referring to the rival coach as Ray "Flattery." The Yankees won the Eastern Division with ridiculous ease. While New York finished with a 10-3-1 record, the three other clubs in the division each had closed at 3-10-1. The stage was set for the first All-America championship game. The Browns, with their superior 12-2 record, would play host to the Yankees on December 22 at Municipal Stadium

A crowd of 40,469 boisterous Cleveland fans braved a dreary blend of freezing drizzle and snow showers to cheer on the Browns. What the crowd lacked in size, it more than made up for in enthusiasm. "It was a young crowd," the *Cleveland Plain Dealer* reported, "a crowd dressed in G.I. hoods and parkas, in hunting caps and olive-drab mufflers, in combat boots and four-buckle antics, wrapped in army blankets and gay plaids. Many were obviously home from school for the holidays and in a holiday mood."

Red Bird and his Musical Majorettes took to the field at halftime and entertained the "overwhelmingly masculine crowd" with a festive "Santa Claus Is Coming To Town." Team mascot Tommy Flynn pranced about the mud-strewn playing surface dressed as ol' Kris Kringle himself.

The festive spirit quickly turned dour after the third quarter began. Orlando (Spec) Sanders burst into Cleveland's end zone, capping an 80-yard drive. The score gave New York a 9-7 lead, a score that held until the 4:13 mark of the fourth quarter. The winning score was provided when Graham hit Lavelli on a 16-yard pass play.

The newly crowned champions were joined on Municipal Stadium's turf by a cheering throng that had stormed the field. As the final gun sounded, Brown started across the field for a perfunctory handshake with Yankee head coach Ray Flaherty when he was swept off his feet and placed triumphantly upon the shoulders of his players and carried to the dugout. Brown and his players darted up the ramp and stormed the dressing room. Over and over, one voice rang out over the others. "We did it! We did it!"

In their wake, the fervent crowd had toppled over each goal post. Beginning in the east end zone, the overzealous fans ripped down the post before traipsing across the gridiron to capture the opposite marker. There, the fans were greeted by a half-dozen of Cleveland's finest who vainly attempted to save the remaining goal post.

Once inside the locker room, Brown was encircled by newsmen, players, radio broadcasters, and more than a few fans who slipped past guards. "Worried? You bet I was worried!" Brown told reporters following the contest. "I didn't stop worrying until it was all over, and then I worried that I might not get off the field in one piece."

The coach generously spread credit for the victory, but reserved special praise for three men: Graham, Lavelli, and Speedie.

"I wouldn't trade these three boys for any six football players in the world," Brown gushed. "Otto was sharp today. I think he played the best game of his career, and that goes a long way. Lavelli had two men on him all afternoon and still caught the ball somehow. And Speedie, well, Speedie makes catches that I don't see how he can possibly get.

"They were all great," Brown emphasized, "played a marvelous game. It was really a team triumph.

"It's great to be champion in your first whirl at this professional game."[13]

Still savoring a dominating season, Brown packed his family into their brand new car (a gift from McBride) and set off for Miami. It was to be a working vacation for Brown. One day was set aside for scouting the Orange Bowl, which pitted Rice against Tennessee. The Brown family returned to Cleveland in time for the January 28 league meetings, where the health of the new league was closely examined.

Even with the championship not taken into consideration, the Browns were the only successful team in the AAFC 's inaugural season. Cleveland took in more than $1 million in gate receipts, but even the substantial sum was not enough to help the franchise turn a profit.

Rental of Cleveland Stadium was $100,000, payment to visiting clubs reached $240,000, the Majorettes charged a fee of $60,000, taxes on admissions ran $230,000. Other operating expenses, salaries, advertising, publicity, and transportation devoured nearly all of the income that remained.

Though McBride would have been pleased making a profit, he well understood the difficulties facing the teams in an upstart league. Unlike several clubs in the AAFC, the Browns' financial affairs had a noticeable upside and Cleveland management was confident that in time the team would show a appreciable profit. What was worrisome to members of the front office was the financial condition of their competitors in the league. While the Browns struggled to break even, the rest of the league was buried in red ink.

Unlike other owners, McBride did not hesitate to spend thousands on publicity to promote Cleveland home games. For his efforts, McBride paid out 40 percent of his gate, yet the Browns only received the $15,000 guarantee for their road dates thanks to his opponents' lack of promotion. The league's weakest franchise, the Miami Seahawks, left Cleveland following their September 6 contest with the Browns without paying their lodging expenses. Interestingly, Miami's accountant did not forget to accept its share of the gate receipts. The Seahawks' cavalier attitude toward obliging its debts rankled Brown. "We have to pay the bills," Brown instructed Frosty Frosberg, the team's business manager. "We can't have people in Cleveland thinking that this league is going to be fly-by-night. It will kill us."

Owned by Harvey Hester, Miami was badly financed from the get-go. An amazing streak of bad luck didn't help the Seahawks' fortunes, either. The club, and the eastern coast of Florida, suffered through three hurricanes, which coincided with three scheduled home games. Hester pleaded with his fellow owners to no avail for patience. The Miami franchise was sold to Baltimore interests and renamed the Colts in time for the 1947 season.

Despite the financial failings of so many clubs, speculation was rampant that the NFL and the AAFC would merge, possibly as soon as the upcoming campaign. Only the strongest franchises—Cleveland, San Francisco, and New York—were under consideration for membership in the established league.

"We haven't come down to earth yet in professional football," Brown said. Both leagues, Brown explained, spent far too much in comparison to the money being taken in. "All the clubs (National and All-American) must level off before you can say that professional football is sound financially. Salaries are sky-high and they probably won't come down until the cutthroat bidding of the two professional leagues get together on some kind of an agreement regarding the drafted players. Then all of us will have a chance to make money."[14]

## seven

**WORLD'S GREATEST
FOOTBALL TEAM**

The story in Cleveland was fresh.

Who was this coach who boasts of having "the most amateur team in captivity"? Arthur Daley of the *New York Times* sought out Brown for a talk about his team and intriguingly innovative methods. "We don't even want to look like professionals," Brown said.

Daley was taken by Brown and his "refreshing" attitude, and found Brown to be "mild-mannered, affable, clear thinking," but also a "strict disciplinarian." He doesn't believe in fining his players, Brown explained. "If they haven't sense enough to behave themselves, I don't want them on my squad."[1]

A few weeks later, after the Browns began the year with victories in each of their first five contests, Brown and his team were profiled in *Time Magazine.* Brown's techniques and his ever-expanding opinions filled the newsweekly piece.

"Days of ranting and raving are over," he said. "This has become a cold, analytical business. You can't bamboozle a professional or even a college or high school player with corn. The desire to win you create that way is short-lived. It blows up with the first adversity. You can't talk a man into doing a job right. He learns only by doing it a hundred times, under exacting supervision.

"Stars are often figments of sportswriters' imaginations. I want high-grade, intelligent men. There's no place on my team for big Butch who talks hard and drinks hard. I like a lean and hungry look.

"If a man learns and studies first, practice doesn't have to be too long. Using the brain saves energy."[2]

It certainly was a new day in the world of pro football. In Cleveland,

Brown was placing as much emphasis on classroom studies as he did on practice field activity.

"I talk to them exactly as I lectured students and I expect them to respond as students,"[3] Brown explained.

There was a judicious explanation for this curious approach to coaching a football team. It was all about teaching.

"First," Brown said, "they write it—they see it.

"Second, they listen to me talk about it—they hear it.

"Third, they work it out on the football field—they do it."[4]

There were tests, also. Periodically, all this information, all this classroom lecturing, would be assessed by an occasional quiz. Football aptitude wasn't the only area checked. Once a year, at the beginning of training camp, every player was given a psychological exam. This, one coach explained, helped separate the quick thinkers from the more slow-witted athletes. The IQ test, Brown insisted, wasn't a determining factor in evaluating a player. "It simply gives us a better understanding of how we must approach individual teaching problems."[5]

Before Brown, a player's speed was calculated in 100-yard sprints. But how often does a player run 100 yards at a stretch? Brown asked himself. Timing a player's speed in a 40-yard dash was a more practical tool for measuring football ability.

"We make no effort to train a player's mind," Brown added. "The use of slogans, pep talks and so on is false and dishonest. You can't teach a player with untruths."[6]

The manner in which Brown put his team through practice was distinctive. While most teams held practice five days a week, once a day, Brown gave his team off Monday and Tuesday. On Wednesday, Thursday, and Friday, there was a classroom session in the morning, which was followed by lunch, and then an afternoon practice. These practices never lasted more than an hour and a half. Ninety minutes was enough time, Brown insisted. If you can't teach in that amount of time, you needed to find a new line of work. On Saturdays, the Browns would hold a thirty-minute run-through, which was always held at the same time as Sunday's kickoff. The Saturday before a home game, the squad would leave League Park and travel together to the Hotel Carter. Dinner as a team was followed by a movie, and then everyone turned in for the night.

It was repetitious, certainly. But there was a distinct method to Brown's propensity for organization; the distinct timetable was reassuring and calming for the whole team.

—⚬⚬—

Brown wasn't the only man making innovative changes to the game. While Brown went to Florida following the championship game, Blanton Collier took an armful of game film home to Kentucky. For six months, Collier devoured the movies, watching them through a viewer that allowed him to slow the film down to a crawl. The resulting "survey" was a cumbersome binder of material, which broke down every single play, every individual movement by each player. Why did a play work or not work? The depth of Collier's meticulous study overwhelmed Brown, as did its groundbreaking look at technical football. The analysis reached far beyond Brown's expectations, arming him with more material for the classroom.

—⚬⚬—

On the first day of camp in 1947, Brown greeted his team with a caveat, "As of this moment we no longer are the champions. The romance is over insofar as our achievements of a year ago are concerned. Right now, we start to do it all over again."[7]

Edward Prell of the *Chicago Tribune* paid a visit to Bowling Green to observe the Browns in training first hand. "They dress neatly. There is no smoking. On the field the workouts are a model of system and precision. Brown knows what he wants and gets it. He commands discipline in a quiet way, setting a fine example in diligence and clean living."

To Prell and most other observers, the Browns appeared to be the frontrunners for the Western Division. Such predictions meant nothing to Brown. He refused to acknowledge that Cleveland was a shoo-in for the title. Sure, the Browns were returning with a nearly identical roster and several significant additions, including former Massillon star Horace Gillom and Ohio State fullback Tony Adamle, but Brown knew his team wasn't a given for anything. "The team that wins ten of fourteen games will win the West. I hope it is us, but I'm not too sure. Yes, we've strengthened a bit, but perhaps not as much as some of the other teams.

"The New York Yankees? They'll win the Eastern championship by a landslide. . . . I'm afraid this team has been strengthened all out of proportion to the other three Eastern clubs."

As the prognosticators predicted, Cleveland easily captured the Western Division. With a 12-1-1 record, the Browns' only slip was a 13-10 loss to the Los Angeles Dons. And in the East, just as Brown expected, the Yankees came out on top. The second All-America championship was held December 15, at a frigid Yankee Stadium. Cleveland was well represented in the stands as more than 3,000 made the trip from Ohio, including the city's mayor, Thomas Burke. They were but a fraction of the more than 61,000 fans that braved the elements and watched the Browns and Yankees struggle to keep their footing on an icy playing surface. Everyone on the field struggled, that is, with the exception of Marion Motley.

Prior to the game Brown pulled Motley to the side. "Marion," Brown asked his star fullback, "you see all those people out there? Guess what they're here for."

Motley, thinking the question was apparent, told his coach that they wanted to see a football game.

"No Marion, the thing they want to know is whether you or Buddy Young is a better man."[8]

Brown's men dominated the fray from the opening kick. They pounded the Yankees to a clear-cut, 14-3 victory. Because of the adverse conditions, Brown altered the Browns' game plan to great effect. Short passes to the ends and backs were prevalent, as well as a whole lot of Marion. It was a Motley 51-yard rumble that set up the Browns' first touchdown late in the first quarter. The fullback had 109 yards on 13 carries.

At the sound of the final gun, hundreds of Browns fans stormed the field. One large group of Harlem rooters swarmed Motley, hoisted him on their shoulders, and carried him halfway to the dressing room. Another group of fans surrounded Horace Gillom and celebrated. With a jubilant jaunt in his step, Brown strode into the Cleveland dressing room. "Great, great, great! Well, we beat them because we played together. Did you ever see any team pull together like ours out there? No fussing, no arguments. We played football like we knew we'd win."[9]

—⁓—

McBride and Brown remained in New York for the AAFC college draft. The two met with the owner of the NFL's Philadelphia Eagles, Alexis Thompson. His Eagles, Thompson informed Brown and Mickey, were operating in the red despite playing before near-capacity crowds at Shibe Park. What the Philadelphia owner wanted was a common draft between the leagues. Escalating salaries, the result of reckless bidding for players, had to be reined in, but what Thompson suggested was too much for his NFL contemporaries. While he had the ear of McBride and Brown, Thompson couldn't convince fellow NFLers to follow his lead. Technically, Thompson's idea failed because NFL bylaws expressed that all proposals must be submitted thirty days prior to a league meeting. Truth be told, though, NFL owners were not about to throw up a white flag of any sort. There would be no peace entreaties. The Nationals were going to wait out the upstarts.

Several weeks later, the *Minneapolis Times* reported in its February 9 edition, "Paul Brown is tired of coaching pro football and despite his $60,000 salary [sic] with the Cleveland Browns, wants to regain his former post at Ohio State."

Four days later Brown was in Columbus promoting the film, "Meet the Browns." The *Minneapolis Times* story had understandably received wide play in the capital, and before the informal conference was a minute old, Lew Byrer of the *Columbus Citizen* questioned Brown about the OSU rumors.

"Would you be interested in returning to Ohio State as a football coach or athletic director?" Byrer asked.

Brown's eyes twinkled and his lips slipped into a wry smile. "This is off the record," Brown told Byrer, "but I don't think I should answer that question. Ohio State has a football coach and athletic director."[10]

Similar rumors surfaced a year earlier, when Paul Bixler suddenly resigned as the Buckeyes head coach after just one year. Almost immediately, the state House of Representatives took a vote, 66-21, in favor of rehiring Brown to fill the opening. The High Street quarterbacks went into full swing hoping to entice Brown back to Columbus. Those in the know, however, knew Brown wouldn't be returning, not as long as Lynn St. John held any sway in the capital city. The rift between Brown and St. John ran too deep. And though St. John was set to retire in June, his replacement, Dick Larkins, had already made overtures to Wes Fesler. Though the job did eventually go to Fesler, Brown's refusal to comment publicly on the OSU vacancy angered St. John and Larkins. Brown's silence, they believed, simply encouraged his supporters in Columbus.

And now, twelve months later, Larkins remained bitter. "Brown has started a terrific drive in Columbus and around Ohio to return as football coach at Ohio State," Larkins stated. The Buckeye A.D. believed Brown had made enough money in the pro game and was now ready to teach college kids again. In the next breath Larkins blasted Brown for "stealing football players off our campus by the dozen. He has done everything in his power to hurt Ohio State."[11]

While visiting with Columbus scribes, Brown touched on a wide array of topics during the three-hour discussion. Not surprisingly, one subject carried more interest than all others: the swirling rumors and Larkins's biting remarks dominated the writer's questions. But Brown wasn't biting. Disgruntled alumni or not, Brown knew Fesler wasn't going anywhere after just one season. And St. John may be gone, but Larkins had no more use for Brown than Old St. John did. No, Brown was staying out of this mess. "I'm not engaged in any such campaign," Brown told Lew Byrer. "I was in Miami catching tuna when the stories were printed."[12]

—⁓—

"It's going to be a tough year in which everybody will be gunning for us," Brown explained. "There isn't a soft touch in the league." With a couple of notable trades, Brown improved an already loaded Browns roster. Cleveland traded the draft rights to Michigan All-American Bob Chappius to Brooklyn for halfback/defensive back Dub Jones. Brown also acquired Chubby Grigg and Alex Agase from the Chicago Rockets. The Browns were the overwhelming favorites to win yet another title in 1948. The loss of Dante Lavelli to a broken ankle during an exhibition loss to the Colts was eased by the great depth of talent Brown had acquired. With Lavelli ably replaced by Horace Gillom, the Browns had secured a record of 7-0 by the time Lavelli returned to the lineup.

The streak continued as the Browns stood at 10-0 after defeating the 49ers 14-7 on  November 14 in front of 82,769 at Municipal Stadium. Following the game, Cleveland embarked on a road trip that took them to New York, Los Angeles, and San Francisco . . . three games in eight days. Brown's boys swept the grueling three-game run, the last of which clinched the Western Division. The championship game itself was anticlimactic. The Browns-49ers battle two weeks earlier had decided who the finest club in the league was; a game Cleveland scraped by to win 31-28 on a gutsy and inspiring performance by Otto Graham.

Graham was still hobbled by a knee injury when the Browns faced Buffalo for the league crown. From the opening kickoff, Cleveland dominated the Bills. With Otto hobbled, Marion Motley rambled for three touchdowns on the sloppy, snow-flecked turf while the Browns' defense stifled any sign of life in the Buffalo offense. Only 22,981 fans watched Cleveland cap a perfect season with its 49-7 victory over an overmatched, overwhelmed Buffalo outfit.

In the locker room, Brown effusively praised his men. It was, Brown said, "the greatest team I've ever coached." He was taken by this group: their spirit, drive, and ingenuity. "This is a very resourceful team. It's one that has tremendous spirit. It's fast and elusive . . . and they're a grand bunch of boys."[13]

A reporter piped in, Would you like to place your team on the field against the National's champion? "We're ready to meet them any place and any time,"[14] Brown said without hesitation. For all the immense satisfaction Brown garnered from the championship campaign, the march to perfection was clouded by uncertainty.

Brown helping Frank Gatski prepare for battle.

On October 21 Brown spoke at the Touchdown Club gathering at the Hallenden Ballroom. Among other topics, Brown announced that the Browns had drafted Doak Walker of SMU. "We were able to select him ahead of other teams in our league because most of them were concentrating on boys they were sure would play next year," he said. Walker still had a year of collegiate eligibility remaining, and neither the Browns nor the Detroit Lions, who selected the wildly talented Walker in the NFL, could sign him until his career at SMU had concluded.

The drafting of Walker was the bright news, but Brown also addressed a more dour topic, one being regurgitated in the sports pages throughout the country: the war between the NFL and AAFC.

"I only hope," Brown told the 400 attendees gathered in the ballroom, "that any moves made by the two professional football leagues will be best for all of football rather than for any particular team or individual. . . . It just seems that it's right for football for the leagues to get together. It's football that counts more than selfish motives."[15]

Alexis Thompson, the youthful and energetic owner of Philadelphia's Eagles had just declared war upon the All-America Football Conference. "Any conciliation between the leagues now is impossible. . . . From now on it's really going to be a battle."

Just one week earlier, Thompson proposed that the two leagues get together in a common draft. The abrupt change of heart occurred after Dan Topping, owner of the New York Yankees, remarked that his NFL rival, the Giants, was in line to lose $200,000 in 1948. Topping's appraisal set off Thompson and several of his NFL contemporaries. Why they would let such an innocuous comment break down a possible reconciliation was curious, but the NFL owners were firm . . . for the moment.

Brown hadn't signed up for this. Brown didn't realize his duties in Cleveland would include arbitrating off-the-field squabbles. The squabbling distracted Brown from coaching and teaching; that was his purpose. "I am disgusted with the bickering and fussing,"[16] he said.

The Browns were the only All-America team to show a profit in the first years of the league, and even that return was minimal. To help keep some of his All-America brethren afloat, McBride reached into his own pockets. But even in Cleveland fan interest had begun to taper off. Each week, McBride's P.R. man was faced with the Herculean task of drumming up interest in yet another mismatch. The lack of competition for the Browns within the conference directly resulted in the falling attendance at Municipal Stadium. Indeed, the 49ers were Cleveland's only viable rival. Even McBride's interest had begun to wane. He failed to visit his club's training camp at Bowling Green earlier in the summer as he had the first two years, and he made only one road trip with the team.

Back in February, Brown told the Columbus press, "If I had my choice between losing before 80,000 and winning before 1,000, I'd rather win."

And though he still stood by those words, Brown had begun to wonder if Cleveland was even a football town. Certainly, in comparison to Massillon and Columbus, the town was lacking. And with the Indians' magical run for the American League pennant, the Browns were a distant second in the thoughts of the city's sports fans. This instability unsettled Brown. The lure of returning to college was very real, and Brown's services were wanted at a number of universities. On the West Coast there were reports that Brown was coming to UCLA to replace Bert LaBrucherie or Jeff Craveth at USC. There were also Pitt and Wisconsin . . . to all of this Brown was noncommittal, saying only that he was under contract through the 1950 season.

—∽—

Shortly after the Browns disposed of the Bills for the AAFC championship, several team owners—James Brevil of Buffalo, Tony Morabito of San Francisco, Dan Topping of New York, and Ben Lindheimer of Los Angeles— joined McBride for an unscheduled meeting at the Hotel Cleveland. They gathered together to discuss a group strategy before boarding the 8:05 train for Philadelphia. The next morning, at 10:30, representatives from both the NFL and the AAFC gathered at the Philadelphia Racquet Club with the hope of bringing some sort of peace to the world of professional football. The December 20 meeting, the first time the two sides sat down at the same table together, extended throughout the day. The give and take found the National owners in control of the deliberations, while the All-America group came to Philadelphia seemingly unprepared. On each occasion a new issue was brought to the table, the AAFC men retired to an adjoining room to discuss the matter before them. The sticking point to tranquility was the Nationals' insistence that Cleveland and San Francisco would be welcome to join the senior circuit. To the rest of the upstart league . . . tough.

While some AAFC owners were content with the chance to escape the business while they still possessed the shirt on their backs, the Baltimore and Buffalo groups both wanted the opportunity to buy into an NFL franchise. This request was refused outright. It was a take-it-or-leave-it offer from the Nationals. No offer of a common draft. No interest in taking on any lesser All-American teams. McBride and San Francisco's Tony Morabito were loyal to their colleagues. Unless everyone was in agreement to dissolve the league, both the Browns and the 49ers would forgo the opportunity to jump to the NFL.

The ten-hour meeting ended in a deadlock. A joint statement was released that revealed little of the negotiations but did contain the hopeful glint that "future meetings might provide some formula for a common understanding between both leagues."[17]

—※—

A few weeks later McBride spoke with the *Cleveland News*. The uncertainty surrounding the AAFC remained a hot topic. "I won't stay in football if there aren't two leagues," he stated. "That's my thinking today and I can't foresee anything in the future to change that."

McBride was asked if the All-America League disbanded, would he accept an invitation to join the Nationals? "No," he ardently replied. "The only chance for success pro football has is to operate with two leagues. Peacefully, I mean, with a world championship playoff between them at the end of the season. There must be two leagues," McBride said emphatically, "or I'm getting out.[18]

"If we go down, I'll go down with the ship. But let me tell you, we're in much better shape than the National League. The owners in our league are all fine men and I'll stick right with them." But his fellow All-America owners weren't of the same thought. McBride then traveled to Coral Gables for a short vacation and left Dan Sherby in control. McBride was oblivious to the feelings of his colleagues.

Shortly after those comments, on January 22, the AAFC hierarchy gathered in Chicago. Ostensibly the conference concerned the Rockets and how to stabilize the struggling franchise. At the conclusion of the confab, the AAFC was reduced from eight teams to seven when the Boston Yanks moved to the Polo Grounds, and the Brooklyn Dodgers consolidated with the New York Yankees. Also the Eastern and Western divisions were condensed to one division, and the schedule was reduced from fourteen to twelve games. The changes were made to strengthen the league as a whole, with the aspiration of making Los Angeles, Chicago, and New York the axis of the circuit.

—⚏—

After leaving the Municipal Stadium playing field following the December 19 conquest of the Bills, Brown declared he wasn't going anywhere. "I don't intend to leave Cleveland and never had," he proclaimed. But these words came in the warm afterglow of another satisfying victory. McBride had heard the rumors all fall, and he too wanted to know Brown's future intentions. He wasn't a newsman looking for a quick quote, Mickey told Brown. He wanted to know if Brown was unhappy, if Brown wanted to move on. At the conclusion of their brief meeting the two men were in agreement: Brown would stay with the Browns, and McBride agreed to extend the coach's contract. They both decided to delay announcing the new five-year agreement. McBride had a train to catch to Philadelphia for the Racquet Club summit between the leagues, and Brown was headed for a short vacation in Florida.

Though the contract was signed on December 31, public notification didn't come for another month, on January 31. In the interim more gossip connecting Brown with open collegiate jobs developed. A Tucson reporter was certain Brown was interested in the University of Arizona, and the Associated Press speculated that Brown would return to Oxford, Ohio, and his alma mater. All this conjecture was based on nothing more than the presumption of Brown being unhappy with the pro game. At a dinner party for Cleveland sportswriters, Brown revealed the contract extension and addressed this issue. He acknowledged the discomfort he felt upon moving to Cleveland. He had been a small-town boy, Brown admitted, and the change took some getting used to. But Katy was happy with the surroundings and pleased with all the friends she'd made, as were the boys. Hoping to put the many rumors to bed, Brown emphasized that Cleveland was the Brown family home.

"I've had a pleasant experience here," he admitted. "The people I've been dealing with have been fair and good with me and I might as well go the route with them. I wouldn't leave these people under these conditions.[19]

"Well," Brown said with a smile, "I'm here to stay,"

Sitting next to Brown, McBride chimed in, "And so am I."

―⚏―

No wives in football. It was one of Brown's tenets preached before every season. But for Brown, Katy was a key ingredient to his success. Hers was a complete devotion to Paul, and it was not an exaggeration to say Katy was adored by all who got to know her. Her tender disposition and sweet smile welcomed friends and strangers alike. There were no wives in football, but Katy did provide a much-needed support system for Paul. And when the team traveled during the season, players' wives gathered together on Sundays. It was a tradition started by Katy when she invited all the coaches' wives to her home for the game. Before long the gathering began to rotate from week to week, with each wife taking a turn at playing hostess. Later in the evening, following the game and dinner, the ladies would all drive to the airport in time to greet the Browns' plane.

It was a family atmosphere, and it was fostered by Katy's gentle touch. The Colliers, the Heislers, the Ewbanks . . . away from the field they all enjoyed one another's company. But none were closer than the Browns and Colliers. Prior to training camp, the two families escaped to Turkey Foot Lake. With Blanton's daughter Kay, Brown would sit at a piano and the two would bang out an old dance hall number. Brown would also gather up all the kids and drive them to the ice cream parlor for treats. In his office desk, Brown always kept a box of chocolates for visiting children. His stony diffidence gave way in the company of children.

―⚏―

The cover of the 1949 Browns press guide bore the bold statement "World's Greatest Football Team." McBride was making no apologies for the braggadocio. "If it's wrong," McBride said, "I'll spend the money to correct whatever is ailing us. I intend to be in pro football a long time and I'm not going to settle for anything but the best."

McBride also tossed out the proposition that his Browns would take on any National League club, "for money or marbles."

The whole league would be gunning for Cleveland, and McBride's brash declaration simply widened the target on the Browns' back. "Our job is getting progressively more difficult," Brown said. "Sometime someone is going to get us, and this year every team in our league is stronger than ever before."[20]

The Browns hadn't lost a game since they played the Los Angeles Dons on October 12, 1947. The amazing streak continued at the start of the new season, though an opening week tie at Buffalo displayed a chink in the Browns' air of invisibility. Against the Bills in the opening week, Cleveland trailed 28-7 with twelve minutes remaining before rallying to a 28-28 draw. The Browns won their next four games before traveling to the West Coast confirming their status as the league's elite team. When asked how to beat the Browns, 49er quarterback Frankie Albert answered, "The way to beat 'em is to outscore 'em." Simplistic? Maybe, but Albert had the right idea. In San Francisco, for the first time in their existence, the Browns were humiliated on the field by Albert and the 49ers, 56-28.

As the final seconds ticked away in the fourth quarter a San Francisco cop came up behind the Cleveland bench. "Hey Coach, what are you going to do now?" Brown seethed, but offered no reply. The defeat embarrassed and angered Brown, but immediately afterward his reaction was thoughtful. "We couldn't go on forever," he said. "The end had to come sometime, and as long as it did, I'm glad it was against San Francisco."

Brown's philosophical outlook vanished by the time the Browns arrived at their hotel in Pasadena. He gathered his players into the ballroom of the Green Hotel and berated them over the Kezar Stadium debacle. "I'm telling you this and its cold turkey," he said. "If those of you who fell down on the job don't bounce back Friday, I'll sell you. . . . I don't care who you are or how important you think you may be, I'll get rid of you."

Brown's outburst continued when he met with the press. "If we don't bounce back against Los Angeles this week, I'm going to rack up this ball-club. I'm going to sell some of these guys while I can still get something for them. . . . There will be a lot of changes,"[21] Brown promised. How much of Brown's verbal explosion was hyperbole was hard to discern. But he was angry with what he interpreted as a lackadaisical performance. The next day, as his team prepared to board their bus outside the Green Hotel in Pasadena, Brown exhorted his players, "Let's go, champions," he chided, a bite of sarcasm evident in his voice.

Brown's explosion made the national wire services and more than one publication took him to task for berating his team after just one loss. *Collier's Magazine* compared Brown's threats to Hitler's snubbing of German athletes who failed to medal at the 1936 Berlin Olympics. There were other editorials that rebuked Brown for the importance he placed on winning. "It wasn't the fact that we lost, but the way we looked in losing," Brown explained. "I knew we had a good football team, but didn't look the part. The players are paid well to do a job for me, and all I want is for them to perform to the maximum of their ability."[22]

The validity of Brown's threat was never tested as the Browns snapped out of their malaise in Los Angeles. Graham threw six touchdowns, four of them to Dante Lavelli, as Cleveland rolled over the Dons 61-14. The victory put the Browns into a first-place tie, and one week later they avenged their loss to San Francisco in front of 71,000 at Municipal Stadium. The impressive turnout was an anomaly. Attendance across the league continued to plummet, and Cleveland was no exception. Their next game, against the Chicago Hornets, drew but 16,506. Though Brown had once insisted that he would gladly play in front of 1,000 as long as he walked away with a victory, the state of professional ball began to alarm him.

"I admit I'm confused about the future," he said. "Now I don't know whether two leagues or one league of two divisions is the answer. And I don't know which cities should be included. But I do know that there'll have to be bigger crowds than some of our games have been drawing to carry on without radical changes."[23]

The Browns weren't the only team struggling. In fact, in comparison, Cleveland was a healthy franchise. Accumulated losses between the leagues had reached an estimated $2 million. Something had to give. Both sides realized that prolonging the fight was fruitless. And so, on December

9, team owners from each league and their representatives converged once again on Philadelphia. The intent was to come away from the conference with some sort of agreement, something to bring financial stability to their game. An accord was met, but not without petty squabbles of self-in-terest and self-preservation. Once it was discovered that only three AAFC teams—Cleveland, Baltimore, and San Francisco— wished to continue operations, the problems became easier to disentangle

"I think it's a peace definitely with honor," Dan E. Sherby said when he emerged from the conference. McBride entrusted Browns minor-ity owner Sherby with the power to act and vote for the franchise while Mickey was in Coral Gables.

"I believe this is a constructive move," Sherby continued. "There will be honest scheduling. As the season goes on, the fans will see the best there is in football and for once we will be crowning a real champion."

Was it peace, or surrender? After all, only three of the All-America clubs decided to carry on, though it was understood that all seven clubs were welcome. The mounting financial losses were just too much for these individual owners to bear. The costly war finally came to a close when the two leagues merged into one thirteen-club circuit. The league was to be called the "National-American Football League." The teams that made up the NFL would all remain intact, while the remaining trio of AAFC clubs would join them. The biggest hurdle for the owners was the distribution of the clubs into divisions. Thirteen owners had thirteen different ideas.

Brown believed Cleveland needed to be placed in the stronger of the two divisions for the franchise to survive. "Unless we get what we need in personnel to fill out gaps plus a place in a division with the better clubs we will not be interested in the new league and we will be out of business," he warned. "We're still on the fence on everything. What I'm afraid is that they're greasing the skids now to give us a poor schedule. We won't go for that."

McBride did not learn of the merger until a reporter tracked him down in Coral Gables and delivered the news. Just three weeks earlier, McBride vowed that he would rather leave football altogether than move his Browns to the NFL. McBride wasn't pleased upon hearing word of the agreement. "Somebody must have thrown in the sponge," he said before catching himself, "I'll have to know what happened. I suppose I'll go ahead with this, so far as I know. I can't make any comments on the new league because I really don't know what happened in Philadelphia. Until I get a full report on the new setup and how the league is going to operate, I can't say whether I'll stay in football."[24]

McBride still believed that two separate leagues were preferable to one. "I have no intentions of entering any blind alleys. Nobody in the new league will bulldoze me as far as scheduling or anything else is concerned. I don't need pro football and I won't stay in it if I don't think the Browns and Cleveland are getting a fair shake."

As the owners bickered among themselves, NFL Commissioner Bert Bell stepped in and arbitrarily assigned teams into two divisions: the National and American. Six teams were placed in each division, slated to play the other clubs in their division on a home-and-home basis. One inter-division contest would be played against a "traditional rival" and each team would play the swing franchise, Baltimore, once, resulting in a twelve-game schedule with one open date.

Cleveland was placed in the American Division, of which Sherby was named president. The merger would result in "a complete reorganization of professional football into one super league consisting of two divisions," Sherby explained. Cleveland fans had become jaded with their perennial championship club and the hope was that the union would rekindle interest in the Browns. Shelby, however, had faith in the market and believed the town would respond to the new configuration.

"We have confidence in Cleveland as a great city and as a great sports center," Shelby declared, "and we will remain in football as long as we can possibly afford it."

Brown wasn't so sure. He had some questions concerning the new divisional alignment. "I am disappointed in the entire settlement of the situation," Brown complained. "This is not to be the distinct two-league set up that I and others had hoped for." Brown then went over Bert Bell's plan. In the Browns' division, the Cardinals, Lions, Colts, and Rams were not good drawing cards. In fact, the only team with the power to bring out fans was the 49ers. The Bears, Eagles, and Giants, all teams on Brown's wish list were placed in the National Division.

"Up to now I don't know too much and there is an awful lot that I must know. . . . If what I read in the morning's paper concerning the shape which the two (divisions) are going to take is true, I don't think I'll be interested in continuing. Mickey McBride is flying up from Miami and I'll have a long talk with him."[25]

Brown spoke with reporters from the cramped meeting room at League Park following a brief practice session for his team. All this merger talk had dominated the headlines and was the leading topic on the mind of most sports fans. But Brown's club had one more contest to play, yet another championship, this one pitting Cleveland against its rivals from San Francisco.

The final score, 21-7, was not indicative of Cleveland's sheer dominance throughout the December 11 championship. It was an exhibition of methodical precision on a day when a muddy track hindered the passing game of both teams. The Browns simply enforced their will upon the 49ers. "The Browns beat the 49ers mentally," Hal Lebovitz wrote, "in the air, on the ground, and most important, in the final score."[26]

Winning never got old. As the clock hit 0:00, Brown burst onto the mud-spattered playing surface, a wide smile of triumph plastered on his mug as he slapped backs and shook hands with his victorious players. Before the Browns exited the field, the small but loyal crowd of 22,500 gave its hometown champions an extended and boisterous round of applause. The band then played taps and the Municipal Stadium grounds crew lowered the flag. Symbolically and literally, the curtain had come down on the All-America Football Conference.

Before allowing the press into the dressing room, Brown spoke privately to his team. He thanked them for a great victory. It was a deserved championship, he assured his players. Brown then brought up the Shamrock Bowl, which was scheduled to be played the following Saturday in

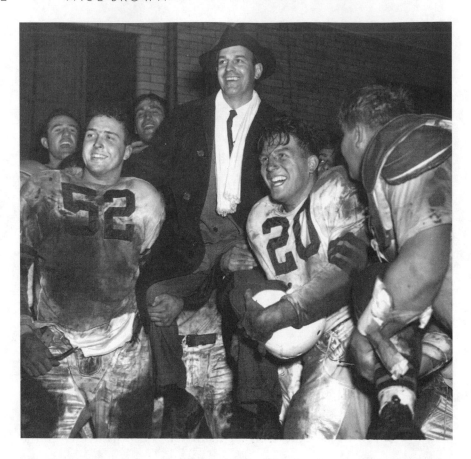

In the locker room following the final AAFC game, George Young (number 52) and Lou Saban (number 20) hold Brown aloft.

Houston, pitting Cleveland against a group of AAFC All-Stars. "Let's enjoy the trip, fellas. . . . I want you to have fun. You can bring your wives along. And I promise you, fellas, I'll not needle you, not once." Brown paused for a moment, took a look around the room, and smiled, "not until next season."[27]

Wives on a road trip! Was Brown delirious? When the newsmen finally entered the locker room, photographers requested a team picture. Several men grabbed their coach and hoisted him upon their shoulders as the cameramen's shutters snapped the shot, a crowning coda for the only champions their league ever knew.

The joy was real, but momentary. What Brown wanted, what he asked for in the locker room after the championship, was a shot at the other league's best. "I'd like nothing better than to play the National League champ as soon as possible,"[28] he said.

But that opportunity wasn't forthcoming. Bert Bell cited the National's constitution, which forbade postseason games. That's why such a contest couldn't be played. Besides, Bell added, "The new organization has adopted the constitution of the NFL." Surely the league charter could be circumvented; these were extenuating circumstances, after all. But by all appearances, the Nationals wanted no part of Cleveland. A loss by the NFL champion at the hands of the Browns would be devastating for the senior circuit's reputation and fan interest.

All Brown was left with was his "hollow title."

A week later, on December 18, the Eagles defeated the Los Angeles Rams for the NFL championship. Afterward Philadelphia coach Greasy Neale was feeling particularly chirpy. "This is the best team ever put together," he crowed. "I don't see why our boys can't do it again. Who is there to beat us?"

From the gaggle of writers before Neale someone called out, "What about Cleveland?"

The mere suggestion put off the Eagles' coach. "Why, all they do is throw the ball," Neale said with a dismissive grunt.

# eight CRASHING THE PARTY

"**All I want is a square shake,**" Mickey McBride spouted, as he prepared to embark for yet another conference in Philadelphia. "I don't want anybody trying to push me around."[1]

Fueled by Brown's repeated objections as well as threats to abandon the pro game altogether, Mickey was standing firm. "I'm not going to do any fighting with these fellows," he declared before departing for the meet. "I have some pretty good ideas about what I consider a fair deal for my team in the way of a schedule and distribution of players."

Cleveland wasn't the only franchise hoping for a better alignment. Each team was looking out for its own best interests, but none was as vocal in its displeasure as the Browns. There were several issues on the table in Philadelphia, including reconciling disputes over draft rights to collegians, how to divide up players from the defunct All-America teams, as well as disputed players claims. Bell advised that any such disputes should be settled between the clubs involved—if a deal couldn't be reached, the commissioner advised a flipped coin should serve as arbiter. In the case of Doak Walker, who was drafted by both the Browns and the Lions, Brown relinquished Cleveland's rights in exchange for Detroit's first-round pick.

Still, nothing was more vital to the league's well-being than the distribution of teams into divisions. Brown's outspoken opposition to Bell's original plan forced the commissioner to reconsider. It took several days before a consensus could be reached; each team had its own agenda. The Chicago teams needed to be separated, as did the New York clubs. Washington's George Marshall insisted that Baltimore not be in the same division as his Redskins so the teams would not have identical home opponents. And both West Coast outfits needed to be placed together to minimize traveling expenses. The final configuration wasn't perfect, but it was the picture of compromise.

| | |
|---|---|
| Cleveland | Chicago Bears |
| New York Giants | Los Angeles Rams |
| Philadelphia Eagles | Detroit Lions |
| Washington Redskins | New York Bulldogs |
| Chicago Cardinals | Green Bay Packers |
| Pittsburgh Steelers | San Francisco 49ers |

Baltimore would serve as the swing team, playing each league member once.

—◊◊◊—

Each team played twelve games: five home and five away against division opponents, one with a "rival" from the other division, and one against Baltimore, the swing team.

It was a setup Brown could live with

—◊◊◊—

Over the Fourth of July holiday Brown took his family to Turkey Foot Lake for a few days of vacation. He took the brief respite to relax and bronze his skin as he anxiously awaited the opening of training camp. Brown admitted to a visiting writer that he was looking forward to the coming campaign more than any previous season.

"Everybody in the National League seems to know much more about us than we know about them," Brown said. "Why, I've only seen a few of those teams in my life, and not too recently at that. So I can't begin to guess how we'll make out against them. That's what amuses me about the people who seem to know already how many times we'll get knocked off."[2]

Brown's cries of ignorance were a bit disingenuous. If ever a man believed in proper preparation, it was Brown, and he certainly wasn't entering this first season in the NFL unaware. The Browns employed freelance scouts—head coaches around the country. These bird dogs were paid $100, $50, or $25, depending on the value placed on their advice. The coaches were invited to Hiram to watch the Browns workout and to see firsthand the quality of athlete in the pros.

"Our business office will send you a check soon after receiving the report," read a standardized letter, "Coach Brown and the rest of the staff appreciate your helping secure data for our draft."[3]

Brown's assistants developed one or two college coaches each who they depended on for scouting tips from the college ranks, but for the pros they relied on their own eyes for information. The previous December, Brown sent Fritz Heisler and Blanton Collier on a scouting assignment to the NFL's championship game. They were to study both Los Angeles and Philadelphia, but it was the Eagles, in particular, that Brown was interested in. Collier, as he did each winter, watched countless hours of game film. So, too, did Brown. More than in any other off season, Brown broke down and studied film. When the team gathered at Bowling Green, Brown and Blanton compared notes on what they'd seen. It was what they'd both believed for the past four years; the Browns could compete in this league. Now all Brown had to do was convince his players that they belonged on the same field with the National Leaguers.

"We've established quite a reputation in four years of All-America Conference competition," Brown said, as he began his opening day address. "But we've been taunted and kidded about playing in an inferior league. It has been said the worst team in the National League the last four years could beat the best in the All-America Conference. . . . We have not only this year at stake, but four years of achievement. I'm asking you to dedicate yourselves more than ever before to preserve the reputation you've made."[4]

The first opportunity to put this practice into play came at Toledo's Glass Bowl. The Browns' opponent for their initial exhibition, the Packers, took the opening kickoff and proceeded to march down the field for a touchdown. For a moment Brown stood on the sideline wondering if just maybe his Browns were in the wrong league. The thought passed when Cleveland scored in just two plays on their first possession on their way to a 38-7 victory.

Cleveland also won the following two weeks and wound up the exhibition season with George Halas's Chicago Bears. From Bears camp in

Mishawaka, Indiana, Halas set out to lower expectations as his team prepared to face the Browns. The Bears' owner claimed his team had little
chance against Brown's powerful band. "The Browns are at the peak of
their game. Their squad is set. The tip-off came when they released John
Yonakor the other day. If Paul Brown's letting go of fellows like big John,
you can bet they're ready. We're nothing like that."[5]

Halas's words reeked of heresy; he was the father of the National
Football League. . . . For four years Mickey McBride hectored Halas re-
lentlessly, trying to wrangle the Bears owner into a winner-take-all contest
between the two franchises. Brown couldn't help but add his two cents.
"When we were in the All-America Conference, I understand we were
called bushers by the other league," he said with a bit of disdain. "Now we
suddenly become the greatest football team of all time."

For the Browns, respect was hard to find. To the Nationals, the
Browns were nothing more than champions of a two-bit league. The media, too, held the reigning four-time AAFC champions in low esteem.
The odds makers also believed Cleveland had little chance now that they'd
hit the big league. Brown joined the parade and downplayed his team's
chances. "I don't care if we get run out of the park, just as long as we get a
chance to prove ourselves."

 Cleveland defeated the Bears, 27-23, but their perfect preseason
schedule did nothing to alter Greasy Neale's contemptuous opinion of
them. Neale and his defending champions were first on the schedule for
Cleveland, not that Greasy was concerned about his unknown opponent.
The Eagles' coach admitted that he hadn't scouted the Browns at all; there
was no need to. "They are just a basketball team," Neale cracked. "All they
do is throw the ball."

Brown and his coaching staff had prepared the team to a fine edge. In
fact, Brown was concerned that his men might peak too early. Since their
inception, the Browns had awaited this opportunity to prove their worth
against a National League outfit, and their coach, too, felt the anxiety as
game time approached. Brown was confident, but his was a cautious optimism. Before departing for the ballpark from the Warwick Hotel, Brown

had some final words for his players. "Just think," Brown said, his voice filled with wonder and sarcasm, "in a few minutes you'll be able to go out and touch Steve Van Buren."*

Philadelphia drew first blood with a field goal, but the Browns responded with three Graham touchdown passes, the last coming early in the third quarter. The 85,000 fans that came to Philadelphia's Municipal Stadium expecting to witness an All-American sacrifice were stunned to see the hometown team behind 21-3. It was a dominating effort by Cleveland, both offensively and defensively. After scoring through the air with ease, the Browns turned to the ground for their final two touchdowns. The score, 35-10, shocked the old guard, none more so than Greasy Neale. "Jeez," he said in wonder, "they got a lot of guns."

The commissioner, too, walked away impressed. The Browns, Bert Bell acknowledged, were "the greatest football club I ever saw."[6]

The Cleveland victory was stunning in its totality. Through the air, Graham completed 21 of 38 pass attempts for 346 yards and three touchdowns. And after rushing the ball just three times in the first half, the Browns ended the day with 141 yards on the ground. In one afternoon the Browns blew up the myth of NFL superiority. "We will not gloat," Brown promised. "This is only the start of a season. We have plenty of games left to play."[7]

The Browns followed the September 16 opener with a decisive 31-0 win at Baltimore before coming home to face Steve Owen's New York Giants. Surprisingly, only 37,467 Cleveland fans ventured to the stadium to watch the Browns' first home NFL game. In a great defensive battle, the Giants dealt Cleveland a 6-0 defeat, the first time ever the Browns were held scoreless. The Browns then beat the Steelers and Cardinals in consecutive weeks before a rematch with the Giants at the Polo Grounds. Offensively, Cleveland struggled again against New York's stout defense. The Browns managed just two field goals and a short-field touchdown following a fumble recovery inside the Giant five-yard line. Thirteen points wasn't enough, though, as New York put 17 on the scoreboard. On the train ride home, Brown vented to reporters. "This team," he said, pointing to the squad riding in the car behind him, "this team is over the hill."

Brown's words had their intended effect. The Browns won their next four contests. Still, they hadn't been sharp since the Philadelphia game, a 31-0 whitewashing of Baltimore notwithstanding. With two weeks remaining in the regular season, the Browns were tied with the Giants for first place at 8-2. It was an open secret that most NFL clubs wanted Cleveland to fail. Coaches from opposing teams shared information about the Browns with one another, exchanging film and philosophies of how to derail Brown's team.

Speaking with a representative from the Associated Press, Greasy Neale openly admitted his anti-Cleveland bias. Neale told the reporter that, if the Eagles couldn't win the division, then he hoped either New York or Pittsburgh came out on top. This disclosure came just days before Philadelphia visited Cleveland aiming for revenge. The elements called for a conservative game plan, but Brown still burned. The memory of Neale's "basketball team" crack continued to rankle. On a rain-plagued afternoon, Cleveland managed to beat Neale's team, 13-7, without a single forward pass.

"It was a grandstand play," Brown explained afterward, "but I wanted to prove we could win the hard way.[8] It's amazing when you think we could go through a whole game without throwing a pass and still not lose our offensive momentum. I don't think Neale really ever forgave us for that."[9]

With that satisfying win, and the subsequent 45-21 victory at Washington, the Browns concluded the season with a 10-2 record; good enough for a first-place tie with the Giants. One more meeting would be needed between New York and Cleveland to determine which club would represent the conference in the championship. Still, even with his team fighting for a berth in the league title game, Brown couldn't escape talk of his returning to the college scene.

On the last day of November, news broke in the *Los Angeles Times* that Brown was a possible candidate for a coaching position at Minnesota and also for the athletic director at Western Reserve University. But, so the *Times* reported, Brown preferred Southern California, a job that was not even open at the time.

Brown was in Washington with his team when the story hit the wires. His reply was an incredulous, "Are you kidding me?"[10] when questioned about the report.

These unsubstantiated rumors only sustained the perception that Brown was unhappy with the pro game, but jumping from the heights of the National Football League to Western Reserve? That conjecture was absurd. However, another more provocative possibility arose on December 9 when Wes Fesler suddenly resigned as OSU head coach. In a 500-word statement released to the press, Fesler claimed health was his chief rationale for resigning. But his physical condition wasn't the sole reason the coach stepped aside. The "people are taking sides," Fesler complained, and the "house is becoming divided." Fesler's comments were interpreted to be directed at OSU alumni and Columbus newspapers, all of whom were critical of the Buckeyes' season-ending 9-3 loss to Michigan two weeks earlier in near-blizzard conditions.

The Ohio State rumors followed Brown throughout the week. At League Park, as his team prepared for the Giants on a snow-covered field, Brown dismissed all inquires on Ohio State. This, Brown didn't need, not right now. "We are getting ready to meet the Giants in a pretty important game Sunday,"[11] was the only comment he would offer.

The December 17 conference title was played under brutal conditions at Municipal Stadium, as the wind whipped in off of Lake Erie, pushing the wind-chill factor below zero. Footing on the icy playing surface was so treacherous that most players wore basketball shoes in place of their football cleats to better manage the hard field.

Similar to their two previous meetings, the Giants and Browns locked into a fierce defensive struggle. Midway through the fourth quarter Cleveland held a precarious 3-0 lead when, with a sudden burst, Giants back Choo Choo Roberts headed for what seemed to be a sure touchdown. Only an amazing effort from Bill Willis prevented the score, as he chased down Roberts at the four-yard line. From there, Cleveland's defense tightened and allowed only a game-tying field goal.

Using Graham's feet rather than his arm, the Browns were able to move the ball into Lou Groza's range. Louie, with a sneaker on his left foot and cleats on his kicking right, came through as he usually did. A late safety made the final score 8-3. For the Browns, the third time against the Giants was the charm. "Now I can get some sleep," Brown said in the locker room. "The Giants are out of the way. We had three games with them and all of them were screwy."[12]

The only obstacle between the Browns and the NFL championship was Cleveland's lost franchise, the Rams. When the Rams stepped from their chartered United Air Lines flight, the temperature in Cleveland was a brisk twenty-four degrees and the forecast for game day, Christmas Eve, was a frigid ten degrees. The conditions dominated the thoughts of Rams' coach Joe Stydahan, who repeatedly complained about the cold. This, Brown thought, was ridiculous. "Why this weather business is greatly exaggerated. It's much more important going from a cold to a warm climate. That's simply an old trick used by coaches for years to give a team a psychological edge,"[13] Brown said.

The freezing temperatures may have been overrated, but the wintry weather kept many Clevelanders home. Only 29,000 witnessed what was an exhilarating and nail-biting contest.

"This one will be remembered a long time," Brown repeatedly said afterward.

The Rams scored on the very first play from scrimmage; an 82-yard touchdown reception by Glen Davis. From that point on, the Browns were playing from behind. Down by the score of 28-27 late in the fourth quarter, the Browns had seemingly moved the ball into field-goal position when Graham coughed up a fumble. Milian Lazetich of the Rams recovered the football at the Los Angeles 24-yard line, giving the visitors possession and a chance to run out the clock. On the sideline, Brown reassured Graham. "Don't worry, Otts; we're still going to get 'em."

Cleveland's defense stiffened, stopping the Rams in their tracks and forcing Los Angeles to punt. This allowed Graham his chance at redemption.

With 1:48 remaining and the ball on their forty, Graham began to march his team down the field. "Go! Go! Go!" rang out from the stands while Graham directed the Browns to the Ram's 12-yard line. Brown was left with a decision: try to put the ball in the end zone or attempt a field goal. Having "the greatest place kicker in the world" on his side made the choice easy for Brown. Under Brown's orders, Graham took a snap and ran the ball to the right, setting up the ball directly in front of the goal posts. From the Los Angeles 16-yard line, Groza's right foot lofted the ball into the air. End over end it sailed through the uprights.

Thousands rushed the field before the final gun rang out. Groza was encircled and lifted up on the shoulders of some exuberant fans. Those who couldn't reach Brown's players found other means to express their happiness. In the center field bleachers a bonfire was built from wastepaper. The goal posts were torn down and carried out of the stadium. Even Brown wasn't immune from the celebrating. His gray felt hat was battered from the hundreds of congratulatory pats on the head he received while trying to escape the frenzy on the playing field. By the time he reached the locker room, the normally composed Brown was visibly dazed—not by the overly enthusiastic celebration, but by his team's stunning comeback victory.

"What the heck was the final score?" Brown called out to the room.

"I never gave up hope," he insisted. "I know this gang too well."

All around him, Brown's players were laughing, slapping backs, hugging, and shouting out in their triumph. Groza was placing a smooch of thanks on his right shoe.

Brown continued, "I know they never quit. This is the greatest football team a coach ever had. Bless 'em all. Next to my wife and family, these guys are my life. What a Merry Christmas they've made it."[14]

The week of the championship game, Mickey McBride addressed the recurring rumors that he was done with professional football. "Win or lose, I have no intention of selling the club," McBride reported. He had threatened to "fold up the franchise" two months earlier when Browns defensive end Len Ford was injured in a game against the Chicago Cardinals. Ford was hurt during a play deemed "too rough" by McBride. The injury put Ford out for the season. "That's all water over the dam now," Mickey said on the eve of the championship. "Ford's accident was unfortunate

Mac Speedie (number 58), Paul Brown, Otto Graham,
and Weeb Ewbank (seated).

and it certainly hurt us, but I guess tempers are bound to flare in a sport
as rough as football."[15]

There was the Ford incident, but also the disappointing turnout at
Municipal Stadium all season. Though McBride acknowledged that the
team had made a "considerable" profit in 1950, attendance for Browns
games was subpar. McBride and Brown both believed interest in their
team would be heightened upon joining the established NFL. Instead,
turnout had dropped. The biggest crowd, 51,076, was for the Bear exhibition contest, while the largest crowd of the regular season, 40,714, was
for the Pittsburgh game. Even taking into account the inclement weather
and the fact that the game was played on Christmas Eve, the weak attendance for the championship was distressing. There was conjecture that the
Browns' thrashing of Philadelphia and the Bears lessened fan curiosity in
the club. But this thought perplexed Brown. Was he supposed to field an

inferior team in order to make events on the field more interesting and thus please the paying customer? Winning, Brown believed, should be pleasing enough for the hometown fans.

Winning certainly brightened McBride's outlook. "It looks as if we at last have this thing rolling," he said one day after the championship game. "Now I want to stay on top and see if we can get 50,000 to 60,000 fans coming out to the stadium regularly. . . . Getting the fans behind us had been a slow process, but I still think this will be the best pro football city in the country. I want to keep on building and winning."

One thing McBride didn't want to do is implement his plan for growing the franchise without Brown. "He's never mentioned leaving the Browns to me," McBride said. "I think he has the best coaching job in the country. He's the boss and he answers to no one. I'm not thinking of anything but having him with us next year."[16]

But the talk of Brown leaving was only getting louder.

—⁂—

On Christmas morning Harold Sauerbrei of the *Plain Dealer* phoned Brown. The call was part personal, part professional. Sauerbrei, like many men who'd covered Brown through the years, had developed a relationship with Brown away from the field. The telephone call wishing the Brown family a Merry Christmas was sincere on the part of Sauerbrei, but the writer couldn't resist asking Brown if he'd made any decision to leave professional football.

"Here it is, Christmas morning and a lot of happiness has come to us," Brown said. "We're just sitting around the Christmas tree and opening packages, Katy, Robin, Mike, Pete, and me." But, as far as his future, Brown couldn't, or wouldn't, offer Sauerbrei any news. "I haven't had time to think yet, everything seems so unreal. . . . All I can say now is that things are status quo."[17]

On the morning of the 26th, Brown, along with Blanton Collier, boarded a train for San Francisco. The two were going to scout the East-West All-Star Game. The leisurely trip across the country allowed Brown and Collier time to plot out a game plan for the Pro Bowl, where Brown was serving as the head coach of the American Conference. After the all-star game, Brown arrived in Los Angeles on New Year's Eve. The next afternoon he and Collier were going to attend their first Rose Bowl. However, before he had the chance set his bags down, reporters began peppering him with questions.

The list was getting lengthy: Minnesota, OSU, USC, and now Stanford were the schools reportedly interested in Brown's services. "Nowhere have I applied for a college coaching job," Brown said. "It would be presumptuous for me to say that I am not interested in a job when it hasn't even been offered to me. I haven't been talking with any college people about a job."

Brown admitted to knowing Southern California Athletic Director Bill Hunter, and though he hadn't been approached, "I'm perfectly willing to talk over the matter with him."[18]

It was an astounding admission by Brown.

"I have had a very pleasant and interesting experience with the Browns," Brown continued. "Arthur McBride has been very kind to me, and I have no reason to believe that I won't be coaching the Browns again next season.

"I just can't commit myself. Who knows, I may be back in the service before next season. If I were certain of my future plans, I would be glad to tell you about them."[19]

Brown was a lieutenant in the Navy reserve, and the war in Korea increased the chance that Brown would be called up. But that was a long shot. Brown would be coaching football in the fall of 1951, but where? USC was interested, and Brown was in their backyard running the American Conference through practices at Bovard Field. This was Brown's first time at the helm of an all-star team, and he took his duties seriously. He ran his players through two drills a day and, with the help of Collier, developed a winning game plan.**

In the midst of one practice, Bill Hunter of USC stopped and paid a visit. To probing reporters Hunter insisted that the coaching vacancy was not discussed; he was just curious to learn what Brown thought of the school's facilities. Trojan alumni were vocally behind bringing Brown to USC. Gwynn Wilson, a member of Southern Cal's Board of Trustees, met with Brown. Despite word that Brown was offered $15,000 a year, talks between Brown and USC never got beyond the preliminary stages. The failure to secure Brown to a contract before he departed California disappointed USC alumni.

The story followed Brown from the coast back to the Midwest. "I have no comment on the situation," Brown said upon arrival at the league meetings in Chicago. "As for myself, I have made no commitments."[20]

Whatever interest Brown might have had in USC was overshadowed by the opening at Ohio State. On the 17th, Fritz Howell, an Ohio-based editor for the Associated Press, served as Brown's agent in the press. "Brown would return to Ohio State as head football coach at $15,000 a year and he would not have to be athletic director. . . . He would insist on picking his own assistants. He will not file an application for the job."[21]

Using Howell as his mouthpiece, Brown was openly flirting with the possibility without actually putting his foot in. Brown was hedging his bets. Five straight titles was immensely satisfying. However, persistent attendance troubles concerned Brown, forcing him to again reconsider the long-term viability of professional football. The Browns' continued success had played out against the franchise at the gate, but the enthusiasm at Ohio State never waned. Brown thrived on the wholesome, energetic atmosphere on campus. Nothing compared to the sensation Brown felt as he brought his team out of the tunnel onto the lush turf of the Horseshoe, leading his squad of Buckeyes into battle on a brisk fall afternoon.

Brown's passion for the college game continued to have a tight hold on him, but he also had legitimate concern for the future of the Cleveland Browns enterprise as a whole. Mickey McBride had volunteered to appear before the Kefauver Committee, which was investigating organized crime. Surely this turn of events played on Brown. Where would the Cleveland franchise be at the close of McBride's testimony? Brown had some knowledge of McBride's colorful background, and there was no telling what would come out in the hearings.

—ɷ—

With a kerchief neatly folded in the pocket of his double-breasted over-coat, a stylish hat atop his head, and a bow tie wrapped tightly around his full neck, Mickey McBride arrived at the Federal Building in Cleveland looking cool and dapper. Over the previous year and a half, his name had come up occasionally in the midst of Congressional hearings on organized crime. The commission put together to conduct this investigation, the Kefauver Committee, was headed by a grandstanding senator from Tennessee, Estes Kefauver. Before he could be subpoenaed, McBride stepped forward and volunteered to testify before the committee. He made his first appearance on January 17, 1951.

What emanated from the stand as McBride answered questions was as interesting as it was entertaining. But first, McBride had something to say. He wanted those in the room to understand, "I never have been engaged in any criminal activity of any kind."[22]

There were three taxi cab companies in Cleveland—the Yellow Cab Company, the Zone Cab Company, and the City Cab Company—all of which were owned by McBride. There were allegations that McBride, with his monopoly on the taxi business, included "fast meters" in his cabs. There were also allegations regarding the hiring of hundreds of drivers, who after being required to pay a $10 initiation fee were dismissed after just a few weeks. The initiation fee was not returned.

This business was raised just to put McBride on the spot. The committee was really interested in more salacious stuff. There were the Chicago mobsters that McBride had done business with, like Murry Humphreys and Anthony Accardo. And they charged that McBride was "making a gift to the Mafia-affiliated mob in Chicago of about $4,000 a week." McBride wouldn't acknowledge the charge nor would he admit to being acquainted with Accardo or Humphreys. But, he admitted, yes, he did know a few fellas of that ilk, but not in that way. Like the real estate deals with Big

Al Polizzi, and the Wood Duck, a yacht McBride sold to John Angersola, aka "King," a Miami resident of questionable character. McBride made no apologies for knowing these fellas. These acquaintances all came about quite naturally through legitimate business.

But what about the Continental Wire Service, and the murder of James M. Ragen? These were the burning questions on the minds of the committee members. Ragen was a friend of McBride's and a partner in the lucrative Continental Press. McBride and Ragen went way back, to the circulation wars when McBride was with the *News,* and Ragen was with the *Leader.* Reportedly, the Capone gang tried to muscle in on Ragen and informed the Irishman that they wanted 40 percent of the take produced by the Midwest News Service, which was the distributor for the Continental News Service. Ragen's refusal to accede to the mobster's demands set forth several acts of retribution, including the slaying of a colleague at Midwest News, Harry "Red" Richmond. A week after Richmond's murder, Ragen burst into a police station on Chicago's South Side claiming that two men were in hot pursuit of him. Their intentions, Ragen told the sergeant at the desk, were nefarious.

Under duress, Ragen revealed to police that local hoodlums were putting pressure on him to part with the wire service. Two months later, on June 24, 1946, Ragen was ambushed while driving near 39th and State Street in the city's South Side. Ragen lingered for some time in a Chicago hospital but died two months later after "they" "slipped him the salt," which was mob parlance for shoving bichloride-of-mercury tablets down his throat.

McBride told his questioners that he'd thought about Ragen's murder, certainly, but despite being pressed, he had no theories on the crime.

It was a lucrative business, this news service, and it could serve the interest of the syndicate in a variety of ways. Continental Press was the sole channel for transmitting results from the tracks to the public . . . and to the bookies. Indeed, the Capone guys visualized the service as a means to control bookmaking throughout the country.

And, according to the Kefauver Committee, this is precisely what came to pass. The committee concluded that, as a result of the national network created by McBride, "the Capone affiliates and the Mafia are now in control of the distribution of racing wire news with a resultant source of enormous power over bookmaking."

But nothing stuck to McBride. After his three days on the stand, investigators came away with nothing but headlines. His testimony was full of intrigue and contained much in the way of entertainment value, but McBride skated away from the Federal Courthouse accused of no crime. McBride's ownership of the club was mentioned in newspaper accounts, but only among a litany of his holdings and never prominently. And, as for Brown's concern, the Cleveland Browns and the NFL came out of the affair unscathed and unsullied.

—⁓—

The *Columbus Dispatch* reported that Brown's name was on the list of "several prospects" to be interviewed by the university's six-man screening committee. Brown remained in Cleveland for a few days waiting for word from the university, delaying his annual winter excursion to Florida.

Some well-heeled alumni began a campaign to bring Brown back to Columbus. The highly publicized crusade forced athletic department members to invite Brown for a formal interview. The meeting was scheduled for Saturday, January 27, at the university Faculty Club, allowing a local radio station a week to drum up turnout for Brown's appearance. The publicity worked. Outside the demure club the scene was festively chaotic. Upward of 500 students began gathering in front of the building at 5:15 P.M., politicking for the selection of Brown. Most pounded the pavement with their feet and rubbed their hands together in an attempt to fight the chill in the air. Several cars drove back and forth in front of the club bearing signs reading, "Bring Back Brown." A jalopy sputtered around Oval Street, promoting the retention of Brown in Cleveland. On the roof of the old car was a large papier-mâché football player dressed in Buckeye scarlet and gray. On the sides of the jalopy were large posters reading, "Cleveland's Browns Want You, Go Home," and "Cleveland Needs You."

A dozen students charged the offending vehicle, grabbed the signs from the car and tore the dummy player from the roof. "I'm from Cleveland," the young man shouted to the angry throng. "We want him there."

Using the papier-mâché Buckeye as kindling, a makeshift fire was built in the middle of the avenue.

Into this bedlam Brown arrived, five minutes before the 6 o'clock meeting was set to begin. Brown emerged from his Cadillac wearing a brown overcoat, suit, tie, and hat. He smiled when he saw the large crowd present to greet him and was quickly engulfed by a sea of clamoring students chanting, "Paul!" and "We want Brown!" With a tip of his hat, Brown proceeded up the walk. When he reached the steps of the club, Brown stopped and turned. The milling crowd fell silent for a moment. "Well, fellas," Brown said, "I guess we might as well go."[23]

While Brown's popularity among the students and alumni hadn't ebbed since he departed for the Navy, many members of the board sitting across from him at the meeting hadn't forgiven Brown for the events of 1945. The conference lasted three hours and forty-eight minutes, in which Brown reportedly told the athletic board that he was "anxious to leave professional football."

When he departed the Faculty Club a little before 10 P.M., the scene had calmed down considerably. The street was cleared of demonstrators and only one reporter waited out the lengthy summit. "No comment," was Brown's initial response, before giving in to the tenacious writer. "It was a very enjoyable meeting. I'm very glad I came."

Did Larkins offer you the job? Brown was asked.

"No, this meeting was merely to iron out a few things and to express views on both sides. All I can say is that I have been 'screened,' as have a number of other candidates. I'm glad I accepted the invitation. It has been a pleasant experience."

Did you actually come down here to get the job?

"I came down here, didn't I?" Brown answered with a sly grin. "That's all you need to know."[24]

—⁂—

Brown wasn't the sole applicant for the open position, just the most publicized. OSU frosh coach Harry Strobel, Missouri's Don Faurot, Warren

Gaer of Drake, Woody Hayes from Miami University, and Massillon's Chuck Mather were all candidates. Each of these men came and went from the Faculty Club with no fanfare. The headlines belonged solely to Brown. Sixteen of twenty-nine Ohio sports editors polled were in favor of Brown receiving the position. The *Columbus Citizen* surveyed its readers: 2,391 out of 2,811 ballots cast selected Brown as their nominee. Lew Byrer, the sports editor of the *Citizen,* though, wasn't so sure that OSU should mortgage the university just to bring back a highly successful football coach. The rumors that there was a slush fund set aside to lure Brown concerned Byrer.

"I'm not anti-Brown," Byrer insisted, "but I definitely am pro-Ohio State on this issue. Brown, the Mr. Big of Football, isn't bigger than Ohio State. . . . Our state institution was here before Paul came and it will be here a long time after he's gone."[25]

Internal politics dominated the process. Larkins vehemently opposed the return of Brown, but his was just one voice. There were several pro-Brown members on the board, also. While the eight-member screening committee was unanimous in its recommendation of Woody Hayes, a fierce battle was waged over the next couple of weeks among the trustees, who were split between Hayes and Brown. While the deliberations continued, Dutch Bergman of NBC reported that Brown was returning to Columbus, barring "a last-minute shift." But Bergman was not privy to the inner machinations of the board. Mid-February arrived and the board was evenly split between Hayes and Brown. The tie-breaking vote belonged to John Bricker, a United States senator and the former governor of Ohio. Though delayed by a snowstorm, the silver-haired Bricker arrived in Columbus in time to voice his considerable opinion. Ninety minutes after Bricker entered the February 16 meeting of the trustees, OSU president Howard Bevis emerged with the news. The new head coach of the scarlet and gray would be Wayne Woodrow Hayes.

Lew Byrer felt for Hayes. OSU had become a graveyard of coaches; the pressure to succeed was overwhelming in an atmosphere that expected success each and every fall. And that's not even mentioning the enormous shadow of Paul Brown continued to loom, and Brown's supporters were a hard bunch to please.

"Here's hoping Woody has a tougher hide than Wid, and Bix, and Fes," Byrer wrote. "He'll need it. For the ring leaders which succeeded in making Wid, Bix, and Fes decide to try their coaching luck elsewhere had one thing in mind. That was to bring about the return of Paul Brown as Ohio State coach.

"They didn't succeed and they're very unhappy about it.

"They'll vent their spleen when Ohio State suffers its first defeat under Woody Hayes.

"They wouldn't have been satisfied with Knute K. Messiah as Ohio State coach, unless he'd changed his name to Paul Brown."[26]

———

Shortly after the announcement was made, Brown was playing a round of golf with Franklin Lewis, the sports editor of the *Cleveland Press.* On the links, Brown began to rewrite the events of the preceding weeks for attribution. He hadn't interviewed for the job, Brown told Lewis, nor had he sought the position.

"I wasn't applying for a job," Brown explained. "No one seemed to have a definite starting point. My name had been mentioned so frequently that I saw no harm in going down there. After all, I never mentioned a word to anyone about Ohio State. Everyone else did the talking in recent months."[27]

It was the only job Brown had ever wanted, and with St. John gone, he wanted it back. But it was Brown's pride, and his ever-expanding ego, that wouldn't allow him to acknowledge that he sought a position and was turned away. To admit that he'd been passed over for a younger, less-experienced coach was too much for Brown.

But it was time to move on. He had put Columbus behind him for good.

After several weeks of golf, swimming, and just plain loafing, Brown was back in the office tending to the usual mundane off-season tasks.

The Brown family: Pete, Mike (with Suzy Q),
Robin, Katy, and Paul.

Details such as signing players to contracts, arranging the exhibition schedule, examining material gathered by his assistants, and penning individual letters to his players awaited Brown when he returned to Cleveland.

"All plans for you and the club will always be made in terms of what we feel, as a staff, to be the best for the team. Everything will be figured in terms of what will give our organization the best possible chance to win. Everything is based on winning."

"I can not emphasize too strongly to you the value of being in condition when you report. We will have far more men in camp than we can hope to keep. Our decision in the retaining of men will be made strictly in accordance with what we feel will best help the club.

"Above all, I would suggest you set up a systematic, long-range program of conditioning—run, run, run. We will still take our football players on the lean and hungry side. Our team is based on speed. I'm certain you will know what I am talking about when we get down to work."

Then, after tending to all the tedious details, Brown retired to a little cottage at Turkey Foot Lake. As they did every summer, the Brown family spent several weeks together relaxing before the grind of another season began.

"We start all over again every year," Brown reminded his players as they reconvened once again at Bowling Green. "We build that broad, new base every season, just like the foundation of a house." The Browns' sixth training camp began on the morning of July 25, when players and coaches joined for breakfast in the Falcon's Nest on the school's campus.

"This is quite a contrast to a year ago, when we were champions of what some folks called an upstart league. We paid a big price, hard work to win the championship. I'm speaking for myself, and I'm sure my old players, when I say I like being football champion of the world and will most zealously defend that ranking."[28]

As champions of the NFL, the Browns had the duty of starting their exhibition season with a contest against the College All-Stars. It was a task Brown took very seriously. As a motivational tool, Brown kept in his desk a well-worn magazine containing an article titled, "The Pros Don't Play Football," by Army coach Earl Blaik. Unknowingly, Blaik inspired Brown with his disparaging portrayal of the pay-for-play brand of football. Cleveland hit the practice field every day, regardless of the weather. A heavy downpour didn't prevent the Browns from scrimmaging several days before the contest. Not a single fan ventured out to watch Brown's club work out in the rain, but there was a lone car sitting stationary on a road overlooking the practice field. Ever suspicious, nay paranoid, Brown was certain that the All-Star coach, Herman Hickman, had sent a mole to watch his boys prepare. Brown grabbed hold of Morrie Kono, the team's assistant trainer, and sent him to investigate. Several minutes later Kono returned. It wasn't a spy operation, he assured Brown. "Looks like an exhausted salesman. The guy is sound asleep."[29]

—m—

Much to Brown's delight, the Browns handled the All-Stars with ease, 33-0. Cleveland went through its elongated 1951 exhibition schedule with a 4-1 record. And though there were minimal changes to the roster—only five new faces joined the squad—Brown proved that no man's job was safe when he demoted Marion Motley to the third string. Motley, the league's leading rusher in 1950, had collided with Tony Adamle while preparing for the All-Star game, aggravating an old knee injury. Motley did play in the contest, but he had to be helped to his car following the game.

"We reward performance, even in training camp," Brown explained. "Cole [Emerson] has looked better doing everything than Motley. So far, Marion hasn't exhibited the speed, the go, and the desire which he showed in past seasons."[30]

They began playing for real on September 30 in San Francisco. On the way to Kezar Stadium, the Browns' bus driver was ticketed for speeding. And the 49ers weren't any more congenial to their old All-American Conference antagonists than the local police were. San Francisco manhandled the Browns, physically beating Brown's team much more decisively than the 24-10 score would indicate. With a weary resignation, Brown told reporters, "It's simply not the ball club it used to be."[31]

He didn't put the entire onus on his players, however. "I feel that I laid one great big egg," Brown admitted. "Everything I did turned out wrong."[32]

It was just one game, and Brown had been known to overreact for effect in the past, but some impartial observers concurred that the Browns' future was, indeed, behind them. One Cleveland scribe pointed out that a year earlier it was a "mad scramble" for Brown's team. "They trailed going into the fourth quarter in seven games. Yes, they managed to win five of them, but no team can maintain such a killing pace for long without cracking up."[33]

With such analysis, it was easy to forget that the Browns had won the 1950 championship and that they still had eleven games remaining on their 1951 schedule. Age, a loss of desire, diminished ability . . . all of this was forgotten as Graham led a revamped offense and a reinvigorated defense down the coast to face the Rams in week two. With a chance at silencing their critics and mollifying their coach, the Browns responded with a 38-23 victory at the Coliseum, and followed up that showing with ten more consecutive wins. Eleven straight, and the Browns were once again playing for their league's championship.

It may have been too much to ask for an even dozen.

The title game was a rematch of the 1950 contest, though this time the Rams enjoyed the home-field advantage and were hell-bent on seeking revenge. The Browns employed three separate aircraft to transport the team and equipment across the country. The first plane encountered rough weather, while the second detachment got hung up in Chicago. Despite arriving in Los Angeles five days prior to the game, the Browns were able to get in only three practices. The first workout took place in a park across the street from the Green Hotel, which housed the Browns in Pasadena. Cleveland players conducted the practice in their street clothes because the third plane containing uniforms was still en route to California.

The game itself, though close in score, was the Browns' worst-played of the season. Cleveland held a precarious 10-7 lead at the half, but that evaporated early in the third quarter. Brown's boys battled back, though, and knotted the score at 17. However, just two plays after Groza kicked off, Rams quarterback Norman Van Brocklin hit left end Tom Fears in stride with a picture-perfect pass as the receiver dashed between two Brown defenders. Fears eluded Cliff Lewis and Warren Larr and took the ball the distance for a 73-yard, game-deciding score.

Just twenty-three seconds had elapsed since the Browns evened the score.

Wearing the hard-bitten smile of a man who came out on the losing end, a gracious Brown walked into the dressing room of the new champions and shook the hand of Tom Fears. Brown said. "Here's the guy who did it, right here."

As could be expected, the Cleveland locker room was subdued. Brown amiably spoke to reporters: "We lost a football game, that's all," he said in a brief post-game conference. "We played as hard as we could. . . . It was [Rams coach] Joe Stydahar's turn."

"It was a strange day," Brown acknowledged. "But that's part of the business. We've had a strange day coming for some time."[34]

The game-breaking Brocklin toss to Fears overshadowed a dazzling performance by Graham. Still, the great champion felt he'd failed his coach and teammates. With his head hanging, he dressed and slowly packed his bag.

Seeing his dejected quarterback, Brown walked across the room. "Get your nose up, Otts," he said.

"I let you down," Graham softly said.

"No you didn't, not in the least, Otts."

"I'll make up for it, Paul, I promise you that."

"It's all a part of living," Brown replied. "Nothing to do now but forget it and start thinking of next season."[35]

—⁓—

Losing the championship game forced Brown to reevaluate Cleveland's roster. There would be drastic changes for the coming season, he promised. This wasn't a drastic, morning-after proclamation. A few weeks away from football, some time with Katy and the boys, and Brown was back on the coast coaching the American Conference in the Pro Bowl. "Eight, maybe more, of the fellas who played in the championship game against the Rams wore Brown uniforms for the last time," Brown informed Arch Ward of the *Chicago Tribune*. "Some won't make the team; others won't be around to try. We'll have to do a complete rebuilding job in '52."

After six years of training at Bowling Green, the Browns announced on April 24 that they were moving their camp to Hiram College beginning the coming summer. Located in northern Portage County, Hiram was smack dab in the middle of nowhere. The college, one writer noted, was "152 years old and as quiet in mid-day as a cemetery at night." This quaint, out-of-the-way town was an ideal location to prepare a football team for the upcoming season.

Age was definitely creeping up on the Browns, and the military draft also weakened the roster. By the time summer rolled around, Brown was acknowledging that it would be another year before they would be ready.

"We'll be very good the year after this one," he promised. "Then our prize draft choices will be coming in, or will be coming out of the Army. Their two years of service will be up. Right now we're sweating out military service for quite a few boys."[36]

A couple of weeks later, as camp was set to open, Brown had changed his tune. He expected nothing short of a title, he told Bob Yonkers of the *Press*. "I relish getting started on recouping what we lost last year. I've never been more serious or more determined about anything in my life than regaining the championship.

"Being anything but the champion is no good," he said with a sharp bite in his voice. "It's not fun."[37]

Champion or nothing was Brown's belief. "Our outlook is not a rosy one, but I do believe we will be more respectable," he said days before the season opener against the Rams. More respectable than American Conference champ? Success breeds lofty expectations, and the Browns' unparalleled six-year run had raised the bar to ridiculous heights. Cleveland fans were spoiled. A few off-the-mark passes and the crowd began chanting for Graham's backup. "We want Ratterman," they shouted, referring to Ohio native George Ratterman. A little on-the-field adversity and suddenly Brown's coaching brilliance came into question. The Browns' play-calling was too predictable; opponents knew what was coming practically every down. Brown lacked imagination, his critics cried.

Still, it wasn't as if the Browns had dropped to the bottom of the standings. Entering the final week of the 1952 season, Cleveland sported an 8-3 record and a one-game lead on Philadelphia. With a victory over the Giants, the Browns would clinch their third straight conference championship. New York did its part to help the Eagles by outscoring Cleveland 37-34, but Philadelphia fell to the lowly Redskins. Brown didn't apologize for "backing in" to the championship game. "I'll go in any old way; I'm not proud."[38]

—⁓—

The Lions had to beat the Rams in a tough playoff game to reach the championship. But even with two weeks to prepare for Detroit, the

Browns couldn't completely heal from the numerous nagging injuries hampering the squad. Nor did the offense get untracked. It was a problem that plagued the Browns all season. They would move the ball fairly easily down the field within the opponent's 10-yard line . . . and then they would stall, settling on Groza's golden toe for three points.

In the third period of the championship, the Lions held a 14-7 lead when Marion Motley broke off a 42-yard run. Motley's well-worn legs carried him to the Detroit five, where he was knocked out of bounds. The Lions defense then stood tough. Three snaps later, the Browns were faced with fourth and goal from the 23-yard line. Brown, believing a touchdown was needed from the drive, opted to go for the end zone on fourth down. Graham's pass fell to the Municipal Stadium turf incomplete. The Browns would not threaten to score again. The Browns dominated the game statistically, 22 first downs to 10, rushing yardage 227 to 199, and passing yardage 157 to 59. Still, despite the lopsided nature of the statistical ledger, the Lions never trailed in the game and led where it counted, on the scoreboard: 17-7

Brown was magnanimous in defeat. Perhaps he was a little too accepting of the loss. The same man who months earlier claimed that nothing short of a championship was acceptable now praised his own team in defeat. "We did pretty well," Brown said, before adding, "That was a great team we played."[39]

—⁓—

Brown departed for Mobile and the Senior Bowl shortly after the conclusion of the title game. Left behind in Cleveland was a controversy over playoff winnings. In previous years, trainer Leo Murphy and equipment manager Morrie Kono were given full playoff shares by the Browns players, but after the loss to Detroit the two were voted partial shares. The news embarrassed Brown as much as it disappointed him. Reached in Alabama for comment on the matter, Brown had little to say other than the whole affair was not "newsworthy." Still the *Cleveland News* ran with the seemingly innocuous bit and played up the cheapskate-player angle to the hilt. The players' decision peeved McBride, as did the adverse publicity. The normally taciturn team owner let loose his anger in the paper, calling the decision to shortchange Murphy and Kono "a lousy deal for the highest-paid football team in the league." It was the only outburst of the sort by McBride throughout his tenure.

Whether the unseemly mess played a part in McBride's decision is unclear, or maybe it was falling short in consecutive championship games, but whatever the reason he began talking about selling his Browns shortly after the first of the year. Five consecutive championships spoiled him. "I don't want to win half championships," McBride said following the loss to Detroit. "I want to win everything. When I can't, it's time to get out."

Some months earlier, Saul Silberman made known his interest in buying the Browns should the team become available. Around the same time another local businessman, Homer Marshman, approached Brown and asked Brown to let him know if McBride ever decided to sell. Rather than compete against one another, Marshman and Silberman approached McBride as one. The two men made no immediate inroads, but the thought had been placed in McBride's mind.

Now, in the spring of 1953, another prospective buyer popped up. Dave R. Jones, a "Cleveland industrialist," had heard through the local sporting grapevine that McBride might be willing to part with his football club. Jones contacted Marshman and Silberman. Would they be interested in joining forces in trying to buy the Browns? This newly formed syndicate, with Jones serving as their figurehead, approached Dan Sherby. Are the Browns for sale? Jones inquired. Though Sherby couldn't speak for McBride, he promised Jones he'd call McBride, who was in Florida attending the funeral of a friend.

"Will you sell the club?"

"I might, if I get what I want," McBride replied. His asking price was $600,000, more than twice the price a professional football team had ever brought.

The close-knit group of Cleveland sportswriters caught wind that the Browns might possibly be sold. To set the record straight, Sherby released a statement for McBride: "Mr. McBride has said definitely that he will sell only under two conditions: One, that we get the money out that we put in. We put over one-half million dollars into the Browns and we want to get that much out. Two, that the purchasers are the kind who will continue to give the city of Cleveland the best in football."[40]

Weeks of negotiations came to a fruitful conclusion in the office of Homer Marshman on June 9, 1953. The syndicate that purchased the Browns was formed by a wide array of local businessmen. Silberman was the owner of Randall Raceway. Jones had served as Cleveland's first boxing commissioner and was a stockholder in the Indians, but it was as president of the Geometric Stamping Co. that he garnered his wealth. Ellis Ryan, former president of the Indians, and Ralph DiChiaro, a Cleveland attorney and business partner of Silberman and Marshman who had tried back in 1935 to organize professional football in town, completed the consortium.

Marshman served as the group's spokesman in his office in the Union Commerce Building. "We will operate the Browns exactly as the past owners operated it as far as we know now," Marshman explained. "Paul Brown knew about the pending deal before he left on his vacation, but we haven't been able to reach him yet to let him know that it has been completed. Brown will be very well satisfied, just as he was with the previous owners."[41]

McBride and Brown hadn't seen one another since the league meetings in Philadelphia a month earlier. And though Brown knew the sale was imminent, McBride had assured him that he would inform Brown before finalizing any deal. Brown went on a Canadian fishing expedition confident that Mickey would be true to his word. McBride, however, felt no need to keep Brown up to speed. The deal was completed without Brown's input or participation.

"I've simply had my fling at football and convinced myself that Cleveland always will buy the best," McBride told newsmen from Marshman's office. "Now I'm getting out. I have a few other things to keep me busy."

The sale included a $50,000 down payment to McBride and an arrangement to pay $250,000 by July 15. This represented half of the sale price. McBride took the $50,000 check and casually placed it in the breast pocket of his checkered coat. "Well, I came out clean after all. Considering what happened to some of the other fellows who started the old All-America Conference with me, this isn't so bad. I never made anything, but I didn't lose anything, either, except maybe a few thousand dollars."[42]

"It's a relief to know Paul is aware of this deal," McBride said with a tinge of bitterness in his voice. "I've been trying to reach him for a week to tell him that we were selling."

For some time there were whispers around town that McBride was having difficulties with Brown, that their relationship, which had never been close, had deteriorated to the point that McBride wanted out. The fun was gone from the whole enterprise. Sure, while the team was winning championships, McBride was riding high. But now, well, things that McBride tolerated before were harder to swallow as the years went on. He had accepted, in fact, willingly given, Brown carte blanche control of football operations. He simply stood back admiringly as Brown fielded some of the finest squads ever assembled.

"Do you have a minute, Paul?' McBride once asked as he approached Brown in the locker room.

"It's time for you to leave," Brown snapped. "We can't have you in here. We have team meetings now."

Without a murmur of protest, McBride turned on his heel and exited the clubhouse. Championships and golden trophies stroked the ego. But moments like Brown's rebuke in front of the entire team were what McBride found tiresome. Though he was a minority stockholder, Brown had no say in the sale, not on the purchase price, or the new buyers. And so, when the time came to sell, McBride had one last chance to let Brown know whose team it really was—a subtle gesture to quell Brown's hubris. Without a second thought, McBride finalized the transaction as Brown sat fishing on some distant Canadian lake.

—◇—

"I called the office Friday morning when I got down out of the bushes," Brown told Paul Hornung of the *Columbus Dispatch* when he returned home from Canada, "and you can believe me, it was quite a surprise to be told the club had been sold."

Actually, Brown learned of the deal in Buffalo, after passing through customs. Brown picked up a copy of the *Buffalo News*. The report surprised and angered him. Upon arrival in Cleveland, Brown stopped by McBride's office and vented. He told Mickey this was no way to do business. "How could you sell the team out from under me?" an incredulous Brown asked. A few more words and accusations, and Brown left McBride's office. The two men would never see one another again.

—⁓—

Brown's own position would remain unchanged; his contract was bought from McBride along with the team. It was an important contingency to the agreement and another frustration of Brown's. He was unable to negotiate a fresh contract with the new owners, an updated pact with more favorable terms. Brown set his dissatisfaction aside when speaking to the press.

"These are fine people," Brown said of the purchasing syndicate. "I haven't met several of them yet, but I know of them and I'm sure they'll want what we've always tried to achieve—the best football possible for Cleveland."

Most prognosticators thought the new owners, headed by President Dave Jones, had bought a team well past their prime. Some in the press mused that the "lean and hungry" player Brown had long touted had turned fat and satiated. Unprecedented success and healthy compensation had sucked the ambition from the team, commentators claimed.

"Only once in my coaching life have I gone into a season not thinking I had a good chance to win," Brown said, referencing the '43 Buckeye team dominated by seventeen-year-olds and 4-Fs. "I'm not conceding anything now," he continued. "We've got problems, yes. There are always problems in this business, but I think we have the material to solve ours. If it turns out we haven't, well, we'll start from scratch."[43]

A November 1953 piece in *Sport Magazine* asked, "Are the Browns over the hill?" In the midst of this public debate, the Browns, past their prime or not, won the first game, then their second, the third. . . . Cleveland continued to win week after week, reeling off victories in the first eleven weeks of the 1953 season. Only a loss in Philadelphia prevented the

In the locker room following Cleveland's eighth straight division
title. Top row: Ken Carpenter. Middle row, from left to right:
Weeb Ewbank, Derrell Palmer, Otto Graham, Chick Jagade,
Abe Gibron. Front row: Paul Brown, Bill Willis.

Browns from recording a perfect regular season.

It had been an amazing run. The Browns were playing in their fourth
straight NFL championship game and Detroit, by once again winning
the Western Conference, had the opportunity to defend its title. Experts
originally favored Cleveland by as much as seven points but altered the
line by game time to a three-point spread.

For the spectators, the title game was a sloppy, mundane affair. On
the sideline, though, the game was tension filled and, for the Browns,
devastating. Briggs Stadium's tenuously soft turf caused numerous slips,
slides, and stumbles. On the second play of the day, Graham dropped

back to pass and fumbled the ball when hit by a Detroit defender. The Lions recovered on the Cleveland 13-yard line and moments later scored a touchdown giving Detroit an early 7-0 lead. The remainder of the first half was replete with stalled drives as each club struggled to get its offense untracked. Graham was so ineffective that toward the end of the second quarter he suggested to Brown that he give George Ratterman a try. Brown did, but for only three plays, which were followed by a missed 51-yard field goal by Groza.

Graham returned for the start of the second half, but his luck and performance fared no better. For the game, Graham completed only two of 15 pass attempts. Still, the Browns hung in there. They even managed a lead late in the fourth quarter, 16-10. But in one moment, the game, the season, the championship, everything slipped away. Jim Doran, who hadn't scored a point all season, slid past Browns defensive back Warren Lahr. A beautifully lofted pass by Lions quarterback Bobby Layne found Doran for a 33-yard touchdown. Doak Walker's successful extra point made the score 17-16. There were two minutes and eight seconds remaining in the game, not enough time for the sputtering Browns offense to mount a scoring drive.

"We worked five months and lost it all in two minutes," a dejected Brown said in the dressing room. "Nobody will ever lose a tougher one."

As could be expected, Graham was a stand-up guy. He didn't offer any excuses for his poor performance following what was perhaps his worst day as a pro. "I was lousy and I admit it," a dejected Graham said. "It was my fault."

The despondency throughout the city and the second-guessing by the team's fans was heartening in its own way. Football had finally penetrated the consciousness of Cleveland sports enthusiasts. Brown's play-calling was brought into question when, just before the close of the first quarter, Len Ford recovered a Lions fumble on the Detroit six-yard line. From there the Cleveland offense bogged down in the mud and settled for a Groza field goal. It wasn't only the fans who were questioning Brown's game management. His players, too, had grown weary of Brown's con-

Studying film. From left to right:
Paul Brown, Fritz Heisler, Weeb Ewbank.

servative play-calling. And it wasn't just this game. Cleveland players had
been griping among themselves the last couple of years. Brown seemed
to tighten in the championship games, they complained. They vowed,
should they get another shot at the title, this would not happen again.

On the train ride back to Cleveland, Brown tried to put the game
out of his mind. He huddled for some time with Weeb Ewbank, the team's
draft coordinator, and the two men went over player ratings together. The
selection process was just weeks away. It was time to put away 1953 and
the Detroit Lions and start looking ahead.

Much of Brown's success could be directly attributed to the men who
served under him. Some of his coaches began to get lured away several
years earlier. Dick Gallagher left following the '49 season for the head
coaching position at Santa Clara. And later, Bob Voigt went to Northwestern. Voigt's successor as tackle coach, Bill Edwards, later left for Van-

derbilt, and John Brickles went to Miami University. All these men left with Brown's blessing. Others, however, would have to wait. Miami University had wanted to talk with Fritz Heisler in 1949 about its head coaching position, but the university never got past Brown. In fact, it wasn't for a number of years that Heisler even knew of Miami's interest and Brown's obstinacy. Some assistants Brown would allow to move on, while others he would keep by his side at all costs.

And now, at the beginning of 1954, the Baltimore Colts were in the market for a head coach. The Colts reassigned their coach, Keith Molesworth, to director of scouting. To replace Molesworth, Baltimore wanted Blanton Collier. But wooing Collier away from Cleveland wouldn't be easy. His loyalty to Brown ran deep, and Brown vowed to do everything in his power to retain his friend.

"Nobody's going to take Collier away from me," Brown pledged. "I'll make it so attractive for him financially that he can't afford to leave us."[44]

The Colts were not able to get past Brown to make an effective offer to Collier. So instead, Baltimore looked to its second choice, Weeb Ewbank.

As they had the previous few years, Brown and Ewbank traveled together to the Senior Bowl. The Colts' general manager, Don Kellet, wasn't going to be repelled by Brown again. While in Mobile, Kellet approached Ewbank directly and offered him the job. Ewbank instantly accepted.

When informed by Ewbank after the game, Brown had no choice but to accept his decision. But he wasn't happy. The Colts had gone behind his back, Brown fumed. And why did Weeb wait so long to tell him? But most importantly, Ewbank was in charge of the Browns' draft. He had all of Cleveland's scouting information, yet he was under contract with the Colts. This was patently unfair, Brown protested. The work Ewbank did while in the employ of the Browns should stay in Cleveland and not benefit the Colts. Brown took his complaint to Bert Bell, and the commissioner ruled in Brown's favor. "The man is paid by the Browns, he will finish his job for them," Bell decreed. Ewbank was to remain with Cleveland until the conclusion of the college draft. And so, Ewbank sat at a table with the Browns' brain trust during the selection process. But something curious happened during the draft session. Several players on the Browns' draft list were picked by Baltimore right before Cleveland had their selection. Most notably, the Colts nabbed receiver Raymond Berry and Ordelle Braase off the Browns' scouting charts.

—⚹—

The week before the championship, a member of the Lions, a man who had once played with the Browns, had received a phone call.

"We have a spy in the Cleveland camp, and we don't want Paul Brown to know. Keep your mouth shut."

There was something to this cloak-and-dagger stuff.

Brown had always been unusually paranoid when it came to protecting his team's secrets. But something curious was happening as the Browns prepared for the Lions. Whatever plays Cleveland practiced in the morning, Detroit had the information in the afternoon. And now, in retrospect, Brown was certain the mole in Cleveland's camp was Weeb Ewbank. Frustration and anger overcame Brown whenever he thought of Ewbank. The way he left, so circuitously. It was unbecoming, unprofessional even. And the events at the draft only added to Brown's scorn. Still, there was no evidence whatsoever that Ewbank had committed such an atrocious transgression. But he had crossed Paul Brown. And that was unforgivable.

—⚹—

Losing Ewbank certainly hurt. And having Baltimore cherry-pick the best player out from under them, that was a significant blow for the Browns. But for Brown, neither affair held the import of Blanton Collier accepting an offer to coach at the University of Kentucky. Before agreeing to go to Kentucky, however, Collier spoke with Brown by phone. He emphasized that he had not applied for the position and that he had not yet made up his mind. He didn't want to leave Brown and the Cleveland organization. But it was true; there was only one post Collier would consider leaving the Browns for, and that was Kentucky.

In early February, university officials persuaded Collier to fly from

Kentucky to Fort Myers, Florida, where Brown was vacationing. A few days earlier, Brown had been stung by a stingray on his ankle and was laid up in bed. Brown and Collier spent an afternoon reminiscing and discussing the future. Brown said he was behind Collier "one hundred and fifty" percent and that their friendship was in no jeopardy.

Collier didn't make his decision until he returned home, and family considerations made it too lucrative to turn down. His three daughters and wife had always remained in Paris, Kentucky, during the school year, and their home was just eighteen miles from campus. On February 28, Collier became the twenty-eighth coach in Wildcat history, replacing Paul "Bear" Bryant, who moved on to Texas A&M.

Through Katy, Paul issued a statement. "He is a wonderful man and an outstanding coach," Brown said of Collier. "He was a big factor in the success of our football, so his leaving is a big loss to us. I shall also feel his loss personally as he had been such a close friend and confidant of mine. I can understand the move he is making and he has made it in his usual high-class manner."[45]

With Collier and Ewbank now gone, Fritz Heisler was the sole remaining member of Brown's original 1946 staff. In March, Paul Bixler joined the Browns, taking the position he had turned down eight years earlier to take the head coaching job at Ohio State. Bixler was named the ends coach and chief scout, succeeding Howard Brinker, who was taking Collier's place as backfield coach. It had been a long, trying eight months for Brown. His confidant and best friend, Collier, had moved on, as had the reliable and proficient Ewbank.

Coaches weren't the only changes to the Browns' makeup.

Eleven veterans from the '53 team were gone. In fact, when Marion Motley retired due to a recurring knee injury, only four original Browns remained on the Cleveland squad: Graham, Groza, Lavelli, and Frank Gatski. There were some promising additions to the roster, including Mike McCormack, who had the daunting job of stepping in for Bill Willis. And there was Curly Morrison, who was obtained from the Bears to fill in for Motley in the backfield. Throughout training camp in the summer of '54, reporters asked Brown how the team would fare.

His assessment was honest and forthright. "[The team] hasn't given any evidence yet that it is as good," Brown said. "Some of our new players will have to come through or things will be mighty rough."[46]

—⚡—

It was an inauspicious beginning to the 1954 campaign. The Browns came out on the losing end of their initial exhibition to the Green Bay Packers, as they did in three of their five total preseason contests.

There was little sign of the Browns' fortunes changing as the regular season began. They lost the first game to Philly, 28-10, and two weeks later the Steelers handed the Browns their worst NFL loss, 55-27. At 1-2, fans and sportswriters were ready to bury the Cleveland dynasty. Even opponents were declaring the Browns to be dead. Buck Shaw of the 49ers stated that the Browns weren't going anywhere, not this season, or anytime in the near future. With a wry grin, Brown responded, "They're going to let us play the schedule, aren't they?"

Even in defeat, Brown found reason for optimism. Two days after the season-opening loss to Philadelphia; Brown studied the game film of the contest. No, they hadn't played a good game, Brown acknowledged, but this squad certainly possessed the potential. And again, following the Pittsburgh loss, Brown didn't believe the lopsided score was indicative of how well his team performed. "You know, we played some pretty good football. Actually the pictures were reassuring. We still are a pretty good football team."

And they went out and proved Brown's flowery appraisal correct on the field by reeling off eight consecutive victories. The eighth, a rousing 42-7 victory over the Steelers, clinched the Eastern Conference, making the Browns the first NFL team to win five consecutive division championships. In the dressing room a photographer brought in a pennant bearing the message, "Cleveland Browns Champs." Brown was asked to pose with the banner. He thought for a moment. "We're not champs yet," he said. But the photographer pressed. The Browns were division champs, after all. The well-thought-out argument eventually persuaded Brown, and the shutterbug got his shot.

Cleveland met with its old antagonist, the Lions, the following Sunday, on December 19, in the only league contest of the week. The game was originally slated for October 3, but the Indians, in the midst of a magical season, needed to use Municipal Stadium for a World Series date with the New York Giants. The rescheduled contest was a meaningless affair, as the Lions, too, had already clinched their conference. The game was little more than dress rehearsal for the championship game one week later in the same locale.

Some tried to read something into the Lions' 14-10 victory; odds makers made Detroit a 2½-point favorite in the game that counted. The prognosticators and analysts amused Brown. "Well, at least they're going to let us play the game, aren't they?"

One year earlier, following Cleveland's second championship loss to Detroit, Brown declared his team to be "over the hill." The statement understandably rubbed a number of Browns players wrong, especially when taking into consideration what they considered Brown's conservative play-calling. His coaching was as much to blame as their performance, these players believed. A number of Cleveland players gathered before meeting Detroit once again for the league title. "If we're going to lose, let's lose our way," was the consensus among these men. If necessary, they decided, Brown's plays would be ignored should the coach turn conservative once again.

The would-be mutiny wasn't necessary, however. Cleveland dominated the Lions all afternoon. The Browns got all the breaks, and though the Lions briefly held a 3-0 lead, the outcome was never in question. Though Graham attempted only 12 passes, he completed nine, three for touchdowns, as Cleveland rolled to a 56-10 win.

A three-year championship drought stirred the Municipal Stadium crowd. On each Browns possession, Cleveland fans implored their team, "Go, Go, Go!!" And, with just over two minutes remaining, Brown made a rare sentimental gesture. He pulled Graham from the ballgame so the hometown fans could say goodbye to the great champion. Months earlier, following the Pro Bowl in January, Graham announced his intention of retiring at the conclusion of the 1954 season. And, just a couple of weeks earlier, Graham confirmed his earlier notice. "I just don't feel up to another season of it," he said in early December, "I'm not trying to kid anybody that I'm as good as I was at one time, but I'm sure my throwing is as good as ever."[47]

As Graham trotted from the playing field, the Cleveland faithful responded raucously. Though most in the crowd wore gloves to insulate their hands from the winter chill, the muffled clapping in time with the rhythmic stomping of thousands of feet created a rousing cacophony of appreciation.

Hundreds of fans anxiously waited for the last moments of the game to expire. They spilled onto the field and gathered along the sideline, waiting for the final seconds to tick away on the clock. At the sound of the final gun, the crowd swarmed the field and engulfed Browns players. The fans split into two groups, each veering off toward opposite goal posts, which were ceremoniously brought to the ground. As the players made their way through the jubilant crowd, dozens of fans followed the team down into the dugout trying vainly to join the celebration in the Cleveland dressing room. "We want the Browns," they clamored, "We want the Browns." Only three valiant policemen kept the cheering throng at bay.

For Brown, this victory ranked right up there with the biggest. He didn't like to rank them, but this team showed resilience. These men were great champions. Before allowing the press in the room, Brown addressed his team. Though he was viewed by most observers as cold and analytical, he could be at times, in fact, an emotional, sentimental man. With tears welling in his eyes, Brown spoke to his team.

"On this day, you were the greatest football team I've ever had." Brown then paused for a moment, and then reminded his players of that bleak October train ride carrying the Browns home from their embarrassing loss to the Steelers in Pittsburgh. Everyone had counted them out after that one. "If anybody had told you then where you'd be today…" Brown's words hung in the air; he needn't finish the thought.

Three years of being a runner-up, three years of frustration. The game may have lacked suspense, but it was long on satisfaction.

# nine   TWO BROWNS

**Brown was in something of denial.** Though Graham had made his intentions perfectly clear to numerous newsmen, Brown wasn't conceding the loss of his quarterback just yet. "Otto has said nothing to me about it," Brown said in his team's clubhouse following the title game. "We'll see what happens next summer when the All-Star Game rolls around. Why should a guy who did what he did out there today retire?"[1]

Certainly, Graham's decision wasn't impetuous. For three years he had been contemplating stepping away from the playing field and devoting more energy to his numerous outside business interests. And Beverly, his wife, had been pleading with her husband to spend more time with the family. Brown respected all of Graham's reasons, and he would proceed to move on without his Otts. But, if his designs fell through, Brown had a contingency plan. . . . Call Otto.

———

Ratterman was the man, Brown declared at the start of camp. "We have not and do not intend to contact him," Brown said, referring, of course, to Graham. "A man must want to play football to play it right. If he says he doesn't want to play, we don't ask him. Graham has said he doesn't. If he himself decides he wants to play he can get in touch with us. We're set to go with George Ratterman as our number one quarterback."[2]

A graduate of Notre Dame, Ratterman began his pro career in 1947 with the Buffalo Bills in the AAFC. Following stops in New York with the Yankees and in Montreal with the Canadian Football League's Alouettes, Ratterman in 1952 came to Cleveland, where he served as Graham's understudy for a couple of years. Now, though, the stage was set to be his. Ratterman's backup, Bobby Freeman, had been signed by the Browns several months earlier, in February. Bringing Freeman aboard, as well as Jack Locklear, both of whom were under contract to the CFL's Winnipeg Blue Bombers, was a direct retaliation by Brown, a response to losing both Mac Speedie and Ken Carpenter, who just a couple of weeks earlier left the Browns for the CFL. This tit-for-tat reached federal court in July. The CFL was asking for an injunction to prevent Freeman and Locklear from playing for the Browns. Judge Paul Jones ruled that Brown had no right signing players from the Canadian Football League. Both men, Jones decreed, were already under contract with the Winnipeg Blue Bombers. The Browns had presented a pathetic case. The team's defense was little more than, "we did it because we could," an argument that carried no weight with Judge Jones, who issued a temporary injunction preventing Freeman from joining Cleveland.*

This setback came directly on the heels of the Browns' loss to the College All-Stars. These events changed everything. It wasn't just losing the services of Freeman that concerned Brown, but Ratterman was lacking in size. He wasn't strong enough to withstand an entire season of pounding in the NFL. Brown had hoped Babe Parilli, the team's third option at quarterback, would get an early discharge from the Air Force. That possibility fell through. Parilli wouldn't be released from the service in time to play in the 1955 season.

What now, Brown was asked. He shook his head, and with a smile of bemusement, admitted, "It appears I'll have to make the call for Otto Graham."[3]

It wasn't Brown's style. He scouted players, he drafted players, he signed players to contracts, but Brown did not go to a player with his hat in his hand, all but begging.  But desperate times call for desperate measures, and Brown reached for a phone and dialed Graham's number. On August 15 they met at a Hiram inn, joined by Beverly Graham. Graham listened to Brown's sales pitch. Seemingly, Graham was inclined to return or he wouldn't have entertained the dinner invitation, but he would be tempting fate by returning to the field following his unbelievable run in '54. It had been a storybook ending. However, the chance to bail out his coach, as well as returning to save his teammates from what promised to be a trying season, was too much to turn away from. Graham was only 33, his competitive desire still burned, and his ventures could wait. With Beverly's blessing, Graham told Brown he would come back for one more season. He'd rejoin the team as soon as he tended to a few business matters.

Less than four months later, Graham was again the toast of Cleveland and was celebrated in song inside a joyous Browns locker room.

—⚏—

They had marched through the season with relative ease, winning their sixth consecutive Eastern Conference title with a 9-2-1 record. Standing between the Browns and their third NFL championship were the Rams, in Los Angeles.

The entire club had taken on the disposition of their coach; there was a certainty among the troops. As they gathered at the Green Hotel and ate breakfast as a team, and later as Brown ran them through a light practice, there was a complete lack of tension. All season long, Graham suffered from anxiety on the day of the game. It was a rare game day when he could keep down much more than a candy bar. But between the lines, he was always poised, self-assured. On this day, while the team waited for the bus ride to the Coliseum, Graham sat alone in the hotel lobby poring over mimeographed play sheets, having no problem keeping his breakfast down.

Brown, too, was unusually relaxed before the game. At the stadium Brown calmly examined each yard marker, stepping off the distance "just to make sure," he said with a wink.

Before a championship-game record crowd of 85,695, Graham put on a splendid exhibition, scoring twice himself and throwing for an additional two. In addition to Graham's impressive performance, the Browns' defense came away with seven interceptions. Offensively and defensively, Cleveland dominated Los Angeles, 38-14. The entire afternoon, everything broke Cleveland's way, a tribute to proper game preparation and luck. "Don't give me too much credit for the win," Brown said following the contest. "It's a guessing game, and when you guess right you look good."[4]

As he had done in Cleveland the year before, Brown pulled Graham from the game with two minutes remaining, allowing Otto a final moment in the sun. The partisan Los Angeles crowd recognized that in Graham they had witnessed football's finest quarterback, its greatest champion. He trotted off the playing field to an appreciative round of applause, which reverberated through the cavernous Coliseum. On the sideline, Graham was greeted with a firm handshake and warm smile by a grateful Paul Brown.

"Thanks," Graham told his coach.

Paul looked to Otts: "Thanks."

This time he was gone for good.

Brown gave his word. He wouldn't try to sway Graham to return. "No," he told questioning scribes, "I imposed on him once, that's enough."[5]

"Nothing would induce me to come back again," Graham said in the dressing room. "I'm glad I ended with a good one."[6]

In the midst of the celebration, the boys broke into song for their pal,

"Hurrah for Otto!"

"Hurrah for Graham!"

"Hurrah for Otto.

"For he is a helluva guy."

When the Browns joined the NFL, Brown decided to take some of the responsibility away from Graham. Prior to 1950 Brown occasionally sent a play in from the sideline, but the bulk of the on-field decision making was left to Graham.

"I have a lot of help during games—the other players, a spotter upstairs, the other coaches. I should be able to tell what the situation is much better than the man playing the game," Brown told Jack Newcombe of *Sport Magazine.*

He stood in behind center at one time, and he understood the responsibilities that fell to the quarterback, and just how much of the field he could see. But what about the quarterback's confidence? Brown was asked. Didn't stripping him of his on-field power diminish his self-assurance?

Paul Brown with Otto Graham.

On the surface, to Brown, the question was absurd, "We're not interested in building confidence or initiative. We're interested in winning football games," he said. "This is a business."[7]

———

Always known for his playful antics on and off the field, George Ratterman wasn't afraid to tweak his coach on occasion. Once Brown sent a play in with guard Joe Skibinski.

"I don't like that play," Ratterman told his teammate, "Go tell Brown to send in another one."

Skibinski stood motionless for a moment before he turned and began to make his way back to the Browns' sideline. Ratterman yelled to Skibinski, "Come back here, we'll use the one you brought."

In the midst of another game, Ratterman was riding the bench watching his teammates go four and out inside their opponent's 10-yard line. After Cleveland gave up possession of the ball, Ratterman looked to Brown: "Hey, Coach, you aren't having such a hot afternoon, are ya?"

Brown was always searching for an edge. The messenger guards served their purpose, but what if there was a better, more efficient means to transport his instructions to the quarterback. For several years, Brown had played with the idea of putting a radio receiver inside his quarterback's helmet. Brown talked with an electronics expert and explained his brainstorm. Could you make this work? Brown asked. The resulting design was a radio receiver placed inside Otto Graham's helmet, slightly larger than a pocket watch. With a four-watt transmitter placed near the Cleveland bench, Brown would speak through a microphone and directly send instructions to his quarterback. The prototype was put to the test at a practice in League Park during the '55 season.

The outcome of the experiment was a mixed bag. Graham could hear the coach's instructions perfectly on some parts of the field, but distortion buzzed his eardrums in other areas. There was also some occasional interference on city wavelengths. Still, despite the complications, Brown thought the results promising enough to keep working on the idea.

Prior to the opening of the '56 training camp, Brown reluctantly confirmed his plans to use the radio receiver in games during the upcoming season.

"Anytime we think it has been perfected, we will use it," Brown acknowledged. It was Brown's intention to spring his innovation on the league with no prior hype. With no messenger guards shuttling to and fro, Cleveland opponents would be wondering what was happening on the Browns' sideline

"I really got the idea because of all the fuss made about my 'messenger' boys. I thought we would perfect this thing and I'd spring it all of a sudden in an exhibition game. Then nobody would have been able to figure out how I was getting in the plays."[8]

Brown had to obtain a shortwave license to operate the radio. A stipulation accompanied the license; no profanity could be used over the transmitter. This proviso did not concern Brown, and he put the new radio system into game use during an exhibition contest with the Lions in Akron. The radio worked fairly well during the game, but occasional thunder and lightning above the Akron skies "scared the hell" out of Ratterman. There were other unforeseen complications for the quarterback. The Lions, having read the many advance notices on Brown's innovation, went headhunting for the contraption inside Ratterman's helmet. George survived, as did the radio, at least for one more attempt.

The next week, during a September 22 exhibition game with the Bears, the contraption worked for a few minutes before going off-line, when Brown was forced to revert back to his messenger guards. Several weeks later, Brown gave the transmitter one more try, this time in a regular season contest with the Giants. Following the game, members of the Giants family crowed to the press. They had intercepted Brown's instructions to Ratterman. "We were able to get the Browns' signals better than they could," New York's general manager, Ray Walsh, crowed. "Finally after three unsuccessful series of plays, they gave it up."[9]

The radio did not work at all that afternoon. Brown's words couldn't make it through ear-bending distortion and feedback, and after three offensive series, Brown scrapped the transmitter for the day. The Giants, in fact, exaggerated their sleuthing skills. Indeed, they made the whole thing up. Walsh simply wanted to make a mockery of Brown's radio system. A number of other clubs felt the same as the Giants, the most outspoken of which were George Halas of the Bears and Washington's George Preston Marshall. The call for barring Brown's instrument forced Bert Bell's hand. Several days after the Giants game, Bell took a poll via the telephone with all twelve teams. By unanimous consent, every club agreed that all electronic devices for use between the sideline and the quarterback would be banned for the remainder of the 1956 season. The embargo did not include telephone lines from the coach's box to the sideline.

Brown's innovative device may have been put on the shelf, but another Brown creation had become a standard part of his players' equipment as well as for a number of teams around the league.

In 1953, and for years before, helmets of the day were open, leaving the player's face exposed to injury. Though Brown had been alarmed for some time about the lack of protection provided by the equipment, it took a gruesome injury to his quarterback to get Brown to act on this concern.

Late in the '53 season, in a contest against the 49ers, Graham dropped back to pass from his own 23. With all his receivers covered, he took off down the field. His feet carried him 19 yards before he was pushed out of bounds by San Francisco defender Fred Bruney. Though Graham was clearly out of the field of play, 49er rookie Art Michalik jumped on the quarterback and viciously drove an elbow into Graham's jaw. A number of Browns, including Paul, crashed onto the field trying to get a pound of flesh from the offending Michalik. Officials stepped in before justice could be handed out, however.

Back on the sideline, a clearly dazed Graham was bleeding profusely from the mouth and needed assistance reaching the Browns' locker room. During halftime, the team's physician, Dr. Vic Ippolito, applied fifteen stitches inside Graham's mouth. Before the start of the second half, Morrie Kono constructed a primitive clear plastic face guard to protect Graham's jaw. Injured or not, Graham returned and completed nine of 10 passes while leading the Browns past the 49ers, 23-21.

Kono's makeshift face mask gave Brown an idea. Brown's first proposal for a face guard was a "plastic mask" that shielded the player's entire face. This initiative had several drawbacks, however. In extreme cold it would break, and in great heat the mask would fog up, hindering the player's vision. Brown went back to the drawing board and came up with a more simplistic idea—a single iron bar that went from ear to ear on the helmet, protecting the player's mouth.

He contacted an acquaintance who worked with the sports equipment maker Riddell. Brown asked Jerry Morgan to manufacture something similar "that will fit across the front of a helmet and will be about as big as my little finger," Brown explained to Morgan. "I want it so it can withstand a stray foot, or a deliberately thrown fist or elbow, and take away the inclination to punch someone."

George Halas and Paul Brown, 1952.

"But," Brown added, "keep it light enough to weigh less than an ounce."[10]

It was elementary, yet no one had previously proposed such a simple device. Like many of Brown's contributions to the game, his face mask quickly became standard fare around the league. He had stirred a revolution within the sport; everywhere one looked, Brown's innovations had drastically altered the game. The old ways had, for the most part, been swept aside. Brown's flurry of innovations had become staples around the league—communication from the sideline to the booth, film studies, stressing intelligence in his ball players, all these initiatives began at Brown's urging. While other clubs had just two assistants, he employed six in Cleveland. The larger staff allowed Brown to use a coach as an advance scout, yet another edge for the Browns. On the field, the development of

the intricate pass pattern could be credited to Brown, as could the imple-
mentation of the zone pass defense. The necessity of the latter came from
Brown's belief that it took just one weak link in the pass defense to derail
a team. These were but a few of the alterations brought about by Brown,
but that were now employed by his rivals. The competitive advantage long
enjoyed by the Browns thanks to their coach's ingenuity was gradually
dwindling.

It was hard to remember that the Browns had won the world championship just several months prior. The Browns' surprise loss to the College All-Stars a year earlier stuck in Brown's craw and he had become
obsessed with avenging the loss. In early June 1956, Brown penned a letter
to each member of his team reminding them of their porous effort against
the All-Stars.

"It was a disgraceful exhibition of football, embarrassing to say the
least. And it isn't going to happen this year."[11]

A month later, as Brown swung open the gates to training camp,
he continued to dwell on the previous year's loss to the college stars. "We
were pathetic. We didn't have a winning attitude. We were full of ourselves, and we showed it."[12]

The strange fixation with the All-Star game paid dividends with a
26-0 Cleveland victory over the collegiates. The Browns, however, had hit
their peak for the season. In the midst of a practice one sunny afternoon,
Brown stood wistfully watching his team workout. "We were so great and
now . . . look at all those old men.[13]

"I've never gone into a season without feeling we could win, and this
year is no different. But there is no question that we're in for an ordeal
week after week."

Brown had reason to be concerned. Five straight exhibition losses
set the pace for a 1956 season in which Cleveland won only five of twelve
regular season games. Following a 17-point loss to the Cardinals in the
final game of the year, a sarcastic Brown cracked, "They've been paid as
champions in the past, but they aren't champions this time."

—⚏—

Virtually every morning, Brown would ride the rapid transit from Shaker Heights to the Terminal Tower downtown. From the Terminal Tower, he would make the hearty walk to the team's offices at Municipal Stadium. One day in the fall of 1956, by happenstance, Brown found a communiqué between some of his players. The subject of the document was the foundation of a player's association.

"This communication had to do with what their initial demands were," Brown later explained. "Their initial concerns were about pensions and health care."

Reading the missive, Brown was taken aback. They may have termed it an "association," but Brown recognized the germination of a union when he saw one. Such an organization was not only unnecessary, Brown believed, but potentially harmful. The players were well provided for and would continue to be. A player's union would only prove to be divisive, pitting management against the players. This could do nothing but harm team unity and morale. The whole conspiracy needed to be nipped in the bud, Brown thought. In fact, the last point in the memo instructed, "Be sure you don't let Paul Brown see this or we won't get off the ground."

Brown gathered his players around him in the cramped League Park dressing room. "Let me tell you something," he began, "I see anybody messing around at all with this player's union, you're gone today, not tomorrow."

Despite Brown's explicit threat, his players were intrigued with the association and what they promised to fight for. In December, the association released a statement of purpose:

"The players obviously want a continuous improvement in their economic condition with some control over their own destiny. . . . Football, like baseball, is a business with obvious economic problems between the players and the owners. The democratic approach on the business side of the game is as important in football as in any business, and the players would like a voice in what so vitally affects each one of them."

The Browns also elected a player representative, Don Colo. Shortly after his selection, Colo was called into Brown's office. It was a talk Colo was dreading, but he also knew it was inevitable. "Well, Paul, I did it because I think there was a need for it, and it was the right thing to do."

He listened intently, but Brown was perplexed by Colo's motives. "You know," Brown said, "you're never going to reap any benefit from this."

Brown correlated unions with organized crime, rife with communist infiltration.

To the players it was representation, a bargaining unit whose end was to procure security for its members. To Brown, the association was a third party intruding into his domain. Brown worked hard to keep the Browns' management from interfering with him and his players, and now a third party wanted to impede this relationship? Nobody should come between him and his players, Brown stridently believed.

Contract negotiations were strictly a one-on-one affair. In fact, Brown customarily mailed contracts to players, whom he expected to sign and return the documents without discussion. "I don't want you to talk to anyone else about this contract and neither will we," Brown advised his players. He ordered his team not to discuss salaries, and the Browns apparently obeyed. Indeed, a number of Cleveland players claimed to have been the first to send back an unsigned contract only to receive a tongue-lashing for their audacity. They all believed they were the first because no one would own up to the seditious act.

"You never negotiated a contract with Paul Brown," Dante Lavelli explained. "It was Paul Brown's way or nothing."

And now there was this association that promised to drive a wedge between Brown and his players. Almost as bothersome to Brown as the formation of a player's union was the man chosen to head the association. Creighton Miller was, at one time, a member of Brown's staff. Miller was a 1944 graduate of Notre Dame, where he starred for the Fighting Irish at halfback. Following his graduation at South Bend, Miller attended Yale Law School. And, after a brief stint with the Browns as a backfield coach, Miller became the club's attorney under Dave Jones. It was Miller who handled the legal technicalities of the sale when the Jones group bought the Cleveland franchise in 1953.

To assuage NFL management, Miller would repeat, almost like a mantra, "We do not consider ourselves a union. We do like to call ourselves an association."

Either way, Brown didn't care for it one bit. The whole thing, Brown said, "was a conspiracy between marginal players and the government."

—⁓—

It was a long fall for the Cleveland Browns and their coach. Ten years, ten championship games, six titles; theirs was a difficult legacy to live up to. Indeed, at 5-7, the Browns had tumbled from grace, and more than a few critics watched Brown's fall with glee.

Brown understood the role of reporters, and he made himself accessible. Still, with the availability came a caveat. They were treated to Brown's version of events, which, of course, were colored by his position and interest. These accounts did not always jibe with the facts. This manipulation, which Cleveland writers took with a grain of salt, exasperated scribes from around the league. When the opportunity arose, some of these men relished poking at the legendary Paul Brown.

"Football has always been the most overcoached sport," wrote Milton Gross of the *New York Post* in the middle of the radio relay controversy, "and Paul Brown, the going genius of the Browns, refined it to the point where an original thought on the part of any of his players was regarded as being on the verge of mutiny."[14]

Brown proffered the image of an unmoving oracle. His word was the only word to be followed. The messenger guard and its offshoot, the radio transmitter, were particular sore points for many in the press corps. Why did Brown feel the need to interject himself into the game? Brown thought of his players as nothing more than chess pieces, interchangeable parts. But these issues were just an easy conduit for writers to reproach Brown. Among some reporters there was a long festering dislike of Brown, which, for some, reached back to Brown's OSU days. New York writers, in particular, did not care for Brown. And Brown did not help matters, often giving New York scribes the old brush-off. There was just something Brown didn't

Catching walleye near Pelle Island, Ontario.

like about the city. His Midwestern sensibilities didn't mesh with the condescending attitude of many New Yorkers. The fans were belligerent, Giant players were not as good as their press clippings, and the press. . . . Brown disliked the New York sportswriters most of all. Not only wouldn't he give those guys the time of day, he'd give them the business sometimes.

The hometown fellas, though, witnessed a fuller picture of Brown. As he had in Massillon with Luther Emery and later with Paul Hornung in Columbus, Brown nurtured a close friendship with local writers. Franklin Lewis, for instance, enjoyed Brown's company, but while "Whitey" Lewis certainly didn't sell out to Brown, he was sympathetic. And there was Chuck Heaton, who in time would develop a close relationship with Brown. These men, as well as other Cleveland writers, helped cultivate a fuller portrait of Paul Brown, a side of the man not known to New York scribes—the man who kept sweets in his office desk drawer for visiting children, whom he liked to scoop up and plop on his lap.

Those many great seasons the Browns enjoyed came with consequences. The fallout of yearly appearances in the championship game delegated Cleveland to the bottom of the heap come draft time. A decade of low draft position had finally caught up with the Browns by 1956. Only Lou Groza remained from those early championships, while the men selected to replace those many Cleveland greats possessed a fraction of their talent.

The first step toward rebuilding the franchise came at the annual draft meeting in Philadelphia. The selection process was held on November 26 at the Bellevue-Stratford Hotel, toward the end of Cleveland's trying 1956 season. Brown entered the draft desperately wanting a quarterback. His hope that Ratterman or Babe Parilli would ably replace Graham was dashed. Neither man rose to the challenge, leaving Brown searching for an answer. Brown was very open in expressing his preference for Len Dawson of Purdue, but second on Brown's wish list was Stanford's John Brodie. However, Brown could only sit and wait, hoping that one of the two quarterbacks would fall to Cleveland.

With the first pick, Rams coach Sid Gillman wanted a running back out of Syracuse University, Jim Brown. Gillman was overruled by Los Angeles ownership, who wanted instead a local boy, USC's Jon Arnett. San Francisco, up next, took John Brodie of Stanford. To sort out who had the third selection, a "flip off" was held between three teams, Pittsburgh, Cleveland, and Green Bay, which all had identical records. The odd man won. Pittsburgh and Cleveland each flipped tails, while the Packers' coin came up heads. With their selection, Green Bay chose Ron Kramer.

Unfortunately for Brown, Len Dawson was also coveted by the Steelers. And when Pittsburgh won yet another coin flip done to break its tie with the Browns, they selected the kid from Purdue.

Brown could not hide his disappointment when he missed out on both Brodie and Dawson. Serendipitously, a four-sport star from Syracuse University fell to the Browns, Jim Brown. Brown played and starred at football, baseball, basketball, lacrosse, and also put the shot for the

Orangemen. An amazing physical specimen, Brown combined speed, power, and agility with startling results . . . if only he played quarterback.

On July 24, Paul Brown played his last round of golf for the year. "Tomorrow," he said, "the animals come in.

"It's like starting all over again. Yes, it could be the start of another cycle. Ten years ago, the Bears went through this same thing.

"Well, it will be very interesting to say the least. We don't have Parilli or Ratterman, but we have six other quarterbacks."[15]

Indeed, the men slated to fill in for Otto Graham, Babe Parilli and George Ratterman, were no longer with the Browns. Brown had obtained Parilli from the Packers several years earlier. When Babe returned from a two-year stint in the service, Brown promised that "much of our future is wrapped up in this man." The statement appeared ill-advised when Parilli stepped in for an injured Ratterman toward the end of the Browns' ill-fated '56 campaign. By December, Brown had seen enough.

With a bite in his soft, tempered voice, Brown told Parilli, "We thought we traded for a quarterback, but we got you."

Gone along with Parilli and Ratterman were twenty other men who finished the 1956 season on the Cleveland roster. Gone were Dante Lavelli, Horace Gillom, and Abe Gibron, as was Frank Gatski. "We went along with the old-timers as long as we were winning," Brown admitted, "but we didn't win last year and we had to make some changes."

Jim Brown wasn't the only key rookie added to the roster. Tackle Paul Wiggin, middle linebacker Vince Costello, and quarterback Milt Plum all contributed to a revitalized Cleveland Browns football team. The resurgent team surprised many experts by finishing the 1957 season 9-2-1 and capturing the Eastern Division. Cleveland's improbable season earned Brown the Coach of the Year honors. Kudos of that ilk was fine, but Brown wanted another championship more than a plaque and a pat on the back.

Standing between Brown and his goal, once again, were Cleveland's rival, the Detroit Lions. The Browns entered the December 29 title game a three-point favorite.

The Lions drove 66 yards for a field goal on their first drive and never looked back. It was an avalanche; an unholy shellacking. It was the most one-sided championship game since 1940, when the Bears white-washed the Redskins, 73-0. The Lions recovered two Browns fumbles and intercepted five Cleveland passes. Offensively, Detroit ran up 433 yards on its way to a 59-14 whipping of the Browns.

"I'm philosophical about it," Brown said, struggling to elicit a slight smile. "We couldn't hear our own signals. That crowd noise was terrific. There's something about this ballpark that makes the crowd noise drown our signals. Finally we just gave up trying to defeat the confusion."[16]

—⚹—

When Brown first arrived in Cleveland, the Indians dominated the local sports scene. Boxing, too, was flourishing in the city, making Cleveland arguably the best fight town in the country. And there were the Barons, the city's pro hockey outfit, who claimed their fair share of fan interest. But finally, after twelve years and all those championship campaigns, Brown was asked to be the keynote speaker at the annual Cleveland Touchdown Club Awards dinner. Don Miller, club president, presented Brown to the crowd with a resounding tribute, "the greatest football coach in the world."

The acrid taste of defeat still lingered as Brown stepped to the dais in the Carter Hotel's Rainbow Room just three weeks removed from the devastating defeat to Detroit. But the past was the past, no matter how recent that past was, and Brown tried earnestly to put a productive spin on the loss.

"It's going to keep us looking forward to next season," Brown assured the packed ballroom. "I can't explain some of what happened myself, but you can bet it'll keep us ouchy until we find out. . . . We resembled a fighter who hadn't fought in eight or ten years."[17]

Six months later, as Brown made his annual address at Hiram, he punctuated all the usual points—the rules, the regulations, and the anticipations. Brown touched on familiar themes, but there was added emphasis this year on the expectation of being a Cleveland Brown. "We've been in business thirteen years," Brown said. "In twelve of them we've won division championships. In several others we've take the whole pot. We're the Ben Hogans, the Joe Louises, the New York Yankees of our game and that's the way we aim to keep it."[18]

—m—

A bad call by an official or a questionable decision by a coach, the slightest thing can disrupt a season of diligence and hard work. The Browns entered the final Sunday of the 1958 season with a 9-2 record, one game better than their opponent, the Giants, who needed a victory to force a playoff for the division title.

On a snow-covered Yankee Stadium field, the Browns and Giants squared off in a tightly contested game. Late in the third quarter, Cleveland held a 10-3 lead and had possession on the Giants 13. On fourth down and five, Brown sent out his field goal team. While Groza lined up for the kick, Bobby Freeman got down on one knee to hold the attempt.

Freeman knelt, but when the ball was snapped, he rose to his feet and tried to skirt the right end. The fake did not surprise the Giants' Harland Svare, who dropped Freeman for an eight-yard loss. The Browns' lead evaporated a short while later. Early in the fourth quarter, the Giants took over possession and drove in for a game-tying touchdown. The game remained tied as the minutes ticked off the game clock.

With little more than two minutes remaining in the game, the Browns were forced to punt the ball. Dick Deschaine shanked the kick, booting the ball just 22 yards, out of bounds at mid-field. Deschaine's poor punt not only gave the Giants good field position, but also stopped the clock.

Moments later the Giants were faced with a third down and the ball at the Cleveland 44. Quarterback Chuck Conerly then connected with Frank Gifford at the Browns' 30-yard line. Gifford hauled in the pass and took several steps before running into Galen Fiss and fumbling the football. The loose ball was scooped up by the Browns' Walt Michaels, who scampered toward the Giants' end zone. After a lengthy hesitation, linesman Charley Berry waved the pass incomplete. Even New York players thought they'd turned the ball over, and several Giants defensive players ran onto the field. But Berry's call stood.

Pat Summerall, who was hindered by a charley horse and had missed two earlier attempts, rushed onto the snow-covered field. Into a fierce wintry wind, Summeral's 49-yard field goal try sailed through the uprights.

The Browns had one last chance and managed to move the ball close enough for one last try from the toe of Groza. The yard markers were beneath a blanket of snow, preventing an exact measurement of Louie's last desperate try. The attempt fell short, as did the Browns, 13-10. It was a three-point loss, exactly what the botched fake field goal would have netted had Brown not recklessly gambled in the third quarter. Three points and a tie, all of which would have been good enough for Cleveland to advance to the championship game.

Once home in Cleveland, Brown fulfilled a previously scheduled appointment to speak before the Touchdown Club in the Manger Hotel. He answered some of the questions being asked throughout Cleveland. "You might do lots of things differently the next day," Brown said to the Monday morning quarterbacks

"Maybe I should have gambled more than we did when we were ahead. We haven't been a free-wheeling outfit, and most victories are won by hard, tough football."[19] He paused for a moment. "It's rather interesting to be on the other end of a second-guess," Brown mused. "You know I don't recall that happening before in Cleveland."

But it was time to put that behind them and look ahead to next week. "We're approaching this game just like all the others this season," Brown insisted. "We're not going beserk and becoming frantic because somebody kicked a 49-yard field goal in a snowstorm. . . . These are the breaks of the game, and without them, its tough to win 'em all.

"Last Sunday we didn't get the break we waited for, but maybe it will come this Sunday."[20]

The break Paul and the Browns were waiting for never came. In the conference championship, held on December 21, the Giants shut out

Cleveland's anemic offense, 10-0, in front of a Yankee Stadium crowd of 61,000.

"We were simply overpowered," Brown explained

"We tried just about everything. There isn't much else we could have done under the conditions. The Giants were inspired, that crowd was out for blood, and they just gave us a total shellacking. "[21]

—⚬—

Like never before, Brown's players found themselves questioning the judgment of their coach. Sure, there was frustration with his conservative play-calling at times, but the fake field goal was something else. Of all times to throw caution to the wind . . . the decision left many Browns shaking their heads. Under their breath, Brown's players had, on pertinent occasions, referred to their coach as "that bastard," which at times was expanded to a more descriptive, "that bald-headed bastard." In the past, though, in the midst of all those championships, the grumbling came with a grudging respect for Brown's abilities. When Brown's techniques began to fail, however, and the titles dried up, well, then the old bastard was out of touch.

Opposing teams had their number, more than a few Browns believed, especially the New York Giants. This, went the common belief, could be attributed to Brown's stubborn tendencies. Defenses had evolved. They had become more deceptive, more mobile; their formation often changed moments before the center snapped the ball. This defensive progression had rendered Brown's play-calling propensity obsolete. Quite often, Brown's messenger guard would carry in a play and, following a defensive adjustment, Brown's call would run right into the teeth of the defense.

Under the Paul Brown system, his quarterback had practically no leeway to alter the play. Opponents were aware of this restriction and game-planned accordingly. An audible at the line of scrimmage was the only option left to combat defensive realignment. Yet ignoring Brown's play placed the quarterback in peril. To make a change and fail would bring piercing contempt from Brown, a fate no Cleveland player wished to tempt. The team was in flux. Though Brown would never admit the necessity, gaining back the faith and confidence of his players would not be an easy task.

—〰—

In December, the Browns were a Pat Summerall kick away from the championship game. But nine months later they began the 1959 season in danger of becoming an also-ran outfit. Two losses out of the gate were followed by five consecutive victories, then two more losses. The only constant through the season was Jim Brown, who, in his third year, had become the finest running back in the game. And without their star fullback, Cleveland was a pushover for opponents, as was evidenced when the Browns visited Yankee Stadium in the season's tenth week.

The Browns entered the contest against the Giants two games behind New York with two remaining. Though their hopes were faint, Cleveland at least maintained hope. On the first play from scrimmage, however, Jim Brown was kicked in the head and suffered from dizziness the rest of the afternoon. Paul Brown pulled his fullback from the game, but Jim was cleared at halftime to return to action by team doctor Vic Ippolito. His return to the game made no difference, however, as the Giants crushed Cleveland, 48-7.

In the waning moments of the contest, thousands of fans stormed the field, engulfing players and coaches. The first incursion occurred with four minutes remaining, and the rowdy fans toppled the goal posts on the western end of the field. As the crowd grew larger, the Cleveland bench was encroached far too close for Brown's comfort, and with 1:53 remaining in the game, Brown pulled his team from the field. Before reaching the locker room, though, Brown had to run a gauntlet of exuberant fury fueled by drink. There was some hitting, pulling, and more than a little cursing.

Referee Harry Brubaker instructed the Giants to restore order. Only the warning of a possible forfeit through the stadium's loudspeaker calmed the rioting crowd. Brubaker then went to the Cleveland dressing room and implored Brown to bring his team back on the field. "Paul was a perfect gentleman about it," Brubaker said. "He agreed immediately."

After the game was halted for twenty minutes, the Browns returned to the field and killed the final moments of the game.

Asked afterward if he considered asking for a forfeit, Brown shook his head. "We didn't even belong on the same field with them today."

On some fronts, Brown was praised for his handling of the on-field riot. "He came out of the melee with added stature,"[22] one New York writer penned.

There were other, not so pleasant, headlines. Why did Brown put an obviously disoriented Jim Brown back into a game? In a boisterous New York locker room, few people were happier to see Paul Brown go down in defeat than Sam Huff. "It couldn't happen to a better man, to get swamped like that," the Giants linebacker exulted. Huff then criticized Brown's decision to play an injured Jim Brown. "His eyes were glassy and he should not have played the second half except for Paul Brown's brutality."[23]

Huff's words stung. Brown offered his defense. "The doctor said that Jim was in shape to play. And he did fairly well in the second half, too. Every football player who plays for us is approved by the team doctor."[24]

Ippolito absolved Brown of any blame, though he didn't offer any explanation for clearing Jim Brown to play. "In my fourteen years as the team doctor, Paul Brown had never put any pressure on me to be allowed to use a player whose physical condition was in question."[25]

Losing to the Giants was bad enough, but on the way to LaGuardia Airport the driver of the Browns' team bus got lost. For more than an hour, the chartered bus circled the island of Manhattan. With sweat forming on his brow, the driver nervously apologized to Brown. "I don't blame you," Brown said. "I blame the person who hired you."

When the bus finally reached the airport, their plane was not there. Incoming flights to LaGuardia had been delayed due to fog, and the airplane hired to carry the Browns home had not arrived. Another craft was substituted and soon in-flight to Cleveland. The replacement plane was not equipped to feed a hungry professional football club, though. The steak dinner ordered for the Browns gave way to cold cuts . . . a fitting end to a brutal day.

"This whole thing's a nightmare,"[26] Brown said, shaking his head in bemused wonder.

—⁊⁊—

On October 11, 1959, while watching the Philadelphia Eagles and Pittsburgh Steelers battle at Franklin Field, Bert Bell suffered a massive heart attack. The commissioner was dead before doctors could transport him to a nearby hospital. Bell was well-respected and liked by everyone in the game. He had been since 1933, when he joined the league as a part-owner of the Philadelphia Eagles, and Bell knew the business of football well. As commissioner, Bell used his powers of persuasion and adroit political skills to sway some of the league's oversized egos. Corralling these personalities and pointing them in the same direction was his gift. Still, under Bell the league remained something of a mom-and-pop operation. Most importantly, Bell was resistant to the advent of television and what the exposure could do for the professional league.

The league had reached a crucial period. One year earlier, after dispatching the Browns, New York played host to the Colts for the 1958 NFL championship. Baltimore's Alan Ameche's overtime plunge into the Giants' end zone captured the world championship for the Colts in what many believed to be the most memorable game ever played. The contest placed professional football in the national consciousness. The NFL was on the cusp, and more than ever, the league needed a strong-minded, business-savvy leader at the helm.

In the interim, until a permanent replacement for Bell could be found, the job fell to Austin Gunsel, the league's treasurer. Weeks passed and no consensus could be found. Two factions of owners drew a line in the sand, each supporting their own favorite-son candidate. One group pushed for Gunsel, while another backed the league's counsel, Marshal Leahy. At one point, Brown's candidate, Leahy, intimated that, should he be selected, the league's offices should be moved to the West Coast. Such a suggestion bordered on blasphemy to the league's old guard. The impasse continued. Something had to give, the dickering had to stop.

"I concur with Art Rooney of Pittsburgh in this," Brown said. "We need leadership. There has been too much public bickering and popping off by owners, coaches, and players.

"We miss Bert Bell and we have to get a strong replacement right away. That should be our first order of business next month."

The winter meetings began January 20, 1960, in Miami Beach. Still, the soothing Florida climate did nothing to break the divide between bickering sides. During the stalemate a number of names were put forth, including the well-respected and admired owner of the Steelers, Art Rooney. Rooney passed on the opportunity. He neither wanted to divest himself of the Steelers nor surrender his dearly loved time at the track.

If not Rooney, then who? Perhaps the answer was sitting amongst them. Frank McNamee, president of the Eagles, stood up and addressed the room. "Gentlemen, the press is laughing at us because we can't make a decision," McNamee said. "We all know there's a man in this room who is qualified and would do a hell of a job. Paul, will you take the job?"

Brown took a look around the hall. "Only if the league offices are west of the Mississippi," he responded, and the room erupted in laughter.

Wisecracks aside, Brown had no aspirations for the title.

Nearly another week passed before a compromise candidate was put forth. Wellington Mara of the Giants joined forces with Brown and the two approached Dan Reeves, owner of the Rams. Brown and Mara asked for Reeves' permission to speak with his general manager, Pete Rozelle.

Rozelle, a thirty-three-year-old wunderkind, had not campaigned for the position. Indeed, he wondered whether he was even up to meeting the challenge. But after a talk with Brown, Rozelle came around. After all, Brown explained, "You are the one person who has never indicated any interest in the job," and so, Brown reasoned, there were no blocs against him. And if elected, Brown continued, you will owe no one anything. "You can come into the job as your own man."[27]

Rozelle was still apprehensive. It was a huge undertaking for anyone, let alone someone of his relative youth. "Don't worry, Pete," Brown assured him, "you'll grow into the job."

The pep talk and slight push from Brown did the trick. Rozelle allowed his name to be placed up for consideration. Whatever debate and argument that may have arisen over the new candidate was stifled when Art Rooney stepped forward and endorsed Rozelle. The compromise commissioner settled into the league's new New York offices, but there was no honeymoon period for Rozelle. Facing the boy czar as he settled into his new role was a budding rival circuit that threatened to break the NFL's monopoly on professional football.

In the late '50s, word was out that the struggling Chicago Cardinals were up for sale. Texas oilman Lamar Hunt inquired about purchasing the Cardinals and relocating the club to Dallas. Another Texan, Bud Adams, made a similar appeal. When both men were turned away, they approached the NFL about the possibility of expansion. Bert Bell listened, but more teams would mean splitting the revenue pie into more pieces. Decreasing his share of the take was unpalatable to Redskins owner George Marshall, and he led the charge to rebuff any talk of expansion.

Hunt would not be denied, however. If the NFL wouldn't have him, he'd launch his own pro football circuit. Founded in 1959, the American Football League took its product to the field a year later. Eight teams began play in 1960 in cities dotting the country. Hunt's creation placed teams in such diverse towns as Dallas and Denver, Houston and Buffalo, Boston and Oakland. Only two AFL cities were already represented by the National League, Los Angeles and New York. The formation of the new league forced the old guard to reconsider their decision not to expand. Dallas would be granted a franchise for the 1960 season and, after much debate, Minnesota was stolen away from the upstart AFL and would begin play in 1961.

Ten years of peace were over. The cost of doing business had just gone up.

—⚏—

On New Year's Eve, 1959, Browns defensive back Junior Wren met with reporters and let loose a torrential attack on Brown. Wren, along with Preston Carpenter, had just been traded to the Steelers.

"I think the reason Preston and I were traded is because Brown knew we were disgusted and might jump to the new league," Wren said. "I was thoroughly fed up with Brown and he knew it."

A regular safety for four years, Wren was benched by Brown for the final game of the 1959 season against the Eagles. "It will be a pleasure next season to play for a coach who treats the players like human beings. I know people are going to say this sounds like sour grapes, but nobody who ever played for Brown will say a good word about him.

"When things are going right, he's all right, but when they go wrong, he's got to find somebody to blame. I'll tell you this; if he doesn't change he's going to lose players to the new league."[28]

Reached by scribes a day later, Carpenter also expressed displeasure with his old coach. "I was going to leave the Browns anyway. I just wasn't having fun playing for the Browns anymore, and that goes for a lot of other men on the team."[29]

Some did attribute the griping to sour grapes; disgruntled players are usually the most boisterous. Others believed the "Brown is a bum" campaign could be attributed to Cleveland missing the playoffs two years in a row, the first time that had ever happened. Brown's management style, difficult to tolerate in the best of times, became insufferable when the championship run dried up. But it wasn't just Brown's dogmatic ways that were coming into question. In recent years, Brown made a number of highly questionable personnel moves. It is true that all teams make occasional mistakes, misjudging talent. But for Brown, there had been too many, in too short a span, for critics to overlook.

Following the '58 season, the Green Bay Packers were in the market for a head coach. The search led Packer brass to Brown. Did Brown have a recommendation? he was asked.

Well, Blanton Collier, certainly, was a worthy candidate, Brown replied. There was also Giants offensive coach Vince Lombardi. In fact, it was Lombardi that Brown pushed harder. And, following Brown's ringing endorsement, the Packers were intrigued by Lombardi. All Lombardi needed was an opening. His enthusiasm for the game was infectious, as was his unmatched intensity. Over the years he had studied Brown, his organization, his coaching techniques, his game planning. Lombardi went into his interview well prepared. The job went to Lombardi and before long Brown was reaching out to his friend. Brown gave Lombardi a list of Cleveland players to choose from, men Brown believed wouldn't make his squad.

Trades were made, two of them in fact, involving three players leaving the Browns for the Packers. The first came in '59, when Brown sent Henry Jordan and Bill Quinlan to Green Bay. A year later, Willie Davis made the same journey. All three players made an immediate impact on a rising Green Bay team, while the draft picks Brown received in return did little to help the Browns.

The Packer giveaway wasn't the beginning. A few years earlier, in 1955, the Pittsburgh Steelers made their notorious decision to release a local boy hoping to catch on with their team. The young man then sent a telegram to Brown requesting a tryout with the Browns. To the surprise of John Unitas, Brown responded to his cable with a phone call. Though he had been frantically searching for an answer behind center just weeks earlier, with the return of Otto Graham from his short retirement Brown felt his needs were covered. His decision unquestionably lacked foresight. Not this year, Brown told John Unitas, but contact me next summer. However, before Brown had a second chance at Johnny U, the Colts signed the young quarterback.

Unitas could have been the answer. Instead, as the 1960 season approached, Brown was still searching for a quarterback. Milt Plum, Jim Ninowski, Tommy O'Connell, each was capable, but none had that special quality of a champion. Just such a player fell in Brown's lap when the Steelers gave up on Len Dawson and traded the third-year player to the Browns. But with Cleveland Dawson didn't receive a fair chance behind center. In 1960, he had 13 pass attempts, and 15 the following year before being released on June 12, 1962.

Hank Stram, head coach of the Dallas Texans, had recruited Dawson for Purdue. With the quarterback now available, Stram called Brown; the two men had been acquainted for a number of years. "We're good friends," Brown advised Stram. "I want to make sure that you understand Lenny isn't the same Lenny that you had in college. His arm is not as strong. He's not a real student of the game. He doesn't have a good attitude."[30]

Stram listened politely to Brown's warning, but he couldn't believe that a boy as talented as Dawson could lose all his ability in such a short span of time. The Texans took a chance on Dawson, a judgment Stram would never regret.

There was also Jim Marshall, the Browns' fourth-round selection in 1960. Brown completely underestimated Marshall's ability and traded the defensive lineman to the expansion Minnesota Vikings, who played their first game in '61. Cleveland fans were left to wonder just how much better the Browns could have been had Brown retained these men. Had his ability to judge talent abandoned him?

Brown had always treated all his players the same—as subordinates. He didn't differentiate between the star and the backup. There was one set of rules for everyone. With Jim Brown, however, Brown came across a personality that refused to acquiesce. When he joined the team in Hiram following an appearance at the College All-Star Game, Jim was initiated to the team by veteran Lenny Ford. Ford, who had some experience with Paul Brown, took Jim aside and offered some sage advice. "First," the veteran said, "when you're running through plays in practice always run twenty yards downfield. Don't just run through the hole and then jog a few steps and flip the ball back. The man doesn't like that. Run hard for twenty yards, even if you feel silly.

"Second, keep your mouth shut when he speaks to you. When he tells you how to run a play, run it the way he tells you. If you have an idea for improving a play, keep it to yourself. Suggestions make the man mad.

"Also, don't initiate anything. You see something wrong, let it go. He does all the talking here."[31]

Jim listened, nodded his head, and did as instructed. Paul Brown was the boss, a fact that the rookie acknowledged. When making public

Along the sideline at Municipal Stadium.

appearances, Jim Brown was almost painfully shy. Though intelligent and well-spoken, he was reluctant to express his opinions and thoughts. His coach appreciated the new fullback's polite disposition and obsequious nature. Indeed, Jim Brown could be the next Marion Motley, Paul Brown prophesized. This was high praise, indeed. And at Hiram a year later, Brown stood by watching Jim work out. "There is the best draft choice we ever made,"[32] he declared to all standing nearby.

The relationship continued to flourish, as Jim Brown developed into the league's finest running back. Surprisingly, Paul Brown went for a running back in the first round of the 1958 draft also—a year after drafting Jim Brown—though Bobby Mitchell was a talent hard to overlook. Lightning fast, with serpentine moves, Mitchell was the perfect compliment to Jim Brown. The two became fast friends, the second-year man taking the rookie under his wing and schooling Mitchell to the finer aspects of professional football.

When given the opportunity, Mitchell played spectacularly. His chances diminished greatly, however, after fumbling several times in the course of one contest. Though Cleveland recovered each of the gaffes, Brown lost faith in the tailback. For the remainder of the season Mitchell remained in Brown's doghouse and played sparingly. Jim Brown witnessed the treatment of his friend and teammate and bristled.

Why did Brown bench Mitchell? Jim Brown wondered. Was this because the team was developing two black stars? he wondered. There were some who witnessed Paul Brown around a variety of people and noticed that the Paul Brown speaking with Bill Willis or Horace Gillom was not the same man they saw talking with Lou Groza or Mike McCormack. This lack of ease could certainly be read by a man as astute as Jim Brown. It brought the question to mind, did Brown subconsciously make decisions on race?

Paul Brown had integrated pro football, admittedly partly out of self-interest. He wanted to win football games, pure and simple, and he wanted the best men available to help achieve that goal. Black and white made no difference to Paul. How could Jim reconcile this with what he saw in Paul's treatment of Bobby Mitchell? He began to doubt a number of Paul Brown's customs. Jim thought Paul's intelligence tests were ridiculous and he wasn't alone. The examinations had been a long-running joke in the Cleveland locker room. How did IQ measure football aptitude? But nobody bucked the system, they took the tests, they just cheated with crib sheets.

One thing no one did, however, was openly resist Paul Brown. That is, no one until Jim Brown. If Jim didn't see reason in an exercise, he resisted. Little things, like running downfield twenty yards in practice. What was the purpose of that? Jim could see none, and after humoring Paul for a couple of years, Jim began to taper off after hitting the hole in practice. Initially, his teammates were shocked by his audacity. But they were even more taken aback by Paul Brown's reaction . . . a silent stare. No reproof. No frosty barb. Just silence.

Jim Brown's impudence spread away from the practice field. There had been one constant in Paul's coaching career. The team bus, train, or plane, would leave precisely on time. 9:05 meant 9:05. On one occasion, Jim Brown was on the telephone as the team bus was waiting to depart. Bobby Mitchell tried desperately to get Jim off the phone and onto the bus. As the two men approached the vehicle, Paul flew off the bus and ran up to the two players. The coach went directly to Mitchell. "Bobby Mitchell, who do you think you are? You know the rules. You're not better than this football team. You'll always be on time."

Paul said not one word to Jim Brown.

While negotiating his contract, Jim also proved obstinate. Though he had received fair and substantial raises in each of his first three seasons, Jim was told by Paul that he had nearly "reached the ceiling" and not to expect much of a salary increase in 1960. This was inherently unfair, Jim said. It was his belief that an arbitrary cap on salaries was unscrupulous; after all, there was no ceiling on how much profit the Cleveland Browns could generate. Why limit a player's earning potential? Unlike most of his peers, however, Jim Brown had leverage. A local boxing promoter approached Brown and offered Jim a $25,000 bonus for his signature on a contract. This very public episode did its job. Jim's brief pugilistic flirtation was enough to prompt Paul to reconsider his earlier assertion. A reasonable and well-earned raise was granted to the star running back.

The shy and soft-spoken rookie who arrived at Hiram in 1957 had grown into a man who had found his voice. Jim Brown was a proud, sensitive, and opinionated black man. He was a natural leader and filled that role decisively, especially among his black teammates. And in the course of Jim Brown's three years in the league, a growing divide developed between Negro and white members of the Cleveland Browns. On the field, the players continued to mesh as one, but in the locker room Paul noticed that his team had begun to split into factions. Black and white players rarely commingled away from the field. Increasingly, black members of the team looked to Jim for his lead, and he was no one's second-class citizen. The movement of Black Power was in its infancy, but Jim Brown

Drawing up a play.

was in tune to the teachings and culture. America was changing and Paul Brown did not necessarily like what he saw. What he saw was division, conflict, and rhetoric. And there was no place in football for all this. Paul Brown took his concerns to his star player. "All the Negro players sit in a group apart from our white players," he said. "People are commenting about this. It doesn't help us look like a team."[33]

We resent being assigned hotel rooms by color, Jim Brown informed Paul. "We are not going to make a show of looking chummy as long as the club assigned us hotel rooms in a manner that suggested we had leprosy," Jim said. If there were an odd number of players, a black player would room alone; likewise, an odd number of whites and a white player would have a room to himself.

Paul listened closely. This, he said, was news to him. And to his credit, Paul vowed to correct this imprudent policy. He had long been responsive to racial issues confronting his players. While most NFL clubs played their exhibition contests in Southern towns, Paul went out of his way to schedule Cleveland games in cities like Akron, where Jim Crow laws would not intrude on his team.

But times were changing. Black empowerment was on the rise, and Paul didn't believe in empowering anyone, black or white, on his roster. Jim Brown may very well be the finest football player on the planet, Paul thought, but what he did not need was for his fullback to play the role of clubhouse lawyer. In the past, intimidation would do the trick. But Paul couldn't bully Jim Brown.

There were a lot of off-the-field distractions, but between the lines the Browns showed marked signs of improvement. Cleveland fielded one of the league's youngest teams in 1960, yet it managed to stay in the race for much of the season. The Browns' 8-3-1 record was good enough to earn Cleveland a spot in the newly hatched "Playoff Bowl," which pitted the second-place club from each conference against one another. The outcome, a Browns loss, didn't diminish Paul Brown's enthusiasm for the future.

Yes sir, things seemed to be looking up for Paul and his Browns.

# ten MELTDOWN IN CLEVELAND

**The 1960 regular season,** which began with some promise, was coming to an unsatisfactory conclusion. Brown could only hope that the harping and backbiting would take leave with the final game. A victory over the Giants would land the Browns in the second-place bowl, a misconceived attempt to reward the also-rans. On the eve of the game, Phil Haber, an attorney for the club, wanted Brown to meet a television salesman of some sort. There, in the Concourse Plaza Hotel, Brown was introduced to Arthur Modell. He was youngish, enthusiastic as hell, and quite courteous. Apparently this kid was part of a group trying to buy the Browns. He seemed nice enough, Brown thought, of this thirty-six-year-old bachelor from Brooklyn, but that was about the extent of consideration Brown gave the encounter. After all, whoever purchased the team made little difference to Brown. His role would remain the same, of that he would make certain.

—⁂—

The seventy-four-year-old Dave Jones frequently dismissed rumors that the team was for sale. In the shadow of Jones's denials, behind-the-scenes machinations had been under way for some time. In fact, these negotiations were an open secret in the local press. This loose chatter followed the team to Miami Beach, where the Browns were to meet the Lions in the Playoff Bowl runner-up game. "I enjoy football and my association with the Browns," Jones told reporters a few days after the New Year. "However, any club is for sale if the price is right."

Later that same afternoon, Brown, too, spoke of the subject. Though he would not admit that a sale was imminent, Brown acknowledged it was a definite possibility. "There won't be any negotiations until I return to Cleveland next week," he said. "We have had other offers before and things haven't worked out. I honestly don't know what will happen." But, Brown added, if a change in ownership took place, "it won't mean any change in the team."[1]

Negotiations, which had begun clandestinely on December 10, concluded January 5, just one day after Jones and Brown spoke with the press. The tentative sale would be taken up at the league meetings, which were scheduled to begin in New York on January 24. A group of New York investors, led by Arthur Modell, beat out an assemblage of Cleveland businessmen headed by Bill Evans of the Diamond Alkai Company. Approval at the league meeting was more of a formality than anything else. The New York group had the necessary financing in place, but first, the purchase was contingent on Brown's approval. Before he gave his blessing, Brown wanted to be sure that his role with the team was clearly defined. Brown consulted with his lawyers and drew up a contract, "just as I wanted it," he later explained. This amended agreement was quickly approved by Modell without question. One issue remained. The new investors offered Brown a significant amount of cash for Brown's stock in the club. And, though he sensed there could be problems ahead with this Modell fellow, Brown acquiesced. He retained a small portion of stock in the franchise, with an option to purchase more. Brown was induced, as men often are, by the allure of money. He wasn't a rich man, and the $500,000 Brown would receive from the sale of his stock was a significant windfall. But with this exchange came less control. Brown was no longer in command of off-the-field ventures, business, and publicity. This capitulation was extraneous, Brown convinced himself. "I retain control of the things I think important."

And so it was, after several weeks of haggling, the sale of the team to the New York syndicate for a record $4 million was officially announced. And, on March 22, Arthur Modell was formally introduced to the city of Cleveland. The Brooklyn native held court that afternoon before an intrigued Cleveland press corps and subtly offered insight into a shift in power in the Browns' hierarchy. Reading between Modell's songs of praise was the clear message: Brown would no longer run the franchise with free rein.

"We'll be consulting frequently," Art informed the newsmen. "I don't like to outline any delineation of duties. We'll be partners in the Browns operation."

The question on every reporter's mind, the single biggest criticism of Brown's coaching philosophy, was the first posed to Modell. "Are the plays still going to be run in from the bench?" a scribe asked.

"As far as I'm concerned Paul Brown can send them in by carrier pigeon," Modell answered with a smile. "In my opinion he has no peer as a football coach. His record speaks for itself. I view our relationship as a working partnership. Paul will attend the league meetings with me. He will decide any questions about player personnel and field operation. I am assuming the responsibility for such things as finances, admissions of new teams to the league, promotion, and that type of thing."

For the media, Brown allowed that he was perfectly comfortable with his new boss. "I still will do the hiring and firing as before and control the factions important to the success or failure of the team. Financial and promotional aspects will be his problems. That's a healthy situation in my opinion. A fellow spending this kind of money has a right to control the finances. The loans are his responsibility."

His words for public consumption were amiable. Privately, though, Brown bristled. Who was this upstart to proclaim they would be "consulting frequently?" He never needed to confer with anyone previously. And what could this advertising executive possibly have to offer in terms of football know-how?

Several hours after the press gathering, Modell roamed the hallways of the Browns' offices, meeting personnel, learning names, trying to ingratiate himself to his employees. He stopped by Brown's office. Modell was anxious to christen the "partnership" that he spoke of at the news conference. A simple salutation, followed by a failed attempt at a joke, and Modell quickly realized that he wasn't welcome. Brown stared steely eyed at the intruder. His domain had been invaded. Brown coldly acknowledged Modell and set his attention back to the business at hand, which was building a winning football club. Modell duly noted the lack of hospitality, while Brown chafed at the very thought of the presumptuous visit.

Brown watching practice at League Park, 1955.

The next afternoon, Modell invited several reporters to his suite at the Sheraton for a more informal bull session. "I'm a conservative, not a circus-type promotion man," he answered when he was asked if he would model himself after former Indians owner Bill Veeck, a man known for outrageous gimmicks. "I'm interested in tasteful, productive promotions, within the limitations of an eight-event schedule. I'm no fast-buck promoter."

Despite his relative youth, Modell had a long and varied resume in the business world. He entered the work force at the age of fifteen, when he obtained a position at the Bethlehem shipping yards in New York City for eighty-seven cents an hour. The job at Bethlehem lasted just a short while, until he quit and enrolled at New York University. Modell's aspirations for higher education were also short-lived. He dropped out of NYU after just five months and entered the Army Air Corps. Following his discharge from the service in 1946, Modell used the GI Bill of Rights to again attend college. With his gained maturity, Art made the most of his second chance and threw himself into studying a new medium that promised to one day rival radio . . . television.

"I was in on the early days of TV," Modell told reporters from his suite. "I produced package programs and for about five years had twelve hours of them on a week. I was fortunate and also worked hard.

"Later I had a measure of success in advertising work, and I also made some good investments. I'm not a speculator, however, and never was. There are not attempts at killings. I look for solid investments."

Modell had long been an avid football fan. As a youth he rooted madly for the Brooklyn Dodgers football team. By the time he returned home from the war, the Dodgers were gone and Modell's allegiance shifted to the New York Giants. An opportunity that he never thought would arise came in 1960 when he was told that a professional football franchise was available. Not just any team, either. The Cleveland Browns. Modell couldn't believe his fortune. The Cleveland Browns . . . the New York Yankees of pro football. It took some time, almost a year, for him to arrange the finances for the deal. Four million dollars was a lot to arrange. After liquidating all his assets, Modell had but $250,000. He found partners, arranged loans, and eventually came up with the necessary cash to seal the deal.

The New York boy, who had never desired to venture beyond the five boroughs, packed up and settled into an apartment in the western Cleveland suburb of Lakewood. He immediately immersed himself in the operations of the front office. Modell even took over the responsibility of hiring personnel, much to the dismay of Brown, who was concerned with employee "loyalty." The most egregious of all Modell's moves following the takeover was his capture of Brown's office. True, it was an office that Brown rarely used, but still, it was the largest and most prestigious in the tower. With a degree of diplomacy, Brown relinquished his office and moved down the hall. Even Brown's players noticed the seemingly cosmetic changes made in the front office. For an ever-growing number of disgruntled Browns, these slight alterations represented a much-needed change in the organization's pecking order. Perhaps now someone would rein in Brown, was the hope. Perhaps now someone would lend an ear to their misgivings.

—⁓—

Away from the field, new life had been breathed into the franchise. Chain smoking Marlboros, Modell looked the part of the young hotshot as he tooled around town in his maroon and black Cadillac. He was a hound for the spotlight. The fledgling owner was everywhere, pushing his product, meeting Cleveland businessmen, schmoozing with the press. He was doing everything he could to curry favor with the locals. None of Modell's promotional efforts could help his team on the field, however. Between the lines things got no better. The Browns were now simply a mediocre outfit, a far cry from the great team that dominated a decade of professional football. They posted an 8-5-1 record in 1961, good enough for a repeat visit to the also-ran bowl. The Browns closed the regular schedule at Yankee Stadium against the Giants on an afternoon that exemplified what many believed was Brown's growing disinterest in his craft. As the clock wound down on the frustrating campaign, news reached the press box that the Eagles had defeated the Lions. The result of that contest meant the Giants would advance to the title game with either a win or a tie.

With fifty-five seconds left on the clock and the scored tied at 7, the Browns possessed the ball, fourth and seven to go. Brown sent the punting unit onto the field. The decision visibly frustrated a number of Browns players including Mike McCormack, who, when he saw the kicking team trotting out, began shouting from his position on the field. McCormack boisterously implored Brown to go for it and try for the victory. Though Cleveland had nothing to lose, Brown refused to yield. His decision stood and the punting team remained on the field.

Across the field, the New York coaching staff was suspicious. Surely Brown wasn't throwing in the towel. Perhaps a fake punt was in order. To guard against such a scheme, and to also avoid a fumbled return should Cleveland actually kick the ball, the Giants didn't even put a return man back. There was no fake, and the booted ball came to rest on the Yankee Stadium turf with forty-three seconds remaining. Y.A. Tittle took the snap from center and gently lay on the ground, effectively running out the clock.

In the clubhouse afterward, Brown offered an explanation of sorts for his call, primarily that the east end zone in Yankee Stadium was frozen. Also, a low mist hovered above the field. His reasons, as they were, baffled onlookers all the more because Brown's team had nothing to lose by opening up the playbook. Brown may have felt no obligation to the Eagles, but to the integrity of the game Brown owed more than was given. The Giants moved on to the championship game, while Brown opted to let the clock run out on a disappointing campaign with an apathetic whimper.

—m—

As the 1961 season wound to a close, the Washington Redskins remained the only member team in the NFL yet to integrate. For years Redskins owner George Preston Marshall had dismissed out of hand all demands to bring a black player to the Redskins. "All the other teams we play have Negroes," Marshall reasoned. "Does it matter which team has the Negroes?"

With the dawn of the new decade, pressure to integrate the Redskins greatly increased. For some time, the loudest voice of dissent came from Sam Lacy of the *Baltimore Afro-American*. Lacy's fight was joined by the most powerful of allies, the federal government. With the arrival of the Kennedy administration came increased pressure on Marshall. Secretary of Interior Stewart L. Udall issued an ultimatum to the Redskins: they either lift their ban on black players or lose the privilege of playing their games at D.C. Stadium, a government facility. It was not a hollow threat, yet no time frame was given and Marshall still made no move to change his position. "Why Negroes particularly?" he asked. "Why not make us hire a player from any other race?"

In the *Washington Post,* columnist Shirley Povich stung Marshall with barbed one-liners. The Redskins' colors were, according to Povich, "burgundy, gold, and Caucasian." And more famously, "The Redskins end zone has frequently been integrated by Negro players," Povich quipped, "but never their lineup."

As the months passed, Udall became frustrated by Marshall's inaction. What was a veiled threat now became explicit. Integrate the Redskins or find a new stadium for your home games in '62, Marshall was told. Reluctantly, in mid-October, Marshall finally set the wheels in motion to acquire the team's first black player. More than any other club, the Browns had expendable black talent. In the Cleveland backfield were two of the finest backs in football. Obviously, Paul wouldn't part with Jim Brown, but Marshall thought Bobby Mitchell could be had for the right price. Marshall approached Brown with a proposal—the Redskins' second-round pick in the upcoming collegiate draft—in exchange for Bobby Mitchell. Brown flatly rejected the offer. "I have a feeling Mr. Marshall is trying to project me into his racial difficulties,"[2] Brown said to a newsman.

Brown's comment was a bit disingenuous. He was more than willing to help Marshall with the Redskins' "difficulties," but Brown wanted to be certain that the recompense merited trading the talented Mitchell. Like most every head coach in pro football, Brown had his eye on Ernie Davis, the star running back from Syracuse University. Brown's imagination was stoked by the image of Davis in the role of a companion back to Jim Brown. He wanted to recreate what Green Bay had in the tandem of Jim Taylor and Paul Hornung. Paul Brown wanted another bruising running back to complement Jim Brown. In addition, Ernie's running style, Brown believed, was conducive for Municipal Stadium's playing surface. Desegregating the Redskins, while not Brown's responsibility, would be a worthy consequence if he could swing the right deal. Bobby Mitchell was more than a great running back; he was intelligent, unpretentious, and exuded class. He would be missed in Cleveland. The swap of a "home run" hitter like Mitchell was on the daring side. It meant giving up an established ballplayer for an untried college star. Still, it was a risk Brown was willing to make.

Brown gave Marshall a counter offer. He didn't want a draft pick, he wanted Davis. The two men made a verbal agreement on the morning of the collegiate draft, December 4. The Redskins would draft Davis and then trade him to Cleveland for Mitchell. The deal would stand even if Davis signed with Buffalo of the AFL, who had previously selected the fullback in their draft. Though the trade was reported as speculation in the press, neither team acknowledged the rumors. In fact, the transaction was kept from the public for nearly two weeks, until the terms of the deal were finally released on December 15.*

Amazingly, all the trade activity took place without the knowledge of Modell. Much to his chagrin, the Cleveland owner only learned of the transaction, not from Brown, but from Marshall.

The Redskins' owner upbraided Modell when he learned that Art was kept in the dark about the trade. "Don't ever let that happen again," Marshall said. "You are the owner. You own the franchise. It's yours."

Marshall's words were still ringing in Modell's ears when he confronted Brown. "You could have consulted with me, or at least given me a warning," he angrily told Brown.

This rationale was lost on Brown. In sixteen years he never consulted with an owner, why would he possibly discuss a deal with a salesman? Preposterous.

"Paul had no idea where I was coming from on this and he didn't care," Modell relayed years later. Modell's anger was soothed, though, when he recognized that the deal was a popular one among both the press and the fans. And, taking advantage of the opportunity for positive personal publicity, Modell took over negotiations with Davis. With a splash, he signed Davis to an astounding $80,000 contract and raised expectations of Cleveland fans for the upcoming season.

Brown fumed. Not only had Modell begun handling contract negotiations, a job that he had always handled, but he gave Davis a "guaranteed contract" a practice Paul despised. Brown argued that "no-cut" agreements were unfair to other members of the squad, depriving them of a legitimate opportunity of making the team in light of a "guaranteed" promise to another teammate. Brown quietly seethed as Modell basked in the glory of Davis's signing. He happily posed for pictures, granted interviews, and predicted future glory for the Cleveland franchise. The publicity-seeking

Modell disgusted Brown. The two men were in disconnect. A relationship that had begun poorly had deteriorated beyond repair. Modell had deliberately undercut his authority and was placing undue pressure on the team by virtually promising a championship in 1962. Paul understood that he was being set up to fail. He had been hearing the whispers.

—⁂—

Publicly, Modell endorsed the legend/coach. "Paul has my unqualified support," he said prior to the season. "I'm a Paul Brown man. I believe in him. He's one of the greatest coaches of all time. I'm sure if there are any adjustments to make, he'll make it."

—⁂—

Whipping through the city was a growing "Brown must go" movement. And what had happened? The anti-Brown sentiment was stoked by scribes, player backbiting, and the growing restlessness of Cleveland fans. The local papers began running letters of discontent from Browns fans. One specific Frank Gibbons column consisted of nothing but the voices of readers venting on the state of their beloved football club. Letters also poured into the *Plain Dealer.* "When we had Otto Graham, we had a team," wrote W.H. Stone of Cleveland. "Graham made the Browns great, not Paul Brown."[3]

Cleveland writers Cobbledick, Scholl, Heaton . . . they all remained squarely in Paul's camp. These men liked Brown personally, but they were also practical. No team could stay on top forever. The previously unwavering Frank Gibbons did, however, elicit a slight crack in his support. "Isn't it possible that they [the Browns players] might realize even greater potentials if they were allowed to share decisions with their coach?" After all, Gibbons concluded in his *Press* column, "Aren't these men college graduates who have to make important decisions in other fields?"[4]

Still, Gibbons's critique was atypical. It was those out-of-town guys, mostly New Yorkers, who did much of the provoking. Brown would tell his players to pay the newspapers no mind. "They'll wrap tomorrow's garbage in today's paper," he would say.

Ignore them. Yet even the most minor censure of his rule, from the smallest suburban paper, would rile Brown. "These guys are trying to ruin our football life," Paul would exhort his players. "They're trying to put us out of business."[5]

It wasn't just the scribes, though. The displeasure rumbling through the Browns' locker room finally reached the public. It had long been a one-way relationship. Brown's players who made a mental or physical error dreaded being on the receiving end of his rebuke. Cursing, shouting, that type of outburst could be more easily accepted than Brown's cutting criticism. A typical barb came during a film session when defensive back Bernie Parrish blew an assignment on one play. Brown ran the play several times before coldly offering the commentary, "Don't tell me that the great ones do it that way."

Before being traded, Bobby Mitchell moaned, "[Brown] isn't using me enough." And Mitchell's backfield mate had the opposite problem. "I was overworked by the coach," Jim Brown said. But those grievances focused on playing time. In late February, quarterback Milt Plum vented his displeasure with the direction of the Browns. "The team is in a rut," Plum complained. "We don't get up for the big games most of the time and often have a struggle with the not-so-strong teams. The attitude of the players was just nothing last year."

Plum continued, "I compare us to an auto with a top speed of 70 miles an hour. We can't go any faster no matter what the situation."[6]

Plum's words received wide play throughout the country, and even if he wished, Brown couldn't ignore his player's outburst. Brown was vacationing in Florida when he was reached for comment on Plum's views.

"Really," Brown said, "I don't care what Plum said or thinks about it. Players get around their friends and families at this time of year and get to talking."[7]

While Paul was dismissing Plum's verbal outburst, Jim Brown was publicly backing his teammate. "I think Milt gave constructive criticism that was well thought out," Brown said. "I think that his only thought was in helping the ball club, and letting Paul know some of the feelings of his players."[8]

As Jim Brown well knew, his coach cared nothing of constructive criticism, not when the criticism was directed at his methods. Nor did Paul concern himself with the feelings of his players. Jim's words were politically motivated. By throwing his support behind his quarterback, he was letting the world, and Paul, know that Plum was not alone in his frustration.

Slightly more than a month later, on March 29, Milt Plum was traded to the Detroit Lions. Though the deal was a three-for-three exchange, the principals of the transaction were Plum for Jim Ninowski, a man who left Cleveland on poor terms and had no desire to return. "I'm pretty disgusted by the whole deal," Ninowski said when he learn of the trade. "I have no intention of going to Cleveland. I'll quit football if I have to."[9]

Trading Plum in the aftermath of his critical comments seemed to be more than coincidental. Was it purely reactionary? Brash or bold? Whatever it was, the trade was startling in as much as Brown admitted a mistake by bringing Ninowski back to the Browns. Still, Brown dismissed the notion that the move was an act of reprisal. "The deal was made strictly on the basis of football," he insisted. "For some time we have wanted an active running type of quarterback to broaden our offense."

In the spring, Modell spoke at the Sigma Delta Chi journalism dinner. During his speech, Modell assured his audience that the Browns would win the coming championship. If not, Modell said, "we'll have a rough time finding excuses."

Modell was increasingly visible and much too verbal for Brown's taste. Certainly he paid his money, but did this buy him exposure and the role as the Brown's unofficial spokesman? Brown certainly didn't believe so. Owners own. If you have an opinion, express it behind closed doors. Don't go spouting off to the press or to someone who might leak your words to the media. Better yet, keep your opinion to yourself. Negativity or raising unreasonable expectations only hurt the club and impedes on the team's goal. Modell had been in football a little more than a year and his unbridled enthusiasm hardly made him an expert in the game.

Still, he kept on talking.

Previous to the Modell takeover, critiques of Brown and his coaching style died on the vine. No one in the previous ownership groups would question Brown's football acumen, at least not publicly. Modell, however, was a different breed of owner. Early in his tenure, he stepped out of the customary role of sports owner and began befriending a number of players on the Browns. He was gregarious and possessed an eagerness to please, which struck some as pathetic. Still, Modell was sincere. He believed the players needed him. He listened to their complaints, helped them with personal problems, offered tax and business advice. Modell always gathered crowds when he regularly held court at the Theatrical Grill, a popular Cleveland nightspot. There, Modell would preside over the room. Telling tales and sharing jokes, the young Modell had the city by the tail.

The cavalier lifestyle of the Browns' impetuous new owner troubled Brown. Modell's freewheeling carousing was one thing, involving his players in these antics was quite another. Modell frequently disregarded Brown's wishes and invited players out on the town. Modell flaunted his complete disregard for Brown's ban on alcohol for Cleveland players. This blatant breach of etiquette outraged Brown more than any of the owner's various transgressions. There was also the question of Art's acquaintances, some of whom had questionable backgrounds. In fact, the Theatrical Grill, Modell's favorite watering hole, was owned by "Mushy" Wexler, a "gambler" with ties to a number of shady characters. Modell relished flaunting his friendships with fellows like Mushy.

Modell's lack of football expertise was cured by many late nights at the Theatrical Grill, where he educated himself to the inner workings of the game from the mouths of the disenchanted. "It didn't take long for me to discover the truth about the Browns," Modell later said. "The team was on the decline. I also had a lot of people telling me that the game was starting to pass Paul Brown by a little bit.

"There was a void I tried to fill," Modell offered in an attempt to justify befriending Brown players.

The truth of the matter was, Modell fueled the embers of discontent until the fire of revolution spread throughout the team's clubhouse.

Brown had a steadfast rule: No player was permitted to have his own radio show. What if a quarterback and a wide receiver had competing programs? Brown would argue. Maybe the quarterback wouldn't throw the ball to the receiver because of ratings envy. Inane though his reasoning might be, Brown believed one man shouldn't place himself before the team. Still, Modell audaciously brokered a deal that partnered Jim Brown with Hal Lebovitz of the *Plain Dealer*. Lebovitz would serve as the ghostwriter of Jim's column in the *Plain Dealer*, and he also wrote the script for Jim Brown's five-minute radio show. Modell's covert efforts to undermine Paul Brown's authority empowered the players to feed the press with headline-worthy material, albeit with anonymously dispensed quotes.

"If anything goes well, it's not us, it's him," came a typical un-attributed barb. "When it goes bad we're to blame, not him. And when he's done with us he discards us. How good has he been since Otto Graham left? Without Graham, what has he done?"

The same man that had been held in the highest esteem by his players in 1952 was largely dismissed by a different collection of men a decade later. Upon first glance, the division could be interpreted as a conflict between generations, and surely at least a fragment of the blame could be attributed to changing times. Still, the preponderance of culpability can be placed at the feet of the coach himself. Paul Brown's refusal to adjust his philosophy and open lines of communication with this new generation of players was the root cause of the escalating insurgency found in the Browns' locker room.

The natural course of change that occurs with each succeeding generation was obvious in the complaints that emanated from the Cleveland clubhouse. Brown's greatest success had been built on the backs of men who had fought Hitler and Hirohito. The oppressive nature of Brown's coaching philosophy was not odious to these men, who had served their country under dire circumstances. Indeed, the culture had changed. The young men now charging into battle for Brown on Sunday afternoons were different from those who took the field in 1946, or 1950, for that matter. Blind faith in the head coach was a thing of the past, and Brown was slow to understand this transformation. He also refused to acknowledge the growing sense of independence found in the modern athlete. Who among the current crop of players had earned a championship with Brown? Paul may have been a legend, but to his players Brown's was a soft reputation. What have you done for me lately? This football genius was a thing of the past.

The same characteristics that propelled Brown to the zenith of pro football's world were in essence providing his downfall. His strength of character, his tenacious sense of self-determination, led to an autocracy. His regime would not accept suggestions or compromise long-held beliefs.

"What happened to Brown as a coaching genius?" another player rhetorically asked before offering his own editorial. "Two things happened. First, Collier left to take the coaching job at Kentucky, and then Graham retired."

Much analysis was bestowed upon Cleveland's post-Graham era. Since the quarterback's retirement, Paul and the Browns had not yet captured another championship. Graham and Brown became the chicken-and-egg syndrome personified. Brown's critics believed that his success was entirely related to Graham's heroics. All the while these same commentators ignored Paul Brown's fine record at Massillon and Ohio State. The criticism reached its apex when *Sport Magazine* asked in its June 1962 issue, "Has Pro Football Passed by Paul Brown?"

The amity that Modell nurtured with Jim Brown was beginning to pay dividends in his covert war on Paul. His unusual relationship with the team's owner allowed Jim Brown the latitude to criticize his coach publicly. The great running back chipped in his two-cents' worth when *Sport* ran its in-depth profile on Paul's ability to call a game.

"They've got us pretty well tabbed," Jim Brown was quoted as saying. "We start out as though we're going to do things differently, but somehow we always seem to fall back in the same old groove. Only in desperation do we loosen up and try anything radical or off beat."

Jim also insisted that some teams, namely the New York Giants, knew what Cleveland was going to call "even before Brown does himself."

Andy Robustelli, an assistant coach with the Giants, concurred with Jim Brown's assessment to a great extent. "Brown's offense depends strictly on superior execution rather than new stuff." Robustelli. said. "We know

Paul Brown and Gern Nagler.

Brown won't vary his style. This makes it simpler for the Giants because we don't have to worry about any defensive adjustments."

Another coach, this one nameless, offered, "Brownie is a smart fellow, but he can't seem to realize how much the game has changed the last few years," the "rival" coach said. "Since he refuses to make corrections to allow for these tremendous changes, other coaches willing to adapt have caught up, and in some cases passed him."

Paul opted not to dignify his critics with any rebuttal. His methods had been time-tested and, if properly executed, would again prove effective. Meanwhile, some of Brown's contemporaries were experimenting with new formations. In San Francisco, Red Hickey was using the "shotgun." And in Philadelphia, Nick Skorich was trying a "stacked deck" formation with great success. Brown seldom borrowed schemes from other coaches. But, on the rare occasion when he did lift an idea, he did so surreptitiously, as if the idea had just come to him. A couple weeks after seeing a play succeed against the Browns on film; Brown would implement the same play into Cleveland's playbook.

Regardless, Brown stayed true to his long-held philosophies. Even as other coaches relinquished some of the play-calling duties to their quarterbacks, Brown refused to yield. He would not call on his players to burden themselves with thought. No, he managed the cerebral aspect of the game. As the sport evolved, though, defenses became quicker and more mobile, often shifting an instant prior to the snap. These adjustments usually neutralized Brown's sideline call.

Modell made an attempt to back his coach in the midst of the brewing controversy. "I find no fault in Paul calling the plays from the bench," Modell said. "With two assistants in the press box and another on the phones at the bench, none of whom worry much about [Gino] Marchetti knocking them on their pants, Paul has a better appraisal of the situation than the quarterback on the field . . . but it's my personal hope that he will liberate the check-offs."

In the aftermath of the exceedingly critical *Sport* article, Modell showed little sympathy for the attack on Brown. "I know a cure-all, Paul," Modell said, as he communicated to Brown via newsprint. "Win the National Football League championship this season for Cleveland . . . for yourself . . . and most of all for me."

The highly publicized analysis and criticism of his coaching was making him "uncomfortable," but to this Paul Brown would never admit publicly.

—∞—

The Browns reported to Hiram looking drastically different from the team that had closed out the 1961 campaign. Eleven members of the '61 squad were gone via trade while eight veterans had joined the team through player transactions.

"I guess you could call this a switch in our thinking," Brown explained of the extensive changes. "We hoped in previous years to make changes through the draft.

"There is the advantage of bringing along the players from college in your own style of football. Draft choices aren't as available anymore because of the two leagues."[10]

As the Browns went through their usual training camp routine at Hiram, their most heralded rookie was undergoing an extensive series of tests 375 miles away in an Evanston, Illinois, hospital. Ernie Davis was training with the College All-Stars at Northwestern University when he went to a local dentist to have his wisdom teeth removed. Shortly after that visit, Davis experienced some swelling about the neck glands. He was admitted to Evanston Hospital on July 30. At first doctors suspected the mumps, and then maybe mononucleosis, but both those illnesses were ruled out fairly quickly. Unspoken, but feared, was the possibility that Ernie had a form of leukemia. When he realized the severity of Davis's condition, Modell flew out to Evanston to be with Ernie.

After conferring with doctors, Modell spoke with the press, though he kept his concerns close to the vest.

"It seems to be a blood disorder," a concerned Modell explained. "Our only thought is to get Ernie well."[11]

On August 3, Modell brought Davis back to the Cleveland Clinic for further examination. At camp in Hiram, Paul thought of the impact this could have on his team. "If he's out for any length of time this could be a crusher," Brown rued. "We have high hopes for Ernie."[12]

It took little time for blood specialists to confirm that Davis, indeed, had leukemia. For the moment, the diagnosis was kept from the public. Davis immediately began treatment for the disorder and was comforted by a visit from three of his teammates, Jim and John Brown as well as John Wooten. The four men sat together and watched the College All-Star Game on television. Not a word was said, though the thought lingered, that Davis should have been suited up for the game rather than viewing it from a hospital bed.

Over the course of the next couple of weeks, Davis visited Hiram and watched the Browns run through drills. Standing on the sideline with a wistful gaze, Ernie ached to join them. The only cheers Davis would hear, though, were prior to Modell's grand doubleheader experiment on August 18. At that game, 77,000 fans erupted when Ernie stepped on the field to acknowledge their good wishes.

—⚬—

Perhaps Brown and Modell had turned the corner. Maybe they could live together, if not happily, then perhaps tolerably. Or maybe it was simply winning; victory could bring together the most ardent adversaries. The season began on a pleasant and harmonious note. The Browns opened the year at home with a 17-7 victory over the Giants, the highlight of which was a triple reverse pass that went for a Cleveland touchdown.

Who called the play? a reporter asked.

"WE did," a giddy Brown replied. "That's our new policy. If you ask Jim (Ninowski) who called any play he'll tell you, 'We.' It's our new policy. I may send in a man, but it may have nothing to do with calling the play. Everything this year is 'WE.' This is a team effort. If it works it's 'we,' if it doesn't it's 'we'."[13]

In the clubhouse afterward, Modell embraced Brown and planted a kiss on his cheek. "You are the architect," a joyous Modell proclaimed. "I'm just the ticket seller."

This good feeling couldn't last, wouldn't last. The relationship was far too tenuous to survive once the losses began. A defeat to Washington was followed by a terrible beating in Philadelphia. During that 35-7 disaster, Modell sat in the press box and openly criticized the play below. In the second half, Modell moved down to the sideline and sat silently on the Browns' bench. The view was no better there.

Fans, players, and Modell were mollified slightly the next week by a win over Dallas, but their appeasement was brief. Against Baltimore on October 14, the frustration of Browns fans swelled until it boiled over. Howls of derision, boos louder than anyone could ever remember hearing from the home crowd, rained down from the Cleveland Stadium stands. There was plenty of blame to go around; nearly every aspect of the Browns' performance was lacking and, by most standards, the coaching staff was equally deficient.

It didn't have to be this way.

Earlier in the year, on January 15, Blanton Collier rejoined Brown's coaching staff. Collier had been dismissed from Kentucky a few weeks earlier after eight years as the Wildcats' head coach. UK boosters never quite took to Collier. They didn't believe the soft-spoken teacher was tough enough to succeed at Kentucky. He won, he just didn't win enough. Toward the end, the Colliers began to receive menacing phone calls at their home. Collier was even hung in effigy on campus. Finally, following a 5-5 1961 season, the university bought out the final three years of his contract.

Brown reached out to his friend. "How would you like to come back to Cleveland?" he asked.

Collier appreciated the offer, but he refused to consider the proposal if it meant any of Brown's assistants would be let go to make room for him. Brown assured him that all the coaches would return. This was no act of charity. Brown recognized Collier's genius for the game, and gave him responsibility to match his brilliance. Besides, it felt good to have a confederate in a splintering clubhouse. And in Collier, Brown was certain he would always have an ally.

During the exhibition season Brown gave Collier some leeway and allowed him to experiment with a check-off system. The results were obvious to all: a 5-0 record in preseason, and an offense that was more productive than any Browns unit had been in years. Frank Gibbons penned a laudatory piece extolling the virtues of Collier's new system.

The article effectively brought the check-off plan to an end. Why? Though he never commented on it, the unanimous opinion was that Brown didn't appreciate his assistant receiving credit. Though a petty thought, there was no other conclusion to draw. It was becoming increasingly obvious that Brown was holding steadfast to old tactics. And it wasn't just the offense. The defensive players were practically in complete revolt.

Brown knew nothing of defensive tactics and strategy, they claimed. How-ard Brinker could put together a good defensive game plan, but Brown would bully his brilliant but mild-mannered assistant. They were better than the Giants, to a man every Brown believed this. Yet, they also knew the Giants would whip their ass when they played. This inevitability was tearing the team apart at the seams. Why couldn't Brown listen? To them? To his coaches? To anyone?

—⁓—

Early in the 1962 season, Modell commented to a Cleveland writer, "If Paul would only let me, I would make him the idol of America."

Art's seemingly innocent comment magnified the dramatic differ-ence between the two men. Modell placed an enormous value on the adu-lation of others. Contrarily, Brown believed admiration and kudos should be earned. Furthermore, Brown felt his record warranted any recognition he had received. As the most successful football coach in the land, Brown neither wanted nor needed assistance from the self-important Modell in the P.R. department.

In the past, Brown patiently recognized the "fan" inherent in each of the Browns' previous owners. In Modell, however, Brown was faced with an unsettling dilemma; Modell was the original fan/owner. He not only rooted madly for his Brownies, but with no previous experience in professional football, he wanted to place himself in the decision-making process.

"When the team loses, I die," he told reporters. Modell wore his emotions on his sleeve, and too often publicly offered his criticisms, which were unschooled and inexpert. The owner would habitually sit among the scribes in the press box questioning Brown's play-calling aloud.

"I consider myself a student of football," he offered, "but not an overly qualified one. All fans are the same.

"If I personally thought something was wrong, I wouldn't say any-thing to Paul. I'm not qualified to express myself scientifically. A coach is a special breed. At the most, I might ask a question out of curiosity."

Modell's proclamation breathed of hypocrisy. Though he refrained from questioning Brown personally, Modell's criticisms reached the coach nonetheless, just as the owner intended. Throughout the '61 season, Modell was at practice practically every day. As his second year with the team wore on, he appeared at League Park less and less. But he still traveled with the team on every road trip. On the train, Modell would gather a few players in his club car. His actions were just another example of the widening gulf between himself, Brown players, and Paul. Cleveland writers were aware of the dysfunctional circumstances surrounding the team. Hell, sports scribes around the country knew of the changing politics in Cleveland's locker room. Brown still had friends in the media, men who tried to explain his persona to Brown's detractors.

Frank Gibbons devoted a column to Brown, his motivations, his shortcomings. "This is a tightly wound man, a man who loves neatness and efficiency, a man who runs the empire from a control tower. . . . He is a perfectionist living in an imperfect world, unwilling to admit that he had imperfections in the fear it would be accepted as weakness.

"Brown," Gibbons continued, "is paying the price this year as he never did before, and he is paying it with his own kind of dignity. There is a tear in his voice at times, but I haven't detected a whine."[14]

A few days later, Gibbons covered the other side of the story. "Art is impetuous, emotional, and is playing for big stakes."

"I admire the man," Modell told Gibbons, speaking of Brown. "If we could win this thing I'd carry him down Euclid Avenue on my shoulders."[15]

Modell desperately wanted Brown's friendship and endorsement, but even Art knew by this late date that this would never come to be. Yet another difference of opinion arose between the two men when Ernie Davis's doctors cleared the running back to play. On the evening of October 4, Davis was informed of the severity of his illness. It seems that Davis was only in temporary remission. Dr. Austin S. Weisenberger of Western Reserve University released a statement on Davis's condition.

"Ernie Davis has had a form of leukemia. He has responded extremely well to the therapy and medication. . . . As long as he remains in this perfect state of remission I see no reason why he cannot play professional football."[16]

His physicians told Davis that there had been cases of people living with the disease for years. This glimmer of hope, and his doctor's permission to begin working out, gave Davis a sense of purpose. Within a few weeks he had put on five pounds, putting him eight pounds above his 1961 playing weight of 210. "I feel as good as I ever felt in my life," Davis said in the midst of a League Park workout. "I'm ready now. It's just up to him,"[17] he said while gesturing toward Brown.

Davis had been attending Browns practices almost daily as a spectator and sat on the bench during Cleveland home contests. With Dr. Weisenberger's diagnosis, Modell turned up pressure on Brown to give Davis the chance to play in a game. "It's entirely up to the coaching staff if and when he plays this season," Modell said. . . . "But, if possible, I would like to see him do some work with the squad for a few weeks so we would know one way or the other."[18]

Modell acknowledged that there was a "raging controversy" among medical experts concerning Davis returning to the playing field, "However," he added, "all those who are against Ernie playing haven't examined him."[19]

"I'm itching to get on the team this season," Davis told reporters, but added, "If I don't make the Browns this season, I'll go all out next July."

—ᴍ—

While the controversy swirled around him, Brown refused to comment publicly. Regardless of Brown's silence, everyone knew his position. He did not want to risk Davis's health just to placate Modell's wishes. This was unfair to Davis. Of course the kid wanted to play, he was a football player; a competitor. Brown thought Modell was simply grandstanding, positioning himself as the good guy while placing unfair pressure on the head coach.

In light of Davis's illness, football should have been deemed insignificant. Still, opinions were drawn, comparisons made. In Washington, Bobby Mitchell was on his way to an All-Pro season, while in Cleveland, fate dealt Ernie Davis a terrible, tragic blow. Not only had the Browns come out on the short end of that deal, but the team had suffered a spate of injuries that included pivotal players Ninowski and Jim Brown. The Browns had won only two of their first five games to start the 1962 season, and scored an anemic 73 points in those contests. Still, Paul wasn't losing hope on the season. "I think our team has earned the right to a little luck. This club has had more happen to it than any I've ever seen."[20]

Injuries, illness . . . these excuses were falling flat. The Browns were mired in mediocrity. They were an underachieving lot. Imagination was absent. Enthusiasm was lacking. The players felt they were nothing more than chess pieces, moved only on the whim of Paul Brown. "He intrudes himself on the contest more than any other coach in the National Football League,"[21] Shirley Povich wrote of Brown. Brown bristled at the implication. How could he begin to intrude on his team, on his football?

The rumors swirled. Brown's days in Cleveland were numbered. There was even talk that Brown was going to Los Angeles to take over the Rams, but this story was quickly quashed by Brown, who said he'd never given a move to L.A. any consideration, "and never talked to anyone about it."

"This (Cleveland) is my home, and my only interest is here."[22]

—⁓—

Following a 12-9 loss in the next-to-last game to the Giants in New York, a small meeting was held by several players on the plane trip home. A coup of sorts was taking place toward the back of the aircraft, in the players' section. The consensus among those involved in the discussion was that Brown should be confronted about player dissatisfaction. Though someone suggested going to Brown immediately, that idea was quashed. No, they believed, Brown would dismiss their complaints as simple bitterness in the aftermath of a loss. Eventually, it was decided that they would wait until the following weekend, prior to the season-ending game in San Francisco.

The Browns returned to Cleveland and began preparing for the season finale with the 49ers. The city was struck by a terrible early-winter storm, and along with the snow came frigid cold. While his players toiled away at League Park in the midst of blizzard conditions, Brown sat in his heated car, which was located a short distance behind the huddled offense. Following each play, Ninowski would walk back to the idling vehicle and wait for Paul to roll down his window and instruct on the next call. That Brown was suffering from the flu mattered none to onlookers. The scene was a vivid snapshot of the gulf Brown had allowed to build between him and his players—the emperor detached from his subjects.

Before the week was out, word of the uprising reached Modell, who quickly quelled the revolt. "Maybe this isn't the right time for the meeting," Modell told one of the organizers, Jim Brown. "Why don't you hold off for a while?"

Though Modell could replace Brown without the support of his players, their endorsement of any such action was vital for Modell. Firing Ohio's greatest sports legend would be difficult under any circumstance. For Modell the carpetbagger to discharge Brown and also save his own skin, he needed to enjoin the players to his side. From the day he took over team ownership, Modell nurtured this relationship.

—⚹—

The final trip of the year was marred when the club's flight to San Francisco was grounded in Sacramento for several hours. While waiting for a fog to lift so the team could continue on to San Francisco, Brown was told that Modell was in the hotel bar buying drinks for a number of Browns.

"That was the final straw," Brown recalled. "The last vestige of anything I had ever stood for was destroyed. Art was totally aware of our rules about drinking, yet he had deliberately gone against my wishes."

By this time, Brown was the only character in this sordid affair that didn't realize the end was at hand. With their victory over the 49ers in San Francisco, the Browns finished the season a disappointing 7-6-1, a far cry from Modell's prediction of a championship some months prior. As far as Modell was concerned, he had more than enough justification for making a move many believed was unthinkable just a short time before. First, however, he wanted to check base with Pete Rozelle before confronting Brown. At the league's annual end-of-season meeting in New York, Modell asked Rozelle for a chance to speak privately. In the commissioner's suite, Modell dropped a bombshell. "I've got to make a coaching change," Art said.

After a lengthy silence, Rozelle reminded Modell that he had only been in the profession a couple of years. "Are you sure you want to do this?"

Indeed, Modell was certain of his decision, "It's either him or me," he said of Brown. "He is determined to drive me out."

The whispers had stopped; the conspirators lay at rest.

—〰—

On January 9, 1963, three weeks after the final gun sounded at Candlestick Park, Modell called Brown and asked the coach to drive into the team's offices for a talk.

"I've made a decision," Modell told Brown. "You have to step down as coach and general manager."

Brown was thunderstruck. Yes, he knew of Modell's machinations behind the scenes. Still, Brown's ego would not allow for the possibility that this young upstart from Brooklyn possessed the audacity to fire him. A numb Brown finally spoke after a lengthy pause. "I really don't know what to say," he said. "I have a contract for six years."

The contract would be fulfilled, Modell assured Brown. He would be reassigned and given different responsibilities. As Modell droned on, Brown's thoughts wandered. He can't do this to me. I have a contract. This is my team. As if in a daze, Brown left Modell's office, got in his car, and drove home to Shaker Heights. After breaking the news to Katy, Brown picked up the telephone and called his son Mike. Immediately, the younger Brown sensed something was amiss. Paul's voice betrayed his emotional state. It was the first time, it would be the only time, Mike ever heard his father's voice waver.

"He's taken my team from me."

## eleven

**DYING BY INCHES**

"Paul E. Brown, head coach and general manager of the Cleveland Browns, will no longer serve the team in those capacities. Brown will remain as a vice president and be assigned other duties. He will finish out the balance of his six-year contract at the same compensation and will continue as a stockholder."

The statement was cold and to the point. There was no celebration of Brown's magnificent record, the championships, the glory. . . . And, though rumblings of discord had been heard for some time, Brown's firing was still shocking. One writer equated Modell's bold decision with the Terminal Tower collapsing.

The next day, Brown went to the office. His belongings were all packed neatly in several cardboard boxes. But what cut the most was, Brown's whole staff was present, studying film as if nothing had happened. Where was the solidarity, the loyalty? He expected his men to have walked away from Modell and all his nonsense, but then it was easy from where Brown sat . . . he was getting paid. These men—Bixler, Heisler, Collier, Brinker—they all had families to support, mortgages to pay. None of this mattered to Brown; in fact, none of these incidentals entered his mind as he turned away from his staff, his old staff.

Brown had nothing for the press, not that day or the next. He needed to gather his thoughts. He also needed to sit down with his attorney, Joseph Little, and meet with Modell and the team's lawyers. This powwow happened on Wednesday morning, the 11th, in the Browns' tower offices. At that meeting, the terms of Brown's duties were spelled out.

"I'm on the shelf now," Brown told reporters afterward. "A vice president of I don't know what.

"I'm under contract for six more years. I can't take another job without breaching the contract. . . . My life is coaching—this has been my life, next to my family.

"I guess Art can do this to me," he mumbled.

The reporters gathered were taken aback. Brown was always in control. Whatever the situation, he was in control. And now he looked worn, interminably old, cast aside by the brash Brooklyn huckster.

Brown said he had no plans other than fulfilling his contractual obligations. He was asked of a reported rift between him and Modell. For the first time, Brown acknowledged a discord, which he attributed to Modell wishing to "take a more active part in the actual team aspects formerly assigned to me as part of my contract."

"Mr. Modell is an enthusiastic young man. He wants to hold a closer rein on things pertaining to the actual playing of the game. My contract gave me complete charge in that area."[1]

The very next afternoon, one day after saying Modell was within his legal rights to fire him, Brown claimed that Modell was in breach of contract. "The entire matter is now in the hands of my legal counsel.[2]

"So far as I'm concerned, I'm still under contract. Under the terms of that contract I can't seek another job, and no National League team would be allowed to dicker with me. No other club could even approach me."

Modell was taken aback by Brown's comments. He and Brown had each signed a gag order of sorts that prohibited either man from discussing the particulars of their agreement, or disparaging the other. "If these statements concerning alleged breach of contract attributed to Paul Brown are accurate, Brown is in violation of our agreement made at an all-day meeting with our attorneys."

The understanding Modell referred to was reached when Modell, Brown, and their lawyers met to hammer out the details of their new arrangement. Part of the agreement reached in writing was that Brown would not criticize the Browns, and Modell likewise would not denigrate his former coach. Modell insisted that he had made a fair offer to Brown in the course of negotiations that would sever Brown's ties to the team. Brown dismissed such talk. "His offer centered around repayment of money that already was mine under a pension and deferred pay program,"[3] Brown explained. This was refreshing to Brown's friends on press row to see Brown regain his voice. Brown wasn't giving Modell anything. He had a contract, and he was owed money. This was Modell's obligation and Brown wasn't going to make things easy for his adversary.

And then Brown went silent. Whatever frustration he felt at being fired was kept under wraps from all but family. While Brown took the high road and squelched any desire he may have had to attack his detractors, Brown's adversaries were quick to give newsmen pliable quotes.

At the time Modell released Brown of his duties, the Cleveland newspapers were in the midst of a four-and-a-half-month strike. The work stoppage, which began before the end of the 1962 regular season, would be the longest newspaper strike in the city's history. In fact, there was much speculation that Art took advantage of the strike to make his move for fear of reprisal in print from Brown's friends in the press box. The information void created by the walkout was filled creatively and industriously by *Plain Dealer* writer Hal Lebovitz. With the normal media outlets closed off to local readers, Cleveland gridiron enthusiasts were able to read of the dismissal in a booklet produced by Lebovitz. *Paul Brown: the Play He Didn't Call* offered much more depth to the subject than Cleveland's newspapers could hope to provide. Paying $75 to each contributor, Lebovitz hired a number of his colleagues to report on the event. Bill Scholl, Bob August, Frank Gibbons, Gordon Cobbleldick, and Bob Dolgan each lent their personal cadence to the publication. In addition to local scribes, Lebovitz reprinted the writing of a number of out-of-town columnists. At twenty-five cents each, Lebovitz sold an astonishing 50,000 copies of his pamphlet to Cleveland's information-starved fans

Mired in the pages was Modell's lament. "It was the toughest decision of my life. I know it's a gamble. I'm prepared to rise or fall on the decision. It was mine and mine alone."

Brown's players offered the most brutal and damning indictments that were to be found in the Lebovitz publication. "I checked with my teammates and I'm virtually certain they were 100 percent in favor of the change," Bernie Parrish said. "I know that five, and maybe seven of them, would have retired rather than play for Brown next year. I was one of them."

As could be expected, anonymous quotes were the most vicious.

"Paul felt he had to live up to an image, that of the all-knowing coach," read one unattributed passage. "He really began to act the part. As a result he stopped trying to learn and he stopped listening to assistants. Finally, he got to the point where he was incompetent as a coach. He didn't have the technical knowledge of football he was given credit for and he did not know defensive football."

Though the Cleveland writers who contributed to *The Play He Didn't Call* were unbiased and fair in their coverage, the overall tone was slanted against Brown. No accredited player quotes were offered in support of the coach. Writers lined up on one side of the fracas or the other; virtually no scribe was neutral in this scrum. Few reporters stood more squarely behind Modell than Jim Murray of the *Los Angeles Times*.

"A man of glacial contempt," Murray wrote of Brown, "spare and fussy, he treated his players as if he had bought them at auction with a ring in their noses and was trying not to notice that they smelled bad."[4]

Seemingly the only words in defense of Brown were in praise of the legend, not necessarily the Paul Brown of 1962. "The Cleveland Browns are his monument," Arthur Daley wrote. "They'll never be able to take that away from him."

—⚋—

Modell spoke with two *Akron Beacon Journal* reporters a week after the firing. The interview with the Akron writers simply reinforced Brown's belief that Modell was disingenuous and self-serving.

"First of all, in all my considered opinion, I don't believe the maximum potential of the ball club was being realized.

"Secondly, it was reliably reported to me that, for various reasons, no less than seven key players—and these weren't rookies, believe me— weren't coming back next year under the same condition.

"This was the beginning of the end for the Browns. . . . it was the start of the complete collapse of our club."

There were, Modell claimed, "as many as twenty-five reasons why I fired Paul Brown, but only two were really important. And they were, not fulfilling potential and players quitting.

"The dissatisfied players didn't approach me as a committee. . . . Some of them talked to me individually, but for the most part, I learned of their feelings through sources even closer to the team than myself."[5]

Perhaps the most vocal critic of Paul, Jim Brown, was restrained when questioned by the *Los Angeles Times.* "If you had asked me for an opinion before he was dismissed I would have given it to you," Brown said. "I have definite ideas about the man, but he is out now and there is no point going into them."[6]

To another reporter, Jim Brown was a little more pointed in his remarks. "I feel Modell had good reason to fire Brown. Football players don't like to be treated as inferiors."[7]

—⁂—

Who would replace Brown? That was certainly the secondary story these days. The conflict between Brown and Modell sparked more interest, but still, life for the Cleveland Browns would carry on. Modell was said to be trying to entice Otto Graham from his coaching position at the U.S. Coast Guard. There was also speculation that Modell was interested in Joe Kuharich of Notre Dame.

The answer, though, was much closer to home.

Modell was watching the Pro Bowl with Blanton Collier when he offered him the job. Initially, Collier demurred. First, he told Modell, he would need to talk with Brown.

Collier wasn't looking for advice or permission, but his sense of loyalty went as deep as Brown's. He needed to make Brown aware of the offer and, at the least, let his benefactor know that the proposal was under consideration.

Brown quietly listened as Collier told him the news. Brown looked at his dear friend. "Blanton," he said softly, "you have to take the job. You owe it to your family."

Collier returned home. He understood that though Brown gave his blessing, things would never again be the same. Collier gathered his family together. He'd made the decision to take the job, he told them, but, "an era in our lives has passed."

There would be no more dual family vacations. No more piano duets between Brown and Collier's young Kay. No more relaxing sojourns for ice cream with the kids. As far as Brown was concerned, there would be no more Blanton Collier.

—⁂—

"You'll be paid for your contract," Modell told Brown moments after relieving him of his coaching duties.

Stripped of his lifeblood, money offered no solace to Brown. For a short while Brown considered the prospect of suing Modell. "I can say to you at this time that I'll have to see my lawyer because I don't believe you can fulfill the terms of a contract just by paying me money," Brown told Modell.

Pete Rozelle, though, dissuaded Brown from taking any legal action. No jury would look sympathetically toward a plaintiff who earned $82,500 for doing virtually nothing, the commissioner advised Brown. Principle mattered to Brown, however. He was hired to run a football team, from the field and the front office. He never agreed to be anyone's "advisor," and, moreover, as long as he remained on Cleveland's payroll, Brown could not negotiate for a position with any other club.

With no professional duties, no office, and no team to see over, Brown was mentally adrift. The vague responsibilities spelled out in his contract were nothing more than window dressing. He and his beloved bride Katy packed up their belongings and reestablished their lives in a faraway place. With nary a glance at what he was leaving behind, Brown slipped out of his adopted hometown. The city that hailed his genius and celebrated his world championships was now a distant memory.

—〽—

Brown then seemingly fell off the radar. He was out of town, escaped to Florida, when Blanton Collier was formerly introduced as the Browns' new head coach at 10 A.M. January 16, 1963, in Modell's oversized Tower B office. Surrounded by reporters, photographers, and TV cameras, Collier explained his football philosophy, and yes, the quarterback would call the majority of the plays. Collier reserved the right, though, "to send in a play whenever I feel it is advisable."

Inevitably, the question of Brown arose. "He's my dear friend," Collier said. "I want to maintain that friendship on a high level." He accepted the job, Collier admitted, with "emotions so conflicting that I find them difficult to explain."[8]

The Browns had turned the page. Indeed, life carries on. Brown's retreat to Florida removed him from Cleveland, but distance could not ease his mind, assuage the hurt, or mend the betrayal. Modell was nothing but the source of a paycheck. Collier, he did what he had to do, but there was no turning back. That friendship, as dear as it was, was now just a memory.

Brown's name stayed out of the news for the next few months. It wasn't until early April that his name reappeared in the headlines. While Brown was out of touch in Florida, the wire services ran unsubstantiated reports that he was interested in buying the Philadelphia Eagles. Upon returning to Ohio, Brown hadn't even set his bags down before the phone in his Shaker Heights home was ringing. On the other end of the line was Chuck Heaton of the *Plain Dealer* in search of news, any news, of Brown's intentions. After dispensing with the inquiries of health and well being, Heaton asked his old friend if he was pursuing the Philadelphia franchise. Brown was noncommittal. "I'll just have to say I have nothing to report on it at all," referring to the Eagles.

When pressed by Heaton, Brown replied, "Remember, I haven't said that I'm interested or disinterested."[9]

As much as Brown wished to get back into the game, he had other, more pressing concerns on his mind. From the time he returned to Cleveland, Brown had been traveling back and forth from Shaker Heights to Dalton, Ohio, visiting his ill mother.

Ida Brown had become one of the Cleveland Browns' biggest fans. At least once a year, Ida would travel to Municipal Stadium to take in a game. When she wasn't at the ballpark, Mrs. Brown was listening to the Browns on the radio. She moved into the Shady Lawn rest home in Dalton some time earlier and, for the previous three years, she had become increasingly infirm. On Monday, June 29, Ida Belle Brown passed away,

—⁄⁄⁄—

On May 3, Brown revealed that he was not interested in the Eagles. It was not the right move to make, not at this time. He had come home to Shaker Heights, but this wasn't where he wanted to be. It was too close to his heartache. At the suggestion of a friend, Paul and Katy traveled to LaJolla, California. What was to be a vacation spot so enraptured the Browns that the couple decided to relocate to the seaside town. There were affairs to be settled, and after a brief return to Shaker Heights, Paul and Katy made a home in LaJolla. Life in southern California was idyllic. The climate was near perfect; the views of the ocean were breathtaking, and most importantly, Brown finally had time to spend with his bride. While in the past Brown had been busy preparing for training camp, he now had the opportunity to take leisurely strolls along the Pacific with Katy.

There was also golf, and lots of it. Brown joined two local country clubs, Rancho Santa Fe and LaJolla Country Club. LaJolla, like Pebble Beach, was laid out along the ocean. If the sea weather was harsh on a given day, Brown and his partners would head inland to Rancho Santa Fe. Four or five times a week, Brown hit the links. He was playing so often that one Cleveland critic quipped, "Only Arnold Palmer and Jack Nicklaus are making more playing golf than Paul Brown."[10]

While Brown fed his newfound passion for golf, Katy took to the swimming pool or a game of bridge with her friends. It was a lifestyle men worked their whole lives to achieve. Still, Brown burned. It was no coincidence that LaJolla was as far from Cleveland as one could get in the continental United States. While Brown tried to physically distance himself from football, the game was never off his mind. He was still on the lookout for another opportunity, the right opportunity. For the moment, he would settle for bliss by the sea, where his neighbors didn't know who Paul Brown, the legend, was. He would bide his time, because he had no other option.

Throughout the winter and spring, Ernie Davis was active. He joined in with a number of his Browns teammates on a basketball squad that played at high schools and small colleges throughout the Cleveland area in games arranged for various charities. Davis also worked for a local soft drink company during the off-season. Seemingly, he was in fine health. On the court, he looked like he hadn't lost a step. Besides basketball, Davis had a position working with the Pepsi Cola Company, and he helped coach the Syracuse alumni at the university's annual spring game.

Then, on May 16, Davis had a regularly scheduled appointment with Dr. Weisberger. However, before he went to the hospital he dropped by Municipal Stadium to see some friends at the Browns' office. Modell, who'd grown especially close to Davis the previous year, warmly greeted him. How are you feeling, Ernie? Modell asked.

"I've felt better," Davis said, "but it's nothing to worry about. My throat hurts a little." Just thirty-seven hours after Davis was admitted to University Hospital, Modell received a phone call from Dr. Weisberger. Davis died at 2 A.M., May 18, 1963.

He never played a down for the Cleveland Browns, but still Art Modell permanently retired the number 45, the number Ernie Davis wore in publicity photos. Modell chartered a United Air Lines DC-7 to bring a group of Cleveland Browns to Elmira, New York, for the funeral. The plane was filled nearly to capacity with radio broadcasters, newspapers writers, and photographers. Blanton Collier's staff was on board, as were a number of front office employees. And Browns players, led by Jim Brown, were well-represented. Lou Groza was there, as was Marion Motley. The man traded for Davis, Bobby Mitchell, even made the trip to Elmira. Not present at the funeral was Paul Brown. His critics would say the cold-hearted Brown didn't care enough to say goodbye to the courageous Davis. But others, more empathetic, thought Brown couldn't go back, he couldn't return to the place, to the people who'd caused so much pain.

—◊—

On Saturday night, August 17, the Cleveland Browns took to the field for the first time without Paul Brown directing them from the sideline. As time was running down in the first quarter, a voice was clearly heard echoing down from the stands, "Bring back Paul Brown." Though the sentiment may have been felt by a portion of the 83,000 fans gathered at Municipal Stadium, a new day had dawned in Cleveland. The past, as glorious as it was, was just a warm memory now. More than eight months had passed since Art Modell shocked the city by sacking Brown, but the surprise fashioned by the move had receded in the ensuing months.

—◊—

Brown's $82,500 salary grated on some. As Brown had said months earlier, he was a vice president in charge of "I don't know what." A meeting with Modell earlier in the spring had spelled out Brown's duties to the satisfaction of both parties. He was to watch several pro and college games a year, not necessarily to scout the contests, but to "observe and recommend" any alteration that might be advantageous to the Cleveland franchise. Indeed, Brown's duties as a vice president of the Browns were nebulous. As a consultant, he didn't actually consult with anyone. Brown did, however, write an occasional report to the team, a report that served primarily as a venue for Brown to editorialize on the state of the profession.

LaJolla was a convenient locale for Brown. Its proximity allowed easy access to AFL games in San Diego, twelve miles to the south, and the NFL in Los Angeles, which was 115 miles to the north. In truth, Brown only went to the games to see friends who ventured out to the coast. Occasionally, they came to see him. Weeb Ewbank visited Brown in LaJolla when his Jets came west to meet the San Diego Chargers. Past differences between the men had since been mended. The visit had a melancholy tinge to it. Before the Jets coach took his leave, Brown reached out.

"Weeb," he told his old friend, holding Ewbank's arm tightly, "Don't ever let them do this to you. I used to think losing was the worst thing in the world, but it's not. No football at all is worse."[11]

A couple of months later, Brown went to the Los Angeles Memorial Coliseum to see Vince Lombardi. While the Packers warmed up on the field, Brown came down from his seat in the stands to have a few words with Lombardi. Following a few minutes of conversation, Lombardi excused himself and receded to the locker room for final game preparations. Standing nearby, a writer witnessed the exchange and approached Brown. The scribe watched as Brown looked out over the field. A deep longing was palpable; an appetite for competition unquenched.

The sportswriter was taken aback when he saw Brown's eyes moisten. "Is it that bad?" he asked Brown.

"I can't tell you how bad it is," Brown answered, absently staring off to the activity on the field. "I can't tell you."[12]

Shortly after the first of the year, Philadelphia called again. The Eagles' new owners were in the market for a new coach. The sale of the franchise had taken some time to go through. In the end, yet another thirty-six-year-old novice had control of a National League franchise. In fact, Jerry Wolman fired Nick Skorich as the Eagles' head coach twenty-four hours before his purchase was approved by the league. Wolman naturally thought of the best coach available and reached out to Brown. Did he have any interest in coaching the Eagles? He was open to the possibility, Brown replied, and an interview was set up for the two sides to meet.

From the jump it was obvious that Wolman and Brown were not a good fit. Brown arrived at the summit only to see Wolman and his partner, Ed Snider, dressed in casual attire. Shirt sleeves, jeans, one of these fellas was even wearing slippers. The three-hour interview went on as scheduled, but both sides recognized it was just a formality. Wolman was put off by Brown and his condescending manner. And by Wolman's account, the entire conversation was overridden by Brown's acerbic attitude toward Modell and the Browns organization. Chiefly because of the rancor that Brown displayed toward Modell, Wolman claimed, the job was not offered to Brown.[13] For his part, Brown was disgusted by the lack of respect he perceived these men were giving him. They weren't football men, Brown convinced himself, and he'd already had enough of that type.

After the Eagles approached Brown, months went by; football had seemingly forgotten about Paul Brown. There was golf and more golf, trips to Mexico, shopping, long walks, and golf. In the fall, Katy and Paul decided to take a lengthy vacation. How far could they get from football? Hong Kong was on their itinerary, as was Tokyo and the Summer Olympics. The Browns departed immediately for the Far East after their son Mike's October 10 wedding to Nancy Lou Houston, which was held at Faith Lutheran Church in Lakewood.

They spent a week in Hong Kong before moving on to Tokyo. The plane ride to Japan turned out to be an unforgettable experience. Shortly after takeoff an engine caught fire. The pilot swiftly turned around and returned to Hong Kong, and only through skillful maneuvering was he able to safely land the aircraft. The return flight was tense and frightening for the passengers. Everyone aboard knew this could be it. As the stewardesses explained how to prepare for a crash landing, Paul and Katy took a moment to express their gratitude and love for one another. The eventual safe landing of the plane signaled to Brown he'd been given a second chance.

The Browns returned to the states in time for the holidays. The entire family—Pete on break from Denison University, Mike and his bride, Paul and Katy—everyone gathered at Robin's home in Arkansas. It was a joyful reunion that did wonders for Paul, a Christmas to remember. It had been easy for him to put football out of his mind for a few months. While he was on his two-month sojourn, though, the Cleveland Browns were in the midst of a magical season.

Two days after Christmas, with his boys by his side, Brown watched as the Cleveland Browns defeated the Baltimore Colts, 27-0, for the 1964 NFL championship. His emotions were mixed, to be certain. For the most part, the players capturing the title were his, and that made Brown proud. But that it was done without him, well, Brown didn't want to examine those feelings

—⁂—

Nearly two years had passed since Cleveland had heard directly from Brown when Bill Scholl of the *Cleveland Press* contacted Brown for a lengthy interview.

"I'm living a very serene existence. . . . Not doing anything exciting, just standing by seeing if anything develops."

The last two years had been difficult, Brown admitted. Tough on him and tough on his boys. "What weighs heavily on the father weighs heavily on the sons. The boys don't say anything about it, but I know it's always on their minds."

The Browns? Yes, he'd seen the championship game, he acknowledged, but that was the extent of the championship run Brown had seen. "I've been following the team as best I can, although it's not easy to get much more than wire reports in California. Nearly everything is either San Diego Chargers or Los Angeles Rams out here."

Brown couldn't hide his restlessness from Scholl. "It's just the day-to-day living to keep myself going. I'm not doing this by choice, but there is nothing I can do about it."[14]

Just a few days later, Brown received a recommendation from an unlikely source. Though the position was already occupied, Bernie Parrish nominated Brown for league commissioner. "We need Paul to run the league," Parrish told Chuck Heaton. "I'm going to work to line up support of the players for this move."

The rank and file of the Player's Association was unhappy with the guidance of Pete Rozelle. Yes, he was outspoken about Brown in the past, Parrish acknowledged, but that was concerning his coaching techniques. He'd always held Brown in high regard personally. "He is a man who knows the problems of the league," Parrish said. "He's been a coach, general manager and part-owner. . . . Paul would bring new and better organization to the league office."[15]

Nothing came of Parrish's proposal, nothing more than a lot of headlines as the story hit the wire services. The league owners were happy with Rozelle at the helm. That the Player's Association was unhappy meant nothing to the owners. The money was rolling in now, thanks to Rozelle's impressive television contracts. And the commissioner's "league think" policy was paying off for the NFL. All for one and one for all, the franchises would share all television income equally under Rozelle's scheme. The only bump in the road for the NFL was the upstart American Football League, and the competition for players which was driving up player salaries.

—ɯ—

In mid-June, a *Plain Dealer* piece reported that Brown was interested in working with the group vying for a franchise in Atlanta should the NFL reward the Georgia city with a team. This rumor continued to percolate for several weeks, even after Brown addressed the issue. "I haven't had any contact with the new owners," Brown said in early July shortly after the franchise was granted to the Atlanta group. Rankin Smith, an insurance executive, was granted the Atlanta franchise on July 1, 1965, for $9.5

million. "I have never talked to Rankin Smith nor have I been in Atlanta to talk with the new owners."

But, Brown added, "I've said on several occasions that if the right opportunity is there, I'd be interested."[16]

Brown wasn't equivocating. Brown hadn't yet met Smith, nor would he a month later when he flew to Chicago for a scheduled conference with the new owner. The trip resulted in more disappointment for Brown. He waited outside Smith's hotel suite. Brown waited and waited. Sixty minutes passed before one of Smith's flunkies informed Brown that Smith was unavailable that day. Angered by the slight, Brown had to shake his head in wonder. Where was the league heading with owners like this Smith. Wolman. Modell. What happened to respect? Where were the football men? As badly as he wanted to be back in the game, Brown couldn't help but think, maybe he was better off on the outside. Maybe he was better off with his memories of the way things were.

Still, that's not to say he wouldn't listen the next time his phone rang.

—◊—

Some of Brown's boys from Ohio State had stayed in close contact with their old coach through the years. One of the them, William Hackett, became a successful veterinarian following graduation, and among the many large farms he serviced in mid-Ohio was John Galbreath's Darby Dan Farms. Galbreath, owner of the Pittsburgh Pirates, knew of Hackett's relationship with Brown and floated an idea to the vet. "Could you ask Paul if he would like to be commissioner of baseball?" Galbreath requested.

Thinking Brown would be flattered by the offer, Hackett carried the message to Brown.

"No, thank you," Brown said, turning down the prestigious position. "What I would like to do is form the sixteenth NFL club."

"Well," Hackett asked, "what do you need?"

"I need some people who will back me. Someone who will give me total control. People I could trust."

Brown had listened to Wolman, waited for Smith, and heard over-tures from several other owners. After all this, Brown knew what he wanted, and what he wanted was his own team. Control over the whole operation. He could see that the NFL was on the verge of expanding. The addition of Atlanta left the league at an uneven number, fifteen, meaning each week one club would have a bye. This situation wasn't practical, Brown reasoned, and would definitely change soon. The Brown family had done its homework. Mike had conducted a study of all major cities without professional football. The criteria used by the younger Brown indicated that Cincinnati was the most attractive of the cities analyzed. Brown re-layed this information to Hackett, and, yes, Brown added, he was so sure of the prospect that he was willing to invest a substantial amount of his own capital in the team.

Even before he hung up the telephone, Hackett immediately thought of someone who fit that bill. John Sawyer, president of Orelton Farms in London, Ohio, had the financial wherewithal and the friends necessary to make something like this go. Sawyer, though a successful businessman in his own right, came from blue blood. His father, Charles Sawyer, served as secretary of commerce under Harry Truman. The Sawyers came from old money in Cincinnati.

Cincinnati was a perfect fit for pro football, thought Hackett. Saw-yer's influence in the Queen City would be helpful, and Hackett knew his friend to be everything Brown was looking for in a partner. Trustworthy above all else, Hackett also knew that Sawyer would be content to stay in the background of any kind of partnership. The two men got together and tossed the idea around. The more they talked, the more they realized this could work. Pro football in Cincinnati, Paul Brown back in Ohio where he belonged. Sawyer spoke with Brown several times on the phone as a way of introduction before Brown came to Ohio to meet in person. Brown flew into Dayton and stayed at Sawyer's farm in Madison County.

The meeting was fruitful. Brown was impressed by what he'd heard, and more importantly, he liked Sawyer. He already knew that he could trust his old guard Hackett, and this Sawyer fella seemed like a stand-up guy himself. Brown explained that the next step was to approach Governor Rhodes, an old acquaintance. It was imperative that James Rhodes be on board; the governor's influence was vital. A new stadium was needed in Cincinnati or the NFL wouldn't give the city a second look.

The whole thing came together very quickly. A corporation was formed: The Ohio Valley Sports Inc. Sawyer served as president, Brown as vice president, general manager, and coach. Hackett performed the duties of treasurer, and Brown's son, Mike, would be the organization's secretary and business manager. The younger Brown graduated from Dartmouth in '57 and then proceeded on to Harvard, where he earned a degree in law. Upon graduation from Harvard, Mike joined the Browns as legal counsel. This brief experience would serve Mike well as the group moved forward.

A luncheon, held at the Sheraton, was organized for Tuesday, December 14, 1965 to announce the group's intentions. Invited to the gathering were 125 leading businessmen and civic leaders of Cincinnati as well as the town's sporting press. The revelation that a group led by Paul Brown wanted to bring professional football to their fair city was as pleasing as it was shocking. And Brown made sure to emphasize as he spoke to the crowd, it wasn't just a pro football team, but a National Football League franchise.

"We'll do our best to bring [a] franchise here," Brown told the business leaders. "We'll be operating and ready to take a go at it, but time is of the essence."[17]

Brown was referring to the NFL league meetings, which were scheduled to be held in Palm Beach on Valentine's Day. The league's owners were to decide then which city would be home to the circuit's sixteenth franchise. Cincinnati faced stiff competition for the coveted slot from several cities, including Boston, New Orleans, Seattle, Houston, Montreal, Phoenix, Memphis, and Portland. A number of issues facilitated the Queen City's candidacy. Cincinnati ranked high in many of the factors being used by the NFL in comparing cities, such as population, per capita income, and highway access. Brown believed Cincinnati competed favorably in all these categories.

"I'm encouraged," Brown told the crowd, "and I believe you're in a better position than you realize."

Most importantly, though, was the establishment of funding for a new stadium. The options then open for football in Cincinnati were Crosley Field and Nippert Stadium. Crosley was primarily a baseball park that seated 28,000, and Nippert was the home field for the University of Cincinnati's Bearcats. Nippert held but 29,000 fans for football games, well under the amount the NFL required. Within a week of the Sheraton luncheon, the governor, city council, county commissioners, and a newly formed stadium steering committee met. Three sites were discussed for a new stadium: just south of Crosley Field, the riverfront, and Blue Ash in the northern suburbs. Within a few weeks, two other towns in the northern suburbs—Sharonville and Springdale—expressed interest in housing a new park.

Local sportswriter Pat Harmon, editor of the *Cincinnati Post*, had tried on a number of occasions to bring professional football to his hometown. Harmon approached the NFL's leaders five times, be it Bert Bell or Pete Rozelle. He had even tried Joe Foss of the AFL on three occasions. The answer from all was always the same. "Get some people with some money to invest and come see us."

Harmon was delighted to see the Brown group make waves that he was never able to rouse. The city couldn't have been more fortunate. The greatest coach the game had ever known wanted to bring pro football to their fair town.

"I've given up any other jobs I've had a chance for," Brown told Harmon. He was done with the game of musical chairs coaches were forced to play. "I'm going to find out if we have a chance to operate a National League franchise in Cincinnati—and I think we have a great chance."[18]

The word "we" had crept into Brown's dialogue when referring to Cincinnati. He had thrown himself headlong into this effort. Brown was commuting back and forth between LaJolla and Cincinnati, all the while keeping Pete Rozelle up-to-date with the group's progress.

James Rhodes, too, was busy pushing, trying to drum up support. The governor vowed that he would speak with every NFL owner prior to the league meetings, but his first priority was Art Modell. On the second day of 1966, Rhodes was Modell's guest at Lambeau Field in Green Bay as the Browns took on the Packers for the NFL championship. Although 335 miles separated Cincinnati from Cleveland, the city was still considered Browns territory, as the team's radio network also ventured into southwestern Ohio. Still, Modell did not hesitate when Rhodes raised the topic of Cincinnati entering the league. He was on board, he assured Rhodes, and he would do anything he could to promote the city to his fellow owners.

Doing his part, Brown flew to Los Angeles for the Pro Bowl on the sixteenth. Two days earlier, Brown met with Pete Rozelle and updated the commissioner on the group's progress. Though Rozelle was encouraging, he didn't promise Brown anything. Truth be told, the commissioner was beginning to think that nothing would be decided in February. There were other, more pressing issues facing the league.

—⟐—

For some time rumors had been traveling through the sporting press that the NFL was seeking a merger with the upstart American Football League. The gossip turned into full-blown negotiations in April 1966. And on June 8, Rozelle announced that the rival leagues had come to an accord. The NFL and AFL agreed to unite under one commissioner and play as a single league by 1970. In the meantime, the NFL and AFL consented to meet in a championship game and to hold a common draft beginning in January 1967.

The merger was prompted by escalating player bidding, which proved costly to both leagues. More than any other contract, the $400,000 paid by the AFL's New York Jets for quarterback Joe Namath set in motion the machinations that culminated with the June 8 announcement.

Among the numerous conditions under the merger terms:

1) The existing franchises were to be retained, and none were to be transferred from their 1966 locations.

2) Two new franchises were to be added by 1968, and "two more as soon as possible thereafter."

3) Pete Rozelle would preside over the new league when the merger was completed in 1970.

—⁓—

In August the story was out that Brown had dropped out of the group trying to bring pro football to Cincinnati and that he was in search of new prospects. Cincinnati City Council had been wavering and had recently decided not to endorse more than $400,000 for additional architect fees. Brown was disheartened by the news. "No question about it, it hurt us," Brown admitted. "I personally assumed when we went into this that everybody was together. It is a disappointment I never bargained for. My support, for what it's worth, is still for Cincinnati. . . . There were rumors that I had walked away. That's not true."[19]

Just three days later, on August 10, the funding for a new stadium was approved by the city council. While the Brown group agreed to a long-term lease should they be granted a franchise, Reds owner Bill DeWitt balked at such a proposition. He was adamant the Reds would play in a publicly financed park, but the team would not sign a long-term lease.

A survey commissioned by the NFL agreed with the study conducted earlier by Mike Brown. Cincinnati placed first among seven potential expansion cities. The criteria used in the review were population, economy, stadium, and competition. And Cincinnati, of course, had something else no other municipality had—Paul Brown. Unfortunately for the Brown group, other factors were in play. Politics and geography dictated the league's decision as much as any other factors, especially politics. And while six months earlier Brown was optimistic about his chances, by the fall he understood that circumstances had changed.

The merger agreement was contingent on Congressional approval. Monopolistic concerns were voiced and lawsuits were threatened. Much maneuvering was necessary by Rozelle to convince Congressional leaders to OK a merger exemption. Two legislators—Louisiana Senator Russell Long and Representative Hale Boggs—specifically met with the commissioner. Before he cast his vote, Boggs waited for Rozelle's promise that New Orleans would be granted the expansion franchise. Following some playful give and take, the boy czar assured the congressman that he could "count on" the owners' approval. Within the hour, the merger exemption had passed.

From the ballroom of New Orleans' Pontchartrain Hotel, Pete Rozelle announced that the Crescent City would be awarded the NFL's sixteenth franchise. A day prior to the November 1, 1966, statement, Rozelle paid a visit to Brown. The commissioner wanted to tell Brown in advance of the league's decision. Traveling to Cincinnati with Rozelle were members of the AFL's expansion committee. Brown's disappointment was masked by his grateful feeling for the support he was given by his friends in the NFL. The AFL, which Brown gave no consideration just a short while earlier, now looked like a viable option. What made Brown reconsider his once-adamant stance was the June merger agreement between the rival leagues.

Brown was not surprised by the decision. "I sort of realized from the start that everyone had his own ideas on which city should get the sixteenth NFL franchise," Brown admitted. "And Louisiana did lead the way in saving the merger. I thought it was a strategic situation."[20]

He came away from the meeting with Rozelle and the expansion committee emboldened. Rozelle informed Brown that Cincinnati had the inside track of becoming the next AFL club. The only competition was Seattle, where voters had turned down a stadium bond issue two months earlier.

"I believe we can have the franchise for 1968 if assurance is given that a new stadium in Cincinnati will be ready in time,"[21] Brown told reporters afterward.

The snag continued to be Bill DeWitt. Through the preceding months pressure began to mount on the Reds owner. Still, DeWitt refused to yield. The local press portrayed the Reds' owner as a villain, the culprit keeping the city from getting professional football. In the pages of his paper, the *Cincinnati Enquirer,* Francis Dale was relentless in his criticism of DeWitt's determined stance that the riverfront location was too risky. Boxed in by the river on one side and a highway on the other, the site would have limited access for fans. The Reds owner preferred a suburban spot. Put the park where the people are, DeWitt thought. Both

Blue Ash and Springdale were more desirable settings than downtown, but location wasn't DeWitt's only misgiving. He did not like the idea of a dual-purpose stadium. Baseball clubs and football teams have different needs, DeWitt thought. Why force them to cohabitate? But DeWitt's thinking went against the grain in 1966. Multipurpose stadia were being built or planned in cities throughout the country. These facilities saved the taxpayer money. It was the two-birds-with-one-stone philosophy.

While DeWitt may have come around to sharing the new park with a football team, a long-term lease without an escape clause was unacceptable. He was civic-minded, however, and if this was what the city wanted, DeWitt wouldn't stand in the way. Finally, on December 6, DeWitt succumbed to the coercion. He wouldn't sign the lease that the city wanted, but he would sell the team. A diverse group of local businessmen and companies, including the *Cincinnati Enquirer,* James and William Williams, Louis Nippert, and Dave Gamble were part of the new Reds ownership group. Also among the investors were prominent members of the football assemblage: Bill Hackett, Dutch Knowlton, and John Sawyer. The new ownership agreed to a forty-year lease on the day of the sale, eliminating what seemingly was the final obstacle for Brown's goal.

By all indications it was a done deal. Cincinnati would now be granted the AFL expansion outfit. But still, months dragged on with no movement or official word. While at home in LaJolla, Brown spoke with Jack Murphy of the *San Diego Union* in mid-May. He was guardedly optimistic, but the wait was killing him. "I have sort of a precedent of not living it up until a thing is completed," admitted Brown. "It's too early to say anything fancy."

He loved the southern California weather, and LaJolla was a charming place to live. "But football is my life," Brown confessed. "I can't walk away from it. Except for my family, there is nothing else. We're steeped in the football business, all of us. That's why I must not build up my hopes about this Cincinnati franchise. I don't want it to break everybody's heart."[22]

Indeed, it was the family business. Mike was a key member of the syndicate fighting for the franchise. As for Pete, Brown had something in mind for him should this new team come to fruition. Robin would continue to personally oversee his array of successful businesses in Arkansas, but if his father's comeback came to fruition, he too would lend a hand in the venture. And then there was Katy. Her health had been deteriorating quickly over the previous few years. She had developed diabetes, and the disease had taken nearly all of her vision. For Paul, the acrimony and strife over losing his job was tempered by the opportunity to tend to Katy's needs. Their time together was a blessing, but still he couldn't stifle the burning desire to return to the sideline. He hadn't made the decision to chase this Cincinnati dream alone. It was a family decision. He already knew where the boys stood; they loved the game, but they also wanted their father to have his chance at redemption. And Katy, when asked, didn't hesitate. "Oh," she told Paul, "we'll go back into football."[23]

And now, as a family, they waited.

—⚏—

On the 23rd of May, 1967, the AFL search committee came to Cincinnati along with Rozelle. The league invited Governor Rhodes to sit in on their discussions, joining City Councilmen Eugene Ruehlmann and Myron Bush, as well as utilities director Wallace Powers and City Manager William Wienman. Through the course of the day, the committee stalled, hemmed and hawed, as hour ran into hour. Rhodes finally spoke up. "You invited me up here," the governor grumbled. "Do something. I came here to hear Cincinnati awarded a franchise and I won't leave until it's done."[24]

Despite the presence of the AFL owners, the NFL, more specifically Pete Rozelle, was calling the shots. The search committee settled its petty squabbling that kept it from reaching a decision—issues that had nothing to do with expansion—and passed the resolution granting Cincinnati the tenth AFL franchise. The new team would pay $8 million for the privilege of joining the exclusive club. The entire fee, as per the merger agreement, was to be split among NFL teams. A promise came from Rozelle that the ownership group would be named in a month. Backgrounds were checked, financing verified. But would old grudges be taken into consideration? One anonymous AFL owner implied that the Brown syndicate was no cinch to be approved "because some people now controlling things are envious of Brown's past success as coach."[25]

Certainly Brown had rubbed some people wrong in the past, but he did have Rozelle on his side. "I'm hopeful," Brown told Chuck Heaton, who reached Brown in LaJolla. "I'm happy that Cincinnati was selected. As far as myself and my group are concerned, another hurdle is ahead."[26]

The first step was naming the city for the next franchise, and now it was choosing which operatives would run it. Though Brown had dominated the headlines for the previous eighteen months, his wasn't the only group vying for the Cincinnati team. Two anonymous factions came forth immediately following the approval of Cincinnati. The only information given on either of these groups was that one was composed of Texans. Another conglomerate was headed by Len Troglio, a food broker from Columbus. But Brown's chief competition for the expansion club was headed by a prominent Cincinnatian, John A. "Socko" Wiethe. Though his pedigree paled in comparison to Brown's football resume, Wiethe had his fair share of experience in the game. Following three years of lettering at Xavier University, he turned pro and played briefly with the Cincinnati Bengals before spending time with the Detroit Lions from 1939-42. In retiring from football, Wiethe's career began. He joined the bar and made a name for himself locally as an aggressive attorney, which led to Wiethe becoming the Democratic chairman of Cincinnati. He was no dilettante. His position as Democratic chair allowed Wiethe to exercise substantial political power in Hamilton County. This influence, Wiethe hoped against hope, would persuade football power brokers to select his group over the more-glamorous Brown contingent.

To try to match Brown's credentials, Wiethe needed to hire a powerful football personality, one that could rival Brown's reputation. He claimed to have talked with fifteen potential coaches, among them Woody Hayes, Bud Wilkinson, Ara Parseghian, and Bear Bryant. What Socko wasn't telling the media was that Bryant had verbally committed to coach the team that was to be named "the Romans." "He's going to be the first millionaire coach," Wiethe told confidants.

Unlike the other three groups competing with Brown, Wiethe's wasn't a fly-by-night venture. He had a name for the team, as well as a logo, which featured a gladiator. Wiethe hired a publicist, but most importantly, he had significant capital behind his effort, including Fleischmann money earned from Charles Fleischmann's yeast fortune. He had been in the fray for more than a year, but no one on the national level was taking Socko seriously. Hell, most of them hadn't even heard of his group. He was homegrown, a Cincinnatian through and through, a fact that he never failed to tout. In fact, that was why he jumped into the fray to begin with. Wiethe didn't believe the Brown group had enough Cincinnati flavor. His consortium certainly wouldn't fall short in that category. Even if the press and the public were overlooking Wiethe, Pete Rozelle wasn't. If nothing else, Wiethe provided the league with leverage when dealing with the Brown group.

In the last week of August, Brown was in New York to meet with Rozelle and AFL President Milt Woodward. Some issues had already been resolved in the previous weeks. Brown's investment group was expanded in response to critics complaining that the group didn't have enough of a Cincinnati quintessence. Francis Dale, publisher of the *Enquirer,* joined the syndicate, as did William and James Williams, David Gamble, and Louis Nippert. All men were native to Cincinnati as well as associated with the Reds. This addition pleased Rozelle, but there still were other concerns left to resolve. First, Brown's stock with the Browns needed to be disposed of. And secondly, the AFL had made some significant alterations concerning television revenue compared to the last expansion. For their first two years, the Cincinnati owners would not share in television receipts, a loss of an estimated $1 million.

In addition, the system for stocking the new team had been changed appreciably. Cincinnati would choose from the remnants after each AFL club "froze" 29 players. In comparison, Miami selected after each team protected 23 players.

Brown did not accept such changes graciously. These modifications would force Cincinnati to field a demonstratively inferior club. Interest in the team would disappear quickly if the league insisted on tying his hands in this manner. Brown was so adamant that he threatened to withdraw his group's bid. Brown's obstinacy threw the whole process into chaos. Surely Brown wasn't serious about retracting his offer; but Brown felt he had been sandbagged. The conditions presented were not what the league previously represented, nor were they anything resembling what the last expansion team, the Miami Dolphins, was given in 1966. Miami, though not receiving a full television share of $850,000, did get $500,000 for their first two seasons.

Brown was furious, but the league was not budging. Woodward was unwavering; there would be no TV money, "That's the way it's going to be. That's final," he said.[27] Finally, in mid-September, Brown was given an ultimatum—sign on to the franchise agreement as is or get out. The AFL meant business. Socko Wiethe was contacted and told to stand by. His group was still in the running. In fact, both the Wiethe and Troglio groups had been approached with the new terms and each readily agreed to the conditions. Brown's hands were tied. This was his chance to get back in the game, to be in complete control. Publicly, he decried what the league had done. Privately, he accepted the terms. But he also made it clear: Don't expect him to do any more for the next expansion club to come down the line.

—⁄⁄⁄—

In the midst of these frustrating negotiations, Brown paused for a day while his career was celebrated in his old backyard. On August 5, 1967, Brown—along with Chuck Bednarik, Bobby Layne, and Daniel F. Reeves—was inducted into the Pro Football Hall of Fame. Two nights before the ceremony, Paul and Katy made their first public appearance since leaving Cleveland four-and-a-half years earlier. The evening started with a quiet dinner at the Massillon Club followed by a special booster-club stag at the American Legion. A steady line of past and present Massillonians took the microphone and saluted Brown, who was seated beneath a banner that read, "Welcome Back Paul"

Dave Stewart remembered back to 1920, when Brown arrived in Massillon from Norwalk. "Nobody made Brown," Stewart said. "He had it."[28]

Others, including Red Bird, Dick Gallagher, and Luther Emery, all paid tribute to Brown before Brown finally stepped to the microphone. He seemed a bit embarrassed by all the fuss.

"It all sounds like a eulogy," he laughed, "but where is the body?"

"I can't express my gratitude. This is my home. My job here was the most rewarding I ever had. The kids believed in me. I could coach more minutely. The public kept them in line. You don't do a job of coaching without the spirit in the community."

When he was finished, Brown was presented with a photograph of a much younger version of himself; a snapshot of him playing center field for Miami University. For a moment, Brown gazed at the picture. "It's hard to believe it was that way once upon a time." Before the night came to a close the 450 persons in attendance had given Brown three standing ovations. It was just the start of an eventful weekend.

The following night Brown and the seven other inductees entering the Hall of Fame with him were feted at a dinner at Canton's Hotel Onesta. And then on Saturday afternoon Brown was presented at the induction ceremony by his old field general, Otto Graham. Now the head coach of the Washington Redskins, Graham left his team's training camp for the occasion. "It's pretty hard to get time off to come back and do something like this," Graham admitted. "In fact, I had to call off practice today in order to get here. This is something Paul Brown never would have done, I guarantee you this. He just doesn't believe in those kinds of things and that's why he was successful, so I probably won't be.

"I must admit that I was a normal American red-blooded boy football player that always didn't like my coach and I used to cuss him out like every boy. . . . I could never understand why he did some things, but I can tell you very honestly now that I'm coaching I even outdo Paul Brown."[29]

Had he not had a new franchise within his grasp, the tribute would have been bittersweet. But circumstances had turned in his favor, and

Brown was able to bask in the glow of the moment. "You might be well aware this is a red-letter day for yours truly and the Brown family," Brown told the crowd gathered together outside the Hall. "I was like, I presume, many of these fellows up here. You think and hope along those lines but you're afraid to think too much about it for fear it might not happen and so, it's a proud day and a very happy one."[30]

At halftime of the exhibition contest between the Browns and Eagles, the newest members of the Hall were introduced to the spectators at Canton's Fawcett Stadium. Brown, who was saved for last, was escorted by Graham and Cindy Carr, a cheerleader for Canton Lehman High School. Brown walked between two lines of the Washington High Swing Band as they belted out "Tiger Rag" in his honor. The tune drifted about in the air, hearkening back to a long-ago era, a simpler time. Brown couldn't help but smile at the memory.

—⁓—

On September 26, 1967, in front of a packed ballroom at the Sheraton Gibson in Cincinnati, Governor James A. Rhodes stepped to the podium. In a bit of hyperbole, Rhodes declared, "This is the greatest step in the history of the city." Rhodes had reason to bask in the spotlight; he had championed the endeavor from the beginning. His political experience and skill for bending an ear and twisting an arm played a large part in the successful conclusion. The governor knew who the gathering wanted to hear from, and after a few words of self-congratulations Rhodes introduced "Mr. Football himself" to the crowd.

Sporting a glowing smile, Brown stepped forward and shook the governor's hand. He then turned and addressed the crowd. "This is like coming home. I'm living again."

"It's a happy day for me and I hope it turns out to be a happy day for Cincinnati and its environs."[31]

Brown then fielded a handful of questions from the reporters present.

Will you coach the team? Brown was asked. The query wasn't so peculiar. Many wondered if Brown, at his advanced age of fifty-nine, would return to the sideline.

"I'll go through the tough part at the beginning," he responded, "but I have no timetable on how long I'll coach."

Because of their severe disadvantage in the expansion draft, Brown emphasized, the team would have to rely heavily on the collegiate draft. "Our team will be comprised of a tremendous amount of college football players. It will be a golden opportunity for a player coming out of college. We'll have to take a young guy and stick with him, hoping he'll do the job for us." Brown maintained his composure under the hot TV lights and a flurry of questions from inquisitive reporters.

Why the long delay in naming his syndicate the winner of the franchise?

"The TV money and draft situation already had been settled. Projection of the stadium and how we were to invest our money caused the delay. . . . It's been a long, tough siege. I feel like I've had one season already."[32]

Under the terms of the partnership agreement there would be no majority stockholder. Because league rules mandated that one individual be responsible to the commissioner, Brown was given voting trust for the club by his "money men," John Sawyer and William Hackett. In the event of Brown's death, control of the franchise would revert to his son, Mike.

"I appoint the board of directors," Brown informed reporters. "I wouldn't have come back unless I was in complete charge. I had it both ways in Cleveland. The players know they cannot bypass me and go to the general manager or the owners. It gives me great advantage over other coaches.

"That is the way it must be," he continued. "Any other way and in time you'll see the whole structure begin to crumble, and all at once a good team will begin to slide. It's inevitable. Look at the history of great football teams and you'll see all the authority concentrated in the coach."

The terms of Brown's contract were released to the media. His salary was set at $60,000 annually for ten years. Severance pay for Brown would be $50,000 a year if Brown should retire within that ten-year span. He also had 10 percent ownership in the club.

—ɯ—

The first hire would be the most important. Brown wanted to organize the personnel department in expectation of the college draft; it was the "life-blood" of any organization. When the possibility first arose of operating a team again, Brown approached Dick Gallagher about running the team's personnel department. Gallagher was very interested in the position, but as the process drifted on slowly, he was offered a similar job with San Francisco. Not knowing when or how the Cincinnati situation would be resolved, Gallagher asked for Brown's blessing to accept the 49ers proposition, which Brown gave. Earlier in the summer, Milt Woodward served as mediator by bringing together Brown and Al LoCasale, one of the finest personnel directors in the game. LoCasale was in the employ of the San Diego Chargers but was hoping for an opportunity to leave the team. Brown invited LoCasale to his LaJolla home, and with the soothing sound of the surf providing a tranquil setting, Brown and LoCasale sat down and discussed business. Over a glass of scotch and a bowl of peppers and cherry tomatoes, LoCasale laid out his stipulations for Brown. He wanted three full-time scouts, which LoCasale would oversee—a "super scout" so to speak. These terms were reasonable, and Brown accepted them without quibbling. LoCasale was the perfect hire. He knew the AFL inside out—the personnel, style of play, everything about the league. LoCasale's experience would be vital to Brown and the fledgling organization.

—ɯ—

There was much work to do. Finding an office, a training camp site, signing the stadium lease, selecting a team name, creating a radio network, and choosing a practice location . . . the list was extensive and diverse. Periodically, the city's utility director, Wally Powers, would check with Brown concerning stadium construction. The Reds were full of demands, including the color of the ballpark's seats (red). Brown, however, worried little about such trivial matters. "I don't care what color they are," Brown told Powers, "I want them filled with asses."

"This is a tremendous undertaking," Brown admitted. "I went through it all before but had almost forgotten all the things to be done. So many details involved. . . . I must be a darn fool to get into all of this, but I have to admit I'm enjoying it."

His days were full and long, but Brown had never felt so alive. The team's offices were temporarily located on the seventeenth floor of the Carew Tower in downtown Cincinnati until the team could relocate one floor above to more sumptuous dwellings. Brown's modest office was furnished simply with a couple of chairs and a desk borrowed from the building. "We had a board meeting in here, and I was kind of pleased," Brown said of his modestly appointed room, which had a large hole in the linoleum floor. "It showed how frugal I am with their money."[33]

Hiring LoCasale was a starting point and a vital ingredient to the team's future. With the scouting department now launched, Brown then looked to set up the front office. John Murdough was brought over from the Reds to serve as the team's business manager, the same position he held with the baseball club. Next in line was engaging a public relations director. Creating good rapport with the local press was imperative for a young and inexperienced franchise. Brown did his homework here. Al Heim was one of the most respected and well-liked men in the city's sporting sect. A genial and cordial man, Heim was the sports editor at the *Enquirer* when Brown offered him the position of publicity director with the new team.

What to name this new team? Shortly after the city was granted the franchise, the *Post and Times Star* held a contest for fans to contribute their ideas. A number of names were submitted via a coupon available in the newspaper. The most popular choice to arrive from the poll was the Buckeyes, which was rejected out of hand by Brown. He wanted to emphasize that the new team would be a regional franchise that Brown hoped would appeal to fans across a four-state area, not just Ohio. Besides, Brown said, "That name is already used by Ohio State."[34]

Other names were suggested—Krauts, Celts, Romans—but Brown believed "they would make us part of just one group, and we want to be part of all groups." After wading through countless suggestions, a name was settled on that reprised Cincinnati's modest pro football history. The

Bengals it would be, Brown revealed at an October 27 press conference. The name was selected by a committee of directors, Brown said, because it had "animation," in addition to being the name of a team that played in Cincinnati from 1937-1941.

"There is a precedent for reviving an old name," Brown explained. "Two present football teams, the Baltimore Colts and Buffalo Bills, are revivals of famous old names."[35] The old Bengals played their games at Xavier University and Crosley Field with a roster consisting of NFL retreads and local products.

Standing nearby listening to Brown's announcement was an old Bengal, Socko Wiethe.

"Wiethe, Dolly Cohen, Jack Farcasin, and their group were very sporting," Brown acknowledged of the rival group vying for the franchise. "They presented their side fairly and didn't try to knock us."

A grateful Wiethe stepped forward to the microphone. "Thank you," he said. "We'll do all we can to help the new team."

A broad smile creased Brown's face as he wrapped an arm around Wiethe's sturdy shoulders. "If you really want to help, come over and play guard for me," Brown suggested.

Still, no matter what Brown said, it was hard to believe that the name Bengals was chosen to honor a failed semi-pro outfit. After all, Brown dismissed the name Panthers in Cleveland that had a similar history. No, the more likely reasoning is what the name Bengals wakened in Brown. His Tigers in Massillon were often dubbed the "Bengals" in *Independent* headlines. The colors, the mascot, it was all too much of a coincidence.

—⚏—

For a couple of months it was just Brown and LoCasale. While away from the game, Brown wasn't just studying players, he was watching coaches coach. When he got back into the game, Brown wanted to know who would comprise his coaching staff. Though he was sometimes reluctant to pass around the glory, Brown well understood that his assistants were vital to his success. He wanted a mix, a good blend of people, and once his group was granted the franchise Brown had a definite idea of who he wanted to contact. The first, Tom Bass, a fine defensive backfield coach in San Diego, received a call from Brown the day after the Chargers' final game of the season. Some, like Jack Donaldson, sought out Brown for an interview. Donaldson and Brown had Weeb Ewbank in common. Donaldson had been coaching for Ewbank in New York during the previous five seasons when he called Brown, but not before he grilled Ewbank about what it was like to be an assistant under Brown. Weeb spent an evening discussing his time with Brown. It was difficult working for a perfectionist like Brown, but an invaluable experience. Another, Bill "Tiger" Johnson was a veteran of the AAFC, having played for the 49ers against Brown's great Cleveland teams. Though he planned on adding to his staff, this is the group of men Brown surrounded himself with as he and LoCasale prepared for the expansion draft, which was coming up on January 15 in Jacksonville. And with the college draft just fifteen days later in New York, the staff pored over scouting reports. Brown's assistants had the AFL covered. Jack Donaldson was from the Eastern Division, while LoCasale and Tom Bass were both from the West. The first order of business was finding a quarterback. After examining their options, which were limited, the Bengals traded their first- and second-round bonus selections in the college draft to the Miami Dolphins for the rights to quarterback John Stofa. Though Stofa was of limited ability, he was the best player available at the position for the Bengals.

"We had to get somebody to get us out of the dressing room, to get us off the ground," Brown said of the Stofa trade in what was hardly a ringing endorsement of the first Bengal. "If we had waited for the player allocation from the other AFL teams, we wouldn't have had a quarterback."[36]

Brown didn't expect to acquire much in the AFL draft, not with the way it was rigged, and he didn't come away from the experience disappointed. "There were," he said, "a couple of mild surprises."

Brown approached the microphone at a press conference following the first day of the draft. "I don't see how we can lose after all we got, fellows," and then with a grin, Brown added, "don't forget to say I laughed."[37]

"I'd say we anticipated about 80 percent of the names that came up," Brown said from the Sheraton in Jacksonville, which was to say, he didn't anticipate much. Frank Buncom, Ernie Wright, Cookie Gilchrist, and Pat Matson were among the best-known players picked by the Bengals. Gilchrist had been a four-time All-Pro fullback, although he would never play again. The others certainly were not household names. "We made up our minds before we came down here; we'll make the best of it no matter what they put up. I'm sure we're not worrying anybody too much."

The expansion draft was just filler, castoffs from other clubs. What would comprise the future of the franchise was the collegiate draft. On the morning of January 30, the Bengal brain trust gathered in the team's new eighteenth-floor offices in the Carew Tower and prepared for their first college draft. With great secrecy Brown and his advisors took final looks at film of prospects, leafed through the Blue Book of College Athletics, and made last-minute phone calls to coaches and athletic departments. Huddled together in the room were Brown and his staff: Rick Forzano, Tom Bass, Bill Johnson, Jack Donaldson, and Bill Walsh, a thirty-six-year-old who had served one season as Oakland's backfield coach before spending the 1967 season with San Jose of the Continental Football League. At San Jose, Walsh filled the dual role of head coach and general manager. In addition to Al LoCasale, these men perused the top college prospects listed on an oversized blackboard.

Looking out from the Bengals' offices, an early-morning haze shrouded the Ohio River; through the fog the Kentucky hillside was barely visible. On the Ohio side, construction was under way on the new sports edifice that would house the Cincinnati Bengals in a just few years. But the future was now. The future's name was already printed on that blackboard set up in a room in the suite of offices.

The team was connected to the draft and the Bengals' man in New York via a "special phone." Newsmen—print, radio, and television reporters—roamed through the halls of the Bengals' offices, but the war room was off limits to all but the team's hierarchy. Mike and Tom Bass came and went, supplying the press with updates on the team's selections. To

LoCasale, Brown said that if he had his druthers, they would draft a center "because we'll be snapping the ball to the punter a lot the first few years."

But to the press, Brown wasn't quite as fatalistic. "You begin by building up the middle because you've got to start an offense with a good ground game." Brown explained. This theory was put into practice when the Bengals selected Bob Johnson, a center from the University of Tennessee, with their first draft pick.

Dick Forbes described the exhilaration within the team's offices. "The Bengals' office girls found it all very exciting at first," Forbes wrote in the *Enquirer*. "When Brown made his official announcement of Cincinnati's choice of Tennessee center Bob Johnson, the television cameras whirled and the reporters crowded around. . . . Four hours later when Brown announced Bill Staley of Utah State as the Bengals' second draft choice, the novelty somehow had worn off. Newsmen were somehow just plain men again."[38]

To be expected, Brown endorsed the number-one pick.

"Johnson has tremendous speed and quickness," Brown appraised. "He's a 'class person.' The kind you build with. You start out in football with first things first," Brown offered. "Taking Johnson as a center to work with John Stofa is like building down the middle on a baseball team. He's like getting a good catcher in baseball to work with your standout pitcher."

Brown closely studied the newest addition to the NFL, the New Orleans Saints, and examined how that franchise put its pieces together. "The Saints chose to build a veteran team, hoping to be successful immediately, partly because they had an 82,000-seat stadium to fill each week, and as a result, they sacrificed the long-range success of the team," Brown later said. "I knew the moment we got our allocation draft that we had to go with our college draft choices and that we had to spend the bulk of our time working with the players who would be part of our future. The main thing we learned from watching New Orleans was how not to do it."

Among others, the Bengals picked running backs Paul Robinson (the last pick of the third round), Essex Johnson (sixth round), and linebacker Al Beauchamp (last pick, fifth round). The Bengals' first choice

The Bengals' training camp at Wilmington, 1968.

in the fourth round was an intriguing selection of running back Jess Phillips out of a Michigan prison where he was serving time for passing bad checks. "He made a mistake," Brown acknowledged. "I, perhaps better than anyone, should know that a man isn't always what his reputation proclaims him to be."

Bengal hierarchy was, indeed, pleased with the quality of players selected in the collegiate, if not the expansion draft. With actual names now filling out his roster, Brown had other, off-the-field business to tend to.

Shortly after the first of the year, following much deliberation, Brown decided on a training camp site. Though several local schools, including

Miami University, invited the Bengals to train on their campuses, Brown struggled finding the perfect setting. During the fall, Paul and Mike made several car trips between Cincinnati and Cleveland. On one such occasion, the Browns stopped at Wilmington College. The Quaker university located forty miles northeast of Cincinnati was an ideal location. The last time Brown had been to Wilmington College was his junior year of college while a member of The Big Red. Visiting the school forty years later, Brown was enchanted. The setting took him back to Hiram—a lush, wholesome campus.

Establishing an extensive radio network was a point of pride for Brown, and he was competing against himself (indirectly) as he set to building a family of stations to carry Bengal games. The network that he had built for the Browns while in Cleveland was vast and covered every square inch of Ohio, plus parts of West Virginia and Pennsylvania. Anchored by WLW in Cincinnati, Brown was able to band together a group of affiliates to air Bengal contests. The fifty-two-station network reached north to Columbus, west beyond Indianapolis, south past Nashville and Knoxville, and east into West Virginia. Brown also signed on to do a weekly "Quarterback Club" television show. The program was patterned after a similar show Brown had in Cleveland.

In mid-February 1968, the club finally decided upon Nippert Stadium as its home until the new one was ready for the fall of 1970. "Nippert had several things going for it," Brown explained. "First, it was designed for football. It offers better seats. Secondly, we hope to add three or four thousand seats to bring the capacity up to 33,000, and this was much easier at UC."

With players in place, a field on which to compete, and a modest radio network to air the contests, all that was needed before training camp was to clothe the cast of misfits.

The concoction decided upon was eerily reminiscent of Cleveland's togs. But instead of the drab orange and brown color scheme, Brown's Bengals would be attired in black and orange with "BENGALS" spelled out in block lettering on their helmets. "You've no idea how many hours we spent selecting this outfit," Brown said. "We almost chose a helmet with stripes down either side, but some visitors told us they didn't like it." The rejected design had black "tiger" stripes running across an otherwise orange helmet. "[We wanted] nothing to flash," Brown explained, "Because nothing is worse than a bad team with a crazy-looking uniform. . . I was determined to avoid anything that might bring ridicule while we struggled to become respectable."

—∙∙∙—

In late February, Bill Scholl of the *Cleveland Press* came to Cincinnati to do the background research for what would later become a nationally syndicated series on Brown's return to football. Scholl spent several days in Cincinnati, visiting with Paul and Katy, who were living temporarily at John Sawyer's forty-four-acre estate in the charming suburban village of Glendale. The writer walked the streets of Glendale with Brown and observed him at the team's Carew Tower offices. "It's quite a rare thing, getting the opportunity of starting another organization from scratch at my age," Brown told Scholl. "This is a chance to recoup my life."[39]

Brown dismissed the notion that he was returning to the game to prove something. "Proving something is beside the point. I want my life to be purposeful. I want to be active and doing something I really love to do."

This was a theme Brown continually returned to when speaking with the press. A few days after sitting down with Scholl, Brown was in New York for the league meetings. During a break in the conference, Brown sat with a large group of reporters. He was visibly pleased when he entered the press room and was greeted by applause from the forty-odd reporters present. In this setting, Brown was especially garrulous. Writers from across the country listened as he talked about his time away from the game. "I felt as though I was wasting my life away," he said. "I want to warn you fellows who may be looking forward to retirement plans that you may be disappointed."[40]

A man who had kept his emotions in check for so many years was talking freely about his feelings. He was grateful for the second chance, the opportunity to bring another football team to life. There would be some rough spots at the beginning that Brown expected. "There are some things you can't hurry in life. When you try to buy in cheap, you mortgage the future."

He was back—back where he belonged, and that was all that mattered. "I was Dying by Inches," Brown said of his exile from the game. "Nothing is very important to me outside of my family and football."

# twelve  **THANK YOU, ART MODELL**

Nearly three years of planning and hard work came to fruition when the Bengals opened training camp for the 1968 season on July 6. "I'm going into this thing with my eyes wide open," Brown declared. "I feel like I've never been away."[1] Just four days earlier, he finally divested himself of his stock in the Browns. Unburdened by the past and enriched by more than a few dollars, Brown sprang into the fourth stage of his professional life with the vitality of a man a fraction of his fifty-nine years. There would be difficulties ahead, certainly. Economically, it would be a struggle for a couple of years. The lack of TV money, of course, handcuffed the franchise, as did the limitations of playing in a park that sat just 30,000 fans. In fact, money would be so tight that the plans for a scouting department Brown promised Al LoCasale months earlier had been jettisoned. Instead, Brown's youngest son Pete would work as LoCasale's assistant and the Bengal coaching staff would be doubling as the team's scouts.

—⚋—

The landscape of pro football was far different from the sport Brown entered at the close of World War II. Putting together a championship-quality club in 1945 for Cleveland was much easier than the endeavor Brown confronted in 1968. The player market was essentially wide open as the war wound to a close. The Hall of Fame-caliber athletes—Lou Groza, Otto Graham, Marion Motley, and Bill Willis—weren't available when Brown assembled his Cincinnati squad.

"The main difference is," Brown said in comparing the two eras, "I think that right after the war it was a free and open market. I was familiar with quite a few people I wanted. Groza, Graham, Motley, and Lilly . . . they weren't under contract to anybody."

Brown also discovered another change in the game, and not for the better as far as he was concerned. Even in the short span of time that had passed since his tenure in Cleveland, the advent of the player agent had drastically altered the "science" of negotiations. "Now," Brown lamented, "when you draft a boy, you get a telegram from someone saying, 'I represent so-and-so.' We never had that before."

Marty Blackman, whose agency Pro Sports Inc. represented several dozen rookies in the NFL, ran into several roadblocks when trying to negotiate contracts for his clients. Among the clubs hindering negotiations were the Bengals. "At Cincinnati," Blackman said, "Paul Brown doesn't understand. He's still thinking it's ten years ago."[2]

Blackman represented two Bengals, Paul Robinson and Les Webster. "Brown is holding to his offer on each player," the agent complained, "and he has notified the players of his refusal to release them or to permit them to negotiate with other teams."[3]

"I've never dealt with an agent and never will," Brown declared. "If a boy insists on having an agent in on the talks, we simply wish him well and send him on his way. I don't object to a boy having an agent, but I don't want to see him."

The Player's Association, just a minor irritation to Brown several years earlier, was now flexing its modest muscles. Capacity crowds greeted most league games each Sunday and television revenue was increasing at such a rate that each club received more than $1 million a year from the networks. The players recognized the financial growth spurt their sport had been enjoying and they wanted to share in the windfall. Prior to training camp, the association threatened to strike. A number of demands were issued, such as increased pay for exhibition games as well as the per diem for players when on the road. The sticking point, though, and the one issue truly worth fighting over, was a boost in pension benefits. The demands were simple, yet owners throughout the league believed their players to be selfish and unconcerned with the future of the game.

"Here they are," one team owner moaned to *Sports Illustrated,* "making an average of about $20,000 for playing a game for half a year, and they think people will have sympathy."[4]

Negotiations began on March 19 and dragged on for nearly four months. Brown was busy preparing to field a team and was not intimately involved in the talks. He was, however, watching the progress closely through the newspapers and reports from colleagues around the league. On July 14, with the first exhibition games just two weeks away, a marathon session at the Waldorf Astoria brought the labor strife to an end. A two-year agreement was the result, with owners consenting to contribute $3 million for increased pension benefits. It was a resounding success for the Player's Association. Twenty-one of the twenty-two demands made by the union were granted. Of the twenty-one issues, three were technical. Of the remaining eighteen, four were financial, four revolved around pension rights, and ten covered labor rights. The players had exhibited a new unity and militancy, a belligerence that surprised and piqued the ire of owners throughout the league. They had a new swagger now, the players did, as their talk of striking and wiping out the entire 1968 season did not appear to be an empty threat. Still, so many of the union's gains seemed elementary, such as the player's right to representation when negotiating a contract. This stipulation Brown would not abide. A few dollars more for exhibition games? OK. The league needed to kick in a bit more for the player's pension fund? Brown could accept that. But sit down with an agent? Never. He had said it before and he wasn't backing down now that it was part of the bargaining agreement. Changing times or not, nobody was getting between Brown and his players.

—※—

His methods, which worked so well in the old rah-rah days, now seemed beyond quaint; they were laughable. Long hair was the norm; facial hair, too, was in fashion. Questioning authority was the mode of the day. How would Brown connect with the youth of this era? It turned out he would communicate as he always had.

Ninety players crammed into a stuffy Wilmington classroom awaiting the arrival of Paul Brown. Those gathered had heard much of the legend. He was a cold, calculating taskmaster, a genius who suffered no fools. The prospective Bengals fidgeted in their cramped seats as Brown entered the room. Physically, Brown did not overwhelm. His lithe frame was covered in a plain white t-shirt and atop his head, a black baseball cap—Brown's typical training camp attire. What the years away from the game had stolen from Brown was not palpable by his outward appearance, which gave no evidence of aging. His weight, 160 pounds, was the same as it had been for nearly three decades. A deep tan gave his unblemished face a vigorous hue.

Brown greeted his team in a 100-seat classroom in Wilmington College's gymnasium and his lengthy discourse was dizzying in its range. "I want to do the job in Cincinnati," Brown began. "I've waited for five long years to do this, and nothing is going to interfere. We're glad to have you here. There is nobody here that we don't think can do the job. We have no pre-conceived ideas and all positions are open. If we were the Cleveland Browns and we were meeting here for the twentieth year, it would be the same way."

As the meeting wore on, Brown introduced the coaching staff, newspaper reporters, as well as the team's radio broadcasters. He then asked every player to rise from his seat, introduce himself, and tell what school he had attended. "Call me Paul," Brown continued. "You're to call your coaches by their first names. These coaches are my selections . . . my friends . . . these coaches will not swear at you. You'll be treated high grade. Pro football is not for spoiled college kids and there'll be no sugarcoating or pampering."

 Much of Brown's oration resembled his annual address at Hiram. That is not to say he ignored the changing societal times. Not a word was spoken as Brown continued in his soft tone for the better part of an hour. "I ask you to wear a sports shirt to dinner. At the table, keep the meal enjoyable. It's no place for pigs. Class always shows. Watch your language. I don't want to hear careless stuff around the locker room. Trips to Columbus, Cincinnati, and Dayton are out of bounds without permission. We'll tell you when you may leave.

"Nothing devastates a football team like a selfish player. It's like a cancer. It isn't going to take me long to recognize the tramp, the boozer, the barroom bum, the ladies man. We might be an expansion team, but we're not going to be like a French Foreign Legion. There's no room for political factions here. I don't care if you're a Republican, Democrat, black or white, Catholic, Jew, what-have-you. If you're good enough to make it you will. If you aren't, you won't. We have no quotas, no nothing. Nothing but the best players. I've waited five bloomin' years to do this, and nobody, but nobody is going to louse it up. "[5]

Before anything else, the players learned the basics. How to stand for the national anthem. How to properly huddle. The little things . . . the players burned to get on the field, but Brown knew it was the little things that made a team professional, and he wanted his team to exude professionalism. On the road, Bengal players were required to wear sport coats, a dress shirt, and a tie.

Five thousand fans were waiting when the team took the field for its first practice. The Bengal sessions were nearly identical to the practices Brown ran in Cleveland two decades earlier. That the personnel failed to execute his direction as well did not bother him. He would move slower with this group, be more deliberate in his teachings this time around. "Patience with this club is an easy virtue," Brown told writer Tex Maule. "There is no fierce pressure on you to win."[6]

As an expansion club the Bengals were permitted to begin training two weeks before the rest of the league. The extra time, necessary for a variety of reasons, was essential to pare down the roster. Before ten days had passed, ninety players became fifty and the team hadn't even scrimmaged yet. Every man was tested in four areas—intelligence, agility, speed, and ability to learn football. "There is no point scrimmaging a boy you know is not going to make your team," Brown explained. "I would rather concentrate my time on the players who will be with me during the season."[7]

The first preseason game came against the Kansas City Chiefs at Nippert Stadium. As expected, Brown's crew looked like an expansion team; the Bengals didn't get their initial first down until the third quarter. When they finally broke that barrier, the home crowd rose and gave their new team an appreciative standing ovation. Despite the 38-14 loss, Brown came away from the Bengals' first contest pleased with the effort. Three weeks later, Cincinnati faced the Pittsburgh Steelers in Morgantown, West Virginia.

That the Steelers were injury-plagued took nothing away from the Bengals' dominating 19-3 victory. Afterward, in an ecstatic locker room, Brown's baby Bengals presented him with the game ball. The gesture brought tears to Brown's eyes. For an instant, the hurt and betrayal vanished. He savored the moment before leaving his team to meet the awaiting media.

"It looks like the old man is back," Brown was overheard to murmur as he walked through the hallway to the press room.

"Welcome me back to football," Brown told the writers.

A young reporter innocuously asked, "That's your first win in five years, isn't it, Coach?

"That's right, son," Brown replied. "It's been a long time."[8]

—m—

The smiles wouldn't be so frequent in the coming months. It would be a long, tough campaign for Brown's group of rookies, misfits, and recycled veterans. During the course of a franchise's inaugural season, it goes without saying that numerous "firsts" would arise. The first regular-season game (and first loss) came Friday night, September 7, at San Diego. The first touchdown, a seven-yard Paul Robinson run, also gave the Bengals their first lead. Eight days later, Cincinnati played its first home game and earned its first victory, 24-10, against Denver.

A crush of cars and pedestrians clogged the streets of Clifton, the neighborhood where the stadium is located, prior to the home opener. The congestion caused the delay of Governor Rhodes' arrival for the pre-game ceremonies. The Bengals waited for the start of the game several hundred yards away from Nippert Stadium in the university field house. The home locker room at Nippert was sauna-like in the late summer heat. Rather than have his team exhausted in the sweltering clubhouse, Brown moved his players up the hill to the field house, while the Broncos remained in their Nippert "sweat box." Whether Brown's gamesmanship played any role in the outcome of the contest, it certainly showed his players that he was looking out for them.

Brown stoically roamed the Nippert side line in a tan summer suit and straw hat, watching his Bengals take it to the Broncos like seasoned veterans. Brown knew the victory was an aberration, that the road ahead would be filled with setbacks and failures. His chief goal in this expansion season was realizing a team concept. The wins would come in time, with good scouting, great organization, and team unity, of that Brown was certain.

As Brown led the Bengals off the field on that first home Sunday, one overly exuberant fan shouted from the stands, "On to the Super Bowl."

—⚭—

Throughout the year, Brown was the focus of media curiosity. The questions would vary, but not by much. Writers were drawn by the intriguing storyline of football's great genius returning from his enforced sabbatical. Some of the queries Brown would appear to answer by rote. Others questions, like those about the expansion draft, raised his dander each time the process was brought up. Occasionally Brown wouldn't wait to be asked; he raised the subject on his own.

"The AFL could have helped itself, and us, by a liberal 'stocking' plan. Instead, the plan was very selfish. If they want us to finish last and draft first, I guess that's the way it has to be. The NFL never would have done it."[9]

Though he risked incurring the wrath of his colleagues, Brown couldn't resist measuring the rival circuits. "The difference is in the ownership, not the players. There's no comparison in the club ownership in the two leagues."

His comments ruffled a few feathers, but Brown's actions raised the ire of the entire league. In an effort to improve the Bengals by any means available, Brown broke a "gentleman's agreement" when he put in claims on several players placed on injured waivers. All of the players in question were retained by their original teams because of the 24-hour recall rule. To some, Brown's combative move hearkened back to his halcyon days in Cleveland. Back then Brown showed little mercy on his opponents, rarely substituting when his Browns held a big lead. At the time he was asked if he considered what the rival coaches would do if he ever fielded an inferior team.

"I'll never be that bad," Brown smugly replied.

Enhancing the Bengals' roster was part of Brown's motive when he claimed those players off injured waivers, but even Al Heim admitted to the press that Brown "didn't feel he got a good shake in the allocation draft, and waivers is one method to stock the team."[10]

The mini-controversy bothered Brown not a bit. While his brand new team struggled through the season with more low spots than highlights, Brown was tickled to be in the mix again. "I just set my mind to what I'd have to go through," he reflected. "Why? I just like the life."[11]

The 1968 season concluded on an early December afternoon in frigid Shea Stadium in New York. Neither the cold, nor the 27-14 loss, dampened Brown's spirits. He sat in the visitor's locker room contemplating the Bengals' 3-11 record. "We're not displeased," an upbeat Brown said. "I felt we did what we could do. Our problem was a simple thing. When the chips were down, we didn't have the strength to do any more than we did."[12]

Sitting nearby, Dick Forbes of the *Enquirer* asked if Brown planned on coaching the team again next year. "I have no plans at present other than to stay with it until I've got the team off the ground. . . . I'll stay as coach until I believe we have the team I want, then I'll step down."

—◊—

It was a budget operation; the coaching staff served as scouts. Each man covered schools in his part of the country and recommended prospects accordingly. During the season, college contests within driving distance of the Bengals' Sunday games were scouted on Saturday, and the coaches would return to the team in time for dinner that evening. As the staff members sat down for their meal, the first words out of Brown's mouth would invariably be, "What did you see today?"

The consensus number-one pick in the 1969 collegiate draft was Southern California star running back O. J. Simpson. There was no denying Simpson's explosive talent, and Buffalo, as expected, selected the Heisman winner with the first overall pick. While Mike, Pete, and all his coaches wanted to go with Bobby Douglass, a quarterback out of Kansas,

Brown had his eye on a charismatic young man in his own backyard. Earlier in the fall, Brown attended the University of Cincinnati and Miami University game. At one point in the contest, the Redskins led 21-6, before the Bearcats came back to win the game, 23-21. Though Brown left the game early, when he heard word of the final score, Brown was convinced. "That quarterback," Brown said, speaking of the architect of the Bearcats' comeback, "that's our draft choice."

With the fifth pick in the draft the Bengals took Greg Cook, a charming and self-assured young man from Chillicothe, Ohio. Cook was presented to the press at the Bengals' Spinney Field headquarters. With his flowing blond hair and a touch of sideburns, Cook had the mod look down. "To be a quarterback you have to be confident, not cocky," Cook told the writers.  He possessed a strong, accurate arm, quick feet, and another difficult-to-demarcate quality—leadership. "My ambition?" Greg said, repeating a question back to his inquisitor. "It's just to be a football player—for my family, my team, and the city of Cincinnati."[13]

Brown had personally scouted Cook on a number of occasions during the fall and this was one draft pick Brown was certain of. "I would have drafted Greg Cook above O.J. Simpson if I had had the chance," Brown proclaimed. "Let's face it, Cincinnati is no glamour city. When we find a good youngster who really wants to play here, it makes things easier."[14]

—⁂—

On January 12, 1969, Brown attended the third championship game between the AFL and NFL. The result of the first two championship contests did little to dispel the notion that the AFL was a "Mickey Mouse" league. Short on talent, long on chutzpah; that was the conventional thinking concerning the renegade league. And in the days leading up to the game between his New York Jets and the Baltimore Colts, quarterback Joe Namath seemed full of the latter. Namath was self-assured to the point of cockiness, and the Jets' unexpected victory in the Super Bowl led credence to the belief that the AFL was ready to play on a level playing field with the venerable NFL. Along with his sons Pete and Mike, as well as an old friend, Lars Hamel, Paul Brown enjoyed watching the Jets' 16-7 victory. "I really got a kick out of it," he admitted.

Brown even took a moment and wrote a brief note to "Wilbur and Lucy" Ewbank.

"Congratulations!" Brown penned to his old friend and coach of the Jets, Weeb Ewbank. "It was a tremendous job and a wonderful thing for our football. You can be very proud."[15]

An unfortunate byproduct of the Super Bowl upset was the distinct possibility that the merger agreement would be set aside and both leagues would continue as already constituted. The Jets and their surprise victory gave some the argument that the two leagues were now on equal footing. Together, though separate. Brown heard the talk and was not pleased with the notion. "The AFL paid $18 million for the merger and to have the right to realign, and we paid millions of dollars for a franchise. You see, the joker is that there are more major cities in the NFL than in the AFL, and that's why there must be a true merger."

League owners met at the El Hotel in Palm Springs beginning March 16. The primary topic during the five-day summit was the alignment of the league's clubs once the merger went into effect for the 1970 season. Before leaving Cincinnati for California, Brown sounded a call of warning to his fellow owners. "If we don't get the realignment we were promised, we have a legal case. They can start refiguring the price of the franchise."[16]

Still, in Palm Springs a joint AFL-NFL expansion committee recommend that the two leagues maintain their exact 16-10 identity of the individual leagues, with the Bengals placed in the AFL East with Boston, Buffalo, Miami, and the New York Jets. To mollify Brown, a guarantee was made that the Bengals would play the Browns once a year. This plan would maintain ancient NFL rivalries, as well as preserve AFL ties. The rival factions would all play under the umbrella of the National Football League. Virtually all NFL owners took the proposal for granted, while the majority of AFL owners reluctantly assumed it was fait accompli. The only realignment suggested would be the NFL's agreement to play "three or four" games annually against AFL opponents.

While his colleagues in the AFL were apathetic about the proposal, Brown was adamant. He demanded what was originally promised; a complete merger, with at least three NFL teams relocating into the "AFL."

Deception—that was his interpretation of the proposal of status quo. His goal was the NFL; he'd only agreed to join the AFL because of the merger agreement. It was a matter of pride, a matter of principle to Brown. And though the Bengals were the new kids on the block, Brown wielded significant influence. "We stand on what was signed and that's tough to answer when anyone is asked how it can be any other way,"[17] Brown said. Under the election by-laws, only three AFL votes were necessary to sandbag the plan, and with some arm-twisting and politicking, Brown landed Miami's and Denver's as well as his own. With the necessary three votes in his pocket, Brown was able to bring the five-day Palm Springs meeting to a close in a deadlock.

Though Brown went to the meetings hoping there would be a resolution to the realignment debate, he came away feeling emboldened. "The thing is in a healthy position now," Brown said at the close of the confab. "The NFL people know we've been here. Our league sure changed around. I'm encouraged. We're on a fair and square track."[18]

Single-handedly, Brown had taken over a divided group of AFL owners and unified them in Palm Springs. He bonded them into a power the NFL could not ignore. Though a number of AFL men were displeased with the NFL's intention of running roughshod over the younger circuit, it took Brown's cajoling and boisterous displeasure to unite the fractured group.

When the owners met again seven weeks later at the St. Regis Hotel in New York, compromise was already on the table. Though some, like Art Modell, proclaimed they wouldn't "stand for something that would emasculate the NFL."

Beginning on May 11, 1969, at 10 A.M., the talks continued virtually uninterrupted past noon the following afternoon. Initially, conjecture had Baltimore, New Orleans, and Atlanta as the most likely franchises to relocate, with Philadelphia, St. Louis, and Minnesota also under consideration. The all-night debate tired Brown. The air was contentious, as no one wanted to be seen as a patsy in the power play. "What's in it for me?" was the outlook of more than a few men in the room. Some participants, like Lamar Hunt, dozed on the floor rather than retreat to their hotel room. Brown, however, opted to retire to his room at 10 o'clock Saturday morning for a shower and a brief nap, while Mike remained behind at the meeting. Before Paul Brown reached his room, a reporter from the *Post-Times Star* stopped him and asked for an update. "I feel like I'm in a dream. Ol' Paul isn't used to this kind of business. I'm a 10:30- 6:30 guy, but when you're fighting for your life…"

Still Brown believed a resolution was in sight. "I can't believe it won't. I think we're getting close. Nothing has been passed or approved as of now. At the moment, we're waiting for a league tax attorney to arrive."

Finally a breakthrough came later that afternoon. Cleveland agreed to move if Pittsburgh would follow, while the Rooneys were willing if Modell was. With those two key teams in accord, Rozelle then went to Carroll Rosenbloom and convinced the Baltimore owner to bring his Colts to the newly named American Football Conference. There were stipulations; Pittsburgh and Cleveland had to be in the same division to make relocation more palatable to their fans. Baltimore, meanwhile, wanted to be placed in the same division as the Jets to avenge their Super Bowl loss.* The commissioner took these terms back to the AFL, who were pleased with the proposal. One owner was something more than pleased; the result of the thirty-six-hour meeting was more than Brown could have hoped for. The Bengals would be in the same division as the Steelers, a natural geographic rival, and the Browns!

An exhausted Paul Brown emerged from the marathon session elated with the result. "I have fulfilled one ambition I had here—to bring National League football into Cincinnati. This is a great day for the Brown clan. It went beyond our fondest hopes.[19]

"Our realignment is really great," Brown enthused. "Our Midwest is our Midwest, our East is our East, and our West is our West. Geographically, they all fit in a nice picture.

"We'll be playing two games with Cleveland and two with Pittsburgh each year, plus three against teams in the other conference. That means we'll be playing seven games a year against present NFL teams"

As the results of the St Regis summit reached the press, many participants were giving the credit for brokering the conciliation to Brown. His leadership and persistence forced a compromise. At breakfast the next morning, Brown's colleagues and adversaries came to offer congratulations. He single-handedly led the coup; the victory was Brown's. "There was only one complete winner," one owner admitted. "He was Paul Brown. You might say Paul Brown won the war."

—⚌—

During the Palm Spring meetings, Al Davis asked for permission to speak with Al LoCasale. Brown recognized LoCasale's personal need to do less traveling, as well as his desire to return to the West Coast. LoCasale's stay with the Bengals was brief, but his two college drafts were fruitful. Paul Robinson won the AFL Rookie of the Year and Bob Johnson proved worthy of the club's first overall selection. The Bengals even got quality lower in the draft; twelfth-round pick Bob Trumpy, a tight end out of Utah, earned a starting spot on the team. The 1969 draft looked equally promising. In addition to Cook, at the suggestion of Robin Brown the Bengals selected middle linebacker Bill Bergey out of Arkansas State. And in the sixth round, the team picked Ken Riley, a cornerback from Florida A&M.

Though Brown was reluctant to excuse LoCasale from his contract, he believed he had a very capable replacement lined up. The scouting department would now be headed by Brown's youngest son Pete. It was a family affair in Cincinnati, but sadly, a key component to the clan was missing.

For years Katy was the strength of the Brown family, the support system for Paul, Robin, Mike, and Pete. She was always there for her boys. Be it basketball, football, or baseball, Katy attended all their games that Paul missed because of his coaching obligations. And then, in the few years following their move from Cleveland, as Katy's health deteriorated rapidly, Paul was there for her. Diabetes had all but taken her sight, and

Katy needed assistance with even the simplest task. Just a few months earlier, during the Bengals' first training camp, many observers were taken by the image of Paul helping his Katy every day in the cafeteria. Finding her a seat, getting their food, and then patiently feeding his bride, the scene was touching and heartbreaking all at once.

And so, when her death came on Sunday, April 13, it was not unexpected. Still, the loss shook Paul to the core. Paul was by Katy's side at LaJolla's Scripps Memorial Hospital when her weakened heart finally gave out. Katy was only 59.

Paul brought her home to Massillon, where the funeral services were held at Katy's church, St. Timothy's. As to be expected, Paul was devastated by the loss. The vision of the emotionally unwavering Brown so grief-stricken was startling to observers, as Brown needed help making his way down the aisle to his pew. Few in the Bengal family had the opportunity to know Katy well in the brief time the Browns were in Cincinnati. But so many friends from Cleveland, Columbus, and Massillon came to pay respect and remember a lady adored by all who met her.

On Friday, July 11, 1969, Brown pulled his white sedan into its parking space behind the dormitory that served as the Bengals' summer home. There the car would remain for the next seven weeks. Oh, there might be a trip into town on occasion, perhaps for a haircut. There was no time for frivolity; all focus was now on our football.

Of course there was the annual address at the opening of camp.

"I won't stand for any Bolsheviks on my team. We weed them out fast. Anybody who doesn't want to be here won't be. We care. We care very much, about each other and about our purpose."[20]

His days began at 6:30 A.M. There was breakfast at the student union, then back to the dormitory's conference hall, where he met with his coaches at 8:15. A topic of discussion covered in these meetings was personnel decisions. Roster cuts were never made on the spur of the moment. "We all sleep on it," Brown explained. Final decisions were announced after the coaches met. Individuals being released were brought to Brown, who personally delivered the bad news. "It is a task I've despised for twenty years, but it is the job of the head coach. No one else."

Showing the kids how it's done.

"Bolshevik"—it was a new addition to Brown's lexicon. The changing times, long hair, draft-resistors, political dissenters. Brown wanted none of this brought into his locker room.

"I'm only interested in men willing to pay a price. And by paying a price I'm referring to how much importance you give to our football team. . . . We're looking for professionals. Real professionals. We don't want you to look like old pros. We want you to look like a bunch of young, eager, go-getters."

Each afternoon at Wilmington, Brown would gather his young go-getters before sending them onto the practice field. Brown would momentarily speak to the team as they pulled on their shoes and helmets. Again, later in the evening, Brown and his assistants made their way to Herman

Paul Brown (right) with Buffalo Bills general manager Bob Lustig, 1969.

Court gymnasium, where Brown spoke to his players once more.

Brown was pleased with his team's progress. Training camp was a success, and on the field in their exhibition games the Bengals were beginning to look like a team to be bargained with. Against Pittsburgh in their third exhibition game, Cook stalwartly stood in the pocket as the Steelers blitzed time and time again. Nothing seemed to faze him as he led the Bengals to a 25-13 triumph over Pittsburgh, which was followed with a victory over Denver to close out the exhibition schedule with three consecutive wins. The young quarterback left Brown with a difficult decision. Should he play it safe and go once again with John Stofa? Or start the season with the rookie Greg Cook behind center? After minimal deliberation, Brown and his staff opted to go with youth. It was a risk, having a rookie lead his team, but Brown saw nothing but the upside in choosing Cook over Stofa. Certainly the kid would have his missteps, but Brown recognized the Bengals' future was tied to Cook's right arm.

And oh, that future did look bright.

The Bengals reeled off three straight victories against Miami, San Diego, and Kansas City to start the season. "We're young and exuberant and we don't know any better,"[21] Brown said, explaining away the early success.

"If he stays with it, I've got myself another Otto Graham," Brown gushed, speaking of his young quarterback. "He just doesn't play like a rookie. He is no ordinary man."[22] Against San Diego, Cook passed for 327 yards and three touchdowns. Justifiably, Brown was enthralled by Cook's early performance. "[He's] a thinking quarterback. He's cool and he's smart."

Sure, it's easy to warm to a fella who's leading your team to victory, but Cook's effervescent personality was impossible for the dour genius from the "Lake Erie shore" to resist.

One afternoon, Cook burst into the locker room with breaking news. "Hey Coach," Greg called out to Brown, "I just had my hair cut."[23]

"Where?" Brown asked with an easy smile.

Following each Bengal touchdown, Cook would race to the sideline and shake hands with Brown. "Since Paul called the play," Greg reasoned, "I had to believe it was a good call and that he deserved to be congratulated.[24]

"He's a football scientist. If I have any poise on the field, it's because I know he's on the bench. He's my security."[25]

Brown showed great patience with his young prodigy. Mistakes were few, but when Cook had an on-field breakdown, Brown would greet him on the sideline and ask for his analysis of the failure. "He is strong, and smart, and he enjoys the game," Brown told the *Los Angeles Times*. "I would think that two or three years from now Cook might be quite a football player. . . .We were more spirited as a result of his success and I think we've played our best game. I think really the main thing is that we're becoming interesting."[26]

The sky, seemingly, was the limit. The future knew no bounds . . . and then the Bengals played Kansas City in the seventh game of the season. In the fourth quarter of that contest, Cook rolled out to pass. Just as he let go of the ball he was sandwiched between Bobby Bell and Willie Lanier of the Chiefs. As he fell to the turf, his right shoulder was driven into the unforgiving playing surface. The severity of Cook's injury was not immediately determined, but he did miss the next three games, all Bengal losses. He came back, maybe too soon. Some of the zip was missing from his balls, but he could still lead his team. Cincinnati defeated Oakland 31-17 in the season's eighth game and followed that victory with a tie in Houston the following week with Cook tossing four touchdown passes.

After the Oiler game, the Bengals' record stood at 4-4-1, impressive for a second-year club. A reporter asked Brown how far he thought his young team could go. Standing nearby was Brown's enthusiastic quarter-back. "As far as I can take the old coach,"[27] Cook chimed in.

The season went sour, however. The Bengals closed the year with five consecutive losses. "I really can't guess how many games we might have won if Cook had been sound all year, but it's probably best we didn't have more success. At this stage of our development we need a good position in the draft."[28]

Following the season-ending game at Mile High Stadium, Brown looked on the bright side. "As I've said 100 times, this thing is just a matter of time," Brown said from his office his feet comfortably propped up on a desk. "You can't hurry it. We had a few games this year when we looked like a good football team, and it's been a better year. We're on our way."[29]

Four victories was a modest achievement, but Brown believed they were on the right course. They were taking some lumps going with the kids, but Brown wasn't wavering. "We're building and we won't mortgage our future in any way."[30]

The press recognized the improvement made in Cincinnati. Brown was named the AFL's coach of the year, while Greg Cook was given the league's offensive rookie of the year award.

—⁓—

Eight months after the drawn-out battle over realignment, the deal was still not ratified. The problem wasn't the three NFL clubs moving over to the AFC. Rather, the dispute was waged on how the divisions broke down in their 4-4-5 alignment. Petty bickering and self-interest seemed to be the rule when football owners gathered. When all sides finally agreed on a suitable alignment, Brown was a part of the committee that brokered the solution. Once again he found himself immersed in league politics.

Brown left LaJolla for Hawaii on March 7, 1970, where he joined a four-man committee. The directive of the group was to discuss a number of topics prior to a gathering of all owners. The topics were varied, from the possible use of a two-point play following touchdowns, as was done in the AFL, to the site of the '71 Super Bowl whether players' names should be on the backs of their jerseys as they were in the AFL, and scouting arrangements in relation to colleges. But the most pressing concern facing the league was a looming labor catastrophe.

Several months later, on July 12, the NFL owners reconvened. This time it was a "secret" meeting in Chicago. At this gathering, an agreement was reached by a vote of 24-1 to lock out veteran players from training camp. This decision was made in reaction to a communication by the Player's Association, which instructed veterans not to report to camp. The only team voting in dissent of the motion was the Cincinnati Bengals.

The following day, the Bengals opened training in Wilmington with only rookies and free agents who had not yet played a regular-season game on hand. When Brown arrived at his room in Pickett Hall he found a plaque positioned on the wall. "Coach Paul Brown and his wife Katy occupied this room during the summer of 1968," an inscription read. "This was the last summer Paul and Katy were together. . . . All this which now we see is but the childhood of eternity."

The pleasant memories of those days warmed Brown's heart, but the labor strife that was currently plaguing the game grieved him. "The very structure [of the game] is being threatened now by a group of young men who will regret it all their life.[31]

"I am deeply concerned with the development that has taken place as we prepare to start this season. . . . Many great players and coaches have dedicated themselves over the years to building what we have today. The things these people stood for, which meant success, are now being threatened by those who would tear it down.

"They do so by attacking the power of the commissioner. He has contributed tremendously to the present state of the game and the players themselves. They are attacking the powers and right of the head coach to be in control of his team."[32]

The issues dividing management and labor were not insurmountable, though it was interesting that Brown inferred that the powers of the head coach were being infringed upon. Nothing in the players' demands involved diminishing the authority of the coach. The primary disagreement centered on the amount ownership would contribute to the pension fund. There were other, ancillary issues. The players wanted Rozelle "legally aligned" on the side of the owners. It would divide the game into two camps, the owners and the commissioner on one side, and the players on the other. This point was non-negotiable. However, the commissioner would continue to rule over the game and the influence held by the office would not be diminished.

The previous winter, Pete Rozelle negotiated a new television contract, which enriched the owner's coffers by $188 million. The players wanted their fair share of this ever-enlarging pie. Brown found all of the players' demands and petition for a bigger piece of the financial boon distasteful. "It's an old, old story—management is always the bad guy," Brown griped from his office in Wilmington. "It's down to a point now where the only thing they want is more money."[33]

Hell, the players were even requesting a $12 per diem for each day spent at training camp. "It's simply a tax dodge," Brown complained. "When you get paid per diem, its non-taxable. It's just another way of getting money." Besides, Brown said, the only expenses the players have at camp are for "toothpaste and shaving cream."[34]

The league had never been in better shape. The merger was to take effect with the coming season. Television revenue was soaring at an incredible rate. Interest in the NFL product had grown to such a point that some observers believed football, not baseball, could now rightfully be called the "national pastime." Still, Brown argued, if management conceded anything, all these improvements would be stifled.

"We were told late last week that negotiations were making good progress. Suddenly, a new militancy has been thrust into the negotiations and the future of our game is at a critical point."

The impasse lasted more than two weeks. Finally, on the evening of July 29, the owners decided to end the lockout. The Player's Association, meanwhile, advised its members not to report. For their part, the Bengals sent a wire to each of their forty-two veterans.

—⚏—

"The Player's Association has been advised that we are opening training camp at 6 P.M. Thursday evening, July 30 to any player wishing to report.

"The Association has stated publicly that it has not called a strike. Therefore, we expect the Association to advise you to live up to your individual contract."

—⚏—

The ball was now in the players' court. Speaking to Dick Forbes of the *Enquirer,* Brown wanted to emphasize that he wouldn't intimidate the Bengals to report. "If a player feels he doesn't want to report and wants to go to work, we have no hard feelings," Brown said.

Brown's implication was clear—football, as an occupation, was not a laborious endeavor. If any Bengals weren't happy with their lot in life as professional football players, then he wouldn't hold them back from entering the work force and getting a real job. And though Brown expected the majority of his players to show up, he admitted he could end up surprised. "I might get a jolt and none will show up." If that was the case, he stated, "We'll have to cancel the season or start canceling games."[35]

This wasn't an idle threat on Brown's part. The Bengals had much riding on the upcoming season. A new stadium, which opened June 30 when the Reds played the Braves, awaited the team, with 49,000 season tickets already sold. And 1970 would be the first season Cincinnati shared in the league's television revenues. Still, Brown implied the difference between the Bengals showing a profit or a loss was the preseason games.

"The money earned in the regular season is almost entirely taken up by player salaries. We can't topple the whole sport for the sake of the few in leadership of the football union. I think most of the players are beginning to realize that their own best interests are not being looked after by their player representatives. It just doesn't make any sense for so many to be hurt by so few."

The solidarity of Cincinnati players with the association was wavering as July came to a close. On the afternoon of the thirtieth, sixteen Bengal veterans met at Princeton High School in suburban Cincinnati to work out on their own. The club's unofficial spokesman, quarterback Sam Wyche, was speaking for a number of his teammates when he told the *Dayton Daily News,* "I can only give you my personal opinion, but I know that I'm going to vote to go to camp. And I'm pretty sure most of the other players feel the same way."[36]

Initially up to forty-two Bengal veterans were going to disregard the Player's Association and report to Wilmington. The possibility of retaliation on the playing field prevented these men from defying the association.

What was a lockout now became a strike.

—⁓—

Following a meeting of player representatives in Chicago, Bengals player rep Ernie Wright met with Brown in Wilmington to report the results of the session. A poll of Bengal veterans revealed that twenty-two men voted to back the union, while four vets wanted to report to camp. The remaining sixteen vets not present all agreed to follow along with the majority. Wright arrived in Wilmington at 12:45 P.M. and stayed closeted with Brown until 1:45. After Wright left, Brown called his assistants into his office. With his veterans toeing the association's line, Brown made the decision he had vowed for three weeks he would not do. He sent the fifteen rookies home and closed camp at Wilmington. Usually verbose and open with the Bengal beat writers, Brown was unusually subdued when speaking with reporters. "We have no choice but to send the rookies home and break camp," he said.

"It's a sad day, but we have no choice but to abandon our operation here.

"Football is like no other team sport," Brown continued. "It takes a long time to attune the split-second timing so necessary to success. What we are presented with now, apparently, is whether we want to offer the public an inferior product."

The first exhibition game was just eight days away and, if those contests had to be canceled, Brown wanted the owners to rescind their offer to the players' pension "because of the change in the financial structure of the clubs due to the loss of income."[37]

Trainer Marv Pollins and equipment manager Tom Gray began packing the team's effects and shipped everything back to Spinney Field. Within a few hours all trace of the Cincinnati Bengals football club had vanished from Wilmington College. As he prepared to jump in his car for the ride south to Cincinnati, Brown had a few final words for the reporters sending him off. "We just assume this is it," a forlorn Brown said. "What else can I say?"

Brown spent the next few days flying between Cincinnati and New York, as the league desperately tried to find a solution to the crisis. The loss of sleep paid off for Brown when an accord was finally reached on August 3. The players had been asking for $25.8 million in pension funds, while the owners offered $18.1 million. They settled on $19.1 million. The four-year contract increased preseason pay and per diem for players, while all the powers of the commissioner's office remained intact. Rozelle only relinquished authority in cases involving injury grievances to an arbiter.

Players arrived at Spinney Field following a settlement between the NFLPA and the league's owners, leaving just four days for the Bengals to prepare for the Redskins and their first game at Riverfront Stadium.

"I know what you hear from your teammates, and what you read in the paper, but this is the truth," Brown told his players.

"Where does that come from?" a player asked.

"It comes from the teletype, from the league office." The notion was simple; it was the truth, as Brown saw it. Everything was black or white.

To prepare for Washington, Brown had his men go through three-a-days, at 9 A.M., 1 P.M., and 7 P.M. They needed to work quickly and efficiently to be ready for the Redskins, but Brown ran into yet another disruption to his plans.

A treaty may have been reached, but the fallout from negotiations was still being felt. An obviously angry Brown talked with reporters in his Spinney Field office. Brown had just received word from the commissioner's office that Rozelle was giving players directly involved in negotiations permission to not report until the weekend. This decision set Brown off. "Rozelle gave these people additional days off and I don't like it. I take strong exception to the commissioner giving any of my players days off. It hurts our team, our morale, and it's not good. It's just another sign of the times."

Ernie Wright, the 31-year-old left tackle, was the Bengal excused by Rozelle, which forced Brown to alter his plans for the upcoming contest with Washington.

"We've had the rug pulled out from under us by our own league office. You can't put any football player in a special category and have morale. It won't work."

—⚭—

Greg Cook checked in at Spinney Field with bated breath. The right arm that held the hopes of the Bengal franchise suffered yet another injury in the off-season. While playing in a pickup basketball game Cook aggressively went up for a rebound. An opponent also going for the ball accidentally grabbed Cook's shoulder from behind. The incident further damaged Cook's arm. Six months of placidity did nothing to heal the injury. At Spinney he took to the field and immediately knew something was seriously wrong. He couldn't throw the ball without severe pain. Obviously, resting the arm wasn't the answer, and so, after a visit to an orthopedic surgeon, Cook underwent surgery to fix the impairment.

Following the procedure, Brown was assured that Cook's shoulder was repaired. The doctor conducting the surgery was "optimistic" but also revealed the quarterback faced a lengthy rehabilitation and definitely would not be available for the upcoming season.

"Only time and maybe some magic healing powers will tell," Brown said. "Meanwhile, we won't go into any game with a losing attitude."[38] Replacing Cook behind center was Virgil Carter. Realizing that Cook was unavailable, the Bengals luckily latched onto Carter, who was acquired off waivers just two weeks before the 1970 season began. Carter was on the market because his "sassy backtalk" to George Halas got him chased from the Bears.

Since obtaining the Cincinnati franchise, Brown had been asked periodically about a future matchup with the Cleveland Browns. Initially, the question was purely hypothetical, but once the merger realignment was ratified, nearly every interviewer broached the enticing topic. Brown's reply was always the same, "I can't lose. They're both my teams." He was nothing if not diplomatic. When asked if he harbored any animosity toward the Cleveland franchise, Brown had a perfunctory reply: "Bitter people bore me."

D.L. Stewart, a twenty-five-year-old reporter for the *Dayton Daily News*, had grown up a Cleveland Browns fan and introduced himself to Brown as such. In the course of the conversation, Stewart mentioned a book, *Return to Glory*. Published shortly after the Browns captured the 1964 world championship, the book covered the team's history up to that point. While by no means a hatchet job on Brown, *Return to Glory* did not portray Brown in a completely favorable light.

Brusquely, Brown interrupted Stewart, saying, "I have not read that book."

Stewart picked up on the point he was trying to make, and again Brown interrupted. "Young man, I have not read that book."

The reporter attempted to ask a question. "What lessons did you learn…" Stewart was cut off before he finished the sentence.

"I know what you're trying to do, young man, and I'm not going into that stuff."

Indeed, bitter people bored Brown, but he couldn't deny the fire inside himself that burned to beat Cleveland, to beat Modell, to beat Collier. Eight long years had passed.

The first opportunity came when the Bengals met the Browns at Riverfront for their third exhibition contest. As usual, Brown was smartly attired in a striped blazer, gray slacks, and white shirt set off by a blue tie. His own ensemble wasn't on Brown's mind, however, as he surveyed the playing field. A bittersweet twinge overtook Brown and tugged at his emotional reserve as he saw the familiar Cleveland uniforms . . . for a moment. And then he remembered. Just a few yards away from Brown stood Blanton Collier. Tradition dictated that the home coach initiate greetings with his visiting opposite, but Brown made no move to acknowledge Collier.

After apathetic performances in their first two preseason games, the Bengals appeared to be heading for a third consecutive poor outing when Cleveland jumped off to a 14-0 lead in the first quarter. Brown paced the sideline in stone silence. Brown's young Bengals, however, did not lie down for the more experienced Cleveland squad. The final score, a 31-24 Cincinnati victory, overjoyed Brown. "A football team may have been born tonight. We discovered what the spirit of the occasion can do," Brown said afterward. "This will help us tremendously."[39]

Bob Johnson presented an appreciative Brown the game ball. "This one, fellas, I'll keep."

At the end of the game, Collier walked to midfield for a customary handshake with Brown. However, Brown made no move toward Collier and instead headed straight for the Bengal locker room. The snub was noticed by many in attendance who were waiting to see how Brown would react to his old friend. The Cleveland media picked up on Brown's cold shoulder and played up the brush-off in the days leading up to the first regular season game between Cincinnati and Cleveland. When questioned about the incident, Brown dismissed the controversy. It was AFL tradition, he claimed, for the coach to leave the field with his team.

Cleveland was at 2-1, while Cincinnati sported a record of 1-2 as the two clubs prepared to meet in the fourth week of the regular season. Brown addressed the matter. "You newspaper people are always trying to build up this Cincinnati-Cleveland game as some kind of personal grudge match. You people just can't realize how much water has gone over the dam since I left,"[40] Brown said, addressing the "rivalry." A lot of water had passed over the dam, but the hurt feelings remained. When speaking of his old team, Brown always said Cleveland. When plural was necessary it was Clevelands, never Browns.

Brown emerged from the visitors' dugout forty-five minutes before the game and headed directly for the Bengals' bench. Coming directly toward Brown at midfield was Collier, who began calling out Brown's name. When Brown reached the fifty-yard line he turned and approached his old friend. In front of a mostly empty stadium, Brown and Collier shook hands and amicably discussed the hullabaloo surrounding the last "meeting." There were a few moments of small talk and mutual agreement that too much was made over all this handshake stuff. And then Brown was back to business.

Following the 30-27 Cleveland victory, Brown again followed AFL custom and trotted off the field with his players, much to the displeasure of the hometown crowd. Boos rained down from Municipal Stadium's stands as Brown once again gave Collier the cold shoulder. The handshake controversy overshadowed the Cleveland win to some extent, as Brown was peppered with questions once again about the clamor. "I haven't [shaken hands following a game] for years, and Blanton knows this. I haven't done it since the league sent out a directive many years ago, back when I was still here, that practice should be eliminated. You never know when someone is going to take a swing at you.[41]

"Blanton understands, and that's all I care about."[42]

One month later, the two teams clashed once again. A record Cincinnati sports crowd of 60,007 watched as the Bengals dug themselves an early hole. Cleveland had a 10-0 lead three minutes into the second quarter. As they had earlier in the summer, though, the Bengals did not quit. Paul Robinson's one-yard touchdown run late in the third quarter gave the Bengals a 14-10 lead, a score that held up until the final gun.

Brown merrily waved his hat above his head as he led his team off the field with a half-dance, half-prance. And in the locker room Brown struggled to keep his emotions in check when presented with the game ball. His eyes moistened and tears trickled down his cheek as he thanked his team for their effort. A collegiate mood swept through the clubhouse as nearly every Cincinnati player expressed his wish to win the game for Brown.

Brown had to take leave of his team to meet his obligation with the press. Encircled by writers, Brown tried in vain to hide his feelings.

"Was this your best victory, Paul?" he was asked.

Brown looked up from the floor to his questioner and answered softly, "This is my best victory."

"For all time?" another writer posed.

"Since you asked it," Brown replied, "I'm talking about it all. This is the best victory of all. It made coming back worthwhile."[43] Three days later, on November 18, Brown appeared on Phil Samp's radio show. Still riding high from the win over Cleveland, Brown took the opportunity to take several verbal swipes at his former employer.

"I would guess that the move was dictated from the top," Brown told Samp, referring to the trade of Paul Warfield for the right to draft quarterback Mike Phipps. The transaction was not popular among Browns' fans, and Brown implied that Phipps was used against the Bengals in order to justify the trade.

"I think they thought if they could use Phipps and win the game, it would be sort of vindication for the deal.

"After the game, the owner of the club circulated the word that Phipps did well. Scoring only ten points isn't much of a vindication. That's the Browns' hangup. [It] really makes it kind of a tough sell. . . . This is the kind of thing that happens when non-football people decide they know how to run a football team."

Modell, of course, had to respond to Brown's stinging comments. "How sad it is that a man can be that embittered after so many years,"[44] Modell said to Chuck Heaton

Sportswriters lived for verbal skirmishes of this nature. Modell's words, of course, were carried to Brown for comment, but Brown had had enough. "It will serve no purpose to pursue this thing," he said from Spinney Field as the Bengals practiced before him. "I just stand on what I said, and that's it."[45]

—ɯ—

The 1970 Bengals followed an opening-week win over Oakland with six consecutive losses. At 1-6 Cincinnati was all but counted out of the Central Division race. "What I like about this team is that it never quits," Brown said following the victory over Cleveland. "I like November teams, teams that comeback later, that just don't quit." That win placed the Bengals at 3-6, an unexceptional record, but in the weak AFC Central, that was good enough to be just one game out of first place behind Cleveland and Pittsburgh. Ridiculous as it may have seemed for a team that had lost twice as many games as it had won, Cincinnati began thinking about winning a division title. They followed the old axiom, and the Bengals took it one week at a time. And victory followed victory. The Bengals had won five consecutive games as they came home to finish out the regular season against the Boston Patriots.

—ɯ—

"Thank you Art Modell," read a banner hanging from the upper deck.

There was more gratitude after the Bengals rolled over Boston 45-7, finishing the season 8-6 and winning the division title. "We're number one," Cincinnati fans chanted as Bengal players carried Brown from the field on their shoulders. The chant continued for more than ten minutes. "We're number one." The record was underwhelming, but a Central Division championship was earned nonetheless. The Bengals had only played three teams with winning records, and those games all came early in the year. Easy schedule or not, Brown's enthusiasm was not dampened. "I left Cleveland under the cover of darkness with the same record," Brown observed in the locker room. "I'm not saying that bitterly, I'm a happy man."

Reporters strained to hear Brown as he softly spoke. "Personally, this is my little dream come true. I didn't know we could do this well. . . . This has been the most interesting and most gratifying season I've known."[46]

The Bengals had just six days, including Christmas, to prepare for their first-ever playoff game. Their opponents, the Baltimore Colts, were

Walking off the field in Buffalo.

led by veteran Johnny Unitas. And, as one writer quipped, between Paul Brown and Johnny U, they'll be calling all the plays in the contest.

From the team's hotel in Baltimore, Brown declared, "We're having a Merry Christmas. We're in the spirit. I was just thinking today, in fact, that the two big reasons we've come this far are luck and spirit. . . . They may be too young to be knowledgeable, but they're enthusiastic. Every day is Christmas."

Brown kept perspective despite his high spirits. "I think it's obvious we're over our heads in Baltimore," he acknowledged. Indeed, the Bengals were overmatched against the Colts. The game was played the day after Christmas in front of Baltimore's first non-sellout in fifty-one games. Baltimore had more talent and more experience and it showed on the field as well as the scoreboard. Played out in a biting cold on Memorial Stadium's dusty surface, the Colts marched to a relatively easy 17-0 win.

They had come further quicker than any expansion team had gone before, and though the loss to Baltimore stung, the sense of achievement among Bengal players and coaches was great. A pleasant surprise greeted the team at Greater Cincinnati airport when they arrived home from Baltimore later that same Saturday evening. Six hundred fans were on hand to welcome their heroes.

"Attaboy champs," someone shouted as the Bengals descended the aircraft stairs. "We still love you."

A couple of months later, the twenty-six owners gathered once again in Palm Springs for their annual March meeting. The game was enjoying unparalleled success, commissioner Rozelle revealed as he addressed team representatives. More fans than ever before were watching the NFL in person at the stadium or at home on their couch. Television revenues continued to grow, and this proliferation showed no signs of abating. Super Bowl V, Rozelle said, was viewed in 29 million homes—more than any other sporting event. Prosperity, however, breeds its own brand of tribulations.

"Success always brings attacks and investigations from all sides in the climate of our country today," lamented Brown. "We are now seeing attacks on individual clubs, attacks on the league as a whole, and this imposes bigger and bigger burdens. The cost of legally defending the clubs and the league against these things keeps spiraling."

With a degree of resignation, Brown added, "There's not much you can do about it, I guess."[47]

Brown lived for the game on Sunday, for planning strategy, and preparing personnel. The off-the-field politics, there wasn't pleasure in all that, but it was imperative that Brown keep abreast of league affairs. Control was a primary consideration. Brown wielded his influence in league issues. Any owner who did not actively campaign for his personal issue would be run roughshod by his colleagues. Protecting his team, his investment, his family's welfare, all these considerations drove Brown when dealing with league business.

—◊—

Brown stepped into the lecture room carrying with him a tattered manila file. Inside the folder were several pages that contained the address he'd given his men at the start of every camp. In front of Brown sat ninety overgrown men, stuffed into cramped wooden chairs, absently listening to Brown's windy discourse. Some of these Bengals players, who'd sat through the talk just a handful of times, had newfound respect for Louie Groza. "My God," they said to one another, "Groza sat through this shit sixteen times."

But to Brown, this talk was a ritual, as vital as conditioning, practice, and classroom lessons. Political strife and civil unrest were dominating the headlines, but Brown emphasized that social issues had no place in his locker room. Discussion of politics would only divide a clubhouse and build hostility between teammates.

"I want you men to realize that whenever you have any questions or complaints, there's no one you can go to but me. I had to have it that way before I returned to pro football. I'm not saying this in a bragging or bulldozing way. I just want you to know that there's no way for you to circumvent my powers."

The talk continued for ninety minutes. "Just remember that everything you do reflects on you as a person and on the Bengals as a team. We may be a young team, but we're going to be brought up right."[48]

—⁓—

Following practice on August 12, Brown held his usual meeting with the press in his office. The regular attendees were there: Marty Williams from the *Dayton Daily News,* Barry Cobb of the *Post,* and Dick Forbes from the *Enquirer,* as well as Al Heim and Mort Sharnik of *Sports Illustrated.* Brown's informal gab sessions with the media were traditionally opened to any member of the media who decided to drop by. This day was different, though. The NFL office had informed Brown that a freelance writer from New York had checked in to the Denver House Hotel in Wilmington.

"I'm Leonard Schecter," a short, stocky man said, as he offered his hand to Brown. Schecter was part of a new breed of sportswriters. He would dig for information rather than take what was given to him. Most famously, Schecter was the co-author along with Jim Bouton of the best-selling baseball memoir, *Ball Four.* In recent years Schecter had profiled several of Brown's friends in football. This was the work that concerned Brown.

Once everyone was seated, Brown looked directly at the newcomer. "Mr. Schecter, are you the one who wrote the article on Vince Lombardi?"

"Yes I am," Schecter replied. "In *Esquire.*"

Brown's eyes narrowed and settled intently on Schecter. "You also wrote the story on Al Davis in *Look*"?

"Yes," the writer replied.

"You're also the one who wrote the article on Pete Rozelle in *Time,*" Brown continued, seemingly aware of Schecter's entire body of work. Leaning back in his chair, Brown continued, "I just want you to know I'm not interested in anything like that pertaining to our football team. I know I can't help what you do to me, but my team is something else."

The writer tried to interject, but Brown interrupted. "I'm not finished yet. Lombardi was a credit to the game," Brown stated. "He literally died for pro football and that article was uncalled for."

But, Schecter offered, "the man is dead now, and I'm not defending him," he said, explaining his work. "I was just trying to present a different point of view."

Brown, unhappy with the response, cut off the writer in mid-sentence. "No, no deal," Brown said in his even-keeled voice. Rising from his seat, Brown opened the door, "OK, leave. I don't have that much time left, and I will not allow you to hurt our football team. That's just the way it is."

Quietly and without rancor, Schecter walked out, but before parting he had one last word for Brown. "If that's the case, then I'll leave. But I don't think you should censor what is written."

Brown closed the door behind Schecter and returned to his place behind the desk. "OK," Brown said to the remaining scribes, "fire away."[49]

The confrontation garnered national headlines. Some columnists derided Brown. He always had bullied the press, and this latest incident was just the most extreme example of his dictatorial ways. Who was he to censor what a writer printed? He didn't have to approve of Schecter's work to give him access. This was an issue of freedom of the press, some argued. "I don't tell Coach Brown how to coach football," Schecter told a representative of the Associated Press. "I would expect that he not tell me so how to write and report it.[50]

"I think the media in this country should stick together on issues like this or, by heaven, they will, indeed, hang separately."

Nothing, within reason, was beyond the boundaries of this new journalism. A fight in the locker room wasn't off limits. A scuffle on the practice field was fodder for Schecter and writers of his ilk. To Brown, moments like these were sacrosanct. Telling tales of these "private" episodes was an invasion of "our football." At each of his stops through the years, Brown befriended at least one writer who shared his values and sensibilities. Massillon had Luther Emery, in Columbus Paul Hornung; in Cleveland it was Chuck Heaton and before him, Whitey Lewis. And, in Cincinnati, Dick Forbes filled the role. To this point, Brown had gotten a free pass in Cincinnati, and understandably so. The fact that the Bengals were an expansion team and were permitted time to mature, and the early success of winning a division title bought the club goodwill. But only Brown's apologist with the *Enquirer,* Forbes, defended Brown's encounter with Schecter. To Forbes, Schecter's style of reporting was "dirty journalism," though his editor at the *Enquirer,* Jim Schottelkotte, took umbrage at Brown's impudent action.

"In effect, by encouraging attendance of those he thinks will write favorable things and discouraging those who might not," Schottelkotte penned, "Brown is, as Schecter charged, exercising a form of censorship. . . . If you don't write favorable things about Paul Brown and the Bengals, you can anticipate the possibility that you will be excluded from the Bengals' press conference and your access to news sources ended."[51]

Brown's response to the debate was straightforward if not broadminded. "I don't have an obligation to be interviewed if it doesn't serve the interest of our club," he said. Censorship, self-preservation, it all depended on one's point of view, and the only point of view that concerned Brown was his own.

As they had done since the day Brown announced that he was bringing professional football to Cincinnati, sportswriters surmised how much longer Brown would coach. A report out of Cleveland had Brown retiring before the 1971 season. This was news to Brown. In fact, he was closer to stepping aside a year earlier, when labor troubles spoiled the summer, than he was now. After the surprise 8-6 showing by his Bengals, Brown was eager to see how they could follow up on that success.

"After winning that division championship last year," Brown said, "this probably would be a good time for me to take a fancy exit. Around the league, I've heard it said that some people believe we 'overachieved.' That's a pretty good word, but it is possible. . . . But despite what we did, I don't feel it's been built in a completely competitive way yet. That's the reason why I'm not quitting."[52]

—⁂—

By frequently parroting his "overachieving" line, Brown played down expectations for the Bengals. And when Virgil Carter suffered a separated shoulder in the third week of the 1971 season, any chance of repeating as division champs went out the window. With Greg Cook still on the shelf with his bum shoulder, the quarterbacking duties for the Bengals fell to rookie Kenny Anderson. But four wins was all Cincinnati could muster behind the inexperienced signal-caller. Even in light of Brown's repeated words of caution, the campaign was a letdown.

"We paid dearly for our quick success last season by being forced to draft in the sixteenth position," complained Brown. "That's by far the highest draft any third-year team ever had to take. That's plain murder when you have to fill gaps like we do." Brown seemed to find conspiratorial machinations behind every Bengal failure. Cincinnati selected where they were slotted, exactly as their 1970 record dictated, yet Brown wanted to keep tilting at windmills, fighting the power that he was a part of.

One bright spot helped redeem the disappointment of a 4-10 record. Kenny Anderson's was a storybook tale. A third-round pick out of Augustana College in Rock Island, Illinois, Anderson was a local hero from nearby Batavia, where his father was the high school janitor. All the finest Big Ten schools wanted Anderson for their programs, but, Kenny explained, "All my life I wanted to go to Augustana."

Pete Brown was tipped off about the talented quarterback from the tiny school and informed his father of Anderson. Brown, in turn, then sent Bill Walsh to take a look. No one in the business recognized quarterback talent and potential better than Walsh, and he recommended to Brown that the Bengals take a chance on Anderson. For a rookie, Anderson showed great promise and grew as the season progressed.

"He has championship potential," Brown said of Anderson. "He has the strength to complete the long pass and throw with real accuracy. That was Cook's great plus when he started."[53]

Following the Bengals' impressive win over Philadelphia in week one of the 1971 season, *Sports Illustrated* profiled Brown and his team.

"I'm not like most other coaches in the league, because I have my own money invested in this club and my sons in the organization. I'm not trying for immediate success trading draft choices for veterans who might be able to help me for a couple years. We're building on youth, and that takes time."

Notwithstanding Brown's cries of deprivation, the Bengals again picked up some quality players in the '71 draft, including Mike Reid and Lemar Parrish, in addition to Kenny Anderson. Publicly, Brown was saying the Bengals were right on schedule. Privately, however, Brown knew his team had played beyond expectations. He savored the moment, but prepared for the inevitable letdown.

# thirteen    SIGN OF THE TIMES

With only one player over the age of thirty, the 1972 Cincinnati Bengals were the youngest team in football.

"The principles haven't changes for forty years," Paul Brown explained, "and the first principle is that you've got to have fun. That means you have to surround yourself with nice people. Good football can only be played by good people—those who are nice people on the inside." A great deal of the Bengals' success and development could be traced to the staff Brown had assembled.

"My coaches," Brown would say with affection. He surrounded himself with men he could trust, whose opinions he valued.

Organization. As always, that was the key. Brown coordinated the coaching staff and served as the daily administrator. From the technical aspect of the game, however, Brown was detached. This he left to his assistants, to whom Brown gave more leeway than most head coaches. "I hired you to do a job," he would say. "You're going to do the job."

To a man, his assistants responded to Brown's leadership. He ceded almost exclusive control to his staff. Each individual developed his area of the team, and then together as a staff, a game plan was prepared. Invariably, Brown accepted the game plans with slight changes. Tiger Johnson had the running game. Bill Walsh handled the passing game, while Jack Donaldson searched for a role in the offense, helping wherever he could. In time, Walsh assumed the role of offensive coordinator, though he never officially was given the title. He took control of offensive meetings, pushing his innovative approach to moving the football. An age-old football adage said you have to run the ball to open up the passing game. Walsh turned this idea on its head. A controlled short-passing game, to the tight ends and running backs, put pressure on the linebackers. Under Walsh's scheme, one dropped pass was unacceptable.

One idea of Walsh's was to take advantage of Bob Trumpy's speed, and use the tight end in different ways. Walsh wanted to "flop" the tight ends, matching Trumpy up against the strong safety. Time and again the play worked in practice, but when Walsh tried to implement it into the game plan he was stifled.

"We're not going to 'flop' the tight end," Brown said. "It'll appear we don't know how to line up."

—⁂—

Organization. Meetings began precisely on time. If Brown called a meeting at 9:03 A.M., Brown walked through the door at 9:03 A.M. When he entered the room, horseplay ceased, grab-assing stopped, jokes were left hanging without a punch line.

At the close of the meeting, after dismissing the players, the assistants remained behind and broke down film. Brown wanted everyone's input. The defensive coaches would sit through offensive tape. "What did you think of that, Stud?" Brown would ask Chuck Studley when an offensive play would break down.

When the defense faltered, Brown looked to Johnson or Walsh. "What happened there?"

Practice never lasted much more than an hour, ninety minutes tops. "If you can't teach them in ninety minutes, you can't teach." Brown had been repeating that mantra for decades. Sessions began at the exact time the game was scheduled for the coming Sunday. At the close of practice, Brown was in his Cadillac rolling out of Spinney Field's parking lot. The assistants, however, stayed behind studying the game plan. There was no sleeping on the office couch, not on Brown's staff. Without fail, the individual coaches would be home in time for dinner.

The experience of working for Brown was rewarding as well as educational. It could also be frustrating.

Brown's composed demeanor occasionally gave way to emotion in the heat of battle. "Isn't there something we can do to slow them down?" Brown would beseech Tom Bass.

"Coach, everything is all right," Bass would reply.

Brown's steel gray eyes cut through his assistant. "You're so calm, cool, and worthless."

At times he could be cruel and biting. The moment, usually, would pass. "Where are you going to work next year?" Brown asked Chuck Studley during the course of a tough game. Following the contest, Brown put his arm around Studley. "Football is a very emotional game. Don't pay any attention to what is said on the sideline."

While Bass called the defense from the sideline, Walsh sat in the booth and called down plays to Tiger Johnson. The emotionally volatile Walsh would occasionally explode in the coaches box when Brown would change a play call. Walsh wasn't the only high-strung member of the staff. Chuck Weber, who replaced Tom Bass as the defensive coordinator after Bass left the Bengals following the 1969 season, was sensitive and excitable. On one occasion, Weber even hyperventilated during a game.

---

Once the season concluded, Brown gathered his coaches together for one final meeting before he headed west to LaJolla. While in California, Paul phoned Mike every day, keeping him abreast of the organization. The staff continued to work through the winter and into the spring. Brown delegated to each individual and designated tasks for each coach to complete. The Senior Bowl, the Blue-Gray Game, the East-West Game, and the assistants would spread out and scout the college all-star games, gathering information for the draft.

---

Brown had privately talked of a "five-year plan" in 1968. Five years had passed, and though the Bengals had one surprise playoff appearance, they were still far removed from being a championship-caliber club. "We're competitive, at least I hope so," Brown told *The Sporting News*. "The problem is that many of our opponents are bigger and stronger. Our quarterback, Ken Anderson, is a little boy."[1]

Brown continued to denigrate his own club in order to lower expectations. When the team did arrive it would be a triumph for the little guy. The smaller, weaker Bengals ended 1972 with double the number of wins they accumulated one year earlier. But 8-6 was only good enough for third place behind Cleveland and the Pittsburgh Steelers, who after forty years of futility finally reached the post-season.

—⁓—

After Katy passed, Paul threw himself headlong into football. What had always been his passion now became his solace.

What little socializing Brown did do was done out of a sense of obligation. While attending a party at a Glendale residence in September 1970, he was introduced to an outgoing and beautiful widow from London, Ohio. Several months later, at the suggestion of her friend, John Sawyer, Mary Rightsell applied for an opening as Brown's secretary. Her bubbly personality brightened the team's office. Brown couldn't help but be drawn by Mary's vivacious character. She had lost her husband several weeks after Katy passed away, but months passed before Mary realized Paul was a widower. In fact, she knew little about Paul Brown at all. Her husband had followed the Browns, and Mary remembered his outrage when Brown was fired in Cleveland. Still, she was blissfully ignorant of the Paul Brown legend. Then one day he made mention of Katy and things fell into place. Now Mary understood why Paul asked her to take care of personal chores for him, little things like Christmas shopping that he needed help with because he had no one at home.

What began as a working friendship flowered into courtship. It had begun innocently. "Have you eaten tonight?" Paul asked one evening as he prepared to leave the office.

"Just soup," Mary replied.

"Well, if you and the girls would like, perhaps we could all get some dinner."

In time, they discovered a mutual passion: golf. And it was while returning from a day on the links that Paul, with a touch of wistful contemplation, asked, "Is there any chance you could call me 'PB'?"

Paul Brown married Mary Rightsell, June 19, 1973.

Mary, who always referred to Brown as "Coach," just laughed at the question. She didn't know where the conversation was heading.

"I decided we should merge households," Paul told Mary as they drove along I-275. Mary was taken aback by the suggestion. Marriage had never entered her thoughts; she was just enjoying Paul's company. She was the mother of four, including twin thirteen-year-old daughters, Melinda and Melissa. Besides, she was twenty years younger than Paul. Still, there was something charming and hopelessly romantic about him, the way he kissed Mary's hand at the end of the day and told her, "It's been very nice to be with you." But marriage wasn't something she signed up for. She needed to sleep on it, she told him. And though she hardly slept, the next morning Mary had an answer for Brown, "Yes."

They were married on June 19, 1973, in Rancho Sante Fe. The wedding was held at the home of Jack Matzinger, a LaJolla businessman and golfing buddy of Paul's. The unassuming ceremony was presided over by Brown's chaplain from Great Lakes, Reverend James Caughey, in front of a handful of friends who had learned of the nuptials earlier in the day.

After exchanging vows, Mary and Paul popped open a bottle of champagne and then retired for a quiet dinner with their wedding guests.

—⁂—

On the eve of training camp Barry Cobb of the *Cincinnati Post* sat down with Brown for a brief talk. The reporter reminded Brown of his "five-year plan" to get the Bengals "competitive." Now that he'd achieved that goal, Cobb asked, where did Brown hope to next lead his team?

"From here on in, we're out to win something. Whether we get it done remains to be seen. I know one thing; we are respected throughout the league. I don't care who we play, they know we aren't going to be a soft touch. If we get our share of breaks, we'll be right in there."[2]

The team, Brown believed, was on the threshold of something special. "You're here for the long haul, and we're not interested in people who just want a job. We expect you to go all out. We shall be successful in exact proportion to the caliber of people you are.

"I want to win something this year. We are more than competitive now, we can play with anybody and we have built some respect."

It was the outside distractions that could pull a team apart. Brown made mention of Pat Matson, the new player representative. "He is welcome to come to me at any time with any problem. But," Brown added, "when a union becomes more important than our football, we're in trouble.

"The old bull is still a bellowing," Brown said as he prepared for his twenty-third professional season. "I'm still in the game because I enjoy the life. I enjoy watching people. People study has to be about the most interesting thing in living.

"At my stage of life I do what I think is right. My biggest commitment is to win."

—⁂—

Greg Cook gave it one last shot. During a skeleton passing drill on July 27, 1973, Cook overthrew receiver Chip Myers by ten yards. After the attempt, Cook removed his helmet and walked to the sideline. Though his shoulder had never healed and the pain hadn't subsided through the years, Cook kept this information to himself. Several surgeries couldn't resurrect the magic in his arm. "I just didn't want to tell anybody," he explained. "The shoulder is as sore now as it was three years ago. . . . This is it. I'm through, unless God puts a new shoulder on me."

The news, though expected, still saddened Brown. Just three years earlier Cook showed promise that held no bounds, and now, less than four months from his twenty-seventh birthday, his career was over. Cook's immortality would be his place as one of football's great "what-if's."

After that telling practice, Dick Forbes questioned Brown about Cook's decision. Though he tried to keep his emotions in check, Brown couldn't help but reflectively contemplate. "He could've been the premier quarterback in the league."[3]

—w—

The 9-4 Bengals traveled to Houston for the final game of the regular season. A victory over the 1-12 Oilers would clinch the Central Division for Cincinnati. And in what could charitably be described as a lackluster performance, the Bengals edged Houston by just three points. An obviously disturbed Brown spent just a few moments with the press before addressing his team. His eyes flashed anger, his words flowed fast, as he spoke. "There are no easy teams in pro football," he said, and that was the tune he repeatedly told his players throughout the preceding week. "We didn't play well and we know it. Our guys aren't happy with themselves. . . I tried to tell them it wasn't going to be an easy game."

Brown emerged from a dour Bengal locker room and assured writers waiting just outside the door, "They understand me now."[4]

The mood lightened on the plane ride home. "Jingle Bells" and other holiday carols were sung by celebrating players. The "Fa-la-la-las" rang out from the rear of the plane and made their way to the front. A slight smile creased Brown's face as he leaned over to Tom Callahan of the *Enquirer* and said, "I hope this doesn't louse up any stories."

—w—

A small, but festive group of fans greeted the Bengals as they arrived at the Cincinnati airport from Houston. What awaited Brown and his team next in the playoffs was the world champion Miami Dolphins, who proceeded to knock the jolly out of the Bengals' holly Christmas. The teams met at the Orange Bowl on Christmas Eve, and practically from the opening kick-off the Dolphins dominated Cincinnati, 34-16. The Bengals' loss, Brown thought, "was as thorough a throttling job of our offense as I've seen."

"Our guys did everything to try and win, but we were no match," Brown said softly. "They defeated us in every aspect of the game."[5]

—m—

Virgil Carter spent the entire 1973 season on the shelf with a separated shoulder. Regardless of the injury, Brown wanted to retain the quarter-back's services as a backup to Ken Anderson. However, while the two sides were negotiating Carter's return, Brown learned that the new upstart World Football League had made overtures to him. Brown wasn't going to get into a bidding war with this WFL, yet he also wanted to squeeze something of value out of Carter. A quick deal was worked out that sent Carter to the San Diego Chargers, but Carter never reported to the Chargers. Shortly after the transaction, he signed with the Chicago Wind, becoming the first name player to jump to the neophyte WFL.

Over the next few weeks the new league made headlines on a regular basis, snagging a number of star NFL players. From the Cowboys, Calvin Hill and Craig Morton were signed. The Raiders had both of their quar-terbacks, Ken Stabler and Daryle Lamonica, ink deals with the World League. But the biggest splash came when three stars from the Super Bowl champion Miami Dolphins were signed by the Memphis Southmen. The coup landed Larry Csonka, Jim Kiick, and Paul Warfield on the cover of *Sports Illustrated* and gave the new league untold publicity.

Brown watched all this with a wary eye. It was just a matter of time before the incursion reached his team. And on April 5, Bengals' defensive tackle Steve Chomyszak signed a "futures" contract with the Philadelphia Bell. Chomyszak agreed to join the WFL club following his option year in

1975. Though Chomyszak wasn't a key component to the Bengals' success, the news of his defection still disturbed Brown. Some weeks earlier the WFL held a draft in which it claimed the rights to NFL players. In the twenty-third round of the draft, the Washington Ambassadors selected Bengal middle linebacker Bill Bergey. Though he was contracted to the Bengals for the 1974 season at a respectable $37,500, Bergey was intrigued enough to make the drive to Washington to see what the new league had to offer.

Once in the District, Bergey met with Ambassadors coach Jack Pardee. "We'll do whatever it takes to bring you here," Pardee promised Bergey. And after a little negotiating, the men came to an agreement that dwarfed Bergey's previous salary. The contract's total value was more than a half-million dollars, of which $150,00 was in bonuses—$40,000 upon signing with Washington, $60,000 more in July, and an additional $50,000 in 1975. All this money would be paid while Bergey remained under contract to the Cincinnati Bengals.

Securing his financial future was a prospect Bergey couldn't ignore. Returning to Ohio, he sat with Brown and informed him of the extraordinary offer. Brown certainly understood, and the Bengals couldn't match numbers like that, so all he could do is offer fatherly advice. "All that glitters isn't gold," Brown told his young star. "But," he added, "you do whatever is best for you and your family." And then he added, "We'll do whatever we have to do."

Before Bergey had officially signed with the WFL, the Bengals called a preemptive press conference on April 15. Brown was visibly agitated as he revealed this news to local reporters that the five-year Bengal veteran had signed a "futures" contract to play with the now-Norfolk Ambassadors beginning in 1976.

"There is nothing we can do," Brown said. "He committed himself before he contacted us." The hard-hitting Bergey was not a free agent. In fact, the linebacker remained under contract to the Bengals for the '74 season and had to play out his option in '75. This point rankled Brown more than anything else. How could a player put forth effort for his current team when he was under contract to play for another in the future?

"It impairs the integrity of any player's performance when he is under contract to one club and paid by another," Brown maintained. That argument became the central point to the Bengals' attempt to thwart the WFL's raid.

On April 19 the franchise filed suit in U.S. District Court, claiming that the WFL, its teams, and owners "have maliciously and tortuously induced Bergey to breach his contract with the Bengals." The complaint claimed that Bergey, "will no longer perform as a player for [Cincinnati] in such a matter as to impact his performance as a middle linebacker for the Cincinnati Bengals. . . . His breaches of contract and his inevitably strained relationships with coaches, fellow players, and the fans will be substantially disruptive of the morale of the Bengal organization."

How could a player put forth effort for one team when he was under contract to play for another in the future? That was the central argument in the Bengals' suit. Though Mike Brown pushed his father to pursue the issue in the court system, Brown agreed with his son. The WFL was invading his province, they were attacking his mores.

The case came before Judge David S. Porter on April 29, and the scene in Porter's courtroom was surreal. The judge himself bore a slight resemblance to Brown. The lawyer representing Bergey, George Moscarino, hailed from Cleveland and was a self-admitted Browns fan. Next to Moscarino sat Bill Bergey, incessantly chewing gum throughout the five-day proceedings. Across the aisle at the plaintiff's table, Paul and Mike sat with the Bengals' team council, John Lloyd, and a few other lawyers. Over the course of the week a long parade of witnesses stepped forward, including every member of Brown's coaching staff, as well as a former Bengal assistant, Vince Costello. In addition to Bergey, six Bengals players took the stand, as did Jack Pardee and former Cleveland assistant Dick Gallagher. In all, the Bengals presented twenty-one witnesses.

Defensive tackle Mike Reid, dressed casually without socks, would not be crossed by the defense attorney. "I repeat what I said before. Such a situation would wreck a football team," Reid said. Reid's testimony was in step with several teammates who had taken the stand. While the players all acknowledged that they would try their best if they were to sign a futures contract, the chemistry of the team would suffer irreparable damage under such circumstance.

Bill Walsh testified to a personal experience similar to Bergey's. Several years earlier, while an assistant at Stanford University, with the school's knowledge, Walsh signed a contract to join the Oakland Raiders staff.

"I found I was not as readily accepted by the other coaches at Stanford," Walsh explained, "and it became even more of a problem from a personal standpoint when I began to receive checks from the Raiders. It took away my enthusiasm."[6]

Another Bengal assistant, Chuck Studley, heatedly snapped at Moscarino that the lawyer's long-winded questioning was "awful repetitious." To which Judge Porter chimed, "sustained."

The stars of the proceedings, however, were Paul Brown and Bill Bergey. Brown took the stand on May 1, the trial's third day.

Brown couldn't emphasize the harm being perpetuated by the WFL enough. In fact, Brown said, the WFL had already damaged the Bengals. "We've been hurt. This is already accomplished. I don't see how there can be any question in anybody's mind but that this has created quite a thing on our team."

If a substantial number of Bengals were signed by the rival league, Brown rued, "it would just decimate us. It would really wreck what was about to become a good football team."[7]

As far as Bergey, Brown said, "He's not as marketable now. I don't know what we can do with him," He then recounted the club's options:

1. "Take him to camp and act like nothing happened."

2. "Keep him, pay him, and not do anything with him, just have him come out every day and work out."

3. "Waive him and get $100" (if another team took the opportunity to claim Bergey).

4. "Trade him, if someone wanted him for a couple of years."

It was, Brown said, "impossible to estimate in dollars the damage done to the franchise. . . . I never anticipated anything like this. This has created quite a thing on our team."

Indeed, Brown acknowledged, he'd never encountered a situation like this in forty years of coaching. To which Moscarino asked, if Brown himself raided another league years earlier and stole away players under contract to another team. Two days earlier, Moscarino had set up his question when Dick Gallagher was on the stand. Back in 1955, Brown had lured two men, Jack Locklear and Bobby Freeman, to play for the Browns while they were still under contract with the Winnipeg Blue Bombers of the Canadian Football League. Brown's actions at the time were in retaliation for losing one of his men the year prior to the CFL.

Questioned by Moscarino about his long-ago deeds, Brown admitted his fault. "It was a retaliatory thing, and I was wrong, I make no bones about it," Brown said.

"That was twenty years ago, and I guess it was the first time I learned it was wrong to sign a football player who was already under contract. In a general sort of way, I kind of figured that was what this hearing was all about."[8]

The next afternoon it was Bergey's turn. The twenty-nine-year-old middle linebacker acquitted himself well on the stand. He spoke well of the Bengals, and of Brown specifically, deferentially referring to Brown as "Coach" throughout his testimony.

"I feel Paul Brown was the most sincere and truthful person that was on the stand," Bergey stated.

Still, Bergey found no fault in his actions. "I didn't think my signing would create a problem. . . . The problem is being created right now by the Cincinnati Bengals in this courtroom. I don't think my signing has caused any problems to the Bengals at all."[9]

As Bergey looked directly into Brown's eyes and testified that he would continue to give an all-out effort for the Bengals, Brown noticeably squirmed in his seat. This whole affair was unseemly, sordid even. Lawsuits were bad enough, but suing one of your own . . . one had to wonder if it was all worth it.

Sitting in the courtroom every day of the trial was Essex Johnson. Even though he wasn't on the witness list, Johnson recognized what was at stake in the hearing: personal autonomy for the players. "It's our freedom to decide our own future," Johnson told Ed Menaker of the Post. "It's just freedom that we don't have now when we sign a contract."[10]

With Brown gone to LaJolla for a twelve-day respite, Judge Porter brought the five-day hearing to a close on May 3, praising both sides of the aisle for the "high caliber of presentation" they brought to his court-room. "There may be reason to retire this witness chair," Porter quipped, "perhaps to the Hall of Fame, observing the qualities of the professionals in this trial—both football and legal."[11]

Shortly after 11 A.M. on May 14, Judge Porter handed down a forty-six-page decision. Summarily, Porter decreed that the WFL was not competing unfairly for players. In his decision, the judge ruled there was no evidence that Bergey had breached his contract, and there was no reason to believe his performance would be of less value to the Bengals during the remaining years of his contract. "The WFL's motive for signing established players is not to cause harm to NFL teams in general, or to the Cincinnati Bengals in particular, but to further the competitive interest of the WFL."[12]

It was a sweeping defeat for the Browns, both Paul and Mike. He had been on the other side, as a maverick with the All-America Football Conference, but to Paul this was different. How do you hold a team to-gether under these circumstances?

Brown took his argument to Federal Appeals Court and was spurned there as well. By early July, the Norfolk Ambassadors had become the Orlando Blazers. After meeting with the team's new owners, Bergey and the club came to an amicable parting. The player rightfully questioned the stability of the franchise, while the Blazers believed Bergey's contract to be "ridiculous."

Mike Brown tried to work out an agreement that would keep Bergey a Bengal, but too many legal briefs had been filed, too many words parsed, too much of everything had passed for Bergey to return to Cincinnati. Be-sides, you don't butt heads with Paul Brown, you don't buck his authority and return to the fold.

"With the uncertainty attending Bill Bergey at this time," Brown announced in a statement, "I feel that this is in the best interests of the team presently and in the future."[13] The Bengals were able to work out a

Surveying the New Orleans Super Dome

deal with the Eagles that sent Bergey to Philadelphia for two first-round selections and a third-round pick in the '77 draft, a satisfactory conclusion to an unpleasant affair.

If it wasn't this, it was that. To some, pro football was seemingly on the road to perdition. Some of Brown's friends wondered amongst themselves if Brown ever regretted returning to the game. The subject of a work stoppage was pertinent once again. Four years had passed since the labor unrest of 1970 and the bargaining agreement was due to expire with the coming season.

"We're seeing what happens when salaries and prices go up," Brown said. "The public keeps paying more and more and we wonder why we have inflation. In the end, it's the fan who is hit the hardest.[14]

"The owners are not in it for a quick buck. And we're not in it to lose money. We have to look at our business on a long-range program. It's not as profitable as it looks. People see a lot of fans in the stands and they think somebody is making a lot of money. They don't ever see the bills for flying 100 men across the country every other week."

While Brown was spewing the company line for management, the Players Association's executive director, Ed Garvey was earning his paycheck by spouting propaganda for his side. Garvey, Brown believed, was "intellectually bankrupt." In light of such antagonism, all signs pointed to a players strike of training camp.

The looming labor problem, the WFL, the federal government, seemingly the game was at a crisis point. Still, Brown wasn't sounding the sirens of alarm. "I've seen it all before. There is nothing really new in any of this. I've been in it so long that nothing surprises me, and it always seems to come out real good. When things look ominous people with good sense seem to prevail.

"'These are incredible times. But contrary to what most people think, it doesn't upset me. I'm intrigued by it all.

"If we have a strike and there are no camps, there are going to be a lot of people with broken hearts and disappointments. Do the players really realize what giving up training camp means? Doesn't anybody give any thought to the qualities of the thing we present to the public?

"Yes, I'm concerned. But I just hope history repeats and calm people prevail."

It was, Brown said, "a sign of the times. Society is all mixed up and I guess we're just reflecting society in general."[15]

Most owners struggled to see the need for player representation. These men played a game for a living. They were provided for rather well. But there was another side to the issue, of course. Football players had a very finite amount of time when they could ply their trade. The average career lasted less than five years.

"No Freedom, No Football" became a catchy slogan and, to many observers, a ridiculous catchphrase. Still, the Players Association would utilize the motto to illustrate its plight. "Freedom" sold better to the public than monetary greed did, but the public struggled to commiserate with men who played games for a living. Picketers wore t-shirts emblazoned with a hairy fist and bearing the association's inventive motto. The issues, the "freedom issues," which resulted in the players calling a strike in late June 1974 were:

1. Impartial arbitration. At the time, Rozelle was the sole arbitrator.

2. Elimination of the waiver procedure.

3. The right to cancel a trade.

4. Elimination of the waiver procedure. The Players Association believed if a player was no longer wanted by one team, he should have the right to negotitate with whoever he wishes rather than be claimed by another club.

5. Protection of player representatives.

6. A revision of the standard player contract, which would do away with the reserve clause that bound a player to his team for an option year.

7. The elimination of club and league fines.

8. Salary arbitration.

—\m—

The strike was in its third week when the Bengals opened camp on July 13. Fifteen rookies and twelve veterans reported to Wilmington, while the remaining vets honored the association's call for a strike. At training sites throughout the NFL, picket lines were set up, but not at Wilmington.

"We're just small-time stuff out here," Brown said, explaining the absence of pickets outside Bengal camp. "This is not a news media center."[16]

The association suffered from a lack of complete unanimity. In San Diego, august veteran Johnny Unitas refused to speak with picketers when he reported to camp. "If they want to pay my salary, I'll join their strike," Unitas said. And though Johnny U wasn't the only player to hold such convictions, the Bengals had a disparate number of veterans cross the picket line. Five days after camp began, four more veterans reported to Wilmington. Many observers ascribed the lack of unity among Cincinnati veterans to the Bengal players' fear of reprisal by Brown. There was conjecture that Brown threatened his players and Bill Curry, president of the NFLPA, claimed that Brown "lured" his players to camp by offering bonuses to players who would cross the line. Curry was mistaken. No bonuses were offered to Bengals players and Brown never implicitly threatened his men, but such thoughts revealed Brown's reputation. This reputation, be it real or imagined, was born from Brown's complete disdain for the Players Association.

A small group of NFLPA representatives announced their plan to come to Wilmington. It was their intention to shore up the Bengals' weak strike front, as Ed Podolak of the Kansas City Chiefs explained. "Our purpose in coming to Cincinnati was to let the Bengals know that there are 1,200 other football players behind them and they don't have to fear Brown," Podolak said. "He was intimidating those who have reported to camp, and we have to correct that."

Pittsburgh Steeler Tom Keating also spoke harshly of Brown and the need to reach out to Bengal players. "Brown may think he can tell everyone what to do and what to say, but he is wrong. He is not going to coerce me into buying his way of thinking. And a lot of other guys are fed up with his style, too."[17]

Before the group arrived at Bengal camp Brown had his players take a vote. Did they want to meet with the association representatives? With a thirty-to-zero unanimous vote, Bengal players elected not to meet or speak with the delegation.

Brown did what he could do. His rule had once been all-encompassing, but what was within his control was deliberately being chipped away. Still, where he could enforce his will, he did. Keating underestimated him. If the players in his camp didn't wish to meet with the association's group coming from Chicago, Brown would turn them away at the gates of Wilmington. As a result of the poll, Brown vowed to give the association neither the time nor a place to assemble.

—⚏—

Brown had always enjoyed this time or year. The preparation, the drills, the teaching . . . he loved to teach. But this summer was different. Outwardly, Brown's appearance was familiar. Each afternoon, Brown stood in the middle of the practice field wearing those same plain beige polyester pants, an old white t-shirt, and the ever-present ball cap. He stood, watching the action around him with his arms folded across his chest, alone and looking much older than he had just a few months earlier.

Every day following practice the beat writers would sit with Brown and chat.

All summer he'd kept a stiff upper lip when it came to the strike. Externally, he refused to act as if anything was amiss, but it was a front. Unlike previous disputes with the Players Association, Brown kept most of his thoughts on the debate to himself. Still, it was evident that he took the labor problems personally. It was a personal rejection, a rejection of our football, our ideals. On a couple of occasions during the strike Brown sparked a conversation with a local reporter. A casual talk morphed into Brown trying to pry information from the scribe. "What were the players saying about him?" The preceding months had been difficult. Much of what Brown knew was in shambles. Renegade leagues inspiring disloyalty among players. Agents interfering with a coach's jurisdiction over his players. . . . Drugs . . . picket lines. . . .

Earlier in the year, Lou Groza was elected to Pro Football's Hall of Fame. As the day of induction came closer, Groza asked his old coach if Brown would do the honor of introducing him at Canton. Though the ceremony would take place in the midst of training camp, Brown readily agreed. "Ah, Louie, my boy Louie. I've been looking forward to this day for quite awhile," he mused. Getting away from the strike and the strife might do him some good, Brown thought. He looked forward to going home, if only for a couple of days.

To join him for the ride up to Canton, Brown invited Ed Menaker of the *Cincinnati Post*. Earlier in the spring, Menaker began covering the Bengals. He was the only reporter present every day at the Bergey trial, and then there was the strike. Though he hadn't had much opportunity to write about football, Menaker had a fresh voice. At the *Enquirer*, Dick Forbes had become complacent in his coverage of the Bengals. Forbes had been known to pen a good column. His writing style was fluid, and very readable. But in the case of Brown, he got too close to his subject. Forbes had been so wedded to the team that he had lost all objectivity in his reporting, not that Brown was complaining, but Forbes's editor, Jim Schottelkotte, was. Brown wanted company on the trip, and there was something about this Menaker kid that Brown liked.

On Friday, July 26, Brown got behind the wheel of his candy-red Cadillac as Menaker hopped into the passenger seat. With a writing tablet on his armrest, Menaker was at the ready, but the reporter never used his pencil. The entire journey was a trip back in time for Brown, a travelogue to a more idealistic age.

He drove to the schoolyards, to the playing fields of his youth.

There's the Tuscarawas River. In the winter I would ice skate there… All these memories, they were Brown's treasure. It was important to Brown that Menaker know these places, these things. This was who Paul Brown was.

The strike, the Bengals' prospects for the coming season, the WFL . . . no contemporary events were discussed between Brown and the writer. That stuff was of another world. For now, for the moment, Brown was home.

The next morning, Menaker went to Brown's hotel room. He found Brown calm and composed.

Aren't you nervous? Menaker asked. Do you have any remarks prepared?

Brown brushed aside the questions. "I don't need anything written down. These people know me."

—⁓—

Brown's reprieve was brief. The strike had even encroached the ceremonies in Canton. The association announced plans to picket the annual Hall of Fame game, which featured Buffalo and St. Louis. The gall infuriated Brown. "Why would anybody want to mar the day of people who have nothing to do with this struggle? What gets me is this guy Garvey. How does this fresh-out-of-college, straight-off-the-campus, big-talking lawyer get the power to sway so many people?"[18]

On August 11, NFL veterans decided to suspend their forty-two-day strike for fourteen days in an effort to resolve the dispute. It was a cooling-off period of sorts, Ed Garvey insisted. But in reality a white flag had been hoisted. The players remained in camp when the two weeks had elapsed and no meaningful strides were made in their Freedom Issues.

"There will be no bitterness on my part toward the returning veteran players," Brown asserted, "but when they come in they better put that [strike] stuff away."[19]

A couple of weeks later the possibility remained that the strike could be resumed. While the exhibition season wound to a close, Cincinnati players gathered and took a vote. As a team, the Bengals decided not to walk out should the Players Association restart the strike. "Their minds are on football," Pat Matson explained. Present at the union meeting were Brown's assistants and Mike Brown.

Everybody had their mind on football. Ownership hadn't budged on any of the contentious issues, and the Players Association didn't have the stomach to reconvene the strike. Freedom would be put aside for the time being. There was football to be played

A promising 4-1 start had descended to 6-3 when the Bengals went to Houston to play their division opponent. Awaiting Brown and his team in Texas was a story written by Ed Menaker. What had been a routine piece, exploring Oilers head coach Sid Gillman's connection with the University of Cincinnati, made the wire services thanks to Gillman's coarse comments about Brown. The article veered off in an unexpected direction when Gillman went out of his way to criticize Brown. The source of Gillman's anger came from Brown's failure to exchange game film with the Oilers. "We don't like people to accuse us of such childish things as holding up films,"[20] Gillman said.

In the midst of his outburst, Gillman claimed Brown was "senile."

Menaker was taken aback. "You want to go on the record as saying Paul Brown is senile?" the reporter asked.

"Write it," Gillman beseeched Menaker, "The old man is senile. He needs to quit football. You write it."

The resulting article devastated Brown. During the contest, a 20-3 Oiler victory, Houston fans filled the spacious Astrodome with a chant, "Brown is senile." Over and over. . . . "Brown is senile."

Following the game, Menaker approached Brown, who was standing alone under the stands. With tears in his eyes, Brown turned to the writer. "Haven't you done enough already?" he implored Menaker. "See," Brown said, the crowd's humiliating chant still ringing in his ears, "See what you've done to me."

Not to excuse Gillman, by any means, but sometimes things are said in anger. Menaker, however, according to Brown, his part in all of this was inexcusable. Brown took the kid with him to Canton earlier in the summer. Just he and Menaker, he had treated the young writer to an exclusive, a chance to see Paul Brown away from the field, in his home area. And then this. Brown understood the business. Coaches coach, players play, and writers, well, they write. But it doesn't need be mean-spirited. This was beyond game coverage or analysis. By Brown's way of thinking, there was nothing to be served by printing Gillman's slur. But Menaker was of another generation, and though the writer respected Brown, and even liked the coach, this was his vocation, and what Gillman said was news. It warranted coverage. Still, Dick Forbes wouldn't have touched the story with a ten-foot pole.

From Houston things continued to spiral downward. A win against Kansas City was followed by two losses. The promise of another season lay broken as the Bengals slogged their way to the end of a frustrating campaign. Much of the disappointment could be attributed to the slew of injuries that struck the club beginning in mid-season. Eight starters, including Ken Anderson, Boobie Clark, Bob Johnson, and Bergey's replacement, Jim LeClair, all missed significant playing time. The season finale in Pittsburgh was played under insufferable conditions. Icy cold, driving sleet, frigid wind. . . . Brown stood on the sidelines boldly, conceding nothing to the inclement weather, as the Steelers ran over his decimated Bengals, 27-3.

On the plane ride home, Brown's defiance gave way. Sitting alone in his first-class seat, Brown resembled a vulnerable old man, swathed in a blanket, shivering away the chill, struggling to find warmth, struggling to forget this long, crucible year.

—⚅—

A 7-7 record fed disenchantment among the team. On the final weekend of the 1974 season, several skirmishes broke out between Bengal teammates, including Chip Myers squaring off against Rob Pritchard, as did Pat Matson and Bernard Jackson, while Stan Walters clashed with an "unidentified"[21] teammate. Some of the discontent could be attributed to a campaign gone sour. Others believed they had been handcuffed by coaching decisions. Royce Berry, a six-year veteran who played his entire career in Cincinnati, took his frustration public. In a story placed on the front page of the *Post,* Berry issued complaints about "management problems" on the Bengals. A starter since 1969, Berry voiced stinging criticism of the coaching staff in the aftermath of the blowout in Pittsburgh.

"What upset me most was that their (Bengal coaches) main thought seemed to be not on winning, but on just not letting the Steelers run up the score," Berry said.

With Ken Anderson sidelined for the Pittsburgh contest, Wayne Clark filled in behind center. The Bengals possessed the number-one passing attack in the AFC, but with Anderson out of action, they only attempted eight passes for twenty-three yards. Berry, a number of his teammates, and members of the press, believed Brown and his coaching staff let the air out of the football against the Steelers.

Berry also believed that there "seemed to be a lack of confidence by the head coach in his assistants. I'm not saying Brown should retire or anything like that. All I'm saying is that the assistants are competent but seem to be under wraps and restrained from doing their jobs.

"This team needs to take a serious, hard look at itself in the off-season. They need to look at the way they are running things right on down the line from management to the lowest rung. There are problems here that extend beyond the players."[22]

Mounting criticism as well as Brown's advancing age—he would turn 67 in September—fed the speculation that Brown might step aside as the Bengals' head coach. "I haven't committed myself on the future," was all Brown would say to such queries. "I make those decisions as time goes by. I won't give it much thought until I'm well rested and away from the hubbub of this season."[23]

—◊—

The attraction to the job remained for Brown. Every weekend, every game, remained a challenge. "The most fascinating thing about it," Brown said, "is to be able to do the right thing at the right time the greatest possible number of times."[24]

Some commentators believed Brown had begun to "mellow" as he inched closer to retirement. When it came to the game, Brown had changed little through the years. Away from the football field, however, Paul Brown was a different, more serene man. This transformation could be attributed to his spirited bride. Mary's sparkling personality was infectious. She brought out a side of Brown that had never surfaced before.

Invitations to social events, invitations that would have been politely declined in the past, were now accepted. "You know, Paul," Mary would tell him, "we need to do this." And to his pleasant surprise, Paul would invariably have the time of his life.

"When you're alone, maybe you grow narrower," he admitted. "When you remarry, all of a sudden it's a different life and a happier way of life. Your interests are rekindled. You do things, you go places, you have something to plan on, somebody to come home and see. You're alive and growing."

Even Brown's old players noticed the change in him. They respected him, but... hell, Brown's players barely knew him. And what little bit of personality he allowed to seep through was hardly lovable. Yes, some of the same men who had hated their coach when they played now observed that Brown had softened. He was warmer, friendlier. Otto Graham pulled Mary aside on one occasion. "You know," he said, "since Coach married you, he realized there was more to life."

For four and a half years, Brown admitted, he was alone. "I'd go home after a golf game and not have much to do."

Each day began with the morning ritual, pulling aside the drapes in their LaJolla home. It was what they called "the unveiling of the day." It wasn't just Mary that rejuvenated him; Brown's teenage stepchildren also invigorated him, though on occasion their exuberance tested his patience. One evening at dinner the girls tied his shoes together under the table.

"Mary," Paul implored, "you need to get these girls under control."

"Look, this isn't football, Paul," Mary replied, "We can't put them on waivers."[25]

Still, their boundless energy and youth inspired Paul to step out of the crusty stereotype and try things that he never before would have dreamed of attempting at his age, like camping. His grandchildren also gave him great joy. Mike's daughter, Katie, was "Pumkin" to her adoring grandfather. And Robin's four children—Kevin, Scott, Brian, and Robin Elizabeth—were each special to Paul.

For a few months, Brown could relax. He trusted his assistants and sons to run the business in Cincinnati, but Mary knew instinctively when training camp was approaching. Paul's carefree demeanor began to transform as he prepared for yet another football campaign. Off-the-field problems, however, cut Brown's vacation time short. Last year's labor problems still lingered, none of the contentious issues had yet been resolved, and the Players Association threatened once again to call the rank-and-file out on strike. In June, Brown traveled to Minneapolis to testify in federal court. The case was a player's suit attempting to break the Rozelle Rule hindering player free agency.

On the stand Brown used tenuous analogies to preach the evils free agency brought to sport. "Some are glamour spots, some are like Siberia to these guys," he said, referring to baseball pitcher Catfish Hunter going from Oakland to New York and basketball star Kareem Abdul-Jabbar going from Milwaukee to Los Angeles, ever though Jabbar was actually traded. Brown compared these moves to his own quarterback, Anderson. "If he were to leave after our investment in him, the disillusionment, general interest to fans and community would hurt tremendously. Compensation would help some but I don't think that much.

"It can be a devastating blow when a team loses a player," Brown said. "The great players become part of the community in the fans' way of thinking. . . . If you want all teams to be competitive, you can't have one team lose players. It would be a tremendous blow. Before, players had more feeling for a football team and their community."[26]

The sticking point in negotiations was the so-called Rozelle Rule, which held that if a player played out his option and joined another club, his former team must be compensated. If the two clubs in question could not come to an agreement on compensation, the commissioner would step in and decree which player or draft choice was to be given to the club that lost the player. This policy was a far cry from free agency, the players argued.

No Freedom, No Football, indeed.

—⟋⟍⟍—

He had made the speech on dozens of occasions before hundreds of men. The substance of the talk changed slightly with the changing times. As Brown stood before his players in the summer of '75 to mark the beginning of yet another training period, Brown hearkened back to the teachings he acquired at Miami University, wisdom the old coach tried to impress upon all the men who'd ever weathered his lengthy discourse.

"Eternal verities . . . the everlasting truths of living—truth, honesty, loyalty, hard work, dedication, your character—these are the kind of things that impress me, and believe me, at my stage of life, I can tell you for sure they are the things that count."

The times were changing. Sometimes it seemed as if the whole world were turned upside down. He still had his rules and preferences. Brown encouraged his players to attend church every Sunday, even on game day. He liked his players to be married, but married or not, Brown let his men know that he would be watching them. No "love nests," Brown declared. He believed that the home a man kept gave the team insight into a man's character. "It doesn't take me long to recognize the tramp, the boozer, the barroom ladies man, the married man with a girlfriend, the cocktail lounge habitué, the guy with the dark glasses on the morning after—any of the many things that tell me the story. And the druggie really wears his badge—his hair longer, crazy clothes, no shoes, bib overalls, you know the signals."

Such scandalous conduct, Brown believed, reflected poorly on the team. If a player misbehaved away from the field, the Bengals were put in a bad light, which put Paul in a bad light. And Brown would not abide by that.

"I don't care what your political beliefs might be, and I don't want you bringing it around our football. No particular social arguments whatsoever are going to be tolerated here. For the period of our four to five and a half months together it's out!"

Politics. No good could come from a dissertation of politics. Brown certainly had his ideas and thoughts on political affairs, but he kept those beliefs close to the vest. He donated to candidates and causes close to his heart, and those candidates tended toward the conservative viewpoint. But the men who worked closest to Brown couldn't recall a single instance of Brown discussing his views. "Republicans and Democrats all buy football tickets," was Brown's philosophy, and Brown refused to offend possible customers from any political faction.

Every year prior to training camp the Bengals would host an outing for the team's families. Wives and children, everybody enjoyed an afternoon of fun and food. After the picnic, though, it was all business. Brown made this explicitly clear. For the next six months, Brown expected every man to devote himself to football. And, as Brown reminded his players in his annual address, "keep the wives out of our football." Wives talk about salary, about whose husband should be playing and whose shouldn't. . . .

He was in complete control, on the field or off. Every week, the night before a game, Brown would gather the team for a movie. Brown's taste in cinema was sorely lacking in adventure. Disney productions were always a favorite, but Brown's criteria were very specific when selecting a film for his team to preview—no X-rated, no R-rated, and no Jim Brown films. On one occasion, Paul Brown was confronted with the choice of *Ice Station Zebra,* which co-starred Brown's former fullback, or *101 Dalmatians.* Brown decided to treat his Bengals to the intrigues of Cruella DeVille.

Even in social circles, Brown directed the evening. Now, with Mary at his side, the Browns would entertain at their Glendale home on occasion. The affair would begin with Brown serving a cocktail. When Brown finished his drink, he would ask the room, "Anyone like another?" After he was through with his second, dinner was served. When Brown pushed away his plate, dessert was served. And when Paul was through with dessert. . . . Good night!

Complete control.

His list of rules was lengthy and all encompassing. One mandate forbade players from cutting grass on Fridays. Brown's reasoning for the tenet: a number of years earlier one of his men was injured mowing his lawn on a Friday. Of course, the "Tuesday Rule" remained on the books, as did the "no agents" decree. Brown had held to his long-ago promise not to do business with any player agents. "You don't need an agent," Brown would tell players. "I'm the one who sees every play. I'm the one who knows the X's and O's." And for a while, Brown's argument held water with his players, as few Bengals brought representation to the bargaining table. But agents were infesting sports now. It was almost impossible to ignore them. Rather than give in, Brown handed over contract negotiations to Mike a couple of years earlier.

"The old way was better," Brown rued. "Pay the players who are carrying the load. Pay them based on their performance. But we'll probably never see those days again, thanks to agents and the union."

The union, player agents . . . sometimes it felt as if the game between the lines was just a memory from long ago. After eighteen months management and the Players Association remained deadlocked. The NFLPA reported that the union had "overwhelmingly rejected" a contract presented by the owners. Brown claimed he "didn't even know a vote was being taken. I don't think our guys even voted on it."

The Bengals, in fact, did not vote on the proposal. What they wanted was more information. They wanted Bob Johnson and Pat Matson to travel to Chicago and gather more information at the next association meeting. Johnson and Matson went to Brown's room and lightly rapped on the door.

"Yes," Brown said, "come in."

"We had a player's only meeting tonight," Johnson told Brown. "And we couldn't come to a decision."

"Yes," Matson added, "and the team wants to send us to the Players Association meeting in Chicago so we can find out more about it."

The two oversized men stood anxiously while the room filled with awkward silence. Then Brown's face began to contort as it turned a deep, angry red. The silence was broken when Brown exploded. "You can all go to Chicago, and for all I care you could keep on going and not come back here at all."

Brown then rose from his seat and began to escort Matson and Johnson from the room. "And tonight's meeting was the last one you'll have on my premises. You'll have to go out and rent a hall for the next one."

Several days later, Mike Brown approached Matson, who was sitting through an offensive film session. "Bring your playbook," Mike told the guard. Those three words could mean but two things: the player in question had been traded or released. For Matson, it was a trade to the Packers for an undisclosed draft choice. Brown couldn't abolish the Players Association, but he could banish the Bengals' player's representative. To replace Matson, Bengal veterans selected Ken Anderson. His reign as rep lasted but twenty minutes before Brown called the quarterback into his office. In no uncertain terms, Anderson was told, "You're not going to be the player representative."

Matson, as Brown proved, was expendable. Anderson was not. He was the leader of the team on the field, the brightest prospect the Bengals had. If Cincinnati were to have any success, Brown reasoned, it would be Anderson's arm guiding the club.

Five days after Cincinnati opened the 1975 season with a 24-17 win over Cleveland, the Players Association voted overwhelmingly to reject the latest proposal. Upon hearing the news, Brown said the only thing he knew for sure was, "games will continue to be played by those who want to play them." Only one team voted to accept the offer . . . the Cincinnati Bengals.

—⚏—

On the eve of his forty-first season as a head coach, Brown's mind was firmly set on the present. Bob Queenan of the *Post* asked Brown to reflect on his illustrious career just prior to the start of the 1975 campaign.

"I've had a very pleasant life. I never have felt that I was working. I can think back on games that I'd like to have won, that might have been won. But I can also look to the ones where we got lucky and won when we shouldn't have."

"Bitter, vindictive people bore me. You win or lose and that's all that happens. I don't dwell on the past. I'm too consumed by what's going on. At my stage of life, things don't bother me. I've lived fully."

"This is that time of year when you have to tell people you can't keep them. We are sincere in our efforts to find a place for them to play. This is the thing that keys everyone up. And after it's all over everyone is relaxed."

This team, Brown thought, could be special. This could finally be the club. Before leaving Wilmington, Brown addressed his players. "We have a good team," he began before pausing and starting again. "We have a very, very good team here. I really believe that if you play together the way I know you can, I think we are going to make a very sincere run at the brass ring."[27]

Brown had great reason to be optimistic. The union wouldn't interfere with the season; there would be no player's strike. And after suffering the greatest barrage of injuries Brown had seen in forty years the year before, the Bengals were healthy. The team responded by barreling out of the gate, winning its first seven games before losing a tightly contested battle against the world champion Steelers. The team's early-season success sparked an interest in the Bengals by the national press.

Ken Anderson out of little Augustana College was a darling for visiting writers. His story played well, the small-town boy who made good. Anderson's favorite target, Isaac Curtis, also garnered the attention of national scribes. *Sport, Sports Illustrated,* and *The Sporting News* all paid heed to the happenings in Cincinnati, and any writer worth his salt couldn't pen a story about the Bengals and not examine their legendary leader.

"I just keep looking forward, never back," Brown told the *Los Angeles Times.* He was enjoying the game more than he had in years, and much of the credit had to go to the rookies who were spurring Cincinnati's great run. The defense, especially, was invigorated by the efforts of first-year players Gary Burley, Bo Harris, Marvin Cobb, and the Bengals' number-one draft selection, Glen Cameron.

"They have given us the zest to play," Brown said of the team's twelve first-year players. "They're young and they're happy. We don't have anyone here with a 'play-me-or-trade-me' attitude."

The influx of youth, Brown enthused, "made for a good situation. The people they are backing up know the young guys are very capable. It would be very difficult for a player not to get caught up in the spirit of things.

"I've kept the same general principles that I've had from the beginning. I really don't leave much for the imagination when I lay out to my players what I expect from them. But then, I never asked a player to do anything without first explaining why you can't fool, lie, or mislead a player." [28]

—⁂—

Everything was on the line when the Bengals traveled to Pittsburgh in the season's thirteenth week. The Steelers entered the game at 11-1, while the Bengals were at 10-2. A victory would pull Cincinnati into a virtual tie with their rivals. However, a loss by the Bengals clinched the Central Division for the Steelers.

Brown was relaxed before the contest as he strolled across the artificial surface of Three Rivers Stadium. He took a look around as the large concrete oval began to fill with fans. "There are more thugs per square inch there (in the stands) than any stadium in the country," Brown remarked to a reporter trailing behind. Yes, Brown said, a crowd in Pittsburgh resembled a "Mafia convention."

Those thugs had much to cheer about as their Steelers dominated the game from the opening kickoff and won by a lopsided 35-14 score. In the locker room Brown sat, slumped in a chair. "They blew us out of here. Just simply blew us out. They outran us, out-passed us, out-defensed us, and out-thought us. And, of course, they out-muscled us.

"It's just another game. You shouldn't feel too bad, I guess, when you lose to a team with such obvious superiority." Brown continued in his praise of the Steelers before he stopped and realized that his club wasn't so bad itself. "We're not through yet."[29]

—⁓—

The Bengals bounced back with a resounding victory over the San Diego Chargers, which qualified the club as the AFC wild-card team. Cincinnati's reward for finishing 11-3 was a playoff trip across the country to the Oakland Coliseum, where they hadn't won in their last four trips.

There were many opportunities throughout the afternoon for the Bengals to lie down and quit. After dominating the first half, the Raiders scored early in the third quarter, giving them a 24-7 lead. And with just over thirteen minutes to play, Oakland held a 31-14 lead. This Bengal team had heart and character, however. They continued to fight, and with less than five minutes to play, Isaac Curtis made a brilliant touchdown catch as he wrestled the ball away from Raider defensive back Neal Colzie. The score brought the Bengals to within three points of Oakland at 31-28. And Brown's boys weren't done yet. Cincinnati took possession of the ball at the Raider thirty-seven-yard line with a little more than four minutes remaining. A sack on first down, though, pushed the Bengals out of field-goal range. Three incomplete passes followed and Cincinnati had run through its final chance.

Speaking to his men afterward, Brown was strangely upbeat. Oddly, he appeared to be satisfied in defeat.

"I was proud of you," he said. "You tried hard. You came back. You did the best you could."

No, Brown wasn't hanging his head after this loss. "I've never been prouder of a football team than the Cincinnati team we brought in here today," Brown told the press. "We gave it our best shot."

As he exited Oakland Coliseum's visiting locker room, Brown said offhandedly to no one in particular, "I'm done, I'm plenty done."[30]

## fourteen  EXIT PAUL BROWN

The Bengals returned home from Oakland, and Brown had come to a decision. He had given much thought to his future on the plane ride across the country, and he had made up his mind. First, he wanted to talk to Mary. The two took a drive to Oxford and walked all around Miami's campus. Later in the evening, Paul returned home and took a stroll with Mike through the village of Glendale. He told them both, as well as Robin and Pete, the conclusion he had reached. And when the news was released, Paul told them all, "I don't want to be anywhere near it."

At the office the next day, Paul pulled Al Heim aside. "Will you be home on New Year's Day?" he asked.

"I will be if you want me to be," Heim replied.

———※———

On Thursday, New Year's Day, 1976, in between the conclusion of the Cotton Bowl and the beginning of the Rose Bowl, Al Heim's phone rang at his home. He was stepping down as the Bengals' head coach, Brown told Heim. Bill Johnson had agreed to replace Brown, and Mike McCormack was going to take over Tiger's position on the staff. "Take it from there," Brown told Heim. "Happy New Year!" And, Brown added, he wished to be out of reach for the next few days.

There would be no news conference. No opportunity for Brown to bask in the spotlight. He'd had his glory. Brown knew this, and his record spoke for itself. There was no need for self-aggrandizing. All Brown wanted was a simple press release, slipped to news organizations on the evening of New Year's Day.

Low-key or not, the announcement triggered bold headlines. EXIT PAUL BROWN read the front page of the *Enquirer.* Certainly there had been speculation nearly every year since 1969 of when Brown would step aside. But the reality of the event was shocking nonetheless. Just two days earlier, the coaching staff was assembled for a meeting and Brown gave no indication that he was retiring. A few hours later, Paul and Mike met with Tiger Johnson at the Queen City Club over lunch. To Johnson's great surprise, Brown told him he not only was stepping down as head coach, but he wanted Tiger to take over the team.

Johnson was a worthy choice. Word was out that the 49ers were interested in him. Apparently they wanted him to replace their coach, Dick Nolan. This news prompted Brown to act quickly. Johnson was well-liked by the players and respected by his peers on Brown's staff. Tiger was a knowledgeable football man, that was certain. Most importantly, though, Johnson knew the Paul Brown system and understood the intricacies that stimulated not only the players, but also management. Johnson possessed many of the same qualities that Brown carried: stoic, reserved, keen attention to detail, and loyal. Johnson was nothing if he wasn't a loyal soldier.

At the time of the news release, Johnson was in Dallas scouting the Cotton Bowl. He was back in Cincinnati on January 4 to meet with the local press. The bespectacled Johnson, his hair streaked silver, appeared older than his forty-nine years. But he remained robust, filling out his 6' 2" frame at 230 pounds. He was as stunned as anyone, Johnson insisted. He had no inkling what Brown had in mind. The question nearly every reporter present wanted to ask was, what role would Brown play in Johnson's coaching? "I think it's gonna be like it's always been," Johnson said in his slow Texas drawl. "We sit down and discuss things, and the final decision is made by Paul."

What about the draft, someone asked?

"We have always discussed the players, and Paul has always listened to what everyone had to say. The final decision on who we took always rested with Paul. He still has final word."[1]

These thoughts were certainly relevant. Paul Brown was well known for his need to control his surroundings. How would Brown react to being in the background? Would he be happy solely in an advisory position, or did he possess a need to pull the strings behind the scenes? These questions were in the minds of all who knew Brown well. How content would he be away from the sidelines?

The next afternoon, Monday, January 5, Brown surfaced from his brief exile. He met the local media at Riverfront Stadium to answer a few questions as well as offer a few explanations of his motivations. "Seclusion, me?" Brown laughed, "I haven't been hiding. I was meeting people who were interested in filling our assistant coaching jobs."

He would miss roaming the sidelines, Brown admitted, and the decision did not come easily. "But I've conditioned myself for some time, and I'll handle it.

"I think you'll see very little difference. [Tiger's] job is strictly coaching football. The players and how they affect the franchise are up to yours truly. My Mike will continue in his own capacity as he always has. We will observe but not step in."

For a moment, Brown thought back to those early years in Carew Tower, when all the team had to its name was a small desk and a telephone. They'd come a long way in a short span of time. He first began mulling the possibility of stepping aside a year earlier in LaJolla, and now the time was right, Brown explained. The Bengals were up and running. The franchise was on "solid" ground.

Much of the coaching staff was reshuffled. Howard Brinker, who joined the Bengals staff in 1974, was moving from linebackers coach to defensive co-coordinator. Jack Donaldson and Chuck Studley each remained in their old positions. And Charley Winner was brought on board to replace Chuck Weber, who had resigned. And, Brown announced, Bill Walsh, who was the quarterbacks-receivers coach, would now work under the title of "offensive coordinator." Though Walsh had ostensibly performed the duties of an offensive coordinator for a number of years, the designation had never been issued before. The promotion for Walsh was deserved, but it was also an act of appeasement. On several occasions in the past few years, Brown intimated to Walsh that he was the heir apparent. However, Brown had made similar statements to Tiger Johnson in the same time span. Walsh was a budding genius, and Brown recognized his offensive brilliance. Still, Walsh was emotionally volatile. His kinetic energy in the midst of games sometimes chafed Brown. When the time came to make a decision, Brown knew exactly what he was getting in Johnson. Walsh? He was a little too photogenic; he liked being in front of the camera too much. He was a wild card.

There had been interest in Walsh previously, and Brown believed that by giving Walsh a "promotion" he would prevent his coach from taking offers from other clubs. The San Diego Chargers and the newly born Seattle Seahawks had both expressed interest in Walsh earlier but were met by resistance. Brown wasn't concerned with the advancement of his assistants. His only concern was the progression of the Cincinnati Bengals. Walsh stewed. Still, he thought his time would come in Cincinnati, and so he waited for his chance with the Bengals.

And then the opportunity finally arose. Walsh liked and respected Johnson, and his words praising Tiger after the announcement were heartfelt. After absorbing the shock of being bypassed, Walsh issued a statement assuring Bengals fans, "There is no question in my mind that [Johnson] will do a great job."[2] Kind words or not, his frustration was conspicuous. It was obvious to Walsh that the opportunity he expected and rightly deserved wouldn't come with the Bengals. San Diego again expressed interest, and this time Walsh didn't allow Brown to deny him. He resigned his position with the Bengals and signed with the Chargers to serve as offensive coordinator under Tommy Prothro. The decision hardly caused a ripple of concern among Bengals enthusiasts.

The college draft, however, was a source of great interest for Cincinnati fans. The Bengals possessed two first-round draft picks, and there was much anticipation that the first choice would be used on two-time Heisman Trophy winner Archie Griffin. Instead, much to the dismay of their fan base, with their initial selection the Bengals grabbed wide receiver Billy Brooks from Oklahoma. Admittedly, Brown sweated through the next thirteen picks as Griffin's name remained on the board. Brown's gamble of waiting until the Bengals chose again in the twenty-fourth slot paid off. Brown got both of the players he coveted, Brooks as well as Griffin.

In the spring, Cincinnati traded talented receiver Charlie Joiner to the Chargers for defensive end Coy Bacon. The Bengals needed more beef up front, Brown explained. "We just weren't good enough in the big ones late last year. It was certainly evident we needed a little more bulk against Pittsburgh."[3] Others questioned the soundness of the trade, at least from the Bengals point of view. "We got a good pair of hands," a member of the San Diego organization said. "The Bengals got a big mouth," referring to the "clubhouse lawyer" Bacon,

Paul and Mary then retreated to LaJolla and "got out the sticks." After several months of relaxation, Brown returned to his home, Massillon, where he was feted in late June with "Paul Brown Week." The celebration climaxed on June 22 with an evening chock-full of festivities, which began at City Hall, where Brown was presented with a key to the city. Following a brief reception for friends and family, Brown was chauffeured to Tiger Stadium, where a large sign reading, "Paul Brown Tiger Stadium," greeted him upon arrival. This was more than he expected. The door to his limousine opened and much to Brown's embarrassment, an attendant rolled out an orange carpet. Brown walked across the carpet onto the playing field, shaking countless hands along the short journey. He made the stroll alone so those fans who came equipped with cameras could snap a picture if they desired. A man in the crowd called out to Brown, "Wait, Paul, one more picture. I want to take this one for Art Modell." Brown smiled weakly, and then inaudibly mumbled a few words. This was no time to bring up that name. He let the awkward moment pass. There were many familiar faces in the crowd that warmed his heart, and he banished Modell from his mind for the evening. After a brief chat with the Tiger cheerleaders, Brown was escorted to the Amherst Civic Center for a banquet held in his honor.

On the dais with Brown were a number of his former players, including Dante Lavelli, Lou Groza, Lin Houston, Tommy James, and Marion Motley. Brown was visibly moved by the events of the day, and during his remarks, he occasionally slipped into sentimentality. Following a litany of speakers, Brown rose and addressed the well-wishers. "You're probably sick and tired of hearing about Paul Brown," he said. "(Most of you) probably couldn't stand me years ago."[4]

―⚬―

"Bill Johnson will be his own man," Brown assured skeptics.

The Bengals were about to embark on their maiden season without Brown on the sideline, and many critics were of the belief that Johnson was simply a figurehead. Brown meant to dispel these notions. His Sunday afternoons would be spent "up in the press box, with my family and friends like anyone else. There's not going to be a phone. And there will be no ranting and raving or giving the officials heck."[5]

And true to his word, Brown receded into the background. But it wasn't easy. It was tough sitting in his private box, it was tough replaying the game in his head on the car ride home, and it was tougher still when the Bengals lost. Throughout the fall, Brown stayed out of sight, surfacing only to comment on several league issues. He was particularly verbose when relishing the demise of the World Football League. The WFL was closing up shop after just two seasons. Throughout its brief existence the league fought an uphill battle. Initially, attendance was impressive, but the highly publicized numbers were misleading. Several teams were "papering" the house with giveaway tickets, failed promotions meant to whet the appetite of the football fans. Before several weeks passed the product was met by fan apathy, and few wished to spend cash on it. Some teams went belly-up while several other franchises relocated, and many debated that same possibility. The type of investor that helped the AFL weather its early storms was missing in this renegade league. The lack of significant moneymen spelled doom for the WFL.

Brown was downright gleeful at the ruination of the rival league. "It sort of takes the prostitution out of it, and by that I don't mean a man shouldn't try to better himself," Brown said. "But there are different ways to do that." The idea of an athlete selling his services to the highest bidder was anathema to Brown. "The guys who would move to the most money without much feeling or loyalty to the city or team they played for have no place to go. As far as the extra money some of them got, most of that went to the government."[6]

Loyalty. Players who wished to improve their situation and prospects were whores, simply put. Where was Brown's allegiance when he cut a player who was no longer of use to our football? Where was the loyalty when a veteran was sent across the country, bartered to another team? Black and white . . . in the world of Paul Brown, loyalty was conditional.

The selection of Johnson was popular with members of the Bengals. Over the years, he had ingratiated himself with the players by his work ethic, integrity, and knowledge of the game. "If you polled the forty-three players, I'm sure they would pick Bill Johnson as the man they wanted to replace Paul Brown," tight end Bob Trumpy revealed. "He is a player-oriented coach. He listened to suggestions. Paul tries to stay clear of the players."[7]

And the players responded well to their new leadership. The Bengals won nine of their first eleven games in 1976. Still, the club fell short of the playoffs at 10-4. The next year they took another step back, finishing 8-6, again barely missing the postseason following a loss to Houston on the season's final Sunday. Two seasons of near-misses proved the franchise could go on without Paul Brown, but excuses and close calls were getting tiresome to Bengals fans. One evening in the midst of Johnson's second season, a particularly rude fan emblazoned the growing frustration among Cincinnati fans. Johnson and his wife Dot were dining out in a Cincinnati eatery when someone seated at a nearby table recognized the Bengal coach and began to boo.

For Tiger, things would only get worse.

—∭—

Though he had relocated to Arkansas years earlier, Robin Brown remained close to his father and brothers. In addition to his thriving business interests in Arkansas, Robin continued to serve as a part-time scout for the Bengals, primarily covering West Coast schools. Using his personal jet, he would fly from college to college, evaluating players. Personable and genial, Robin was a favorite among the coaches and writers covering the team, and so when the news came in early 1978 that Robin was diagnosed with colon cancer, sadness extended beyond the Browns' immediate family. At one stage of the illness Robin underwent surgery on his lower bowel as well as continuing chemotherapy. Tragically, his body rejected all treatment. But through it all he never stopped living. As he had every summer for the past ten, Robin was at Wilmington College with his four children and wife.

Just a day before he passed, Robin had been jogging, and while his death at forty-six was shocking, it wasn't a surprise. He died on July 28, a day before Paul Brown was to present his old friend, Weeb Ewbank, at the annual Hall of Fame inductions. Understandably, the grief-stricken Brown couldn't be in Canton for the ceremonies. His life was far from an open book. What happened on the playing field each Sunday was all the public need be privy to. Brown's feelings, beliefs, anguish, and sorrow, none of that had anything to do with "our football."

He only offered one comment on Robin's passing, and that came years later. "Burying him," Brown admitted, "was the hardest thing I have ever done."

—⁂—

Shortly after the start of the 1978 season, Paul celebrated his seventieth birthday. Mary, Paul, and Pete spent the evening at Mike and Nancy's over a quiet dinner and a couple of drinks. A year earlier, Mary had found a home for her and Paul in suburban Indian Hill, and soon after Mike and Pete bought homes nearby. Brown wasn't making a fuss about his milestone birthday, but some in the press wanted to play up the "lion in winter" angle. His seventieth came two days before the Bengals traveled to Cleveland for the second game of the year. An old acquaintance from the *Plain Dealer* was one of the writers who paid a visit to Brown at his Riverfront office.

"I still have responsibilities. I have control for years to come," Brown explained to Chuck Heaton. "It's vested in me, then Mike if I should retire."

Brown spoke to Heaton from behind an oversized desk. On the wall behind Brown was a painting of a leaping tiger, on the floor in front of the desk lay a tiger skin rug, head and all a gift from a Cleveland businessman a few years earlier. "I feel like I always felt," Brown assured Heaton. "I have a very happy existence. There have been some blows of course, just recently with Robin, Katy, that thing in Cleveland."[8]

—⁓—

In the second half of the Bengals' final exhibition game before the start of the '78 season, Ken Anderson fractured a bone in his throwing hand, an injury that would cause the quarterback to miss the first four games of the season. Why was the team's star playing so deep into a meaningless game? Brown was furious with his coach's decision-making. With Anderson out, the Bengals got off to the worst start in team history. The heat was on Tiger Johnson and only getting hotter. Brown tried to alleviate the pressure on Johnson.

"He's the coach," Brown said a few weeks into the season. "We're just now starting to get some of the main players back. Give this thing a sporting chance."[9]

In the season's fifth week Cincinnati traveled to San Francisco, where they lost 28-12 to the lowly 49ers. The next morning, the Bengals found they were the butt of many a joke in Cincinnati and San Francisco.

"The 49ers finally found somebody they can beat," a West Coast radio personality quipped.

Back home in Cincinnati, t-shirts were on sale bearing the slogan, "I survived the Bengals of '78." They were at 0-5 and team unity was in disarray. All local media—print, radio, and television—had a field day at the Bengals' expense. The players, coaching staff, and team management, no one at Spinney Field was free from the ever-growing criticism. Brown would later comment that he'd never seen a season open on a more devastating basis.

The afternoon after the embarrassing loss at Candlestick Park, Brown arrived at Spinney Field ready to review film of the previous day's debacle.

There was a rap on the office door. It was Tiger Johnson.

"Can I talk to you?" Johnson asked.

Brown looked up from his desk, "Sure, have a seat," he said.

"I know things are in a terrible shambles. . . . I think something has to be done."

With a nod, Brown grimly nodded. "I think so, too, Bill. It's a difficult thing you're going through, and I'm going through it, too."

Brown accepted Johnson's oblique resignation. He then called in Johnson and his entire staff and informed the whole group of his decision. Every man in the room liked and respected Tiger. Some had been together since that first training camp at Wilmington. The ordinarily stoic Johnson wore his emotions on his sleeve as he went around the room shaking hands and thanking his friends.

A few minutes after Johnson and the rest of the staff left Brown's office, Homer Rice was called in and asked if he would like the job. Without hesitation, Rice answered affirmatively. Indeed, this was his great aspiration, a head coaching position in the NFL! The answer wasn't "Yes." It was "Hell, yes." Rice had known Brown since attending Brown's coaching clinics in the fifties. "I have idolized the man from that point on," Rice admitted. "I used to keep notebooks on everything he said. Paul Brown is seldom wrong."[10]

The highlight of Rice's coaching record was a fifty-game winning streak at Highlands High School in Northern Kentucky. He parlayed his success at the high school level into an unimpressive 12-28-2 combined record while coaching at the University of Cincinnati and Rice University. Having joined the Bengals' staff as quarterbacks coach on May 1, 1978, Rice had a sum total of five professional games on his resume.

How could Brown justify passing over more experienced and worthy candidates already on the Bengals' payroll? Rice was a nice enough guy, but this was a slap in the face to men like Chuck Studley, who had the credentials and had been with the organization for a decade. To stem a possible mutiny, Brown gathered his coaches and offered justification for his selection.

"I could make Mike McCormack the coach, but then I'd have to hire someone to fill his spot," Brown explained. "I could make Chuck Studley the coach, but then I'd need to hire a defensive line coach." Or, he could hire Homer Rice and not fill the position of quarterbacks coach. The staff sat dumbfounded listening to Brown's rationalization, but it all made perfect sense to Brown. This was the least disruptive move to the team, he reasoned, and besides, the season could still be salvaged.

To the already-skeptical press, Brown defended his decision with a lukewarm endorsement of his new coach. "Rice fits into the picture with fine-type coaching and an administration background which is well known in Cincinnati." And no, Brown assured them, he never considered filling the vacancy with himself. "I've given you your last shot at me."

—m—

"A change was made," Bill Johnson later said, diplomatic and loyal to the end. "Let's leave it at that."[11] It was a resignation. Still, many around town couldn't differentiate between it and a firing. That evening, Bob Trumpy was sitting in a local pub when the news came across the television screen. Trumpy knew Tiger well and hated to see what had happened to his old coach in the past two-plus years. The former Bengals tight end had retired at the end of the previous season and begun to work full-time as a radio talk show host. Using a microphone as a bully pulpit, Trumpy unleashed a torrent of criticism on Brown and his tactics.

Brown, Trumpy declared later that evening, didn't give Johnson enough power. And the morale on the Bengals had never been so low. "When Paul Brown came to Cincinnati, he wanted total control of his own destiny. But I don't think he offered Bill Johnson the same opportunity. Control by the head coach has to include a lot more than just between 1 P.M. and 4 P.M. on Sunday and at the weekday practices." Trumpy believed that Brown had interfered with Johnson too much. "He doesn't get his nose into the day-to-day workings of the team, but he determines draft choices and makes deals."

The following afternoon, Trumpy paid a visit to Spinney Field. He wanted to see Brown face to face and tell his old coach what had been broadcast on the radio the night before.

"I don't have to read it," Brown said, waving off a transcript of the show. "I heard it. Mike heard. Nancy heard. Mary heard it. We all heard it."

For the next ninety minutes, Brown berated his former player. He had drafted Trumpy, Brown said, because of his fine character. What happened? What changed you?

Brown stared through Trumpy as Bob tried to defend his point of view. "Paul, you didn't treat him fairly. You didn't let him do his job."

"You're ungrateful," Brown responded. After all that Brown had done for him, this is how he was repaid. What would Trumpy have without the Bengals and Paul Brown? Where was the loyalty?

"You're ungrateful. Now you get off the property."

Trumpy's may have been the loudest, but it wasn't the only voice sounding criticism of Brown. Johnson was well thought of throughout the Cincinnati press contingent, the majority of whom thought Johnson was a scapegoat for the Bengals' horrid start. During games, Mike and Paul sat in the back of the box, behind the coaches. They made decisions on personnel, and they decided who would fill out Johnson's staff. On game day, Johnson and his assistants had been left to their own devices, but the shadow of Paul Brown loomed over each play call.

Brown disputed this notion, and he assured cynics that Rice would run his own program. "Contrary to what people think we (he and Mike) have to be interested because it's part of our job. But we never get into the football aspect of it."[12] Try as he might, however, Brown could not convince his critics that he was not meddling from the front office.

—⚏—

On the field, the results were not discernibly better under Rice. Cincinnati fell to 0-8 before finally registering its first victory. Four consecutive losses followed, placing the Bengal franchise at its lowest ebb in the team's short history. The frustration of a trying season spilled forth from Reggie Williams when he gave an illuminating interview to Mark Purdy of the *Enquirer*. The Bengal organization, according to the third-year linebacker, was lacking in numerous areas. One of the more intelligent, introspective players on the Bengals, Williams gave as numerous examples: below average salaries, a sterile front office, inconsistent publicity efforts, and lack of family atmosphere. Similar complaints were made in the past by Bengal players, in particular, Sherman White and Lemar Parrish, who each demanded to be traded and were both granted their wish.

"As long as the Brown family has been in football, I would assume they knew all the ways to motivate players," Williams stated. "But I would venture to say that 100 percent effort isn't being made to motivate all of them here. Right now, I feel everyone isn't receiving the same motivation, be it in salary, publicity, respect, cordiality, or certain fringe benefits that are inherent to pro football.

"We aren't paid well. Here they use your love for the game, they use that intangible against you (in contract negotiations). . . . That's the one thing that burns me up. . . . But money is really an insignificant part of all this."

How badly did Paul Brown want to win? Williams wasn't the only person in town questioning Brown's impetus. Shortly after stepping aside as head coach, Tiger Johnson confided to a member of the team's front office, "I think Paul wants to win football games, though I wonder how many."[13]

The Bengals tried to salvage their lost season by winning their final three games. The victories may have been nothing more than false hope, but they were enough for Brown to warrant bringing Rice back for another year. Three days after Cincinnati soundly defeated Cleveland, Brown revealed that he was lifting the "interim" tag from Rice's title.

"We feel Homer has done an excellent job of bringing the team back together," Brown explained. "He has earned the right to start from the beginning and get his philosophy and discipline installed."

For his part, Rice was pleased with the work he had done picking up the pieces of the broken season. "I'm totally satisfied," he admitted. "My goal when I was named head coach was to pull it together, finish strong, and put our program in the right atmosphere. I think we have momentum going for us now."[14]

Rice painted a rosy picture in bleak times. A new season stifled whatever momentum he believed his team might have. "The biggest surprise of the 1979 NFL season is the Cincinnati Bengals," a perplexed Brown told a newsman. "I thought that we were going to be a pretty good football team."[15] Cincinnati kicked off the new campaign with six consecutive losses. The ineptitude brought the franchise recognition and notice, for all the wrong reasons. Around town, the team had picked up the sardonic moniker "the Bungles," which was introduced to readers across the country by *Sports Illustrated.* The widely read sports weekly examined the plight of the Bengals. "Everything's gone wrong in Cincinnati, and Paul Brown is getting all the blame," the magazine stated.

Team management was often criticized for its "strictly business" attitude with Bengal players. "They negotiate your salary, they pay you your salary, you play, and that's it,"[16] one veteran complained to Joe Marshall of *Sports Illustrated.*

The Bengals and their miserly ways were a hot topic on the talk shows, and the Bengals, as everyone understood, were Paul Brown. However, more and more Paul was relying on Mike, giving his son significant responsibility running the franchise. Mike's increased profile was a sore spot with some players and the focal point of growing criticism of the team. Highly intelligent and very personable, Mike was sorely lacking in diplomacy when discussing salaries with Bengals players. Since taking over contract negotiations from his father, Mike had increasingly alienated players with his ploys at the table. Ray Buck summarized the growing estrangement on the Bengals in a *Football Digest* piece.

"...the Bengals will remain a lost cause as long as the players resent Mike Brown. Mike has become the dupe for player deficiencies. It's Catch 22. The Bengals are unhappy. They are preoccupied with their own misery. They don't need a strength coach; they need a psychologist."[17]

"If you could divorce a team, I'd divorce this one for mental cruelty,"[18] stated wide receiver Billy Brooks.

Bob Trumpy's repeated barbs on his evening talk show cost him employment on the Bengals' preseason telecasts, and Brown had also banned him from team charter flights. "Paul Brown is a powerful man with a lot of connections," Trumpy explained. "I could have lost my job. He does not forgive. He hasn't forgiven me or Art Modell."

—◊—

Just a short while earlier, at the close of the '75 season, the Bengals were seemingly a team on the cusp of greatness. Their division rivals, the Pittsburgh Steelers, were the foremost obstacle between the Bengals and a possible AFC championship. Theirs was a young squad, and in the coming four college drafts, Cincinnati possessed nine first-round draft picks. And then this, the complete collapse of the franchise. Too many of those first-round picks were wasted on "good guys" and not necessarily good football players.

Brown defended this approach. "It only makes sense to have players who share your beliefs, principles, and ideas," Brown claimed. "These are the principles of Middle America, and Cincinnati is Middle America.

"It's hard enough to win football games when things are relatively pleasant and stable," he continued. "It's almost impossible if somebody is stirring things up."[19]

—◊—

The *Enquirer* ran a poll in the fall that asked readers, "What is wrong with the Bengals?" One-third placed the blame on Brown. But when he looked down from his box, Brown couldn't see himself playing on the field or coaching on the sideline. He was particularly disturbed by the Bengals' sloppy play in the final weeks. On several occasions, including a key play in the next-to-last game of the year during a Redskin touchdown drive, the Bengals' defense had only ten men on the field. "That," Brown said flatly following the game, "should never happen." That contest at RFK

Stadium was the final straw. Attendance had dropped drastically at Riverfront and interest in Cincinnati was waning. The fans were in full revolt. Only 25,336 came out to Riverfront for the Bengals' December 3 game against Atlanta. And for the season finale against Cleveland, there were more than 12,000 no-shows. That they won the final game against the Browns, 16-12, was of little consolation. Brown woke up the day after realizing a change had to be made.

The Bengals called a press conference, where Brown addressed the media for three-quarters of an hour. Several times in the course of talking, Brown repeated how difficult it was to let Rice go. "I dreaded to get up this morning," he said. But, he added, "it was obvious to all we had to do something, because we just weren't getting it done."

"I'd go out week after week hopeful, but things began to happen so much of the time. Something always seemed to be happening to us. These little things have to be controlled."[20]

There was speculation around town that Brown would step aside as general manager and allow Mike to take full control of the operation. Perhaps, some thought, this would be the only possibility for a strong personality to come to Cincinnati and coach, lifting the long shadow of the legend. But Brown wasn't going anywhere now or in the near future. It remained his show to run. Maybe he and Mike needed to reevaluate how they did things, but he wasn't going anywhere, Brown assured all listeners. When asked by a scribe if he would continue on as general manager, Brown was short and to the point. "I sure as hell will."

Eleven days later, Rice's replacement was named at a December 28 press conference. After the Bengals' second straight 4-12 season, Brown knew what he was looking for in Rice's replacement. "He has to be a strong type of personality. He has to be someone who knows the game but who, at the same time, is strong in a demanding way." Brown's choice fit that bill perfectly. Forrest Gregg earned a place in the Pro Football Hall of Fame playing tackle for Vince Lombardi's fabled Packer teams. Nine Pro Bowl nominations awarded to Gregg together equal the praise Lombardi gave when he once referred to him as "the finest player I coached."

Brown had been in contact with Gregg several times throughout the season. And though Gregg thought a change might be made on the Cincinnati staff, he never inquired about the position, nor did Brown show his hand. At the end of the season, however, Brown called Gregg, who was in Florida on a scouting trip.

"Forrest, would you be interested in the coaching job?"

Without hesitation, Gregg snapped, "Yes sir!"

"When could you come up here?" Brown asked.

"I'll be on the next flight."

The next flight, though, was to Toronto. To keep the press off his trail, Gregg flew into Toronto, then to Columbus, where he rented a car and drove to Brown's Indian Hill home. With Mike present, the three men discussed the job, what the Browns expected from their head coach, and how they ran their organization. At the close of the meeting all were in agreement, but first Gregg had to get out of a contractual obligation.

Gregg had served as an assistant in Green Bay, Dallas, and San Diego before landing a place in Cleveland on Nick Skorich's staff in 1974. After finishing at the bottom of the Central Division standings in '74, Art Modell fired Skorich and selected Gregg as the replacement. His record in Cleveland was a mixed bag. A last-place 3-11 season was followed by a respectable 9-5 record one year later. However, all that Gregg had built in his first two seasons collapsed in the third. After a 6-4 start, the Browns lost their final four games of the season to finish with a disappointing 6-8 record. Hounded by player backbiting and intense media scrutiny, Gregg was fired prior to the year's final game.

"Good riddance," was the attitude of most Cleveland players. Gregg was a disciplinarian cut in the mold of his former coach. Of Vince Lombardi, it was said, "He treats all players the same, like dogs.' The same could be said of his protégé.

From Cleveland, Gregg went north of the border to the Canadian Football League and the Toronto Argonauts. There were two more years remaining on his Toronto contract when Brown approached him with the offer to coach the Bengals. Later, commentators would criticize Brown for not requesting permission from Toronto management to speak with Gregg. And Gregg would also come under fire for deserting a team to which he was under contract, but the CFL certainly wasn't the NFL. With great reluctance, Argonauts President Lew Hayman released Gregg from his contract. "I have mixed emotions about leaving Toronto," Gregg admitted to the *Toronto Star.* "I do not, however, feel I'm doing anything dishonorable as some people have suggested."[21]

—ⲙ—

"He's a fundamentalist," Brown said as he introduced Gregg to the Cincinnati press. "I don't know about all this Lombardi stuff. All I know is they sure blocked and tackled when we played them [Cleveland]. We picked him because we wanted to win."[22]

What many players deeply resented in Cleveland, Gregg's stern discipline, was sorely needed in Cincinnati. And Gregg promised to bring that same order to the Bengals, whether his players liked him or not. "I'm in this business to win football games," he explained. "I'm not in this business to be loved. There is talent here to win. What we want to do is put that talent together and step forward from this day on.[23]

"Let me say this about Paul Brown. I'm confident that the coaching decisions are mine, and I'll succeed or fail with my concepts. Paul and I are both working toward the same end, to win a championship."[24]

Several years earlier, in the midst of the 1975 season, a freelance sportswriter named Jack Clary came to Cincinnati while working on a book titled *The Game Makers,* which was backed by NFL Properties. *The Game Makers* was not a traditional study of X's and O's, but rather an examination of people-management skills by the game's great coaches. Brown served as the subject for one of the book's chapters. Clary spent considerable time with Brown, watching him consult with his staff, work with his players, and take long walks through Glendale. The Boston writer couldn't help but be impressed by Brown, and after returning to his New England home Clary wrote Brown a letter of thanks. As a postscript, the author mentioned that

Brown needed to leave a record of his legacy behind by putting his story down on paper. At that moment, Brown couldn't be bothered with such. He was focused on coaching; memories and legacy would have to wait.

A year into Brown's retirement from coaching, Clary wrote Brown again. The letter was placed in the mail the same day Brown was posting a note of his own to Clary. He was ready to take a nice, leisurely jaunt down memory lane, Brown penned, and from there he took the lead. With Clary securely in the passenger seat, Brown got behind the wheel of his Cadillac and the two began retracing Brown's steps through life. A journey to Norwalk, a few days in Massillon, a stop in Columbus, even a trip across the state line to Sharon, Pennsylvania, where they paid a visit to Dave Stewart. Through it all, Clary had a tape recorder running capturing Brown's every thought.

The expedition to Sharon was delayed slightly when Clary ran into car problems before meeting up with Brown, which set them behind their timetable. Brown notoriously adhered to schedules, a trait he picked up from his high school coach years ago.

"Brown, you are never on time," Stewart bellowed as Brown pulled into the drive twenty minutes late.

The two men shared history and genuine affection, but Stewart didn't defer to his legendary pupil. To him, Paul was simply "Brown."

The experience of writing his memoirs was rewarding. Reliving past glories, explaining his tactics, Brown had become more sentimental about his players as the years rolled past, and working on the book gave Brown a chance to toss some compliments around to the men who captured all those championships. The resulting work, *PB: The Paul Brown Story,* was published in October 1979 by Athenum. The book's dust jacket promised:

"After a long silence, it is the first full and complete account of his stormy relationship with famed running back Jim Brown and Browns' owner Art Modell."

Prior to the book's official release several newspapers serialized select portions of the text. Athenum chose some of the more salacious material to excerpt. The most controversial topic centered on Brown's allegation that Art Modell wanted Brown to enter the terminally ill Ernie Davis into a contest back in '62. "Put him in the game and let him play," Brown quoted Modell as saying. "We have a large investment in him and I'd like the chance to get some of it back. . . . If he has to go, why not let him have a little fun."

Upon reading Brown's words in the *Cleveland Plain Dealer,* Modell issued a statement vehemently denying the callous words. He also filed a grievance with the National Football League, claiming Brown's accusations in *PB* violated a league by-law against a member of one club publicly criticizing another club or its members.

"That Paul Brown is guilty of such conduct is irrefutable. In fact, it is difficult to envision a more blatant disregard of this prohibition," wrote the general counsel for the Cleveland Browns, James N. Baily, to Rozelle.

"Paul Brown's portrayal of Art Modell represents nothing more or less than a self-serving distortion of the facts. It can only be surmised that Paul Brown has lost all sight of objectivity in his effort to enhance his own image."[25]

The duty of reviewing *PB* fell to Brown's longtime friend, Hal Lebovitz, of the *Plain Dealer.* With reluctance, Lebovitz regrettably declared the work "one of the most self-serving autobiographies I have ever read."

"For a man who has achieved so much, attained the pinnacle of his profession and great wealth through it, the gross amount of backbiting is unnecessary and redundant. If there were some contrast, it might be palatable. There is none."[26]

The commissioner couldn't help but be drawn into the storm. While attending a Browns-Oilers game in Houston, Rozelle was questioned by a Cleveland writer about Brown's autobiography. "I was greatly disturbed by some of the clips I saw," he admitted. And yes, Rozelle said, he had spoken with Modell on the matter, but for the time being the commissioner would add nothing.

An ambitious Cleveland writer, Russell Schneider, compared an earlier work by Jack Clary, *The Cleveland Browns,* published in 1973, with *PB.* There were many instances in which the two books had distinctly different versions of the exact same events. Brown also angered Leonard Tose, the owner of the Philadelphia Eagles, in his telling of the Bill Bergey affair. Brown directly implied in his autobiography that Tose made an "under-the-table" payment of $10,000 to the Orlando franchise of the WFL in order to release Bergey from his contract. Tose took his complaint to the commissioner and also penned a letter to Brown venting his anger: "Your direct quote attributed to me . . . was nothing short of slander. . . . I have the documents and checks releasing Bill Bergey from his contracts, all very legal and proper."[27] Brown's accusation was refuted in detail by Bergey's attorney, Bart A. Brown, and Tose threatened Brown with litigation.

Through it all, Brown did not back away from his words. While on a tour promoting his autobiography in Massillon, Brown was perplexed by all the fuss but made no apologies for the content of the book.

"I'll stand by every word in the book. Those are the facts. I never dreamed there would be any controversy. I just put down what happened."[28]

He repeated these words on every stop of the promotional tour.

Several months later, just after the first of the year, Pete Rozelle rebuked Brown in a formal letter. ". . . it is clear that chapter twelve of your book contains numerous attacks on Art Modell's business judgment and motivation and, more seriously, on his integrity and character. Particularly distasteful are your characterizations of Art as a person who ran roughshod over his contracts and obligations, who would use a dying young man for his own financial gain.

"The violations lie in publicly critical commentary, which can only have a disruptive effect on league efforts to maintain a positive, stable, and unified public perception. Ironically, your own stature and reputation may even heighten the damage that such statements can occasion."[29] The punishment handed down by the league was a $10,000 fine pursuant to Article VIII, Section 8.13 of the NFL Constitution and By-Laws.

Brown accepted the punishment put down by the commissioner but did not repent. In fact, he continued to stand by his words, which only caused the controversy to be rehashed again and again in the press. "I have sent him [Rozelle] his check," Brown said. "However, I stand by the book as written.

"I might add that in his letter to me, the commissioner specifically

No hard feelings. Bill Bergey with Paul Brown
at a 1977 awards ceremony.

stated that, 'The question of truth, falsity, and privilege, and the like . . .
are not pertinent in this contest.' His action, therefore, is not a judgment
on the facts."[30]

Brown's complete lack of contrition angered Modell, as did Brown's
flaunting of the league's by-laws. The Cleveland Browns' owner also wasn't
appeased at all by the relatively insignificant fine levied by Rozelle. "He
has not only used his announcement of the fine to further disseminate his
slander, he has twisted your own words to lend credence to it,"[31] Modell
complained to the commissioner in a letter.

The book was a missed opportunity, practically void of self-analysis.
What made Paul Brown tick? He certainly wasn't giving away any secrets,
just some stories, a little finger-pointing, and more than a little self-congratulations.

# fifteen    I LIVE FOR SUNDAYS

Under Homer Rice the Bengals, according to one player, were "[48] men going in six different directions."[1] Forrest Gregg guided the entire team in one track.

"We picked Forrest because we want to win," Brown said. By stating the obvious, some people read something into Paul's declaration. What about Tiger and Homer? Did the Bengals not want to win then? There was the strong belief that Johnson was Brown's puppet, and despite Rice's denials, similar thoughts carried on through his tenure with the Bengals.

And now with Gregg . . . would he be his own man? Could he?

Gregg began to answer these questions early, at his first training camp to kick off the 1980 season.

The chairs were laid out in an orderly fashion, and affixed to each chair was a piece of tape upon which were written individual player names. It had been like this for decades. Neat, orderly, organized, typical of Paul Brown, who wanted to know where each player sat. This practice continued under Johnson and later Rice.

Forrest Gregg neither wanted, nor needed, tape on chairs. If he saw an empty seat, Gregg instinctively knew who was missing. Upon entering the meeting hall for the first time, he took a look around the room and called for the team's equipment manager, Tom Gray. Please remove all the tape, Gregg asked Gray.

The next day Gregg arrived at the group meeting room and saw that the tape and the names were back.

Again he called on Gray.

"What's this?" the coach asked.

"Paul wants everyone's name on their desks," explained Gray.

"Take 'em off."

The next afternoon, the scenario played out exactly the same. After three days, Gray pleaded with Gregg for mercy. "Please. Help me. I'm spending forty-five minutes a day putting names on pieces of tape."

With poor Tom Gray as the middleman, Forrest Gregg won the small battle of wills.

There was also the playbook, which was renumbered by Gregg. The playbook had remained virtually unchanged since 1968. Even before that, this was Brown's playbook in Cleveland. But Gregg altered the playbook so severely that it was nearly unrecognizable to Brown.

The new coach also displayed his independence when he cut four-year defensive back Marvin Cobb, who had been a starter, and the second-round selection in the 1980 draft, Kirby Criswell.

All the changes didn't seem to have an effect on the field, however. Ken Anderson spent much of the year hampered by injuries, and the Bengals' offense struggled all season long, finishing twenty-eighth in scoring. "We got better as the season went on," Gregg said. "We will improve next year."[2]

The step forward came on the Bengals' offensive line. Cincinnati possessed the number-three pick overall in the 1980 college draft. It was vital that the Bengals not falter with the selection, as they had done with their top pick several times in recent years. First-round selections Bill Kollar, Archie Griffin, and Mike Cobb hadn't lived up to expectations, nor had second-round choices Charlie Davis, Al Krevis, and Glenn Bujnoch. Brown sent his new head coach to California to personally evaluate USC tackle Anthony Munoz. Though an eye-catching 6'6" and 280 pounds, Munoz was a risky selection to take that high in the draft. He had suffered through surgeries to both knees while at USC, limiting him to only eight games in his junior and senior seasons combined.

Gregg came away from his visit thoroughly impressed by Munoz—his character, personality, and unlimited potential on the football field. While his strength was remarkable, his graceful agility and quick feet had Gregg gushing. Munoz is our guy, Gregg told Brown upon returning to Cincinnati.

He had inherited a team conditioned to losing, and Gregg spent his entire first season trying to alter the infectious attitude that hung like a cloud over Spinney Field. As that 1980 season went on there was progress, though the evolution was hardly perceptible to the casual fan. Gregg's players were buying into his system, and though the resulting 6-10 record didn't suitably convey the steps forward, Gregg had sound reason to feel optimistic.

—⚉—

Like Brown, Gregg spoke to the team. But his speech lacked some of the refinement and cordiality of Brown's well-rehearsed talk. Upon meeting his club for the first time in Wilmington the next summer, Gregg was frank and to the point. "You guys are never going to win until you become more aggressive."

As he had every year as the head coach, Brown addressed his team each summer at the start of training camp. The speech had been re-titled, "Opening Talk as General Manager," and touched on some of the same points Brown emphasized for years. But for the most part, Brown wanted to illustrate the organizational structure of the Bengals. This was his only business and he had everything staked in it.

"We have three major owners," Brown explained, "and I am one of them. We put our money on the line for the franchise. We put up the risk capital. The other two owners are not football people, and the total control of this football team is vested in me, by way of a trust."

In the Cincinnati organization, the buck stopped with him, Brown explained. "Forrest Gregg is the head coach and will operate in this capacity in every sense of the word. He is responsible for and is given total and full opportunity to coach the team. I back Forrest and the staff completely."

Yes, they would see him, Mike, and Pete at practices. "It is our job and we make no apologies for being there." [3]

—⚉—

The Bengals took to the field sporting a new, flashy look. Stripes were added to the jerseys and pant legs of the Cincinnati uniform, as well as to their helmet. Those helmets, the same headgear Brown had cast aside for being too brassy in 1968, were brought out of the dustbin for the new season.

It was an auspicious beginning to the 1981 season. Cincinnati was down 21-0 to the Seahawks before the end of the first quarter. As the home crowd filled the air with a deluge of jeers, Gregg lifted the ineffective Kenny Anderson from the game. Because backup quarterback Jack Thompson was out with an injury, the choice to step in for Anderson fell to third-stringer Turk Schonert. Behind Schonert, the Bengals came all the way back and beat Seattle by the score of 27-21.

Though thrilled with the victory, Gregg was left with a dilemma. Who would start behind center against the Jets in week two? Initially the coach committed to Schonert. However, almost as soon as the words left his mouth, Gregg began to rethink his decision. The next morning, even as the day's newspapers trumpeted his selection, Gregg paid a visit to Brown's office.

"I need to speak with you," Gregg told Brown.

They discussed Anderson. They talked about Schonert. Brown had been down this road before and he could commiserate with Gregg.

"Well, we're playing the Jets," Brown began. "The Jets have two monster defensive ends. Kenny is bigger, stronger, and has more experience. I'd go with Kenny." What he couldn't convey to Gregg was how well he knew Anderson had the competitive drive to go along with his considerable talent. Gregg would have to learn that on his own.

Gregg listened intently, thanked Brown for his thoughts, and left the office. Before finalizing his decision, Gregg needed to know that Anderson wanted to be the Bengals' starting quarterback. He called him in and directly asked him the question.

With conviction in his voice, Anderson looked Gregg in the eye and assured his coach that he wanted to lead the Bengals on the field.

—m—

Brown had a ritual every Monday morning during the season. He would arrive at Spinney Field carrying his lunch—one egg sandwich, three or four olives, a couple of Oreo cookies, and a few apple slices—in a brown paper sack. He then settled in and watched hours of film. And with the knowledge he gathered from his own personal film session, Brown was asked by a reporter, did he interfere with Gregg's decision-making?

Interfere? That was a peculiar question. He was, after all, the team's general manager. "I say what I want to say," Brown replied. "Like, say one end of the field freezes up. Make sure the defensive backs backpedal on that side of the field so they will know what it's like in the game."

Gregg took advantage of Brown's vast experience in the game, as well as his enormous football knowledge. They would sit together on the bus that chauffeured the Bengals from their hotel to the stadium, and on the plane ride that shuttled the team to and from its away games. Saturdays before an away game were always a slow day for the team. There was a workout at the opponent's field, but not much else was happening. Gregg cherished using these Saturdays, sitting back and listening to Brown reminisce about the old All-America Football Conference, those great Browns teams that dominated, about joining the NFL. This wasn't interfering, Gregg thought, this was tapping into a reservoir of knowledge.

—␣—

At the halfway point of the 1981 season, the Bengals stood at 5-3. Good, but not exactly what Gregg had envisioned. This team had too much talent for a 5-3 record. And though it took some time to get going, the Bengals began to show it on the field. Cincinnati reeled off five straight wins, before being stymied by the 49ers. Still, a victory over Pittsburgh in the season's fifteenth week, and the Bengals would clinch the AFC's Central Division

Throughout the seventies, the Pittsburgh Steelers, with four Super Bowl crowns, were the class of the NFL. Before Gregg's arrival in Cincinnati, they had lost eight of the ten meetings with Pittsburgh over the previous five seasons. The aura surrounding the Steelers intimidated teams throughout the league, the Bengals included. On bitter cold days, Steeler offensive linemen would take to the field with their shirtsleeves rolled up, baring their biceps, ignoring the biting weather. Physically, talent-wise, and psychologically, for the better part of a decade, Pittsburgh held the edge over Cincinnati. The Steelers had been the bullies of the AFC Central, but 1981 was a new day. The sheen was off Pittsburgh's crown.

Winning at home would have been nice, but knocking out the Steelers in front of their home crowd was particularly pleasing. Brown sat in the owner's box while those Three Rivers thugs sat in the upper deck watching helplessly as the Bengals roared to a 17-10 victory. While the team celebrated afterward in the locker room, Brown receded into the background.

"I sort of restrained myself, you know," he explained. "Don't get me wrong. I'm happy about what's been accomplished this season. But it's just my nature to think about the next step."[4]

The next step would come in a few weeks when the Bills came to Cincinnati for a first-round playoff game. The Bengals' 12-4 record and first division title in twelve years had done wonders for fan interest in the city. Winning will certainly do that to a town. The spirit was infectious. A local brewery began packaging a beer dedicated to the home town team. "Hu Dey?" was manufactured by Hudepohl Brewery. The name came from a rally cry heard throughout the city. "Who Dey Think Gonna Beat Dem Bengals?" A call answered with a resounding, "Noooooooo-body!"

The fan frenzy grew following the Bengals' 28-21 cliffhanger over Buffalo in their first playoff game. The excitement, Brown told Dick Forbes over lunch, was almost too much for him. The two old friends sat together at the Queen City Club two days before the Bengals met the San Diego Chargers in the AFC championship game.

"It's actually easier when you're involved as the coach and all you're thinking about is football," Brown said. "I don't think I ever thought about the tension (as a coach).

"Now, well, I get upset. It might not show it, but I feel it. During the games now, up there in our box, I get up and walk around in the back.

"It was a game of tension, long, drawn-out. Each play was a hold-your-breath job. It weighs on me."[5]

—∿—

As Cincinnatians awoke January 10, 1982, the morning of the championship game, they were greeted by unbearable cold. A newsman on a local radio station warned his listeners to "Keep all animals inside. Keep your dogs and cats inside." It was fifty-nine degrees below zero with the windchill factor, and while dogs and cats were to be kept safely inside, more than 46,000 people filed into Riverfront Stadium. The Bengals were one game away from the Super Bowl, the furthest the team had ever advanced, and even the brutal weather conditions wouldn't keep away the most diehard fans. John Murdough, the team's business manager, arrived at the stadium at 5 A.M. There was much to prepare for. The water lines had frozen in all the private boxes, as had every toilet in the stadium. Removing the tarpaulin from the field proved to be more daunting than anticipated. The twenty-five-man grounds crew fought the cold and wind for an hour and forty-five minutes before finally rolling up the tarp.

Murdough also had to make preparations to protect fans from their own over-exuberance. Riverfront personnel were instructed to rush any fans directly to the stadium's first-aid stations that, for the benefit of television cameras, stripped to the waist.

"People have been known to die from that kind of exposure,"[6] Brown explained.

The game itself was almost an afterthought compared to the record-setting cold.Outside the ballpark, steam rose from the Ohio River, creating an eerie ambiance. Inside, the Bengals knew the only way to combat the frigid cold was to score early and often. "There's nothing we can do about the weather," Gregg told his team before the game. "You have to assume you're going to be uncomfortable and play around it." Led by Anthony Munoz, the Cincinnati offensive line borrowed from the Steelers and took to the field in short sleeves. It was a sign of solidarity, intimidation, and practicality; the Chargers defensive linemen wouldn't have extra material to latch onto. It was also a bit batty, but the Cincinnati linemen made for an impressive and intimidating sight when they took to the field. Looking down from his box, Brown shook his head. He admired their chutzpah, if lack of self-preservation and comfort.

Cincinnati went up early with a field goal and only got stronger as the game went on. A touchdown pass to M.L. Harris put Cincinnati up 10-0. Early in the second quarter, the Chargers were able to close the gap with a touchdown, but that's as close as San Diego would get as the Bengals won with relative ease, if not comfort, 27-7.

In the locker room a jubilant Ken Anderson sought out Brown. The quarterback embraced his old coach, "We made it, PB!"

Next up for the Bengals were the San Francisco 49ers and the sixteenth Super Bowl. The location, the Pontiac Silverdome, in the Detroit suburb of Pontiac, Michigan, was the first Super Bowl to be played in a cold-weather site.

The NFL had learned some years earlier that its premier event was more than just a football championship game. It had become an entertainment spectacle. Rather than play the game the Sunday following the conference championships, the Super Bowl wouldn't come for two weeks to enhance the hype.

On Monday, January 18, the Bengals arrived at their home base for the week, the Troy Hilton Hotel, and Brown immediately retired to his suite. The next day, during the media crush on the Silverdome field, Brown remained in his room. On Wednesday, when the press arrived en masse at the Troy Hilton, Brown was noticeably absent. Finally, on Thursday, Brown came down from his suite. He'd been fighting a cold by taking numerous naps, Brown explained. Then, with some reluctance, Brown agreed to speak with reporters. About ten writers followed him to an out-of-the-way banquet room and, for the next forty-five minutes, he answered their questions and told a few stories.

Always nattily dressed, Brown wore his houndstooth jacket and snap-brim hat, which was adorned with a colorful feather. "I was probably the first football coach to dress up," he admitted with more than a hint of pride.

He'd been keeping a low profile, Brown explained, because he didn't want to siphon any of the spotlight away from Forrest Gregg. But once he began talking, Brown warmly reminisced. He went back to that first NFL title, his most satisfying win in the pros.

Looking around the room at all the writers scribbling down his every word, he said, "These are exciting days. You guys rather intrigue me. This whole scene does. We never experienced anything like this at those championship games in Cleveland. We didn't have media like this."

Did he anticipate the NFL turning into this? a reporter asked, referring to the grand spectacle the league's championship had become.

No, he replied, he couldn't foresee this. The Super Bowl was a $10 million game that would have 100 million viewers. He remembered the time in Cleveland many years ago when he was approached by a local station that wanted to broadcast Browns' games. The offer was to broadcast the contests for free. The station thought it would be good publicity for the team to be seen on television, and that exposure would be compensation enough. But Brown held out. He sold the rights to Cleveland Gas and Electric for $5,000. "I was trying to get the idea started that it was worth something to broadcast our games.

"I didn't visualize this progressing to the degree that it's progressed," he admitted. "I think television is the reason it has."[7]

All the attention paid Brown during the week embarrassed him. "I won't be going to many Super Bowl parties," he said. "But anyone would be mistaken to think that this doesn't mean a great deal to me. I want with all my heart to win. Cincinnati deserves to win.[8]

"I was a teacher. If I've helped some of the other people around the league learn something, then I'm proud of that. Of course, working under me, they might have learned what not to do. But, these are exciting days, to be sure. As soon as you're 50, you know, a segment of society wishes you would blow away. The Cleveland thing, that fades into nothing."[9]

That "Cleveland thing" wouldn't go away. Art Modell was in Detroit, too, but he didn't have much to say. "What little we had evaporated when he wrote his book," Modell said of Brown and his autobiography, which the Cleveland owner referred to as "libelous and trash."

Brown certainly didn't want to rehash those old, tired memories, certainly not in these happy days. Still, the primary storyline to the game, the story that every reporter worth his salt tried to get an angle on, was Bill Walsh and Paul Brown, the student and the mentor, and the unreported grudge between the two.

Walsh became the 49ers' head coach in 1979 after two years as head coach at Stanford. In only three seasons Walsh turned the 49ers around from 2-14 to the NFC representative in the Super Bowl. If he harbored any bitterness toward Brown and the Bengals, Walsh refused to reveal his feelings to the dozens of reporters questioning him.

"It was a great experience for me to be with the Bengal organization for eight years," Walsh said. "I wouldn't be where I am now if not for the many lessons I learned in Paul Brown's organization.[10]

"I had aspirations for the Bengal job," Walsh admitted. "I had hopes. But there was no bitterness toward Tiger Johnson. . . . No bitterness on my part at all, only vast disappointment."

Both Brown and Walsh dismissed the notion that a "feud" existed between them. That stuff was just newspaper hype; they had to fill their papers with something. In fact, Brown demurred when the question of Walsh came up. He did not wish to discuss "the Bill Walsh matter." But people close to both men told a different story, that Walsh hoped for nothing more than to spoil the day of the man that he was certain tried to hold him back.

—⁓—

Once the game began, there were too many lapses, too many turnovers. The 49ers built up a 20-0 lead at halftime, which, despite the Bengals' best efforts, proved too much to overcome. That's not to say they quit. To the contrary, Cincinnati clawed its way back to within nine at one point, 23-14, before San Francisco embarked on a time-consuming drive that resulted in a back-breaking field goal.

"Too many mistakes against too fine a team," Brown said afterward. And that was the only comment he had on the heartbreaking 26-21 loss. "I don't have anything to say. I've been through it."[11]

Brown came up behind Gregg in the locker room. "Forrest," Brown said as he extended his right hand, "congratulations on a good season."

Taking Brown's hand, Gregg forced a smile. "We came up a little short," the chagrined coach replied.

"You had a fine season, a fine season."

Later that evening, more than two hundred invited guests came to a Bengal "victory" party at the Troy Hilton. The event was planned by Paul and his son Mike, "win or lose." An eight-piece band performed for the guests. It was dance music, none of that rock and roll. While others celebrated an improbable season, from 6-10 to the Super Bowl, Brown retired early. As the music played and the dancers danced, Brown quietly retreated to his room.

—⁂—

"I've always had a strong belief in the value of truth, honesty, character, and loyalty," Brown told a reporter for the *Los Angeles Times* on the telephone. "I'm not trying to sound like a sanctimonious angel. It's just that I think those qualities are keys to success in both football and life in the larger world. And I must admit these values seem to have been diluted among today's athletes."

In the course of the conversation with Chris Cobbs of the *Times,* Brown intimated that his retirement, while clearly a concession to his advancing age, was also rooted in his growing frustration with the modern athlete, as well as the increasing influence of the Players Association. A distinct threat of a strike was again in the air. "A strike would hurt, but strikes are the way of the world. We have to work to insure that we keep football pretty much as it is now. Our game is fun to watch."[12]

The ever-increasing popularity of the NFL was a boon for the league's owners, but the Players Association wanted its share of that pie. For a couple of years, the union had been politicking for a larger share of the gross revenues. But the owners didn't yield a thing. Negotiations for a new collective bargaining agreement took place throughout the exhibition season and into the regular season. With no sign of an accord in sight, the association's Board of Player Representatives voted to call a strike following the second weekend of games in the 1982 season. The walkout officially began on September 19.

The fear on both sides of the dispute was, if the strike wasn't settled quickly, then there was an excellent chance the work stoppage would become a drawn-out affair that would threaten the remainder of the season. Brown no better understood the reasoning behind this strike than he did eight years earlier, in 1974. The players were being used, he believed, by Ed Garvey and other leaders of the association. "They are beginning to realize they are just pawns,"[13] Brown said.

There was some backlash from a few Bengal players who were offended by Brown's paternalistic statement. This ripple of controversy forced Brown to amend his comment . . . slightly.

"What I said was that I think the players are just Garvey's pawns. I just think Garvey is using them. I don't think a lot of our guys are aware of where he's trying to lead them. If this thing goes much longer," Brown stated, "the season will be jeopardized."[14]

One month later, the dispute was no closer to being settled. "If owners were to give in to those demands, what they would be doing would be giving up control of the game they have built up in the past sixty-two years."[15]

What did the players have invested in the well-being of the league? It was their job. To Brown, the game was his lifeblood. Brown and the other owners were not about to give up the store, not for Ed Garvey, not for anybody. "That's just management's position from the beginning that the control of the football league would have to be with the people who had invested in it."[16]

The season was saved when the Players Association capitulated following a fifty-seven-day walkout. The players did achieve some modest gains, including severance pay, a raise in minimum salaries, pre-season pay, and a pension increase. But they did not realize their main goal of attaining a higher percentage of gross revenues.

Yes, the season was salvaged, but barely. The integrity of the sixteen-game schedule was thrown aside in favor of a nine-game season. The number of teams participating in the playoffs was expanded to sixteen, of which the Bengals, with their 7-2 record, were one. A 44-17 first-round drubbing at Riverfront by the Jets, however, quickly ended Cincinnati's season.

—⁓—

For all its unprecedented growth and prosperity, the NFL was at a cross-roads. Fan loyalty was tested when the strike forced the cancellation of regular-season games for the first time in the league's history. And now a new upstart league, the United States Football League, was set to challenge the NFL monopoly on pro football. After some consideration, the new league opted not to go head to head with the NFL. Instead, the USFL scheduled its games for the spring and summer. After two years of planning and research, the new twelve-team league took to the field in the spring of '83

They may not have been competing head to head, but both leagues were in competition for players and coaches.

—⁓—

The summer was the beginning of the most trying period for the Bengals and Brown since 1974. Two prominent members of the team, Ross Browner and Pete Johnson, were suspended by Pete Rozelle for four games. Both men testified in a Cincinnati courthouse against a local drug peddler. Johnson and Browner each admitted to buying cocaine on numerous occasions in 1980 and '81. These two Bengals weren't alone in their habits. Drug use was up around the league; some might say it was rampant. Other names were brought out in the papers, but many guilty parties were hidden from public identification. For his part, Brown had no sympathy for the guilty.

"A guy who is on drugs needs money to keep the habit going, and I guess they'll do anything if they need it," Brown said, alluding to the possibility of point-shaving or even throwing a game.

"It's terrible to have it in our midst," Brown said of the league's, and, more specifically, the Bengals' widening drug problem. "I'm thinking what it might do to our sport. You never know what these guys might do and I think that's why Pete [Rozelle] has finally decided that you have to do something. I don't think this business of sending people off [individual clubs sending players for treatment] is stopping the practice."[17]

Drugs. Brown was a man out of step and out of place with the times.

A four-game suspension. Back in the day Brown would have shown a player the door if he was caught using drugs. But the commissioner's reprimand of Browner and Johnson would have to suffice. Not for a moment did Brown consider appealing the suspension. Paul could never understand the betrayal to the team by these drug users. The betrayal, purely for self-gratification, both angered and saddened him.

Money. Some things never change. Everybody wants to be paid what they're worth, and maybe a little more. But what had changed was Brown's ability to dictate contractual terms to his players. The Bengals' finest player, Anthony Munoz, used the only weapon at his disposal and held out for the first thirteen days of training camp. Other Cincinnati players looked to the USFL to sweeten their deal. First tight end Dan Ross signed to play with the Boston Breakers, and then wide receiver Cris Collinsworth agreed to a futures contract with the Tampa Bay Bandits in 1985.

Brown had little respect for the men running the USFL. "These people aren't football people," Brown said. "Actually, it's a ridiculous financial risk they are taking."[18] Dan Ross's contract, in particular, provoked Brown. Boston gave Ross a three-year, $1.5 million deal. "The first thing Danny is going to find out is that he gives half of it back to the government," Brown said, condescendingly. "And there's no severance, no pension, no stability."[19]

The Jacksonville Bulls then asked the Bengals for permission to speak with Cincinnati's offensive coordinator, Lindy Infante. Brown flatly refused the request. Still, the Bulls went ahead and reached out to the Bengal assistant. Infante had been waiting patiently for a head coaching opportunity in the NFL, and when the Bulls approached he listened. Four days before the start of camp in 1983, Infante agreed to coach the Jacksonville team when his contract with the Bengals expired on January 31, 1984.

Typically, Brown was unyielding. The day after Infante came to an agreement with Jacksonville he was fired. Allowing a coach under contract to another team to remain with the Bengals was akin to allowing the "fox in the henhouse." There would be no lame-duck coaches on his team. No, Infante's action, Brown said, was a conflict of interest and a breach of contract.

Forrest Gregg wanted to keep Infante on his staff. When Brown adamantly refused to retain the offensive coordinator, Gregg expressed his desire to fill the vacancy. Brown declined this request also. He wouldn't pilfer a coach from another team, not this close to the start of the season. No, Brown wouldn't do to another club what the Bengals had done to them. This decision, as well as Brown allowing players to be signed away by the USFL without a fight, frustrated Gregg. How much of this stubbornness could be attributed to cost-saving measures is unclear, but Gregg's hands were tied nonetheless.

Despite a strong finish, a 7-9 record was all the Bengals could muster in 1983 thanks to six losses in the season's first seven games. Six days after Cincinnati concluded the season with a 20-14 loss at Minnesota, Forrest Gregg signed to coach his old team, the Green Bay Packers. It had long been a dream of Gregg's, returning to the place of his former glory, and Brown did not stand in his way. He gave the Packers permission to speak with Gregg. He recognized that, despite the infusion of discipline Gregg brought to Cincinnati, it was time for Gregg and the Bengals to part ways. One scribe described the deterioration as "a gradual falling out between two strong-willed men."[20]

Again, as the season neared its conclusion, Brown made a personnel decision based on dollars and cents. Following a spate of injuries, Gregg wanted to bring a player in so the Bengals would be at full strength. The request was declined, which forced the coach to prepare for a game one man shy of the allowable forty-nine. "You can't win if you can't sign your players," Gregg was heard to mumble, but for the record he took the high road. When he addressed the media to announce his move to Green Bay, any dissatisfaction Gregg may have had with Brown was not on display. Gregg had too much respect for Brown to denigrate him in the press. Brown had earned that.

"I will always be grateful to Paul Brown for giving me the chance to coach again in the National Football League," Gregg said. "I think it is something that worked out well for him, and I think it worked out well for me. That I will never forget.

"We started this as friends and we have ended it as friends."[21]

—m—

Speculation in the local press was that the leading candidates to fill Gregg's vacancy were Bengal defensive assistants Hank Bullough and Dick LeBeau, along with BYU head coach LaVell Edwards. But for their next coach, Mike and Paul Brown looked backward, to one of the original Bengals. The thirty-eight-year-old Sam Wyche had previously been offered a position with Cincinnati. In 1980, when Forrest Gregg was putting together his staff, Wyche was interviewed for the position of offensive coordinator. Gregg and Brown, who sat in on the meeting, both came away impressed with Wyche. The job was offered, but, according to Brown, the 49ers would not release Wyche from his contract. He had joined Bill Walsh's staff in 1979, where Wyche remained until 1983, when he became the head coach at Indiana University.

Wyche never applied for the Bengals job, but he was, according to Brown, "the first and only man interviewed for the job."

Brown made the statement on December 30, 1983, two days after the hiring of Wyche was announced. For those forty-eight hours, the Bengals' new coach was out of reach to the press. Now, however, Brown sat next to Wyche as he was introduced to the Cincinnati media.

"He was the man we wanted from the beginning and we are very happy he has elected to be with us," Brown continued. "There are always those who, for what reasons I'll never know, like to project it like it's a puppet situation. Don't kid yourself. Don't be misled. And it wasn't before. Sam is his own man."

Following an opening statement by Wyche, a question was posed to Wyche concerning the "puppet situation" involved when working for Paul Brown.

Wyche looked to PB. "What should I say now, Paul?"

After the laughter over Wyche's comment died down, Brown piped in. The phones in the owner's box were for emergency use only, he explained. The lines didn't even reach the bench.

"Can I get to you from down there if I need you?" Wyche quipped.

"No," Brown replied tersely.

"Third and three is all mine?" a smiling Wyche asked.

Brown obviously failed to see the humor in the exchange. "You know, it gets to be rather ridiculous after seven years."[22]

In Wyche the Bengals had a different personality at the helm. As a player, he was known to be a practical jokester, and as a coach, Wyche liked to indulge in magic tricks. But Brown wasn't searching for a comedian or a conjurer when he looked to Wyche. What he wanted was his brilliant and innovative offensive mind. His Hoosiers only recorded a 3-8 record in Wyche's one season at Indiana, but offensively the team made great strides as the year wore on. Despite the losing record, Wyche brought excitement to Indiana with a sophisticated passing attack. Brown wanted some of that excitement brought to Riverfront Stadium.

—⁓—

The USFL made a splash signing collegiate stars directly out of school, including the previous two Heisman Trophy winners, Herschel Walker and Mike Rozier, and Reggie White, the finest defensive lineman in the country. The league had also raided NFL rosters, and no team was hit harder by these incursions than the Cincinnati Bengals. Ross and Collinsworth were just the beginning. Offensive lineman Dave Lapham signed with the New Jersey Generals, as did twelve-year veteran linebacker Jim LeClair. And Tom Dinkel opted to go with the Jacksonville Bulls. Typically, Brown was dismissive of the whole state of affairs. Who did Ross sign with, Brown asked hypothetically, the "New Jersey Colonels?"

His new coach took a more understanding position about the player defections. "If players are in a business," Wyche said, "this is their free enterprise. Their product is themselves, so they market themselves."[23]

Why were the Bengals affected more than any other club? Was the USFL specifically targeting Cincinnati because of Brown's alleged cheapness? Agents who were asked that specific question said it was just a coincidence, but maybe Bengal players were more receptive to USFL offers. The Browns again were accused of stinginess when the Bengals' number-one draft pick, Rickey Hunley, couldn't come to terms with the team. Hunley's holdout lasted the entire summer before Paul and Mike Brown traded his rights to Denver for the Broncos' number-one pick in the '85 draft in addition to a conditional pick.

The turmoil was all in the past, Brown believed, the Hunley contract squabble notwithstanding. "This is a happy time for us," Brown said as the 1984 season was set to kick-off. "We don't have guys coming in and telling us what they're going to do if we don't pay 'em. We don't have a coach leaving right before camp."

Maybe things were more stable in 1984, but the best the Bengals could muster was an 8-8 record.

—⁓—

In the fall of '82, Pete Rozelle negotiated a $2 billion television contract with the three major networks, bringing $14 million annually to each franchise for the next five years. That's $14 million before a single person passed through the gates. It was the most successful sports league on the planet, yet turmoil and strife continued to plague the National Football League

A few years earlier, in 1980, Al Davis attempted to relocate his Oakland Raiders down the California coast, to Los Angeles. The move, however, was blocked by a court injunction. To this, Davis responded by filing an antitrust suit against the NFL. Brown got into this business to coach, to teach, and now it had become this. Teams shouldn't relocate, this Paul believed, but neither should the league prevent such moves. Still, the Davis lawsuit saddened Brown. The NFL should not be run through the courts. The league should be governed internally. But for two years, as Davis and Pete Rozelle battled one another in the press and courtroom, the league had its dirty laundry aired out for the public to see and scrutinize. And though Brown lamented Davis's decision, Brown respected the right to do with his franchise what he felt was best. So when Davis won the lawsuit in

1982 and relocated the Raiders to Los Angeles, the floodgates were open. In the winter of '84, the Colts bolted Baltimore in the dead of night and set up shop in Indianapolis.

The USFL continued to be a costly nuisance to the NFL. Across the league some owners got into the frenzy and tried to match the offers made by USFL owners. Some, like Eddie DeBartolo in San Francisco, simply egged on the escalating salaries, an action that led to increased pay across the board. Obstinately, Brown was in favor of holding the line on player salaries. If this spending spree continued, Brown believed, the new league would spend itself into oblivion and then we can get back to business. It wasn't all bad news for the Bengals, though. After losing several key players, Cincinnati finally had some good news concerning defections to the new league. The team's lanky star receiver, Cris Collinsworth, was to begin service with the Tampa Bay Bandits in February 1985. The deal fell through when Lloyd's of London refused to issue an insurance policy on Collinsworth due to the player's chronic ankle problems.

Truth be told, Tampa Bay was thankful to be relieved of the obligation. What was a promising idea began to founder as too many teams overextended to make a splash in the headlines. After their first season, several USFL owners proposed moving their games to the fall, where they would directly compete with the NFL. However, the small group of men who originally designed and planned the league was adamantly opposed to such a proposal. "Newcomers" like Donald Trump, owner of the New Jersey Generals, pushed for the move, a move that they dreamed would force a merger with the NFL. This new breed forced the issue, and in October of '84 it was announced that beginning in the fall of '86 the USFL would take on the NFL directly.

Almost simultaneously, the USFL filed an antitrust lawsuit claiming the NFL held a monopoly in respect to access to some stadiums as well as television broadcasts. The USFL was reaching for damages of $567 million, which under antitrust law would have been trebled to $1.7 billion. The suit went to trial in the spring of 1986, and no one knew which way the jury would lean. When the verdict came down on July 29, Paul and Mike were riding together in a car listening to the news on the radio. The jury found that the NFL was indeed a monopoly. Paul and Mike looked at one another. What were the damages? they each wondered silently. And then it came.

One dollar . . . one dollar

—⚏—

His passion for the game hadn't faded. And Brown did like what Wyche was building. It was exciting, unpredictable.

After accumulating 8-8 and 7-9 records in 1984, and '85, respectively, the Bengals finished 10-6 in Wyche's third season and were a team seemingly on the cusp of something big as they entered the 1987 campaign. An opening week win at Indianapolis was followed by one of the most distressing and embarrassing losses in the Bengals' twenty-year history.

Six seconds remained in the game as the Bengals led San Francisco 26-21 and possessed the ball on their own thirty-yard line. Rather than punt on fourth and twenty-five, Wyche inexplicably opted to run a sweep. The play lost five yards and the 49ers took over with two seconds remaining. Two seconds was quite enough time for Joe Montana to hit Jerry Rice for a game-winning touchdown.

The local talk shows and newspapers were all calling for Wyche's head following the debacle at Riverfront. Brown, however, thought talk of Wyche's job being in jeopardy was nonsense. "Ridiculous," he said. "Of course it's not in jeopardy. He's the head coach of our team and he'll continue to be the head coach."[24]

He might have been Brown's man, but Wyche would be coaching nobody the following Sunday. For the second time in five years, the NFL-PA called a strike in the midst of the regular season.

—⚏—

The Bengals, led by third-year quarterback Boomer Esiason, were among the most militant strikers in the league. On the first day of picketing, thirty-nine Cincinnati players walked the line in the morning, and thirty did so later in the afternoon. Three players, including Esiason, sat in front of the entrance gate prohibiting a bus containing replacement players from entering the facility. The town quickly turned on its fair-haired quarterback. Cincinnati had long been a conservative city, and Esiason's provocative and belligerent action drew ridicule and criticism on talk shows and in the local newspapers.

Without using his quarterback's name, Sam Wyche censured Esiason in the press. "I want guys to be independent enough to be evaluated whether they want to be on a picket line lying in front of buses, acting silly," said Wyche, "or whether they want to be professional adult men and live in this community after football is over and respected after it's over with."[25] Brown allowed his coach to do the talking. Unlike previous squabbles with the Players Association, Brown remained silent. Speaking out in the press would serve no purpose, he believed. This time around things were very different. Owners anticipated and prepared for a strike by paying replacement players a weekly stipend of $1,000 in case the regular players walked out. Unlike 1982, only one week of games was canceled in 1987. Beginning with the second week of the strike, the league put on official games with scabs dressed in NFL uniforms. Unlike some teams, the Bengals didn't put a lot of thought or effort into building a replacement team. In fact, neither of the club's two scab quarterbacks had played Division I college football. Upon meeting his replacement players, Wyche went directly to the basics. Holding a football up in one hand, Sam began. "This," he explained, "is a football."[26]

—◊◊◊—

The games went on, fans came to the stadiums, and the television networks put the show on as if nothing were amiss. Indeed, the product was inferior, ratings were down, and attendance suffered, but still the games went on. Upon the first replacement contest, the union began to feel cracks in its solidarity. Eventually eighty-nine association members crossed the pickets and shattered whatever chance the union had of succeeding. One game was canceled outright, while three others were replacement farces, and the twenty-four-day strike ended much as it began, with ownership in control of the game and the players crawling back to work without a collective bargaining agreement.

"A battle has been won," Cris Collinsworth acknowledged, "and our side didn't win. It's the end of the Civil War. They've taken Atlanta. Let's get the furniture before they burn it, too."[27]

The Bengals were 1-1 when the strike began and 2-3 when it concluded on their way to an immensely disappointing 4-11 campaign. As the year came to a close, Wyche's job security was topic one in Cincinnati sports circles. Surely his job was in jeopardy after a season like that. But Brown liked Wyche. He liked him personally, and he also believed Wyche was a fine coach with enormous potential. But there were some things that Sam needed to change. Rather than fire Wyche, Brown instead sat his coach down and talked with him. He presented Wyche with a list of stipulations. If Wyche agreed with these "suggestions," then he could return for the final year of his five-year contract.

"I make no apologies for believing in certain things," Brown flatly stated. "We talked about the things that I felt had to be changed or improved. Most of them dealt with Sam's personal discipline and his organizational and practice procedures. That was the way we operated, period."

On a plane ride home from an away game Wyche once wondered aloud what the airline might offer to eat on the trip. "I haven't eaten in twenty-four hours," Wyche mentioned to Brown. This was unacceptable, as was Wyche's habit of staying in the office until all hours of the night and reappearing before the first morning's light.

"I told Sam to eat properly," Brown offered. "And I told all of our coaches to go home early every night. No more sleeping on cots. That's ridiculous."

Wyche certainly had a different style from Brown. He allowed the offensive unit and defensive units to straggle onto the field separately where they gathered in a number of smaller groups. Running backs gathered together in circles, as did linemen, receivers, etc. and the individual position coaches would then go over new plays that had been installed the night before.

This was no way to run a team.

As a coach Brown always gathered the entire team together in the meeting room. They sat as Brown made several announcements, informing his players of everything they needed to know before they hit the field. When dismissed by Brown, everyone would then slip on their cleats, which they removed because the meeting room had tile floors. They would then gather in a breezeway before taking the field . . . as a team.

Brown pushed this practice on Wyche. "I wanted all the players and all the coaches sitting in the same classroom when Sam walked in," he said. "And there was no two-minute warning. The clock was on the wall."

Brown also told Wyche not to argue with refs. Far too often Wyche was confrontational with officials. Indeed, Brown reiterated, Wyche needed to get his emotions in check. "You're a better head coach when you're not steamed up," Brown said.

There was also the issue of the coach's weekly press conference. Wyche regularly sat with the media on Tuesday, the players' day off. But in 1987 these weekly gatherings grew increasingly contentious as the season wore on and Wyche's comportment grew testy. Following the more confrontational sessions, Wyche's outbursts and impatient remarks would be replayed all week on news outlets throughout the city. At times he seemed to be a coach on an emotional ledge.

"Sam would prepare for those things," Brown explained. "He meant well, and he was just trying to do what the job called for. But he would take time out from his work schedule to do that. We wanted that time spent on football."

Months later Brown reflected on his decision to retain Wyche. "It was my feeling that last season was an aberration," Brown explained to *Football Digest*. "With the strike and the replacement games and all that went on, there were a lot of things that were beyond the coach's control. I didn't think it was fair to judge [Wyche] on the basis of that season."[28]

The strike had brought a division to the Bengal locker room. Wyche worked throughout the off-season and into training camp trying to bring his squad together. One avenue that might help team unity would be more accommodating weight facilities. The weight room at Spinney Field was lacking in atmosphere, comfort, and equipment. Wyche looked into the problem and discovered the entire team could get a membership to the downtown YMCA and have access to its top-of-the-line amenities.

Wyche approached Brown with his idea. It cost $5,000 for a team membership, Wyche explained. Brown shook his head. The strike was still fresh in his mind. "They got their money," Brown snapped. "Let them pay for it."

Despite Brown's disapproval, Wyche went ahead with his plan. He told the director to just bill him personally, which came to $9 a visit for the coach. Once at Wilmington, Wyche tried other avenues to bring his team together. He redid rooming assignments, drawing up new pairings from scratch. He mixed black and white, offensive players and defensive players. They were a team, and they would do everything as a team. All barriers between them were torn down.

For all his team-building, Wyche encountered numerous problems at Wilmington. At the beginning of the '88 season number-one pick Rickey Dixon held out, missing all of training camp. He did not sign until the first week of the season. Three veterans—Larry Kinnebrew, Robert Jackson, and Dave Rimington—were released from the team when they could not come to a contractual accord. And two Bengal veterans—Emanuel King and Daryl Smith—received thirty-day suspensions for failing drug tests. And though he was present and accounted for, number-two draft pick Elbert "Ickey" Woods arrived at Wilmington sporting a ponytail, a disconcerting site for Brown, indeed.

If Woods's ponytail was the Bengals' biggest problem of the season, the team would be in fine shape. Still, the running back's choice of hair style was another sign of the changing times. And, as Brown's eightieth birthday neared, many writers sought out the old man for thoughts on the current state of the game. Art Rooney had just died a month earlier, and the passing of the Pittsburgh Steelers' patriarch prompted a flood of memories and thoughts from Brown.

"It's not as much fun as it used to be. I think any long-time owner will tell you that.

"We have more problems now than we've ever had. Part of that is the change we're seeing at the top. The owners who really lived the game, men like Art Rooney and George Halas, are gone. They are being replaced by all these entrepreneurs.

"They don't understand the game. They operate by the philosophy, more is better. They hire the biggest front office, the biggest coaching staff, the biggest everything. Last year one owner [San Francisco's Ed De-Bartolo] offered his players a bonus if they won the division. The idea is to buy everything.

"What's happening is the system is out of whack. We're spending millions on first-round picks, and only one-third of them ever pan out.

"The [old] way was better. Pay the players who are carrying the load. Pay them based on their performance. But we'll probably never see those days again, thanks to the agents and the union."

It wasn't all bad. Not by a long shot. "It's a great game," Brown said. "I can't get it out of my system. There may come a time when I say, 'That's it. I've had enough.' I reached that point with coaching and I'll probably reach that point with what I'm doing now.

"I don't know when that will be. I could live without the Monday-Friday part of it now. But I can't give up Sunday. I live for Sundays."[29]

Indeed, a number of reporters contacted Brown and asked him to look back on his eighty years. Memories, there were plenty of them, and Brown was happy to rehash them. But the present was on his mind. "Reluctantly, I've had to let some things become acceptable that I wish I didn't have to. I'm talking about the drug problems and things of that sort. Years ago, I could be a lot more strict about those things. But now, society just keeps beating you down and you have to go along with the way things are. I don't like it, but I do it. Of course, it's a little easier for me today because I'm not coaching anymore, which means I'm not as directly involved with these things as I used to be."

The biggest problem confronting Brown in his role as the Bengals' general manager? "It would have to be the labor situation and such related issues as free agency," Brown admitted. "The thing that people forget is the reason we have our rules is to equalize competition so the smaller markets can compete with the bigger markets. We're trying to keep it so all twenty-eight teams can play and you know there's a chance it's going to be a ballgame right down to the end."[30]

Yes, there were difficulties and distractions, but the game itself still brought joy. And on the field the Bengals were enjoying their finest season since 1981. They caught the city by storm by winning their first six games. Wyche and his stirring no-huddle offense exploded on the league. Just one year earlier, his innovation was the subject of ridicule and scorn, but now everything was clicking. Wyche took the idea of the hurry-up offense used in a two-minute drill and implemented the style into the Bengals' offense regardless of the time on the clock. This "no-huddle" device kept defenses off balance by not allowing situational substitution and time to regroup and recover before the next snap. This freewheeling style enraptured Cincinnati fans and confounded Bengal opponents.

Rookie running back Ickey Woods became something of a cult hero in town when he unveiled an ingenious dance step following a touchdown. The dance, if it could be called that, was a simple move. Three hops on the right leg, and then three on the left . . . a new craze was born, the Ickey Shuffle.

A song hit the airwaves in Cincinnati:

*Have you heard of the dance that's taken the town;*
*It starts in the jungle and spreads all around*
*His name's Ickey Woods, running with muscle;*
*Now even Paul Brown does the Ickey Shuffle*

As the wins piled up even the staid, crotchety Paul Brown got into the spirit. "That little dance you do," he told Ickey. "I don't think much of it, but my wife likes it."

But winning is infectious, and Brown couldn't resist trying Ickey's jig himself in front of a shocked and amused audience. "If you can't do the Ickey Shuffle, you can't do any dancing at all,"[31] Brown laughed.

They rode the wave to a 12-4 record and a spot in the playoffs, where the roll continued. First up were the Seahawks, who the Bengals handled with ease, 21-13, before they played host to the Buffalo Bills for the AFC

Championship. An hour and fifty minutes before the game, Buffalo coach Marv Levy strong-armed the league. Levy argued that the Bengals' "no-huddle" style was outside the rules and spirit of the game. Shortly before kickoff, the NFL issued a statement specifying that officials would nullify plays in which, in their judgment, "the offense gained an unreasonable and unfair advantage by a quick snap of the ball, e.g. a quick snap which is intended to cause the defense to be penalized for too many players on the field."

Wyche was apoplectic. They had used the no-huddle extensively all season and sporadically for the three years before, and now, moments before kickoff the Bengals were told they might be penalized if the scheme was used. A week earlier the Seahawks angered Wyche when several players feigned injury, thus stopping the clock and allowing time for defensive substitutions. Levy threatened to do the same.

Come game time, Wyche ignored the league's newly instituted restrictions as well as Levy's threats. The Bengals took to the Riverfront turf and ran their offense as they had all year without incident. The resulting 24-10 victory catapulted Cincinnati to Miami and its second Super Bowl appearance. The opponent would once again be Bill Walsh and his 49ers.

The storyline was similar: Walsh versus his mentor Brown. But that was old news. Wyche versus his mentor, Walsh, however, that story was fresh. But reporters still sought out Brown and however much he tried to downplay it, Brown couldn't conceal his excitement. This was the one trophy that had eluded him, and as could be expected, Brown was a focal point for reporters once the team arrived in Miami. The story of the old master returning to the championship still had legs, as did the recap of Brown's enormous legacy to the game. But the attention was misplaced, he insisted. This was Wyche's game, not his. "It's nice for Sam's sake," he said. "I keep trying to make a point that it's no crown for me, it's for the coaches and players who went through it all."[32]

—⚍—

The heartbreak began the night before the game.

Two years earlier, Bengals running back Stanley Wilson was suspended by the league for the 1987 season due to a substance abuse problem. The next summer, prior to training camp, Brown sat with Wyche and running backs coach Jim Anderson when Wilson was eligible to return. Brown's instincts told him not to take Wilson back, but against his better judgment, Brown allowed Wyche and Anderson to persuade him. Wilson came back and became a key contributor to the team's offense.

In Miami, Wilson's troubled past was out of mind. The eve before the Super Bowl the Bengals were housed at the Holiday Inn in Plantation. On the way to a meeting with a couple of teammates, Wilson stopped. "I forgot my playbook," he said. "I'll meet you guys downstairs."

Wyche was set to begin the meeting when he noticed Wilson's chair empty. He gave Wilson a few moments to arrive. Fifteen minutes later, however, Wilson was still absent and Wyche left to investigate. Attempts to call his room went unanswered as did knocks on Wilson's hotel room door. Eventually the door was broken down by the Cincinnati police chief, Larry Whalen, who had accompanied the Bengals as their security chief. Jim Anderson entered the room and found Wilson on the bathroom floor in a drug-induced haze.

When Wyche returned to the meeting room there were tears in his eyes. Stanley "had a relapse," Sam told his team. As the words left his mouth, Wyche broke down and left the room for a moment to compose himself. He had no choice but to leave Wilson off the team's roster for the game. Mike Brown, who was brought up to speed on the situation by Wyche, went to his father's hotel room.

"I need to talk to my dad," he told Mary, who had answered the knock on the door.

Brown came out from the back of the suite to see his son. He listened quietly to Mike and took a moment to digest the news. "I told you . . . one bad apple," Brown said, as he shook his head in dismay.

"It was like he stuck a pin in our hearts," Brown later said. How much of a difference Wilson could have made in the game will never be known, but the slick, sloppy field condition was conducive to Wilson's straight-ahead style. Instead, while his teammates were battling for the world championship at Joe Robbie Stadium, Stanley Wilson was prowling the streets of Miami in search of cocaine.

The Bengals tried to put the Wilson tragedy behind them, but earlier in the contest they suffered a devastating injury when defensive catalyst Tim Krumrie shattered two bones in his left leg. Still, after years of lopsided games, Super Bowl XXIII was destined to be a classic. The teams went to halftime knotted at three, the first time a Super Bowl had been tied at intermission. The game remained close throughout the second half, and when Jim Breech kicked his third field goal of the game with 3:20 remaining in the fourth quarter, the Bengals held the lead, 16-13.

Following the kickoff, San Francisco took over on its own eight-yard line.

A teammate sidled up to Cris Collinsworth. "We got them where we want them," he said.

"Have you seen who's quarterbacking for the other side?" Collinsworth answered.

Over the next eleven plays, Joe Montana skillfully moved his team the length of the field, capping the 92-yard drive with a 14-yard touchdown pass to John Taylor. In spectacular fashion, Montana had deflated the Bengals' championship hopes and stole from Paul Brown the one trophy that continued to elude him.

# sixteen   **IT'S BEEN A GOOD LIFE**

**The next morning** Brown met with a reporter from the *Enquirer.* Though undoubtedly disappointed with the game's outcome, PB was sanguine. "The older you get, the better you handle these things. If I am less solemn, it was because this was a tremendous football game. When you lose a cliffhanger like this it is easier to handle."[1]

Later in the afternoon, Brown joined members of the Bengal family at Fountain Square downtown as 3,000 fans came out to show their appreciation for the great year. Brown briefly addressed the crowd, thanking them for their season-long support, but his mind was already on preparations for the coming months. The first order of business was to meet with Wyche and discuss a new contract. Once he and Wyche came to an agreement, there was a trip to Indianapolis for the college combine, then player personnel talks and discussions covering the team's needs for the draft. Indeed, Brown's schedule was still full, but not as loaded as it once was. Much of the winter, like always, would be spent in LaJolla where he would play golf daily, weather permitting.

"That's the thing about these games. If you win, there is really no time to enjoy it. You have to start thinking about what you are going to do next.[2]

"I think it's a way of life," Brown reasoned. "I'm in bed most nights at 9:30. I eat right, I get exercise, I play golf. I'm fortunate. When I was a coach, I looked forward to the game, but I slept the night before and I slept the night after. Always. I can shut it off. . . . It's been a good life. The only thing I can find fault with is your blooming years go by so fast."[3]

—⋙—

Brown commenting to fans who had gathered the day
after the Bengals lost the Super Bowl.

The Stanley Wilson tragedy lingered. The questions continued to be asked. Why? Of course, why did Stanley succumb to temptation in Miami? Was it a conspiracy, or, more likely an untimely character failure on Wilson's part? In the early spring, Reggie Turner, Wilson's agent, bandied the story that there were other Bengals in the Plantation, Florida, hotel room with Stanley.

Brown dismissed Turner's allegation. "I don't put much credit in an agent who's trying to sell somebody's story,"[4] he said. But the story continued to follow the Bengals as they broke camp at Wilmington. A news report was published stating that Wilson had sold his tale to *Penthouse* magazine, and in it he would name five teammates who were allegedly in his hotel room the night before the Super Bowl. They were all free-basing cocaine, Wilson claimed. The names of the Bengals supposedly with Wilson were leaked to the press prior to the magazine's publication, forcing each man to defend his reputation while trying to prepare for the upcoming campaign.*

The Wilson controversy wasn't the only crisis hindering the Bengals.

At the start of camp a couple of players were hampered by injury while several others held out over contract disputes. This had become a common occurrence at Wilmington. Throughout the decade the Bengals organization had earned the reputation of being tightfisted. Cincinnati perennially was among the last teams to sign its first-round draft pick. "I get the image of being cheap, and I certainly don't want to lose it," Brown said while addressing the topic. "But we feel no obligation to subsidize a team for a city. It has to be a business venture. I make no apologies for that."[5]

The Bengals also had the fewest number of assistants in the league at nine. Some teams had as many as nineteen. What was a "quality control" coach anyway? Brown certainly didn't know. There was also criticism from fans and writers that the Bengals only brought in half as many players to training camp as other clubs. It had to be a cost-saving measure, they moaned.

"Some teams bring 150 to 200 players to camp," Brown acknowledged. "We brought in seventy-six last summer. We hold mini-camp and cut those who don't belong. We want our coaches to coach guys they are going to keep, not spend time with players who are going to be cut."

With a slight chuckle, Brown added, "Right away, I can hear people saying, 'Oh sure, the Bengals have fewer coaches and take fewer player to camp. That's typical of cheap old Brown.'

"I don't want to lose that image. It has nothing to do with finance. If spending more money would help, we would do it. We have a nice practice facility. We just didn't spend a million dollars on it."[6]

Criticism of Brown came from reporters, players, agents, and fans. He was miserly, was the general assessment. Paul and, in his ever-increasing role as team vice president, Mike Brown wouldn't spend the money necessary to field a championship-caliber football team. That the Bengals had just reached, and nearly won, one of the most exciting championship games did not quell such censure. Even members of the ownership fraternity spoke out on Brown's evolving role on the league's competition committee. Brown's approach to the committee, Cowboys owner Tex Schramm claimed, had become an act of self-interest.

On January 23, 1989, three thousand fans greeted Paul and Mary Brown on Fountain Square in Cincinnati.

"Speaking candidly," Schramm said, "Brown was a great motivator when he was coaching and also an individualist. He was a person who would do things his way and not worry about what others did or thought. Now he's profit-motivated and advocates programs and policies to keep other teams from doing things he doesn't want to have to pay to do in order to keep up."[7]

"League-think" was becoming a thing of the past. A new breed of owners had begun to infiltrate the league, and with their addition came an emphasis on profit. To these newcomers the well-being of the sport was secondary to making a buck. Further shaking things up, the brilliant architect of the communal system under which the league thrived, Pete Rozelle, announced his retirement on March 22, 1989.

Brown declared his intention to help in the search for Rozelle's replacement. "I'll do whatever I'm asked, but I've served my one time on this in a central role," Brown said. "The poor guy, he needs to be just like Pete.

He needs a football background, a touch with media and public relations, and the way things are now, he needs to be politically knowledgeable."[8]

There was much at stake with the selection, Brown explained. "Within the next three years new television contracts, collective bargaining, and expansion are some of the primary things he will have to deal with."

Finding a successor for Rozelle proved to be an arduous task. Brown was solidly behind longtime executive Jim Finks for the position, as was much of the league's old guard, such as Wellington Mara, Lamar Hunt, and Art Modell. Finks was well thought-of around the game as a "football man." The newer group of owners was piqued at being left off of the original search committee. These men, with interests outside the sport, wanted a commissioner who was more involved in the marketing and business aspect of the sport. Paul Tagliabue, a senior partner with the NFL's principal legal counsel, Covington and Burling, was the preference of the second cluster of owners.

Through three meetings, in three cities, with three selection committees and more than fifty hours of debate, a consensus could not be reached. Thirteen owners sat solid on one side and another thirteen were on the other side of the fence, while Dan Rooney and Al Davis abstained. They were on the verge of throwing out both candidates and starting from scratch when a compromise was finally reached. The ridiculous tug of war ended when the old guard realized that the votes just weren't there for their man, Finks. And Tagliabue's experience wasn't anything to sneeze at; he had been advising Rozelle for the past two decades. A man of varied talents, Tagliabue was a wise, intuitive choice to lead the National Football League into a new era.

—⁂—

On the field, the Bengals suffered from a Super Bowl hangover. The team struggled through an injury-plagued 8-8 season, one that saw the Bengals barely miss the playoffs when they concluded the year with a 29-21 loss at Minnesota. The next season was filled with more mediocrity, though in 1990 their 9-7 record was good enough for first place in the AFC's Central Division. A convincing victory over Houston in the wild card round

(41-14) was followed by a 20-10 defeat to the Raiders in Los Angeles.

While his team toiled on the field, Brown suffered from health problems for much of the year. Earlier, in March, an inner ear difficulty prevented him from attending the owner's meetings. The ailment lingered for months. By late summer, though, he was well enough to attend the annual "Meet the Bengals" luncheon on September 7. Feeling a bit playful, Brown invited the attendees to serenade him with "Happy Birthday."

His head coach continued to make life interesting. Following the Bengals' October 1, 1990, game in Seattle, Wyche chased Denise Tom, a reporter with *USA Today,* from the Cincinnati locker room. Commissioner Tagliabue was not amused by Wyche's action and called him on the carpet. By ordering Wyche to his New York office, the commissioner would be taking Wyche from his team for a couple of days. This, Brown declared, was unacceptable.

Brown called Taglibue and freely vented his feelings. Brown's voice rose to such a pitch that he could be heard out in the office hallway. Taking a coach away from his team for two days threw off the league's competitive balance, Brown contended. His argument was persuasive. A substantial $30,000 fine was handed down to Wyche by the commissioner, but Wyche remained in Cincinnati.

"Let's just say we had a healthy exchange of ideas," Tagliabue later said.

A couple of weeks later Brown suffered a setback. He missed his first Bengal game when he didn't travel to Cleveland for the team's October 22 contest against the Browns. He downplayed the significance of his absence saying, "I'd be in a booth anyway, probably watching the TV like I would at home."

And then, on December 9, he was admitted to Christ Hospital with a blood clot in his leg. Brown was in a hospital bed while the Bengals were losing an overtime contest to San Francisco at Riverfront. He hadn't traveled with the team since the Cleveland game, and now this was the first time he had missed a game in Cincinnati.

Local reporters were given scant details on Brown's health. "There was no pain, just some swelling," Bengals team physician Robert Heidt explained. "What you do in a situation like this is to put the person to bed for a few days and give them some medication. Then the clot disappears, and it's over. Overall he's in excellent health."[9]

By the end of the week, Brown was out of the hospital and sorely missed at Spinney Field. "If it was up to him, he would have been here today," Wyche told a reporter. He and his staff had just studied the film of the San Francisco contest, a weekly review that Brown always participated in. "This is his team, no one else's. He makes that clear."

Shortly after his release from Christ Hospital, Brown dropped in on writers at Spinney Field one afternoon. "I've never had to stay in the hospital before," he said. "They want you to stay still and keep quiet for forty-eight hours. [It's] boring. Embarrassing. But the old buzzard's still alive; just wanted you to know."[10]

—◊◊◊—

While Brown had recovered from the inner-ear affliction and the blood clot, he suffered another health impediment several months into the new year, 1991. In March, while in Tempe with Pete for the college combines, both Browns became very ill. When they were well enough to travel Mary drove Paul to LaJolla for further recuperation. And though his doctor in California warned Paul that the virus hadn't left his body, he felt good. He was instructed to take it easy and to get some bed rest. Though he was slowed, Paul failed to heed his doctor's instructions. In fact, a month later he was in Cincinnati attending the Bengals' mini-camp. As a concession to his recent health difficulties, though, Brown took in the workouts with the aid of a golf cart. And in mid-April he was at Riverfront Stadium for the team's draft meeting. Brown arrived at the office at noon for the summit and remained until eleven. Despite recent health complications, he kept up to date with film and scouting reports.

"I love (Alfred) Williams from Colorado and (Florida's Huey) Richardson," Brown told a reporter.

A couple of weeks later, in early May, Brown contracted pneumonia. Following a brief hospitalization, he was permitted to return to his Indian Hill home, though his health hadn't improved dramatically. How much time he had left, Brown wasn't sure, but whatever there was wouldn't be spent in a hospital bed. For a time his condition worsened; he became too weak to even speak on the telephone. But he rallied enough to consent to a few interviews, including an arduous six-hour talk with a *Massillon Independent* reporter.

"I know I'm at a high age," Brown admitted, and he readily acknowledged his lingering health problems. "But I feel fine. I enjoy coming to work."

He had long savored his role on the NFL competition committee, and he was the only original member remaining on the twenty-five-year-old group.

"I enjoy that job," he said of his role with the committee. "They call me 'The Grand Kahuna.'"

"We have to guard the game. The TV money is fine, as long as we still control the game."

He talked of the state of the game and his role in it, but Brown still recognized the inevitable. "I know it can come to a close at any time. But that will take care of itself.

"I'm really a fortunate man . . . to be congenially working with my sons all the days of my life."[11]

Mike and Pete each paid a daily visit to their father. Even from his sickbed, Paul continued to offer advice and suggestions to his sons. A quarterback out of the University of Houston, David Klingler, was getting a lot of notice. But there was something about the kid that Brown didn't like, something in his mechanics. "Don't draft Klinger," he told his sons. "He will never make the big scene."

Pete and Mike carried with them to their father's house league reports and updates on the Bengals. Not all the news was good. Draft picks were holding out and free agency was being bandied about by the Players Association. Several weeks before the start of training camp, Brown spoke with a young reporter from the *Enquirer*, Paul Daugherty. Brown still had his well-formed opinions, and some issues needed to be addressed. Only time would tell, but this little talk with Daugherty might be his last forum to express these thoughts.

The onus for the holdouts couldn't be placed on the Bengals, Brown insisted. It was those damn agents.

"The agents have worked in concert not to sign people until a certain late date. It looks like we may have some real problems at getting people in on time. These people have to play. They have to make a living. It's almost that time."

Free agency? "It doesn't really concern me," Brown said. "It could be five or ten years away. What we [the owners] are trying to do is reach some kind of agreement with the players. The game will survive. It always does."[12]

In the midst of his conversation with Daugherty, Brown mentioned that he might not be present when camp opened in a few weeks. The comment received little notice mixed in an article filled with a number of thought-provoking remarks. When the team arrived at its training facilities at Wilmington for the 1991 season without Brown, however, members of the Bengals family and local media feared the worst. As the summer wore on and Brown's health showed no sign of improving, Brown's family protected his privacy. His absence at Wilmington was the first public admission of the gravity of Brown's condition. It was the first time that Brown failed to greet his team at the start of camp and deliver his annual address.

His mind remained clear, but his body was failing him. His days were numbered and this he knew. But this fact was difficult for his boys to accept. Their father was sick, both Mike and Pete understood this, but surely he would rally. Paul recognized their denial and called his sons to his bedside. Time was running short, he told them. He wanted to be buried in Massillon, Brown told his boys, out of your mother's church, St. Timothy's. Pete and Mike each listened to their father, though neither wished to concede to the inevitable.

Paul Brown at Wilmington with grandson Paul.

Staying in the hospital was never an option for Brown. Whatever days he had remaining, Brown was going to live out in his own home. Mary made him as comfortable as possible, though on several occasions she had to push the "panic" button, which called for help from their Indian Hill neighborhood security post.

"Coach is really sick," Mary informed the rangers, "and he doesn't want anyone to know." She needed their assistance in moving him, and after that incident the rangers checked with Mary every morning and helped with anything she needed.

For years Brown had kept two bird feeders in his yard—one a regular feeder, the other a crushed peanut feeder. One particular red-bellied woodpecker frequented the Brown property. Paul kept an eye out for the bird and named it "The Duke." After her husband became bedridden, Mary had one of the feeders moved around so Paul could see it from the bedroom window. The Duke was a little reminder of God's beauty and the simple pleasures of life.

It was Brown's wish that he be given privacy, and visitors were kept to a minimum. Paul and Katy's godchild, Katie Leech, came and stayed at the house for a couple of days. And Marian, Paul's sister, flew into Cincinnati the first week of August for one final visit with her brother.

—⁂—

On Saturday, August 2, the Bengals traveled to Detroit for a pre-season game. Mike stayed behind and watched the game on television with his dad. It was the first time in the 460-game history of the team that Mike had missed a contest. This signaled to everyone in the Bengal family that the end was near. He still kept a close eye on his team and offered an unblinking critique on his Bengals. At one point during the course of the contest Mike thought his father had dozed off when Paul piped up, "Why'd they put him in?"

The next day, Mike stopped by again following Bengals practice at Wilmington. Paul handed his son his traditional birthday check, though Mike's birthday wasn't for another six days. It's about time, Paul told his son.

At 4:20 A.M. the following morning, Monday, August 5, 1991, without a struggle, Paul Brown took his last breath.

—⁂—

"His lungs gave way, but his mind stayed solid," Mike said in a statement. "I know that was important to him. He was desirous that as little be made over his passing as possible. That was his nature, as I'm sure everyone who knew him well would understand."[13]

It was Brown's wish that his funeral be simple and unadorned, similar to Katy's service. The service was held on Wednesday morning, August 7. Mourners began arriving outside the 160-year-old stone building at 8 A.M. "The whole town is sad," Al Drabney told a reporter. Drabney was a fair representative of his hometown. He was an iron worker and years earlier served as the team trainer for Massillon's 1970 championship club. "We'd be a ghost town without football. That's all this town is: Paul Brown, football, and steel mills."[14]

The mills that kept the town running through the Depression were now mostly shuttered and boarded up. What kept the town going now was Tiger football. Indeed, Massillon was football, and Paul Brown was Massillon. In his last years, Brown had returned to his hometown on a number of occasions. While in Massillon he would stay at Marian's house, where his sister would bring Paulie up to date on the town's happenings. And on each visit, Paul would take a ride alone around Massillon, and inevitably he ended the drive at the high school field named in his honor. He would get out of his car and stroll around the grounds. There he encountered some kids who looked at the old man, but did not see him. They knew nothing of the history, the genius, the legend walking before them.

And now, on a warm August morning under clear skies, townspeople stood in reverence, prepared to lay their favorite son to rest. They lined Third Street and stood on the small hill that placidly lay in front of the church waiting for the service to begin.

Shortly after 10 A.M. Wednesday morning, the current group of Massillon Tigers, wearing white shirts with orange ties, marched two by two up Third Street onto the lush green grass in front of St. Timothy's. Dignitaries from throughout pro football descended on Massillon to pay their respects and offer a word on a life well-lived.

The former "boy czar," Pete Rozelle, and present commissioner Paul Tagliabue each spoke of Brown's profound influence on professional football. The maverick owner of the Los Angeles Raiders, Al Davis, acknowledged that Brown "dared me to dream. And I dreamt of building the finest organization in all sports."

Brown's longtime understudy, Bill Walsh, was now widely considered a genius in his own right. "My feeling was to make the 49ers team, as best I could, a reflection of the Browns teams of the 1950s and '60s.

My approach to the game, my work ethic, and my moral ethic all came from him."[15]

Nearly all present offered a tribute or a story. Many of Brown's players came. Graham, Motley, Lavelli, Groza, Willis, and Bobby Mitchell were several of Brown's Cleveland players in attendance. The pallbearers represented every stop he had made from Massillon to Cincinnati. There were Tommy James, Lin Houston, Gene Fekete, Reggie Williams, Ken Anderson, and Dave Lapham

The limited seating inside St. Timothy's wouldn't permit access to all the mourners. The difficult task of deciding who was in and who was not was left to Earl Biederman. The church sanctuary was filled with 350, while another 100 listened in the chapel as sound of the service was piped into the smaller room. The Reverend Henry G. Harris presided over the brief, eighteen-minute funeral. He read from the Episcopal Book of Common Prayer, the 23rd Psalm.

"Yea, though I walk through the valley of the shadow of death,
I will fear no evil. For thou art with me."

There was more prayer, a hymn, and a short tribute to Brown by Rev. Harris. That was all, and that is all that Brown wanted.

"God's love will bring Paul new and unending life. In God's mansion a place has been prepared for him."

At the conclusion of the service the procession traveled down Lincoln Way to Wales Road. All along the route, people lined the streets as the limousines filed by. Some held signs aloft with words bearing their appreciation. Others simply bowed their heads. Down Wales Road they continued to Rose Hill Memorial Park, near the Massillon city limits. At 11:30, Wednesday morning, before a private ceremony of forty members of his immediate family, Paul Brown was laid to rest beside his lovely Katy.

—〰—

It's all black and white . . . truth, honesty, and character, these eternal verities remained.

Paul Brown died just one month shy of his eighty-third birthday with his vast legacy firmly secure. Indeed, the very game he loved was changed forever by his fertile and innovative mind. The honors, achievements, and records were nowhere to be found at his final resting place. No, the notice was simple and to the point.

Paul E Brown
September 7, 1908 - August 5, 1991

There had been more than enough fuss made already. It was time now to get back to business; there was football to be played.

# ENDNOTES

**PROLOGUE: Living Again**

1. *The Game Makers: Winning Philosophies of Eight NFL Coaches.*

**CHAPTER 1  Paulie Boy**

1. *Cleveland Plain Dealer*, 2-11-45.
2. *Return to Glory.*

**CHAPTER 2  Tiger Town**

1. Paul Brown Collection, Box 14.
2. 1935 letter to candidates for Washington High Football Club.
3. 1938 letter to candidates for Washington High Football Club.
4. Massillon Independent, 11-6-40.
5. *Akron Beacon Journal*, 11-2-40.
6. *Akron Beacon Journal*, 12-23-40.
7. *OSU Monthly*, 5-44.

**CHAPTER 3  Lean and Hungry**

1. *OSU Monthly*, 1-41.
2. *OSU Monthly*, 1-41.
3. OSU archives, letter dated January 1, 1941.
4. *Columbus Dispatch*, 1-7-41.
5. *Columbus Citizen*, 1-13-41.
6. *Columbus Citizen*, 1-14-41.
7. *Columbus Citizen*, 1-14-41.
8. *Columbus Dispatch*, 1-1-41.
9. *Columbus Dispatch*, 1-16-41.
10. *Columbus Citizen*, 1-19-41.
11. *OSU Monthly*, 3-41.
12. *Canton Repository*, 2-15-41.
13. *OSU Monthly*, 6-41.

14. *OSU Monthly*, 4-41.
15. *OSU Monthly*, 4-41.
16. *Columbus Citizen*, 9-14-41.
17. *Columbus Citizen*, 9-29-41.
18. *Los Angeles Times*, 10-5-41.
19. *Columbus Citizen*, 10-26-41.
20. *Columbus Dispatch*, 11-16-41.
21. *Columbus Dispatch*, 11-25-41.

**CHAPTER 4**  We Won, We Won

1. 8-14-42 Brown letter "To all Candidates for the 1942 Ohio State University Football Team."
2. *Columbus Dispatch*, 9-27-42.
3. *Columbus Citizen*, 10-4-42.
4. *Columbus Dispatch*, 10-18-42.
5. *Columbus Citizen*, 10-24-42.
6. *Columbus Dispatch*, 10-31-42.
7. *Columbus Dispatch*, 11-18-42.
8. *Columbus Dispatch*, 11-18-42.
9. *Columbus Dispatch*, 11-27-42.
10. *Columbus Dispatch*, 11-29-42.
11. *Columbus Citizen*, 12-13-42.
12. *OSU Monthly*, 2-43.
13. *New York Times*, 4-7-43.
14. *Columbus Citizen*, 10-3-43.
15. *Columbus Dispatch*, 10-10-43.
16. *Columbus Citizen*, 10-17-43.
17. *Columbus Dispatch*, 10-24-43.
18. *Columbus Dispatch*, 11-7-43.
19. *Ohio State: 100 Years of Football*.
20. *Cleveland Press*, 11-24-43.
21. *OSU Monthly*, 1-44.
22. *New York Times*, 2-13-44.
23. *Columbus Dispatch*, 2-15-44.
24. *OSU Monthly*, 5-44.
25. *OSU Monthly*, 5-44.

**CHAPTER 5  First Get A Ball**

* Topping brought his franchise, which was the Brooklyn Dodgers, to the AAFC from the NFL in December 1945. His first choice was to stay in the established league and move his team's home games to New York city, but was prevented from doing so because the territorial rights to New York City were held by Tim Mara and his New York Giants.

** The United States League and the Trans America League had both fallen by the way-side. Lack of organization and qualified investors spelled doom for both would be organizations.

1. *Cleveland Plain Dealer,* 11-10-44.
2. *Cleveland News,* 12-10-49.
3. *Columbus Citizen,* 10-21-44.
4. *Columbus Dispatch,* 10-19-44.
5. *OSU Monthly,* Feb 1946—Reportedly OSU freshman coach Sam Selby was present to hear this exchange.
6. *Columbus Dispatch,* 10-22-44.
7. *PB: The Paul Brown Story.*
8. *New York Times,* 2-9-45.
9. *Chicago Tribune,* 2-9-45.
10. *Cleveland Press,* 2-9-45.
11. *Columbus Dispatch,* 2-20-45.
12. *Akron Beacon Journal,* 2-10-45.
13. *Cleveland Plain Dealer,* 2-11-45.
14. *Chicago Tribune,* 2-10-45.
15. *Cleveland Press,* 4-2-45.
16. *Columbus Dispatch,* 4-1-45.
17. Paul Brown Collection, Box 2, folder 7.
18. *Ohio State Monthly,* February, 1946.
19. Associated Press, 5-4-45.
20. *Chicago Tribune,* 4-21-45.

**CHAPTER 6  Hey Elmer!**

* A second bond of $1,000 was awarded to a William S. Thompson, a veteran of World War I.

**The Rams had signed two Negroes in March, 1946—Kenny Washington and Woody Strode.

***All three men were later cleared of charges.

1. *PB: The Paul Brown Story.*
2. *Cleveland News,* 12-19-45.
3. *Cleveland News,* 12-28-45.
4. *Great Years.*
5. *Cleveland Plain Dealer,* 8-10-46.
6. *The Game That Was.*
7. *Columbus Sunday Dispatch,* 10-20-46.
8. *Cleveland Press,* 9-7-46.
9. *Cleveland Press,* 9-7-46.
10. *Cleveland Plain Dealer,* 11-26-46.
11. *Cleveland News,* 12-7-46.
12. *Return to Glory.*
13. *New York Times,* 12-23-46.
14. *Cleveland Press,* 8-21-47

**CHAPTER 7** World's Greatest Football Team

1. *New York Times,* 9-14-47.
2. *Time* Magazine, 10-27-47.
3. *Time* Magazine, 10-27-47.
4. *Sport* Magazine, December, 1954.
5. *Sport* Magazine, December, 1954.
6. *Sport* Magazine, December, 1954.
7. *Return to Glory.*
8. *Sport* Magazine, Nov. 1948.
9. *Cleveland Press,* 12-15-47.
10. *Columbus Citizen,* 2-13-48.
11. *Sport* Magazine, November, 1948.
12. *Columbus Citizen,* 2-13-48.
13. *Cleveland Plain Dealer,* 12-20-48.
14. *Cleveland Plain Dealer,* 12-20-48.
15. *Cleveland Press,* 10-22-48.
16. *Newsweek,* 11-1-1948.
17. *Washington Post,* 12-21-48.
18. *Cleveland News,* 1-15-49.
19. *Cleveland News,* 2-1-49.
20. *Chicago Daily Tribune,* 8-7-49.
21. *Cleveland News,* 10-10-49.
22. *Return to Glory.*

**CHAPTER 7** World's Greatest Football Team *(continued)*

23. *Cleveland News,* 11-8-4924. *Cleveland Plain Dealer,* 12-10-49.
24. *Cleveland Plain Dealer,* 12-10-49.
25. *Cleveland News,* 12-12-49.
26. *Cleveland News,* 12-12-49.
27. *Cleveland News,* 12-12-49.
28. *Cleveland News,* 12-29-49.


**CHAPTER 8** Crashing the Party

\* Van Buren, star running back of the Eagles and reigning MVP of the NFL, would suit up for the game but not play due to an injury incurred in a preseason contest.
\*\* On January 14, the Americans defeated Joe Stydaham's National squad, 28-27.
1. *Cleveland Press,* 1-17-50.
2. *Cleveland Press,* 7-6-50
3. Weeb Ewbank Papers, Cradle of Coaches Collection, Miami University.
4. *Return to Glory.*
5. *Chicago Tribune,* 8-30-49.
6. *Los Angeles Times,* 9-17-50.
7. *Los Angeles Times,* 9-17-50.
8. *Cleveland Plain Dealer,* 12-4-50.
9. *Great Teams, Great Years.*
10. *Los Angeles Times,* 12-1-50.
11. *Chicago Daily Tribune,* 12-16-50.
12. *Washington Post,* 12-18-50.
13. *Washington Post,* 12-22-50.
14. *Cleveland Plain Dealer,* 12-25-50.
15. *Cleveland Press,* 12-20-50.
16. *Cleveland Plain Dealer,* 12-26-50.
17. *Cleveland Plain Dealer,* 12-26-50.
18. *Los Angeles Times,* 1-1-51.
19. *Los Angeles Times,* 1-1-51.
20. *New York Times,* 1-21-51.
21. *Los Angeles Times,* 1-18-51.
22. Investigation of Organized Crime in Interstate Commerce Testimony, January 17, 18, 19, and February 19, 1951.
23. *Columbus Dispatch,* 1-28-51.
24. *Columbus Citizen,* 1-28-51.
25. *Columbus Citizen,* 2-6-51.

26. *Columbus Citizen*, 2-19-51.

27. *Return to Glory.*

28. *Chicago Daily Tribune*, 7-26-51.

29. *Return to Glory.*

30. *Chicago Daily Tribune*, 8-1-51.

31. *Los Angeles Times*, 10-2-51.

32. *Cleveland News*, 10-2-51.

33. *Los Angeles Times*, 10-2-51.

34. *Los Angeles Times*, 12-24-51.

35. *Cleveland Press*, 12-24-51.

36. *Cleveland News*, 7-17-52.

37. *Cleveland Press*, 8-5-52.

38. *Washington Post*, 12-15-52.

39. *Cleveland Plain Dealer*, 12-29-52.

40. *Return to Glory.*

41. *Cleveland Plain Dealer*, 6-11-53.

42. *Cleveland Plain Dealer*, 6-11-53.

43. *Sport* Magazine, November, 1953.

44. *12th Man in the Huddle.*

45. *Cleveland News*, 2-11-54.

46. *Los Angeles Times*, 8-26-54.

47. *Washington Post*, 12-8-54.

**CHAPTER 9** Two Browns

* Locklear had quit football due to poor health.

1. *Cleveland Plain Dealer*, 12-27-54.

2. *Chicago Tribune*, 7-8-55.

3. *Cleveland Press*, 8-16-55.

4. *Washington Post*, 12-27-55.

5. *Cleveland Press*, 12-27-55.

6. *Cleveland Plain Dealer*, 12-27-55.

7. *Sport* Magazine, 12-54.

8. *Los Angeles Times*, 7-21-56.

9. *Chicago Daily Tribune*, 10-16-56.

10. *PB: The Paul Brown Story.*

11. *Cleveland Plain Dealer*, 6-8-56.

12. *Cleveland Plain Dealer*, 7-20-56.

13. *Chicago Daily Tribune*, 7-21-56.

**CHAPTER 9  Two Browns** *(continued)*

14. *New York Post,* 10-16-56.
15. *Cleveland Press,* 7-25-57.
16. *Washington Post,* 12-30-57.
17. *Cleveland Plain Dealer,* 1-15-58.
18. *Cleveland Plain Dealer,* 7-24-58.
19. *Cleveland News,* 12-16-58.
20. *Washington Post,* 12-19-58.
21. *Cleveland News,* 12-22-58.
22. *New York Tribune,* 12-9-59.
23. *Cleveland Press,* 12-8-59.
24. *Cleveland Plain Dealer,* 12-15-59.
25. *Cleveland Plain Dealer,* 12-15-59.
26. *Chicago Daily Tribune,* 12-8-59.
27. *PB: The Paul Brown Story.*
28. *Washington Post,* 1-1-60.
29. *Los Angeles Times,* 1-2-60.
30. "Going Long."
31. The Case Against Paul Brown.
32. *Cleveland News,* 8-2-58.
33. The Case Against Paul Brown.

**CHAPTER 10  Meltdown in Cleveland**

* The Browns included halfback Leroy Jackson in the deal. Jackson was the team's second pick in the first round of the college draft.

1. *Chicago Tribune,* 1-5-61.
2. *Washington Post,* 10-19-61.
3. *Cleveland Plain Dealer,* 12-15-61.
4. *Cleveland Press,* 12-20-61.
5. *Off My Chest.*
6. *Washington Post,* 2-21-62.
7. *Washington Post,* 2-21-62.
8. *Los Angeles Times,* 3-2-62.
9. *Chicago Daily Tribune,* 3-30-62.
10. *Washington Post,* 7-22-62.
11. *Cleveland Plain Dealer,* 8-1-62.
12. *Cleveland Plain Dealer,* 8-1-62.
13. *Cleveland Plain Dealer,* 9-17-62.
14. *Cleveland Press,* 10-26-62.

15. *Cleveland Press,* 10-31-62.
16. *Cleveland Press,* 10-5-62.
17. *Washington Post,* 11-7-62.
18. *Cleveland Press,* 11-7-62.
19. *New York Times,* 11-3-62.
20. *Washington Post,* 10-17-62.
21. *Washington Post,* 12-12-62.
22. *Los Angeles Times,* 10-31-62.

**CHAPTER 11** Dying by Inches

1. *Chicago Daily Tribune,* 1-12-63.
2. Associated Press, 1-11-63.
3. *Chicago Daily Tribune,* 1-12-63.
4. *Los Angeles Times,* 1-27-63.
5. *Washington Post,* 1-16-63.
6. *Los Angeles Times,* 1-11-63.
7. *Chicago Defender,* 1-15-63.
8. *Cleveland Plain Dealer,* 1-17-63.
9. *Cleveland Plain Dealer,* 4-21-63.
10. *New York Times,* 10-13-63.
11. *The Last Season of Weeb Ewbank.*
12. *Sports Illustrated,* 8-12-68.
13. Letter from James N. Baily to Edward Bennett Williams 11-15-79.
14. *Cleveland Press,* 1-5-65.
15. *Cleveland Plain Dealer,* 1-13-65.
16. *Washington Post,* 7-3-65.
17. *Cleveland Plain Dealer,* 12-15-65.
18. *Cincinnati Post and Times Star,* 1-25-66.
19. *Cincinnati Post and Times Star,* 8-4-66.
20. *Cleveland Plain Dealer,* 12-16-66.
21. *Chicago Tribune,* 11-3-66.
22. *San Diego Union,* 5-18-66.
23. *PB: The Paul Brown Story.*
24. *Cincinnati Post and Times Star,* 5-25-67.
25. *Washington Post,* 5-25-67.
26. *Cleveland Plain Dealer,* 5-25-67.
27. *Cincinnati Post and Times Star,* 9-19-67.
28. *Massillon Independent,* 8-4-67.
29. The 1967 Pro Football Hall of Fame Enshrinement Program.

**CHAPTER 11  Dying by Inches** *(continued)*

30. The 1967 Pro Football Hall of Fame Enshrinement Program.
31. *Cincinnati Enquirer,* 9-27-67.
32. *Cincinnati Post and Times Star,* 9-27-67.
33. *Cincinnati Enquirer,* 12-8-67.
34. *Cincinnati Post and Times Star,* 10-27-67.
35. *Cincinnati Post and Times Star,* 10-27-67.
36. *Los Angeles Times,* 2-21-67.
37. *Cincinnati Enquirer,* 1-16-67.
38. *Cincinnati Enquirer,* 1-31-67.
39. *Cleveland Press,* 2-19-68.
40. *Washington Post,* 2-21-68.

**CHAPTER 12  Thank You, Art Modell**

* Each franchise also received $3million for relocating.
1. *New York Times,* 7-7-68.
2. *New York Times,* 7-4-68.
3. *New York Times,* 7-4-68.
4. *Sports Illustrated,* 5-27-68.
5. *Cincinnati Enquirer,* 7-12-68.
6. *Sports Illustrated,* 8-12-68.
7. *Sports Illustrated,* 8-12-68.
8. *Cincinnati Enquirer,* 8-26-68.
9. *Buffalo Courier Express,* 9-21-68.
10. *Oakland Tribune,* 10-24-68.
11. *Boston Globe,* 12-7-68.
12. *Cincinnati Enquirer,* 12-9-68.
13. *Cincinnati Enquirer,* 1-29-69.
14. *Miami Herald,* 10-1-69.
15. Letter from Paul Brown to Weeb Ewbank dated Jan. 13, 1969. Weeb Ewbank Collection, Cradle of Coaches Collection, Miami University.
16. *Cincinnati Post,* 3-12-69.
17. *Cincinnati Post-Times Star,* 3-19-69.
18. *Cincinnati Enquirer,* 3-23-69.
19. *The Sporting News,* 5-31-69.
20. *Miami Herald,* 10-1-69.
21. *Sports Illustrated,* 10-13-69.
22. *Washington Post,* 9-28-69.
23. *New York Times,* 11-23-69.

24. *Miami News*, 10-1-69.

25. *Los Angeles Times*, 9-25-69.

26. *Super Stripes*.

27. *San Diego Union*, 12-28-69.

28. *Cincinnati Enquirer*, 12-15-69.

29. *Washington Post*, 12-12-69.

30. *Cincinnati Enquirer*, 7-14-70.

31. *Cincinnati Post*, 7-14-70.

32. *Cincinnati Enquirer*, 7-18-70.

33. *Chicago Tribune*, 7-24-70.

34. *Cincinnati Enquirer*, 7-30-70.

35. *Dayton Daily News*, 7-29-70.

36. *New York Times*, 8-1-70.

37. *Canton Repository*, 9-7-70.

38. *Cincinnati Enquirer*, 8-30-70.

39. *Dayton Daily News*, 10-11-70.

40. *Cleveland Press*, 10-12-70.

41. *Cincinnati Enquirer*, 10-12-70.

42. *Cincinnati Enquirer*, 11-18-70.

43. *Cleveland Plain Dealer*, 11-29-70.

44. *Cincinnati Enquirer*, 11-26-70.

45. *Cincinnati Enquirer*, 12-21-70.

46. *Cincinnati Enquirer*, 3-24-71.

47. *Dayton Daily News*, 7-18-71.

48. *Cincinnati Enquirer*, 8-13-71 and *Washington Post*, 8-13-71.

49. *Cincinnati Enquirer*, 8-18-71.

50. *Cincinnati Enquirer*, 8-22-71.

51. *Cincinnati Enquirer*, 7-15-71.

52. *Dayton Journal News*, 10-28-71.

53. *Sports Illustrated*, 9-27-71.

**CHAPTER 13  Sign of the Times**

1. The *Sporting* News, 11-18-72.

2. *Cincinnati Post*, 6-19-73.

3. *Cincinnati Enquirer*, 7-28-73.

4. *Cincinnati Post*, 12-17-73.

5. *Cincinnati Enquirer*, 12-24-73.

6. *Cincinnati Enquirer*, 5-1-74.

7. *Cincinnati Post*, 5-2-74.

**CHAPTER 13  Sign of the Times** *(continued)*

8. *Cincinnati Enquirer,* 5-2-74.

9. *Cincinnati Enquirer,* 5-3-74.

10. *Cincinnati Post,* 5-2-74.

11. *Cincinnati Enquirer,* 5-3-74.

12. *Cincinnati Post,* 5-14-74.

13. *Cincinnati Enquirer,* 7-11-74.

14. Associated Press, 2-25-74.

15. *Cincinnati Post,* 7-22-74.

16. *Chicago Tribune,* 7-14-74.

17. Associated Press, 9-18-74.

18. *Cincinnati Post,* 7-28-74.

19. *Chicago Tribune,* 8-13-74.

20. *Cincinnati Post,* 11-16-74.

21. *Los Angeles Times,* 12-19-74.

22. *Cincinnati Post,* 12-16-74.

23. TSN, 1-4-75.

24. Copley News Service, 4-15-75.

25. Interview with Mary Brown, 10-29-2007.

26. Cincinnati, 6-19-75.

27. *Trump.*

28. *Los Angeles Times,* 11-20-75.

29. *Chicago Tribune,* 12-14-75.

30. *Cincinnati Enquirer,* 1-4-76.


**CHAPTER 14  Exit Paul Brown**

1. *Cincinnati Enquirer,* 1-5-76.

2. *Cincinnati Post,* 1-2-76.

3. *Washington Post,* 4-2-76.

4. *Akron Beacon Journal,* 6-23-76.

5. *Washington Post,* 7-8-76.

6. *Cincinnati Post,* 11-19-75.

7. *Cincinnati Enquirer,* 1-3-76.

8. *Cleveland Plain Dealer,* 9-8-78.

9. *Cincinnati Enquirer,* 9-28-78.

10. *Cincinnati Enquirer,* 10-3-78.

11. Interview with Bill Johnson, 10-02-06.

12. *Cincinnati Enquirer,* 10-5-78.

13. *Cincinnati Enquirer,*    12-9-78.

14. *Los Angeles Times,* 12-20-78.

15. *Sports Illustrated,* 11-5-79.

16. *Sports Illustrated,* 11-5-79.

17. *Football Digest,* June, 1979.

18. *Football Digest,* June, 1979.

19. *Los Angeles Times,* 10-21-72.

20. *New York Times,* 12-18-79.

21. *Toronto Star,* 12-28-79.

22. *New York Times,* 12-29-79.

23. *New York Times,* 12-29-79.

24. *Super Stripes.*

25. Letter dated 9-26-79, James N.Bailey to Pete Rozelle.

26. *Cleveland Plain Dealer,* 9-23-79.

27. Letter dated 11-9-79, Leonard Tose to Paul Brown.

28. *Canton Repository,* 10-20-79.

29. Letter dated 1-2-80, Pete Rozelle to Paul Brown.

30. *Chicago Tribune,* 1-22-80.

31. Letter dated 1-31-80, Art Modell to Pete Rozelle.

**CHAPTER 15**  **I Live for Sundays**

1. *Washington Post,* 1-5-82.

2. *Super Stripes.*

3. Paul Brown Collection, Box 5, folder 2.

4. *Cincinnati Post,* 12-15-81.

5. *Los Angeles Times,* 1-10-82.

6. *Super Stripes.*

7. *Cincinnati Enquirer,* 1-22-82.

8. *Columbus Dispatch,* 1-21-82.

9. *Chicago Tribune,* 1-22-82.

10. *New York Times,* 1-13-82.

11. *New York Times,* 1-26-82.

12. *Los Angeles Times,* 11-3-81.

13. *Cincinnati Post,* 10-5-82.

14. *Cincinnati Post,* 10-5-82.

15. *Dayton Journal Herald,* 10-10-82.

16. *Dayton Journal Herald,* 11-16-82.

17. *Chicago Tribune,* 8-4—83.

18. *Cincinnati Post,* 12-24-83.

19. *Cincinnati Post,* 12-24-83.

**CHAPTER 15 I Live for Sundays** *(continued)*

20. *Cincinnati Post,* 12-23-83.
21. *Cincinnati Post,* 12-26-83.
22. *Cincinnati Post,* 12-30-83.
23. *Cincinnati Post,* 12-31-84.
24. *Dayton Daily News,* 9-22-87.
25. *Cincinnati Enquirer,* 9-23-87.
26. *Orlando Sentinel,* 10-30-2007.
27. *Dayton Daily News,* 10-16-87.
28. *Football Digest,* February, 1989.
29. *Football Digest,* February, 1989.
30. *Game Day* National Issue, Vol XIX, Number 4, 1988 Paul Brown at 80.
31. *Columbus Dispatch,* 11-28-88.
32. *Washington Post,* 1-14-89.

**CHAPTER 16 It's Been a Good Life**

\* *Penthouse* delayed publication of the story until February, 1990. When the article was finally made public three players were named by Wilson as being in the hotel room, Eddie Brown, Rickey Dixon, and Daryl Smith. Wilson claimed he did drugs with Smith and Dixon. Brown was not implicated in the use of narcotics. All three men denied Wilson's allegation, including Brown who said the story was "fabricated" to make money. The NFL did not believe there was enough information in the *Penthouse* piece to warrant further investigation.

1. *Cincinnati Enquirer,* 1-24-89.
2. *Cincinnati Enquirer,* 1-24-89.
3. *Newsday,* 9-4-88.
4. *New York Times,* 4-25-89.
5. *Louisville Courier-Journal,* 12-24-88.
6. *Miami Herald,* 1-8-89.
7. *Cincinnati Enquirer,* 9-8-88.
8. *Canton Repository,* 3-24-89.
9. *Cincinnati Enquirer,* 12-10-90.
10. *Cincinnati Enquirer,* 12-19-90.
11. *Massillon Independent,* 6-15-91.
12. *Cincinnati Enquirer,* 7-15-91.
13. *Cincinnati Enquirer,* 8-6-91.
14. *Cleveland Plain Dealer,* 8-8-91.
15. *Cleveland Plain Dealer,* 8-8-91.

# BIBLIOGRAPHY
## BOOKS

Brown, Jim, and Myron Cope. *Off My Chest*. Garden City. NY: Doubleday, 1964.

Brown, Paul E., and Jack Clary. *PB: The Paul Brown Story*. New York: Atheneum, 1979.

Clary, Jack. *Cleveland Browns: Great Teams, Great Years*. New York: Macmillan, 1973.

Clary, Jack. *The Game Makers: Winning Philosophies of Eight NFL Coaches*. Chicago: Follet Publishing Co., 1976.

Collett, Ritter. *Super Stripes: PB and the Super Bowl Bengals*. Dayton, Ohio: Landfall Press, 1982.

Cope, Myron. *The Game That Was: The Early Days of Pro Football*. Cleveland: World Publishing, 1970.

Levy, William V. *Return to Glory: The Story of the Cleveland Browns*. Cleveland: World Publishing Co., 1965.

Miller, Jeff. *Going Long: The Wild Ten Year Saga of the Renegade American Football League in the Words of Those Who Lived It*. New York: McGraw-Hill, 2004.

Zimmerman, Paul. *The Last Season of Weeb Ewbank*. New York: Farrar, Straus and Giroux, 1974.

## MAGAZINES

The 1967 Pro Football Hall of Fame Enshrinement Program

"Aw Come On, Coach, Relax." *Collier's*, December 10, 1949.

"Big League Browns." *Time* Magazine, November 27, 1950.

"Brown Ohio." *Newsweek*, December 30, 1946.

Brown, Paul. "Interview." *Pro Quarterback*, November, 1969.

Brown, Paul and Bernard Fay. "I Watch the Quarterbacks." *Colliers*, December 10, 1949.

Brown, Paul and Harry T. Paxton. "I Call the Plays For the Browns." *Saturday Evening Post*, December 12, 1953.

Buck, Ray. "Has Paul Brown Ruined the Bengals." *Football Digest*, May-June, 1979.

Clowser, Jack. "Brown of the Browns." *Sport*, December, 1946.

Cobbledick, Gordon. "12th Man in the Huddle." *Collier's*, November 12, 1949.

Cobbledick, Gordon. "Are the Browns Over the Hill?" *Sport*, November, 1953.

Cobbledick, Gordon. "The Cleveland Browns." *Sport*, November, 1952.

Critchton, Kyle. "Mr. Brown Goes to Town." *Collier's*, October 18, 1942.

Dailey, James. "Paul Brown: Ohio Storm Center." *Sport*, November, 1948.

## MAGAZINES *(continued)*

Deindorfer, Robert. "Has Pro Football Passed By Paul Brown." *Sport*, June, 1962.

Didinger, Ray. "Paul Brown: The NFL's Elder Statesman." *Football Digest*, February, 1989.

Grow, Doug. "Has Pro Football Caught Up With Paul Brown?" *Sport*, November, 1974.

Grow, Doug. "Paul Brown Has Mellowed At 66- A Little." *Sport*, November, 1975.

Lebovitz, Hal. Exclusive—Paul Brown: The Play He Didn't Call

Magee, Jack. "Paul Brown: This Legend Is Still Working." *Football Digest*, October, 1982.

Marshal, Joe. "Bengals Bungles." *Sports Illustrated*, November 5, 1979.

Maule, Tex. "A Man for This Season." *Sports Illustrated*, September 10, 1962.

Maule, Tex. "Big Brown Boom." *Sports Illustrated*, October 7, 1963.

Maule, Tex. "No One Holds These Tigers." *Sports Illustrated*, September 27, 1971.

Maule, Tex. "Rude Welcome Back for Paul." *Sports Illustrated*, August 12, 1968.

Maule, Tex. "Youth Will Have It . . . Oops!" *Sports Illustrated*, October 13, 1969

Newcombe, Jack. "Paul Brown: Football Licensed Genius." *Sport*, December, 1954.

"Paul Brown at 80." Game Day National Issue, Vol. XIX No. 4, 1988.

Rain, Ron. "They're A Winning Combination." *Sports Illustrated*, October 20, 1975.

"Well Browned." *Newsweek*, October 24, 1949.

## NEWSPAPERS

*Akron Beacon Journal*
*The Boston Globe*
*Buffalo Courier-Express*
*Canton Repository*
*Chicago Daily Tribune*
*Chicago Defender*
*The Enquirer* (Cincinnati)
*The Cincinnati Post & Times Star*
*Cleveland News*
*The Plain Dealer* (Cleveland)
*Cleveland Press*
*The Columbus Citizen*
*The Columbus Dispatch*
*Dayton Daily News*
*The Journal-Herald* (Dayton)

*Los Angeles Times*
*The Courier-Journal* (Louisville)
*The Independent* (Massillon, OH)
*The Miami Herald*
*Newsday*
*New York Post*
*The New York Times*
*New York Tribune*
*The Oakland Tribune*
*The Ohio State University Monthly*
*Orlando Sentinel*
*Pittsburgh Press*
*The San Diego Union-Tribune*
*The Toronto Star*
*The Washington Post*

## INTERVIEWS

Bob August
Tom Bass
Bill Bergey
Mary Brown
Mike Brown
Jack Clary
Jenny Cline
Vince Costello
T. Dendui
Bill DeWitt Jr.
Bob Dolgan
Jack Donaldson

Forrest Gregg
Pat Harmon
Evelyn Heisler
Tiger Johnson
Kaye Kessler
Brian McBride
Dr. Kay Collier
  McLaughlin
Ed Menaker
John Murdough
Bernie Parrish
Wally Powers

Bob Queenan
Jenny Sauerbrei Baron
John Sawyer
Jim Schottlekottee
D. L. Stewart
Junie Studer
Chuck Studley
Bob Trumpy
Michael Wiethe
Sam Wyche
Bob Yonkers

## LIBRARIES

Cincinnati Public Library
Dayton Public Library
Columbus Public Library
Massillon Public Library
Cleveland Public Library
State Library of Ohio
University of Cincinnati Langsam Library
Cradle of Coaches Collection, Special Collections & Archives, King Library,
    Miami University
Paul Brown Collection, Cincinnati Bengals-Paul Brown Stadium
Cincinnati Bengals Archives, Paul Brown Stadium
Cleveland Browns Archives, Cleveland Browns Stadium
National Archives
Great Lakes Naval Training Base Library and Archives
Pro Football Hall of Fame Library and Museum

# ABOUT THE AUTHOR

Andrew O'Toole is a lifelong football fan who has authored six books, most recently *Winning in the Trenches: A Lifetime of Football* (with Forrest Gregg) and *Sweet William: The Life of Billy Conn.* A native of Pittsburgh, he resides in Lebanon, Ohio, with his wife, Mickie.